INTERMEDIATE CONVERSATIONAL
FRENCH

Intermediate

Conversational

FRENCH

Julian Harris
André Lévêque
University of Wisconsin

HOLT, RINEHART AND WINSTON, INC.
NEW YORK

Back cover photograph by
Henri Cartier-Bresson, Magnum Photos

June, 1961

33480–1110

Printed in the United States of America

CONTENTS

[v]

REFERENCE MATERIALS

INTRODUCTION

Like the other Harris-Lévêque books, *Intermediate Conversational French* is based upon three assumptions: (1) that language is something you do, (2) that the natural and most efficient way to go about learning a foreign language is to practice using it — first by hearing and speaking and then by reading and writing, and (3) that, at least for literate adults, a systematic study of practical grammar is an indispensable aid.

Following the pattern of our *Basic Conversational French,* we have alternated conversation and grammar units, systematically providing practice in the use of phrases before describing grammatical principles that they exemplify.

As we have often been asked why we "put the cart before the horse" instead of proceeding from the abstract to the concrete, perhaps we should mention what seem to us the advantages of proceeding from the concrete to the abstract. In the first place, students like to generalize. They overdo it. The older they are, the more they tend to *figure* things out instead of *trying* them out. Therefore they often get the idea that the structure of the language is the important thing and that learning the language itself is just a matter of memorizing a certain number of basic words and idioms. Moreover, when students start out with grammatical explanations, some understand clearly but passively, others understand only partially, and those who have learned the technique of getting by in other courses by the practice of "outlining and memorizing" never really understand anything at all. As most members of a class can not possibly understand a succinct explanation of a complicated principle of grammar, the teacher necessarily spends much time in explaining the explanations. Some students have been known to ask questions merely to postpone the moment when they must confront the exercises which call for active participation on their part. In a word, however logical it may be to proceed from the general to the particular in some disciplines, in our field it seems to give more emphasis to learning *about* the foreign language than to learning the language itself.

On the positive side, we find that when correct examples are "planted" in conversations, most students can grasp almost at a glance the meaning of the grammatical explanations that follow in a subsequent unit. Moreover, in these circumstances they accept the explanations as a series of generalizations that are relevant, that make sense, and that are immediately useful. And as the examples used in grammar units are taken from conversations that have a modicum of human interest, the context of the models carries over into the grammar units and supplies flesh and blood for the otherwise dry bones of the structure of the language. Most important of all is the fact that this arrangement gives the students the habit of using correct patterns of the language instead of teaching them to figure out "how you would say . . ." something or other in the foreign language.

The exercises that accompany the conversations are constructed so that they will give the students practice in hearing, understanding, repeating, using, and varying the phrases of the models. We have dispensed with the "Dites en français" exercise that always appears as exercise A with conversations in our earlier books because we believe that the average student of French at the intermediate level can read the conversations and understand them in French. However, we have included a translation of the conversations that can be used for this kind of exercise or as a prompt-script from which students can practice saying the French sentences of the conversations at home. Moreover, for the students who feel that they must know precisely how every phrase would be expressed in English — and who tend, therefore, to look up every word and write a translation (often meaningless) between the lines — we believe that an easy, idiomatic English version of the models may help them to get the habit of dwelling upon the meaning of the French instead of lapsing into the semi-conscious state that seems normal to a student who is thumbing absent-mindedly through a vocabulary and making a word for word mistranslation of the text. If students can see at once precisely what the French phrase means, they will perhaps avoid this practice and learn to read phrases, understand, repeat, use, vary and remember them.

But no matter how much oral practice students may have, when they are trying to carry on in French they sometimes want to say something they do not know how to say and, consequently, they lapse into English. The real advantage of having students work from the English translation back to the original French conversation is that it teaches them how to get back into French when they find themselves thinking in English. For example, a student might know perfectly well the expression "Ça ne fait rien" and still find himself at a loss as to how to say "If it is all right with you." After using the English translation of the first conversation as a prompt-script, however, he would know that "Si ça ne vous fait rien" is what he is looking for. Most students think "take" is always "prendre" in French; but when they see that "How long does it take . . ." is "Combien de temps faut-il . . ." they are pried a little further from the state of "hardening of the vocabulary" that must be overcome even in studying one's native language.

The grammar units are frankly intended to give the students a clear grasp of the morphology and syntax of the language. We have made it a point to present grammar in large blocks rather than to split it up into small parcels; for while small parcels may be easier to master from day to day, they are also easy to forget, whereas larger blocks are much more helpful for a second year student who aspires to attaining some real mastery of the language. If you study different uses of the *imparfait* piecemeal, for example, you never really understand the nature of this tense. Moreover, we find that at this level, students can appropriately confront the treatment of a large subject such as irregular verbs; although that unit will appear at first to be discouragingly long, there is real value in looking at a subject in the large once in a while: once the students realize that irregular verbs fall into groups that are easily recognized and remembered, they master the irregular forms much more painlessly than by trying to memorize them individually. To take another example, the time to study the forms of the present subjunctive is obviously the moment when you are learning to use this tense. The association between form and function that is achieved by the combination makes of the lesson a "learning experience" rather than a guide for getting through the course.

The exercises of the grammar units consist of a variety of devices to give the student practice in using phrases that exemplify the principles concerned and the forms that are being studied. While we do not hesitate to use drills (English to French) to give students practice in using forms that appear in a lesson, we recommend particularly that the exercises in which both question and answer are in French be used systematically. When such exercises are done orally, the student hears the question in French, understands it in French, answers it in French and, if he makes a mistake, has it corrected in French — an experience in the use of the language that teaches him far more than a mere translation exercise which may be full of mistakes. It should never be forgotten that a student does *not* learn by making mistakes. As we wrote long ago, "You do not learn to do it right by doing it wrong;" and certainly if you practice doing it wrong, you will learn only how to do it wrong!

Although intermediate books usually take it for granted that pronunciation has been mastered in first year French — as it should of course be — we find that many intermediate students need systematic help in improving their pronunciation. Consequently, we have included a considerable section entitled "Improving your Accent" that is intended to provide such help. An important part of this section is a transcription into the International Phonetic Alphabet of the conversations. Some teachers will want to use it for entire classes and others may leave it to individual students. We have tried to make this section simple enough for students to use by themselves.

We would like to thank Professor Karl Bottke for reading the I.P.A. transcription of the conversations both in MS and in proof although we do not want to imply that he is responsible for the errors that may appear. We have deliberately transcribed the monosyllables **mes, ses, des,** etc. with an *open* "e" instead of with a *closed* "e" as that pronunciation seems to be more and more current in France.

We are indebted to so many colleagues both at Wisconsin and in other institutions for suggestions and help in planning and writing this book that it would be impossible to say here precisely what we owe them. It would be ungracious, however, not to say we have made use of many ideas and hints that have been sent us by a number of correspondents during the last few years. We are grateful to them and we hope their letters have all been duly acknowledged; in any case, it is certain that the book would be very different without their suggestions.

J. H.
A. L.

The University of Wisconsin
Madison, Wisconsin.

How to Improve Your French Accent

Although most second year students of French have learned to speak simple French with some skill, there are few who would not profit by (1) a glance at the basic differences between the way we speak English and the way French is spoken and (2) a careful study of the pronunciation of the sounds of the French language.

The first step towards getting a good accent is to learn to utter words and groups of words in French without stressing some syllables and slighting others; the second step is to learn to pronounce the individual sounds of French as French people do.

Specific suggestions and exercises on both points will be found on pages 193-203.

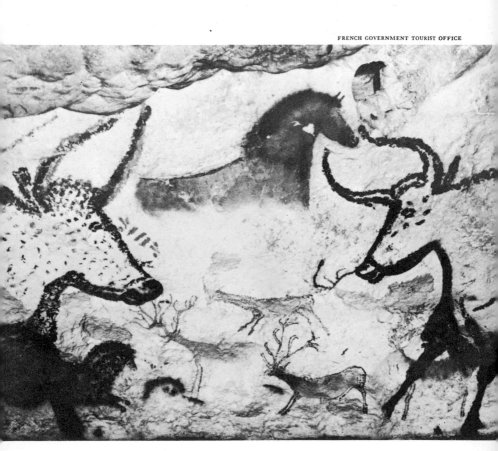

Grotte de Lascaux. Dessins préhistoriques.

Les origines

Monuments préhistoriques dans la campagne bretonne.

Le Pont du Gard, ancien aqueduc romain.

La Maison carrée. Temple romain à Nîmes.

Saintes. Arc de Triomphe romain.

Arles. Les Arènes. Au fond (in the background), théâtre antique.

Ville fortifiée du moyen âge (Carcassonne).

hIC:MILITES: FESTINA VERY

Tapisserie de la Conquête de l'Angleterre par les Normands.

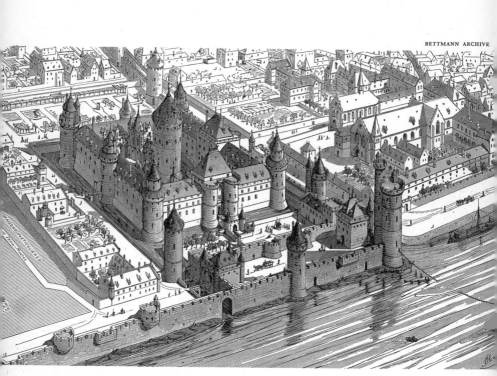

L'Ancien Louvre construit par Charles V.

Le Mont Saint-Michel.

La France au moyen âge

Église romane de Vézelay.

JEAN ROUBIER, RAPHO-GUILLUMETTE

Cloître roman de Moissac.
(Romanesque cloister at Moissac.)

La Cathédrale de Rouen.

L'Agriculture au moyen âge.

Calendrier des travaux des mois. (Juillet)

Le Travail de la laine. Tapisserie française du moyen âge. (Sheep shearing and making wool thread.)

Petit garçon en train de dessiner une tapisserie au Louvre.

INTERMEDIATE CONVERSATIONAL
FRENCH

I

Retour à Paris

De passage à Paris après une longue absence, John Hughes décide d'aller revoir ses amis parisiens, Roger et Marie Duplessis, maintenant mariés et qui demeurent depuis quelque temps à Saint-Cloud.* Il vient de faire signe à un chauffeur de taxi. Le taxi s'arrête.

Passing through Paris after a long absence, John Hughes decides to go to see his Parisian friends again—Roger and Marie Duplessis (who are) married now and who have been living for some time in Saint-Cloud. He has just signalled to a taxi driver. The taxi stops.

LE CHAUFFEUR. —[1]Où allez-vous, monsieur?

JOHN. —[2]13, avenue du Palais, à Saint-Cloud. [3]C'est près du pont de Saint-Cloud, à l'entrée de l'autoroute de l'Ouest.

LE CHAUFFEUR. —[4]Entendu. Montez, s'il vous plaît.

JOHN. —[5]Volontiers. Il y a dix minutes que j'attends un taxi. (John monte dans le taxi.)

LE CHAUFFEUR. —[6]Si ça ne vous fait rien, je vais prendre les quais.† [7]C'est peut-être un peu plus long, mais on perd moins de temps.

JOHN. —[8]Comment ça?

THE DRIVER. —[1]Where are you going, sir?

JOHN. —[2]13 Avenue du Palais in Saint-Cloud. [3]It's near the Saint-Cloud bridge at the entrance to the freeway to the West.

THE DRIVER. —[4]Okay. Get in, please.

JOHN. —[5]Glad to. I have been waiting for a cab for ten minutes. (John gets into the taxi.)

THE DRIVER. —[6]If it is all right with you, I am going to follow the river. [7]It is perhaps a little longer, but you lose less time.

JOHN. —[8]How's that?

---

* Saint-Cloud is a pleasant suburb to the west of Paris. It has a fine park and was once the site of a royal palace.

† Les quais are the streets along the river.

[1]

LE CHAUFFEUR. —⁹Le long des quais, toutes les voitures vont dans le même sens. ¹⁰Ça va beaucoup plus vite.

THE DRIVER. —⁹Along the river, all the cars go in the same direction. ¹⁰It goes much faster.

JOHN. —¹¹Combien de temps faut-il pour aller à Saint-Cloud?

JOHN. —¹¹How long does it take to go to Saint-Cloud?

LE CHAUFFEUR. —¹²Il faut environ une demi-heure, tout au plus.

THE DRIVER. —¹²It takes about a half hour, at the very most.

(*Un peu plus tard*)
JOHN —¹³Sommes-nous déjà à Saint-Cloud?

(*A little later*)
JOHN —¹³Are we already in Saint-Cloud?

LE CHAUFFEUR. —¹⁴Non, monsieur. Vous êtes toujours à Paris. ¹⁵On ne sait jamais où Paris commence et où il finit.

THE DRIVER. —¹⁴No, sir. You are still in Paris. ¹⁵You never know where Paris begins and where it ends.

A. *Répondez en français par une phrase complète à chacune des questions suivantes:*

1. Où est John? 2. A-t-il des amis à Paris? 3. Qui sont ses amis parisiens? 4. Qu'est-ce qu'il décide de faire? 5. Où demeurent Roger et Marie? 6. Demeurent-ils à Saint-Cloud depuis longtemps? 7. Est-ce que Saint-Cloud est près de Paris? 8. Comment John décide-t-il d'aller à Saint-Cloud? 9. Qu'est-ce qu'il fait pour avoir un taxi? 10. Que fait le taxi quand John fait signe au chauffeur? 11. Qu'est-ce que le chauffeur demande à John? 12. Quelle adresse John donne-t-il au chauffeur? 13. Est-ce près du pont de Saint-Cloud? 14. Quelle est l'autoroute qui commence près de là? 15. Combien de temps y a-t-il que John attend un taxi? 16. Quelle route le chauffeur va-t-il prendre? 17. Est-ce que c'est plus court? 18. Alors, pourquoi le chauffeur va-t-il prendre cette route? 19. Pourquoi les voitures vont-elles plus vite le long des quais? 20. Combien de temps faut-il pour aller à Saint-Cloud? 21. Quelle question John pose-t-il au chauffeur

un peu plus tard? 22. Que répond le chauffeur? 23. Est-ce que John est toujours à Paris quand il pose cette question au chauffeur? 24. Est-ce qu'on sait toujours où une ville commence et où elle finit?

B. *Répondez en français à chacune des phrases suivantes en employant les expressions indiquées:*

(Le présent de l'indicatif des verbes **être, aller,** et **venir** est employé dans les exercices. Pour les formes de ces verbes, voir "Reference Materials" pp. 244, 250, and 273.)

(*a*) **Depuis, il y a . . . que**

1. John est-il à Paris depuis quelques jours.? 2. Les Duplessis sont-ils à Saint-Cloud depuis longtemps? 3. Êtes-vous ici depuis longtemps? 4. Y a-t-il longtemps que John est à Paris? 5. Y a-t-il longtemps que les Duplessis sont à Saint-Cloud? 6. Y a-t-il longtemps que vous êtes ici?

(*b*) **il faut**

1. Faut-il longtemps pour aller de Paris à Saint-Cloud? 2. Combien de temps faut-il? 3. Faut-il plus d'une demi-heure?

(*c*) **venir de**

1. John vient-il d'arriver à Paris? 2. Venez-vous d'arriver ici? 3. John est-il à Paris depuis longtemps? 4. Y a-t-il longtemps que vous êtes ici?

(*d*) **aller, aller voir**

1. Où John va-t-il? 2. Pourquoi va-t-il à Saint-Cloud? 3. Pourquoi les voitures vont-elles plus vite le long des quais? 4. Allez-vous souvent en voyage? 5. Allez-vous voir des amis quand vous êtes de passage dans une ville?

C. *Demandez en français à quelqu'un:*

1. combien de temps il faut pour aller à Saint-Cloud. 2. combien de temps il faut pour aller de New-York à Paris. 3. combien de temps il faut pour aller de Paris à Versailles.

D. *Posez une question en employant l'expression «Combien de temps y a-t-il que?» avec chacune des phrases suivantes:*

1. John est à Paris.   2. Il est de retour à Paris.   3. Il attend un taxi. 4. Les Duplessis sont mariés.   5. Ils demeurent à Saint-Cloud.

E. *Dites en français:*

1. How long does it take to go by car from Paris to Lyons?   2. It takes about ten hours at the most.   3. It takes a long time.   4. How long have they been living in Saint-Cloud?   5. They have been living in Saint-Cloud for some time.   6. They have been living near the Saint-Cloud bridge for two months.   7. They have been married for two years.   8. Along the *quais.*   9. Along the Seine.   10. Along the Champs-Élysées.

F. *Thème:*

    John is passing through Paris. He has been there for three days. He decides to go and see Roger and Marie who now live in Saint-Cloud. He takes a taxi. It takes a half-hour to go to Saint-Cloud. The taxi stops near the Saint-Cloud bridge. John gets out (**descend**) and walks along the Avenue du Palais. He arrives at number 13 (**au numéro 13**) where his friends live. He is very happy to see his Parisian friends.

II   GRAMMAR UNIT

Présent de l'indicatif

1. THE TENSES OF FRENCH VERBS.

The tenses of French verbs correspond in part with those of English verbs, *but only in part.* Even the present indicative should be studied with care. For example, in English the present tense takes three different forms (*I speak, I am speaking, I do speak*) ; but in French the single form **Je parle** is used with all three meanings. The present tense in French also has other special uses.

2. USES OF THE PRESENT INDICATIVE COMMON TO FRENCH AND ENGLISH.

(1) The present indicative is used to express an action that takes place or to describe a situation that exists at the present time.

John est à Paris.	*John is* in Paris.
Il décide d'aller voir ses amis.	*He decides* to go to see his friends.
Il fait signe à un taxi.	*He signals* a taxi.
Le taxi s'arrête.	*The taxi stops.*

(2) It is used to express an action in progress at the present time.

— Où **allez-vous?**	Where *are you going?*
— **Je vais** à Saint-Cloud.	*I am going* to Saint-Cloud.
— Que **faites-vous?**	What *are you doing?*
— **J'attends** un taxi.	*I am waiting* for a taxi.

(3) It is used to express habitual actions in the present.

Que **faites-vous** le samedi?	What *do you do* on Saturdays?
Le samedi, **je vais** au cinéma.	On Saturdays, *I go* to the movies.

[5]

(4) It is used to express action in the near future.

Que **faites-vous** ce soir?	What *are you doing* tonight?
Je reste à la maison.	*I am staying* at home.

3. SPECIAL USES OF THE PRESENT INDICATIVE IN FRENCH.

(1) With **depuis, il y a . . . que,** or **voilà . . . que** and an expression of time, the present tense is used to express an action (or to describe a situation) that began in the past and is still going on at present.

— **Depuis** combien de temps **attendez-vous** un taxi?	
OR: — Combien de temps **y a-t-il que vous attendez** un taxi?	How long *have you been waiting* for a taxi?
— **J'attends depuis** dix minutes.	
OR: — **Il y a** dix minutes **que j'attends.**	*I have been waiting* for ten minutes.
OR: — **Voilà** dix minutes **que j'attends.**	

(2) The present tense of **venir** followed by **de** and an infinitive expresses an action of the immediate past.

John **vient de faire** signe à un chauffeur de taxi.	John *has just signalled* to a taxi driver.
Le taxi **vient de s'arrêter.**	The taxi *has just stopped.*

4. FORMS OF THE PRESENT INDICATIVE.

(1) Affirmative forms of the present indicative of regular verbs and of **avoir** and **être** will be found on pp. 239 and 244.

(2) Negative.

Saint-Cloud **n'est pas** loin de Paris.	Saint-Cloud *is not* far from Paris.
On **ne sait pas** où Paris commence.	You *don't know* where Paris begins.

Ça ne fait rien.	That *makes no* difference.
On ne sait jamais.	You *never know*.

Note that **ne** precedes the verb and that **pas** (or **rien** or **jamais**) follows it. In compound tenses **ne** precedes the auxiliary, **pas** (**rien, jamais**) follows it.

(3) Interrogative.

(a) With est-ce que?

Any declarative statement becomes a question if it is preceded by the expression **est-ce que?**

John est à Paris.	— Est-ce que John est à Paris?
Il est Américain.	— Est-ce qu'il est Américain?

(b) By inversion.

If the subject of the verb is a personal pronoun, you can ask a question by inverting the order of pronoun and verb.

Il est à Paris.	— Est-il à Paris?
Il a des amis.	— A-t-il des amis?

If the subject of the verb is a noun, you can ask a question by inserting the appropriate pronoun after the verb.

John est à Paris.	— John est-il à Paris?
John a des amis.	— John a-t-il des amis?

When a question consists only of a noun, a verb, and an interrogative expression (**Où? Combien? Quel?** etc.), the noun itself may follow the verb.

— Comment va John?
— A quelle distance est Saint-Cloud?
— Combien coûte cette voiture?
— Où demeurent les Duplessis?

(c) Other ways of asking questions.

You often ask a question by simply adding **n'est-ce pas?** to a declarative statement — especially when you expect an answer which agrees with what you say. This expression corresponds to a number of English expressions such as: "Don't you?" "Wouldn't he?" "Shall I not?" "Didn't they?"

> — Ses amis demeurent à Saint-Cloud, n'est-ce pas?
> — Ça ne vous fait rien, n'est-ce pas?

Or, omitting n'est-ce pas? you can ask a question simply by uttering a declarative sentence with a questioning tone.

> — Ça ne vous fait rien?
> — Nous sommes à Saint-Cloud?

This pattern is more common in French than in English.

Americans tend to use the est-ce que? forms of questions to the exclusion of the rather commoner pattern of inversion. Both forms should be mastered.

Note, however, that for the first person singular, the inverted form is rarely used. For the first person singular, you normally say: Est-ce que je parle? Est-ce que je suis? Est-ce que j'ai? etc.

A. *Répondez en français par une phrase complète à chacune des questions suivantes:*

1. Êtes-vous Américain?   2. Avez-vous des amis à Paris?   3. Où demeurent vos parents?   4. A quelle heure arrivez-vous en classe?   5. A quelle heure finissent vos cours aujourd'hui?   6. Attendez-vous souvent un autobus?   7. Perdez-vous beaucoup de temps le soir?   8. A quelle heure commencez-vous à travailler le soir?   9. A quelle heure finissez-vous d'habitude?   10. Allez-vous souvent au cinéma?   11. Aimez-vous aller au cinéma?   12. Combien de temps faut-il pour aller en ville?

B. *Mettez chacune des phrases suivantes à la forme interrogative par l'inversion du pronom sujet et du verbe:*

1. Vous êtes de retour.   2. Il est marié.   3. Ils demeurent ici.   4. C'est près d'ici.   5. Il y a une pharmacie près d'ici.   6. John est de retour. 7. Les Duplessis habitent à Saint-Cloud.   8. Roger va voir ses amis. 9. John décide de prendre un taxi.   10. Les Duplessis sont contents de revoir John.

C. *Demandez à un autre étudiant (à une autre étudiante):*

1. s'il (si elle) est Américain(e). 2. si Roger et Marie sont Français.
3. si Roger et Marie sont mariés. 4. si Roger et Marie ont des **amis**
américains. 5. si Roger et Marie demeurent à Paris. 6. où Roger **et**
Marie demeurent. 7. depuis quand Roger et Marie demeurent **à**
Saint-Cloud. 8. s'il (si elle) demeure à Saint-Cloud. 9. où il (elle)
demeure. 10. à quelle heure sa classe finit. 11. à quelle heure il (elle)
finit son travail. 12. à quelle heure il (elle) commence à travailler **le**
soir. 13. s'il (si elle) va au cinéma ce soir. 14. où il (elle) **va.**
15. s'il (si elle) attend souvent un autobus. 16. combien de temps **il**
faut pour aller de New-York à Paris. 17. combien de temps il **faut**
pour aller de Paris à Saint-Cloud. 18. depuis combien de temps **il**
(elle) est ici.

D. *Donnez deux réponses à chacune des questions suivantes en vous servant des expressions* depuis *and* il y a . . . que:

1. Depuis combien de temps êtes-vous ici? 2. Y a-t-il longtemps **que**
vous étudiez le français? 3. Depuis combien de temps demeurez-vous
ici? 4. Combien de temps y a-t-il que vous jouez au tennis?

E. *Répétez chacune des phrases suivantes en remplaçant* **le** *passé composé par le présent de l'expression* venir de *et l'infinitif:*

1. John est arrivé à Paris. 2. Il a déjeuné. 3. Il a fait signe à **un**
taxi. 4. J'ai déjeuné. 5. J'ai joué au tennis. 6. J'ai acheté une **voi-**
ture. 7. Êtes-vous arrivé? 8. Avez-vous pris des photos? 9. **Avez-**
vous vu ce film?

F. *Verb drills. Dites en français:*

(a) **être** *and* **avoir**

1. I am. 2. We are. 3. We have. 4. Have you? 5. Has he?
6. Have they? 7. Are they? 8. They are not. 9. They have not.

10. You are not. 11. Are you not? 12. Is she? 13. Has she? 14. Has she not? 15. Is she not?

(*b*) **aimer, décider (de), chercher, monter, rester, fumer, étudier**

1. He likes. 2. They like. 3. Do you like? 4. We do not like. 5. He decides to take a taxi. 6. He looks for a taxi. 7. He gets into a taxi. 8. She decides to stay at home. 9. We are staying home tonight. 10. Are you staying home? 11. No, I am not staying home. 12. Don't you like to smoke? 13. No, I don't smoke. 14. Do you smoke? 15. I am looking for a number. 16. I study French. 17. We are studying. 18. She does not study much.

(*c*) **finir, réussir (à + *inf*.), choisir, obéir (à)**

1. What time do you finish? 2. I finish early. 3. Do you always succeed? 4. Do you always succeed in finishing before midnight? 5. No, I do not always succeed. 6. Do you always obey? 7. I always obey the law (**à la loi**). 8. My little brothers do not always obey. 9. We choose. 10. They choose.

(*d*) **perdre, attendre, entendre, vendre, descendre**

1. I waste a great deal of time. 2. He is wasting his time. 3. What are you waiting for? 4. I am waiting for a bus. 5. I have been waiting for five minutes. 6. I hear a bus. 7. Where are you getting off? 8. I am getting off at the Place de la Concorde. 9. Where do they sell stamps (**des timbres**)? 10. They sell stamps at the post office (**à la poste**).

G. *Posez en français la question à laquelle répondrait chacune des phrases suivantes:*

1. J'ai le temps d'acheter un journal. 2. La représentation commence à huit heures. 3. Il y a dix minutes que j'attends. 4. Je ne perds jamais mon temps. 5. Je ne finis jamais mon travail avant onze heures. 6. Il vient d'arriver. 7. Il vient nous voir tous les samedis. 8. Je descends de l'autobus sur la place. 9. Il y a dix jours que je suis ici. 10. J'étudie tous les soirs.

H. *Dictée* (Verbs that have two stems, see pp. 241-243) :

1. Où achetez-vous votre journal? 2. J'achète mon journal au bureau de tabac. 3. Quelle saison préférez-vous? 4. Je préfère l'été. 5. Il gèle aujourd'hui. 6. Cette route mène à Saint-Cloud. 7. Combien pesez-vous? 8. Je pèse 70 kilos. 9. Nous commençons à 8 heures. 10. J'espère qu'il est à la maison. 11. Je lève la main. 12. Nous levons la main. 13. Comment vous appelez-vous? 14. Je m'appelle Henri (Henriette).

III CONVERSATION UNIT

Chez les Duplessis

Roger a reçu John à bras ouverts, et John a été très heureux de retrouver son ami. Malheureusement, Marie était sortie au moment de l'arrivée de John. En attendant son retour, nos deux amis parlent de ce qu'ils ont fait au cours des deux dernières années.

Roger welcomed John with open arms, and John was very happy to be with his friend again. Unfortunately, Marie was out when John got there. While waiting for her (return), our two friends talk of what they have done in the course of the last two years.

ROGER. —[1]Vous n'avez pas mal voyagé depuis votre départ il y a deux ans, n'est-ce pas?

JOHN. —[2]Et comment! [3]Comme vous le savez, en quittant Paris, je suis retourné à Philadelphie. [4]De là, je suis allé à Pittsburgh, où j'ai passé quelques mois dans les laboratoires d'une compagnie de pétrole. [5]Puis on m'a envoyé au Vénézuéla.

ROGER. —[6]Vous êtes allé aussi dans le Proche-Orient, n'est-ce pas?

JOHN. —[7]Attendez! Je n'ai pas encore fini de parler de mes voyages . . . [8]Du Vénézuéla, je suis parti pour le Soudan. [9]J'ai quitté le Soudan pour l'Égypte, l'Égypte pour l'Arabie saoudite.

ROGER. —[1]You have travelled a good deal since your departure two years ago, haven't you?

JOHN. —[2]And how! [3]As you know, when I left Paris, I went back to Philadelphia. [4]From there I went to Pittsburgh, where I spent several months in the laboratories of an oil company. [5]Then they sent me to Venezuela.

ROGER. —[6]You also went to the Near East, didn't you?

JOHN. —[7]Wait! I haven't finished telling about my travels . . . [8]From Venezuela, I set out for the Sudan. [9]I left the Sudan for Egypt, Egypt for Saudi Arabia. [10]Now they are send-

[10]On m'envoie maintenant aux États-Unis, passer un congé de trois mois que je n'ai pas volé.

ROGER. —[11]Comparée à la vôtre, ma vie a été bien tranquille. [12]Depuis notre mariage, Marie et moi nous sommes restés bien sagement à la maison, [13]sauf bien entendu quelques petits voyages d'agrément.

JOHN. —[14]J'ai reçu l'invitation à votre mariage quand j'étais dans la jungle vénézuélienne. [15]Je n'ai pas pu venir assister à la cérémonie. C'était trop loin.

ROGER. —[16]En tout cas, restez dîner avec nous ce soir. [17]Marie sera enchantée de vous revoir, et nous reparlerons du bon vieux temps.

ing me to the United States for a three months leave—which I have really earned (which I have not stolen).

ROGER. —[11]My life has been very calm in comparison to yours. [12]Since our marriage, Marie and I have remained very quietly at home, [13]except, of course, for a few little pleasure trips.

JOHN. —[14]I got the invitation to your marriage when I was in the jungle of Venezuela. [15]I couldn't come to (be present at) the wedding ceremony. It was too far.

ROGER. —[16]In any case, stay to dinner with us this evening. [17]Marie will be delighted to see you again, and we will talk over the good old days again.

A. *Répondez en français par une phrase complète à chacune des questions suivantes:*

1. Comment Roger a-t-il reçu John? 2. Où était Marie au moment de l'arrivée de John? 3. De quoi les deux amis parlent-ils en attendant son retour? 4. Quand John a-t-il quitté la France? 5. A-t-il beaucoup voyagé? (Oui, il n'a pas mal voyagé.) 6. Où est-il allé en quittant Paris? 7. Où est-il allé en quittant Philadelphie? 8. Combien de temps a-t-il passé à Pittsburgh? 9. Où a-t-il travaillé à Pittsburgh? 10. Où l'a-t-on envoyé ensuite? 11. Est-il allé directement du Vénézuéla dans le Proche-Orient? 12. Dans quels pays d'Afrique est-il allé? 13. Où va-t-il maintenant? 14. Pourquoi l'envoie-t-on aux États-Unis? 15. Qu'est-ce que John pense de son congé? 16. Est-ce

que Roger et Marie ont beaucoup voyagé depuis leur mariage?
17. Quelle sorte de voyages ont-ils faits? 18. Où était John quand il
a reçu l'invitation à leur mariage? 19. Est-ce qu'il a assisté à la cérémonie? 20. Pourquoi n'a-t-il pas pu venir? 21. Est-ce que John va
rester dîner? 22. Marie sera-t-elle contente de revoir John? 23. De
quoi parleront-ils ensemble?

B. *Employez une des expressions indiquées en réponse à
chacune des questions suivantes:*

(*a*) **arrivée** (*f*), **retour** (*m*), **départ** (*m*)

1. Qu'a fait John depuis son départ de Paris? 2. De quoi Roger et
John parlent-ils en attendant le retour de Marie? 3. Que vont-ils
faire à l'arrivée de Marie? 4. John est-il de retour à Paris depuis
longtemps?

(*b*) **au moment de, au moment où**

1. Où était Marie au moment de l'arrivée de John? 2. Où était
John au moment du mariage de Roger? 3. Où était Marie au moment où John est arrivé à Saint-Cloud? 4. Où était John au moment
où il a reçu l'annonce du mariage de ses amis?

(*c*) **assister à**

1. John a-t-il assisté à la cérémonie du mariage des Duplessis? 2. Pourquoi n'a-t-il pas pu assister au mariage? 3. Assistez-vous souvent à
des concerts?

(*d*) **ne . . . rien, ne . . . jamais**

1. Êtes-vous jamais allé au Japon? 2. Avez-vous jamais assisté à un
match de rugby? 3. Avez-vous acheté quelque chose en ville ce matin?
4. Avez-vous dit quelque chose? 5. Qu'est-ce que vous avez dit?
6. Qu'est-ce que vous avez fait hier soir?

C. *Demandez en français à quelqu'un:*

1. où habitent les Duplessis depuis qu'ils ont quitté Paris. 2. où ils
habitent depuis leur départ de Paris. 3. où était Marie quand John
est arrivé chez les Duplessis. 4. où elle était à l'arrivée de John.

5. où elle était au moment de son arrivée.   6. si John est content d'être de
retour à Paris.   7. si John a assisté au mariage des Duplessis.   8. pourquoi il n'a pas assisté au mariage.

D. *Dites en français:*

(*u*) assister à, aller à*

1. Did you attend the concert yesterday?   2. No, I attended a lecture.
3. Where did she attend college?   4. She never attended college.   5. I
just went to (attended) an interesting lecture.

(*b*) rester

1. Stay and have dinner with us tonight.   2. I stayed home last night.
3. I never stay home at night.   4. I am going to stay to finish my work.

(*c*) retrouver

1. John is very happy to meet his friends again.   2. I am going to
meet you at four o'clock.   3. Where are you going to meet me?

(*d*) sauf

1. Except a few little trips.   2. Except a few days.   3. Except a table
and a chair.   4. Except for his friends.

E. *Thème:*

When John arrives at the Duplessis, Marie is not at home. She is
in town. Roger hopes that she is going to be back soon. She is buying
a loaf of bread. But sometimes it takes a long time to buy a loaf of
bread. Sometimes you (**on**) meet your (**ses**) friends. You never know.
Sometimes you waste a great deal of time.

While waiting for Marie to come back (Marie's return), John and
Roger talk together. John talks about what he had done since he left
Paris two years ago.

---

* **Assister à** is used to refer to specific *events*: performances, lectures, church
services, etc.; but not to *places* such as schools, theatres, movie house, stadiums.
Ex.: Elle a assisté à la cérémonie, à la représentation, à un match. **Elle est
allée au** cinéma, à l'école, au stade, au théâtre.

IV

Passé composé. Article défini.
Prépositions de et à

5. THE *passé composé* AND THE *imparfait*.

The *passé composé* and the *imparfait* are both used to express an action or state of being in the past: the *passé composé* is used to tell WHAT HAPPENED, whereas the *imparfait* is used primarily to tell what was going on at the time when the action took place. The *passé composé* is the normal past tense in spoken French; the *imparfait* is a special tense that is used only in special cases. Its use will be described in Unit VI.

6. EXAMPLES OF THE USE OF THE *passé composé*.

(1)

— Qu'est-ce que **vous avez fait** pendant les vacances?

What *did you do* during the vacation?

— **J'ai voyagé.**

I took a trip.

Je suis allé en Californie.

I went to California.

En route, **nous avons visité** le parc de Yellowstone.

On the way, *we visited* Yellowstone Park.

Et vous, qu'**avez-vous fait?**

And what *did you do?*

— Moi, **j'ai été** malade.

I was sick.

J'ai eu une **crise d'**appendicite.

I had appendicitis.

On m'a opéré. Il y a eu des complications. **J'ai passé** trois semaines à l'hôpital. **Je n'ai pas pu** quitter mon lit. **J'ai** même **cru** un jour que j'allais (*imparfait*) mourir.

I was operated on. There were complications. *I spent* three weeks in the hospital. *I couldn't* leave my bed. One day, *I even thought* I was going to die.

[16]

(2)

— **Avez-vous vu** le film de Walt   *Have you seen* the Disney film?
   Disney?
— Oui. **Je l'ai trouvé** excellent.   Yes. *I thought* it was excellent.
   Est-ce qu'**il** vous **a plu?**   *Did you like* it?
— Oh! **Je l'ai trouvé** comme ci   Oh! *I thought* it was so-so.
   comme ça.

(3)

— Cet hiver **a été** très rigoureux,   This winter *was* very severe
   n'est-ce pas?   wasn't it?
— Oui, **il a fait** froid tout l'hiver   Yes. *It was* cold all winter and
   et **il a neigé** tout le temps.   *it snowed* all the time.
   Le soleil **n'a pas paru** une   The sun *did not come out* once
   seule fois au mois de jan-   in January.
   vier.

Note with care that in the above examples the *passé composé*
is used regardless of what you would say in English. Students
often suppose that if you say: I was, I had, I could, I thought,
etc. in English, the French *imparfait* would automatically be
called for; but this is frequently not the case.

7. FORMS OF THE *passé composé*.

The forms of the *passé composé* will be found on p. 236.

For the negative and interrogative forms of the *passé composé,* you use the negative and interrogative forms of the
auxiliary verb. Ex.: **Vous avez voyagé. Avez-vous** voyagé? **Je
n'ai pas** voyagé.

8. FORMS OF THE PAST PARTICIPLE.

Past participles have four forms: masculine and feminine
singular and masculine and feminine plural, aimé, aimée, aimés,
aimées; fini, finie, finis, finies; perdu, perdue, perdus, perdues.
All four forms of these (and most other participles) are pronounced alike. In the case of irregular verbs whose participle

ends in t, the t is pronounced only in the feminine forms; ouvert, ouverte, ouverts, ouvertes; fait, faite, faits, faites. Likewise, the s of participles ending in s is silent in masculine forms and is pronounced z in feminine forms: pris, prise, pris, prises; mis, mise, mis, mises.

9. AGREEMENT OF THE PAST PARTICIPLE OF VERBS CONJUGATED WITH avoir.

The past participle of these verbs is invariable except when the verb is preceded by a direct object; but when the verb *is* preceded by a direct object, the past participle agrees with it in gender and number.

> Marie a été malade. (*No agreement.*)
>
> Elle a eu une crise d'appendicite. (*No agreement.*)
>
> On l'a opérée. (*Agreement with preceding direct object* l'—*which refers to Marie.*)
>
> J'ai acheté des fleurs. (*No agreement.*)
>
> Voilà les fleurs que j'ai achetées. (*Agreement with preceding direct object* que—*which refers to* les fleurs.)
>
> Je les ai achetées dans la rue. (*Agreement with preceding direct object* les—*which refers to flowers.*)

Note, however, that the past participle does not agree with **en:**

> Marie en a acheté aussi. (*No agreement, even though* en *refers to* les fleurs.)

10. VERBS CONJUGATED WITH être.

The following verbs which denote motion or change of condition (and a few others) are conjugated with the auxiliary verb être:

INFINITIVE	PAST PARTICIPLE	
aller	allé	*to go*
venir	venu	*to come*
sortir	sorti	*to go out*
entrer	entré	*to go in*

INFINITIVE	PAST PARTICIPLE	
partir	parti	*to go away, to leave*
arriver	arrivé	*to arrive*
monter	monté	*to go up*
descendre	descendu	*to go down*
tomber	tombé	*to fall, to fall down*
rester	resté	*to stay, to remain*
naître	né	*to be born*
devenir	devenu	*to become*
mourir	mort	*to die*
retourner	retourné	*to return*

Compounds of these verbs (**revenir, ressortir, rentrer, repartir, remonter, redescendre, retomber,** etc.) are also normally conjugated with **être.**

Note that **rentrer** means *to go back home,* **revenir** *to come back to the place from which you started,* and **retourner** *to go back where you were.* Ex.: **Avant de rentrer** à la maison, **nous sommes retournés** au bureau de tabac acheter des timbres.

11. AGREEMENT OF THE PAST PARTICIPLE OF VERBS CONJUGATED WITH **être** (EXCEPT REFLEXIVE VERBS).

(1) The past participle of these verbs agrees with the subject.

{Le petit **Michel** est né à Saint-Cloud.
{**Marie** est née en Bretagne.
{**John et Roger** sont allés en ville.
{**Marie et sa mère** sont allées en ville.
 Nous (*m* or *m* and *f*) sommes partis.
 Nous (*f*) sommes parties.
 Vous (*m sg*) êtes parti.
 Vous (*f sg*) êtes partie.
 Vous (*m pl* or *m* and *f*) êtes partis.
 Vous (*f pl*) êtes parties.

(2) When **monter, descendre, sortir,** and **rentrer** are used

as transitive verbs (that is, when they take a direct object), they are conjugated with **avoir**.

> **J'ai monté** (descendu) les bagages.
> **J'ai sorti** (rentré) le chien.

Note also that many verbs that seem to imply motion are conjugated regularly with **avoir**. Ex.: **J'ai quitté** la maison. **J'ai voyagé** tout l'été. **J'ai marché** un peu. **J'ai couru. J'ai avancé. J'ai reculé.**

12. DEFINITE ARTICLES **le, la, les** AND PREPOSITIONS **de** *(of, from)* and **à** *(to, at)*.

(1) Forms used with masculine singular nouns beginning with a consonant — other than a mute **h**:

> **le:**　le taxi, **le** chauffeur
> **du:**　**du** taxi, **du** chauffeur
> **au:**　**au** taxi, **au** chauffeur

(2) Forms used with feminine singular nouns beginning with a consonant — other than a mute "h":

> **la:**　la voiture, **la** maison
> **de la:**　**de la** voiture, **de la** maison
> **à la:**　**à la** voiture, **à la** maison

(3) Forms used with all singular nouns beginning with a vowel or mute **h**:

> **l':**　l'ami, l'homme *(m)*
> 　　　l'entrée, l'annonce *(f)*
> **de l':**　**de** l'ami, **de** l'homme
> 　　　　**de** l'entrée, **de** l'annonce
> **à l':**　**à** l'ami, **à** l'homme
> 　　　　**à** l'entrée, **à** l'annonce

(4) Forms used with plural nouns of both genders:

> **les:**　**les** taxis, **les** voitures
> **des:**　**des** taxis, **des** voitures
> **aux:**　**aux** taxis, **aux** voitures

13. USE OF THE DEFINITE ARTICLE.

The definite article is normally expressed in French either when the noun is used in a specific sense (The books are on the table) or in a general sense (Books are useful). Note the difference between English and French usage.

Le jus d'orange est bon pour la santé.	*Orange juice* is good for the health.
Le déjeuner est à midi.	*Lunch* is at noon.
L'homme aime la liberté.	*Man* loves *liberty*.
Le départ de John.	John's *departure*.
Le retour de Marie.	Marie's *return*.
Je vais à l'école.	I go *to school*.
Le prix de la pension.	The price *of room and board*.

The definite article is not used with nouns that are in apposition (**M. Adam, professeur à la Sorbonne**); in references (**Imparfait; paragraphe 13, page 47**); in lists (**Hommes, femmes, enfants, tout le monde s'amusait. Il n'a ni père, ni mère, ni proches parents.**); or with nouns denoting nationality or professions when they follow the verb **être** (**Il est avocat. Nous sommes Américains.**).

14. PREPOSITIONS AND DEFINITE ARTICLES WITH GEOGRAPHICAL NAMES.

(1) With names of countries that are masculine:

au (aux) (*to* or *in*)	Mon père est **au Canada.**
	Je vais **aux États-Unis.**
	On a envoyé John **au Vénézuéla.**
du (des) (*from*)	Je suis parti **du Mexique.**
	John vient **des États-Unis.**

Most countries in the Western Hemisphere are masculine. Ex.: **les États-Unis, le Mexique, le Canada, le Brésil, le Pérou, le Chili, le Nicaragua,** etc.

(2) With names of continents, and countries that are feminine:

en (*to* or *in*)	John est allé **en France.**
	On l'a envoyé **en Égypte** et **en Arabie.**
	Roger et Marie habitent **en Europe.**
de (*from*)	John vient **d'Égypte.** Il vient **d'Afrique.**

All the continents and most European countries are feminine. Ex.: **la Suisse, la Russie, la Suède, la Belgique, l'Allemagne.**

(3) With names of cities:

à (*to* or *in*)	Il est **à Paris.**
	Il va **à Genève.**
	Son père est **à Londres.**
de (*from*)	Il vient **de Philadelphie.**

In the case of cities whose names have a definite article (Le Havre, La Nouvelle Orléans) you use the forms **au** and **du** and **à la** and **de la** as you would expect: **au Havre, à La Nouvelle-Orléans.**

A. *Répondez en français par une phrase complète à chacune des questions suivantes:*

1. Qu'est-ce que vous avez fait l'été dernier?   2. Comment avez-vous passé les vacances?   3. Avez-vous voyagé?   4. Voyagez-vous tous les étés?   5. Avez-vous été malade?   6. Avez-vous eu une crise d'appendicite?   7. Quel temps a-t-il fait l'été dernier?   8. L'été a-t-il été très chaud?   9. Est-ce qu'il a beaucoup plu?   10. Avez-vous jamais visité Yellowstone?   11. Avez-vous trouvé Yellowstone intéressant? 12. Combien de temps avez-vous passé à Yellowstone?   13. Quand avez-vous quitté la maison?   14. Vos parents voyagent-ils souvent? 15. Ont-ils voyagé l'été dernier?   16. Ont-ils jamais vu les Chutes du Niagara?   17. Comment ont-ils trouvé les Chutes du Niagara?

B. *Mettez les phrases suivantes au passé composé:*

1. Je vais en ville.   2. Il vient lundi.   3. Il revient lundi.   4. Il sort tout de suite.   5. Il ressort tout de suite.   6. Il entre.   7. Il rentre.

8. Nous partons mardi.   9. Nous repartons samedi.   10. Ils montent
dans le taxi.   11. Elle remonte dans sa chambre.   12. A quelle heure
allez-vous en ville?   13. A quelle heure retournez-vous en ville?
14. Qu'est-ce qu'il devient? (*What's becoming of him?*)

C. *Répondez affirmativement en français par une phrase complète:*

1. Êtes-vous sorti hier soir?   2. A quelle heure avez-vous quitté la maison?   3. Avez-vous dîné au restaurant?   4. Combien de temps êtes-
vous resté au restaurant?   5. Où avez-vous passé la soirée? (**au
théâtre**.)   6. A quelle heure avez-vous quitté le théâtre?   7. En quittant le théâtre êtes-vous retourné au restaurant?   8. A quelle heure
êtes-vous rentré chez vous?

D. *Exercice sur* **aller, partir, sortir, quitter, retourner, revenir, rentrer.** *Demandez à quelqu'un:*

1. s'il est allé au Canada l'été dernier.   2. quel jour il a quitté la maison.   3. quand il est parti des États-Unis.   4. s'il est allé à Montréal.
5. s'il est allé à Québec en quittant Montréal.   6. s'il est allé voir l'Île
d'Orléans.   7. s'il est retourné à Montréal.   8. quand il est revenu
aux États-Unis.   9. quand il est rentré à la maison.

E. *Exercice sur l'emploi de l'article défini. Dites en français:*

1. Dinner is at seven.   2. Milk is good for the health.   3. French
people like wine.   4. Americans like automobiles.   5. Boys like girls.
6. Children go to school.   7. Men love liberty.   8. Women prefer
luxury (*le luxe*).   9. School begins at 8:30.   10. At the entrance of
the freeway to the West.   11. Near the Saint-Cloud bridge.   12. Near
the entrance.   13. John has just signalled to a taxi driver.   14. He
has just signalled to the driver.   15. He finds Roger at the door of
the house.

F. *Emploi des expressions:*

1. *Employez* **près de** *avec chacun des noms suivants:*
    le pont, l'hôtel, la Seine, l'entrée, les quais, la voiture;

2. *Employez* **le long de** *avec chacun des mots suivants:*
   la rue, le boulevard, la Seine, les quais, le parc, l'avenue (*f*);
3. *Employez* **Il fait signe à** *avec chacun des mots suivants:*
   le chauffeur, le garçon, l'homme, le professeur, la jeune fille;
4. *Employez* **au cours de** *avec chacun des mots suivants:*
   le voyage, la conversation, l'année, les vacances;
5. *Employez la préposition* **à** (*at, on, upon*) *avec chacune des expressions suivantes:*
   l'arrivée de mon père, le départ de John Hughes, le retour de mon ami;
6. *Employez* **Nous allons à** *avec les mots suivants:*
   la maison, le parc, les Champs-Élysées, le théâtre, le cinéma, l'hôtel, le cours (*course*) de français;
7. *Employez* **Il s'arrête à** *avec les mots suivants:*
   l'entrée, la sortie, le parc, le kiosque, le bureau de tabac;
8. *Employez* **Je vais à** *avec chacun des noms suivants:*
   le Canada, les États-Unis, le Brésil, le Japon, le Danemark; Genève, Lyon, Bruxelles, Le Havre, La Nouvelle Orléans.
9. *Employez* **Je viens de** *avec les mêmes noms.*
10. *Employez* **Je vais en** *avec les noms suivants:*
    l'Afrique, la Hollande, l'Angleterre, la Chine, l'Allemagne, la Russie, la Suisse, l'Asie, l'Amérique.
11. *Employez* **Je viens de** *avec les mêmes noms.*

G. *Thème:*

We decided to have dinner downtown. We looked for a restaurant. We went in. We ordered (**commander**) a good dinner. The waiter brought the dinner. We finished early. We left the restaurant. We got into a taxi. The driver lost his way. He wasted a lot of time. We got home very late.

V CONVERSATION UNIT

Conversation à table

JOHN. —[1]Marie, votre dîner était délicieux. [2]Je ne savais pas du tout, il y a deux ans, que vous étiez si bonne cuisinière.

MARIE. —[3]J'apprécie vivement votre compliment. [4]Mais dites-nous un peu* ce que vous avez fait au cours de ces deux dernières années.

JOHN. —[5]L'année dernière, à cette date, j'étais en Égypte. [6]Vous souvenez-vous du terrible accident qui a eu lieu sur le Nil?

ROGER. —[7]Je me souviens de quelque chose—[8]un bateau qui transportait des passagers sur le Nil, n'est-ce pas?

JOHN. —[9]J'étais dans le voisinage au moment de l'accident. [10]Le lendemain, j'ai accompagné un de mes amis qui voulait prendre des photos pour un journal.

ROGER. —[11]Qu'est-ce qui est arrivé, exactement?

JOHN. —[1]Marie, your dinner was delicious. [2]I didn't have any idea two years ago that you were such a good cook.

MARIE. —[3]I appreciate your compliment very much (keenly). [4]But how about telling us what you have done in the course of these last two years?

JOHN. —[5]Last year, on this date, I was in Egypt. [6]Do you remember the terrible accident that took place on the Nile?

ROGER. —[7]I remember something —[8]a boat that was carrying passengers on the Nile, wasn't it?

JOHN. —[9]I was in the neighborhood at the time of the accident. [10]The next day, I went with a friend of mine who wanted to take pictures for a paper.

ROGER. —[11]Just what happened? (What happened, precisely?)

---

* This use of **un peu** merely softens the imperative. It does not mean "a little." Cf. **Voyons un peu**, *Let's take a look.*

[25]

JOHN. —[12]C'était un très vieux bateau. [13]Depuis soixante-dix ans il transportait des passagers sur le Nil. [14]Il y avait de la place pour une soixantaine de passagers. [15]Le jour de l'accident, on en a embarqué plus de cent cinquante. [16]Le bateau venait à peine de quitter la rive lorsque l'eau a commencé à entrer à l'intérieur.

MARIE. —[17]Pourquoi le capitaine n'est-il pas retourné au bord?

JOHN. —[18]Il a essayé. [19]Le bateau était à quelques mètres du bord quand l'accident a eu lieu. [20]Il était même si près du bord [21]qu'on a lancé des cordes à des gens sur la rive du fleuve. [22]Naturellement, plus ils tiraient sur les cordes plus le bateau s'inclinait. [23]Il a fini par chavirer. [24]Une centaine de personnes se sont noyées. [25]La plupart des passagers ne savaient pas nager.

MARIE. —[26]C'est en vérité une bien triste histoire. [27]Quand ils sont montés dans le bateau, ces pauvres gens ne savaient pas que leur dernière heure était proche.

ROGER. —[28]Oh! telle est la vie! ... [29]Si nous allions prendre le café au salon?

JOHN. —[12]It was a very old boat. [13]For seventy years, it had been carrying passengers on the Nile. [14]There was room for about sixty passengers. [15]The day of the accident, they took on more than a hundred and fifty. [16]The boat had scarcely left the shore when water began to come in.

MARIE. —[17]Why didn't the captain go back to shore?

JOHN. —[18]He tried to. [19]The boat was just a few yards from the shore when the accident took place. [20]It was so near the shore, even, [21]that they threw ropes to people on the bank of the river. [22]Naturally, the more they pulled on the ropes, the more the boat listed. [23]It finally turned over on its side. [24]About a hundred persons were drowned. [25]Most of the passengers didn't know how to swim.

MARIE. —[26]That is really a very sad story. [27]When they went on board the boat, those poor people didn't know that their last hour was near.

ROGER. —[28]Oh! such is life . . . [29]How about going into the living room to have coffee.

A. *Répondez en français par une phrase complète à chacune des questions suivantes:*

1. Comment John a-t-il trouvé le dîner de Marie?   2. Savait-il qu'elle était si bonne cuisinière?   3. Est-ce qu'elle apprécie son compliment? 4. Qu'est-ce qu'elle demande à John de leur dire?   5. Où était John l'année dernière à cette date?   6. Où l'accident a-t-il eu lieu?   7. Où est le Nil?   8. Est-ce que Roger se souvient de l'accident?   9. Qu'est-ce que le bateau transportait?   10. Où était John au moment de l'accident?   12. Le bateau était-il vieux?   13. Depuis combien de temps transportait-il des passagers?   14. Pour combien de passagers y avait-il de la place?   15. Combien de passagers a-t-on embarqué le jour de l'accident?   16. Qu'est-ce qui est arrivé quand le bateau a quitté la rive?   17. Qu'est-ce que le capitaine a essayé de faire?   18. A quelle distance le bateau était-il du bord quand l'accident a eu lieu?   19. A qui a-t-on lancé des cordes?   20. Qu'est-ce qui est arrivé quand les gens qui étaient sur la rive ont tiré sur les cordes?   21. Est-ce que le bateau a réussi à retourner au bord?   22. Combien de personnes se sont noyées?   23. Est-ce que tous les passagers savaient nager?   24. Est-ce que ces pauvres gens savaient que leur dernière heure était proche? 25. Que pensez-vous de cette histoire?

B. *Dites en français en employant les expressions indiquées:*

(a) **venait de**

1. The boat had just left the shore.   2. John had just arrived in Egypt. 3. They had just taken on more than a hundred and fifty people. 4. They had just thrown ropes to people on the bank of the river.

(b) **finir par**

1. The boat finally turned over.   2. The boat finally left the shore. 3. They finally took on more than a hundred and fifty passengers. 4. John finally left Egypt.

(c) **plus . . . plus; plus . . . moins**

1. The more they pulled, the more the boat listed.   2. The more the

boat listed, the more (the) water came in. 3. The more the water came in, the more the boat listed. 4. The more they tried, the less they succeeded.

(d) il y a

1. Two years ago. 2. An hour ago. 3. A few minutes ago. 4. A week ago.

(e) il y avait

1. There was room for sixty passengers. 2. There was room for about sixty passengers. 3. There was no room for more than sixty persons. 4. There was no room for more than about sixty persons. 5. There was no more room for us.

(f) être à . . . ; à quelle distance?

1. The boat was a few yards from the shore. 2. Versailles is a few kilometers from Paris. 3. New York is 5000 kilometers from Paris. 4. How far is Cairo (Le Caire) from Marseille? 5. How far is it from Le Havre to Southampton?

C. Demandez à quelqu'un:

1. ce que John pense du dîner de Marie. 2. quand John était à Paris. 3. s'il savait que Marie était bonne cuisinière. 4. ce que John a fait au cours des deux dernières années. 5. où a eu lieu l'accident dont parle John. 6. où il était au moment de l'accident. 7. ce qu'il a fait le lendemain. 8. ce qui est arrivé. 9. depuis quand le bateau transportait des passagers. 10. combien de passagers il y avait le jour de l'accident. 11. à quel moment l'eau a commencé à entrer à l'intérieur. 12. pourquoi le bateau a chaviré. 13. si le bateau était loin du bord quand il a chaviré. 14. où Roger propose d'aller prendre le café.

D. Remplacez le passé composé par l'expression **finir** **par** avec un infinitif:

1. Le bateau a chaviré. 2. On a embarqué plus de 150 personnes. 3. Il est retourné au bord. 4. Tous les passagers sont montés dans le bateau.

E. *Répétez les phrases suivantes en commençant chacune d'elles par l'expression* **la plupart (de):**

1. Les passagers ne savaient pas nager. 2. Les gens ont tiré sur les cordes. 3. Les chauffeurs de taxi sont bavards (*chatty*). 4. Les jeunes gens aiment les sports.

F. *Thème:*

Two years ago I was on a boat on the Mississippi near Saint Louis. It was an old boat which had been carrying passengers on the river for more than fifty years. It had hardly left the shore when they (**on**) told the captain that water was coming in. Immediately, the captain stopped the boat and gave orders (**l'ordre**) to go back to the shore. He told the passengers that there was no danger if they remained calm. Most of them knew how to swim and were not at all afraid.

The captain finally succeeded in returning to shore. All's well that ends well.

VI

Imparfait. Partitif

15. The *passé composé* and the *imparfait*.

In a conversation or narration about the past, both the *passé composé* and the *imparfait* are commonly used in French. As we have seen, the *passé composé* reports occurrences as they took place one after the other:

> Hier, **je suis allé** en ville. **J'ai pris** l'autobus. Dans l'autobus, **j'ai rencontré** Hélène. En descendant de l'autobus, **nous sommes allés** prendre un Coca-Cola.

On the other hand, the *imparfait* is used to report other occurrences that were taking place, or situations that existed at the time when the above-mentioned occurrences took place:

> Hier, **il faisait** beau quand je suis allé en ville. J'ai pris l'autobus, car **il était** tard et **je n'avais pas** le temps d'aller en ville à pied. Dans l'autobus, j'ai rencontré Hélène, **qui allait** aussi en ville. En descendant de l'autobus, **nous avions soif** et nous sommes allés prendre un Coca-Cola.

For the forms of the *imparfait,* see p. 235.

16. Commonest uses of the *imparfait*.

(1) The *imparfait* is used with the *passé composé:*

(*a*) to describe what was going on when an occurrence took place:

> Il **faisait** beau quand je suis allé en ville.
> Le bateau **était** à quelques mètres du bord quand l'accident a eu lieu.
> J'ai rencontré Hélène, qui **allait** aussi en ville.

(*b*) to explain why an occurrence took place (or didn't take place) :

J'ai pris l'autobus, car je n'avais pas le temps d'aller en ville à pied.
Je n'ai pas pu aller assister à la cérémonie. C'était trop loin.

(2) The *imparfait* is used in connection with another *imparfait:*

(*a*) to describe habitual action in the past:

Quand j'étais dans la jungle, j'allais au travail à six heures du matin. Je faisais la sieste tous les jours. Je finissais à six heures du soir.

(*b*) to describe two actions that were going on at the same time or two situations that existed concurrently:

Plus ils tiraient sur les cordes, plus le bateau s'inclinait.
Je voulais vous écrire, mais je ne savais pas votre adresse.

(3) The *imparfait* is used to describe the situation at the time of or prior to a past action:

Je pensais que vous étiez malade (*before I saw you*).
Il y avait de la place pour 60 personnes (*when the boat was built*).
Je ne savais pas que vous étiez si bonne cuisinière (*before eating dinner*).
La plupart des passagers ne savaient pas nager (*when the boat turned over*).

17. Special uses of the *imparfait*.

(1) With **depuis** or **il y avait . . . que** and an expression of time, the *imparfait* is used to report an action that had been going on for a specified period before another occurrence:

J'attendais depuis dix minutes quand le taxi est arrivé.
Depuis soixante-dix ans il transportait des passagers sur le Nil.

(2) The *imparfait* of **venir de** with an infinitive is used to express an action that had immediately preceded another past occurrence:

Le bateau venait de quitter la rive quand l'eau a commencé à entrer à l'intérieur.
Je venais de partir quand vous avez téléphoné.

(3) with the conjunction *si,* the *imparfait* is used to express
a mild request or a suggestion:

Si nous **allions** prendre le café au salon?
Si nous **dînions** en ville ce soir?

(4) For the use of the *imparfait* in *if*-clauses of conditional
sentences, see p. 107.

(5) The *imparfait* is used to express present action in indirect discourse depending upon a verb in the *passé composé:*

Il a dit: «Je vais en Égypte.» (*Direct discourse.*)
Il a dit qu'il **allait** en Égypte. (*Indirect discourse.*)

18. COMPARISON OF THE MEANING OF THE *passé composé*
AND THE *imparfait.*

Je ne **croyais** pas Versailles si grand (*before I saw it*).
Je ne vous **croyais** pas si bonne cuisinière (*before eating dinner*).
Je n'**ai** pas **cru** ce qu'il m'a dit (*after he told me*).
L'avion **survolait** la ville pendant la cérémonie. (*What was hap-
    pening . . .*)
L'avion **a survolé** la ville plusieurs fois. (*What happened.*)
J'**avais** peur d'être en retard car mon auto ne **marchait** pas bien.
Quand j'ai vu l'agent de police près de mon auto, j'**ai eu** peur.

We say "I was afraid" in both cases in English; but **j'ai eu
peur** in the last example describes the speaker's reaction to a
specific past action, whereas **j'avais peur** merely describes the
way he felt when something else was going on.

19. NOUNS USED IN A PARTITIVE SENSE.

French usage in regard to expressing the partitive idea is
very strict: a noun used in a partitive sense must be preceded
by the word **de** — either in combination with the definite article
or alone. It is not always easy for English speaking people to
know when a noun is used in a partitive sense, because we
sometimes express the partitive idea by the word "some" or
"any" but, more often, we merely *imply* it. Most people would

say: "Do you want coffee?" rather than "Do you want some coffee?" or "Do you want any coffee?" But in French, if you refer to *a part of* whatever you are talking about, you are using the noun in a partitive sense and you must express the partitive idea. Compare the following:

Le beurre est un aliment.	Butter is a food (*all butter*).
J'ai acheté **du beurre** ce matin.	I bought butter this morning (*a part of the butter that they had for sale at the store*).
Le beurre est dans le réfrigérateur.	The butter is in the refrigerator (*all the butter I bought*).
Voulez-vous **du beurre?**	Do you want butter? (*a part of the butter I bought*).

As a general rule, verbs such as **avoir, acheter, manger, vouloir** are usually followed by nouns used in a partitive sense: **J'ai des amis, J'achète du tabac, Je mange de la viande, Je voudrais du rosbif;** but verbs like **aimer, préférer, détester, admirer** are usually followed by nouns in a general or specific sense: **J'aime** (je n'aime pas) **le café noir; Je préfère le café au lait, Je déteste les bananes, J'admire les peintures de Renoir.** "I like *some* coffee" means "I like *some kinds of* coffee" — a nuance which is not expressed by the partitive in French.

20. USE OF PARTITIVE FORMS du, de la, de l', des, AND de.

(1) When a noun used in a partitive sense is the direct object of an affirmative or interrogative form of a verb, it is preceded by **du, de la,** or **des** — depending upon the gender and number of the noun: Voulez-vous **du café? de la crème? des fruits?** If the noun begins with a vowel, the form **de l'** is used for both *m* and *f sing.* nouns: Donnez-moi **de l'argent, de l'eau.**

(2) When a noun used in a partitive sense is the direct object of a negative form of a verb it is preceded by **de** (or **d'**) alone, regardless of gender or number:

Je ne bois **pas de café (pas de crème, pas d'eau minérale, pas de vin)**.	I don't drink coffee (cream, mineral water, wine).
Je ne prends **plus de café**.	I no longer take coffee.
Je ne prends **guère de café**.	I hardly take any coffee.
Je ne prends **jamais de café**.	I never take coffee.

(*a*) Note, however, that **ne . . . que** (only) is not negative and must be followed by **du, de la,** etc.

Je **ne** prends **que du café (que de la crème, que de l'eau,** etc.).

(*b*) Note also that when nouns are *not* used in a partitive sense, the form of the article is the same after a negative as after other forms of the verb:

J'aime **le café** (la crème, l'eau minérale, le vin).
Je n'aime **pas le café** (la crème, l'eau minérale, le vin).

21. SPECIAL USES OF **de** ALONE:

(1) After expressions of quantity: **beaucoup de** sucre, **un peu de** crème, **un kilo de** beurre, **des quantités de** fruits, **un tas de** choses, **une bouteille de** lait.

(2) Ordinarily **de** is used instead of **des** when a plural noun is preceded by an adjective: **de bons restaurants, d'autres restaurants, d'autres idées** (note exceptions in par. 29, 3, 4, 5).

22. THE INDEFINITE ARTICLE **un, une, (des).**

J'ai **un frère**.	J'ai **des frères**.
J'ai **une sœur**.	J'ai **des sœurs**.

The partitive form **des** can be thought of as the plural of **un, une.**

When the verb is negative, both **un, une,** and **des** are replaced by **de** alone.

Je n'ai pas de frère (de frères).
Je n'ai pas de sœur (de sœurs).

A. *Répondez en français à chacune des questions suivantes:*

1. Le dîner était-il bon?   2. Est-ce que Marie était bonne cuisinière il y a deux ans?   3. Savait-elle faire la cuisine il y a deux ans?   4. Où John était-il l'année dernière?   5. Qu'est-ce qu'il faisait en Égypte? 6 Était-il sur le bateau qui a chaviré?   7. Qu'est-ce que son ami voulait faire le lendemain?   8. Que faisait John quand il était à Paris il y a deux ans? (Il était ingénieur-chimiste.)   9. Que faisait-il quand il était à Pittsburgh?   10. Que faisait-il au Vénézuéla?   11. Est-ce qu'il faisait chaud lorsque John était en Arabie?   12. Faisait-il encore plus chaud au Soudan?   13. Est-ce qu'il pleuvait souvent au Vénézuéla?

B. *Dites en français:*

1. Suppose we go to the living room to have coffee.   2. Suppose you stay to dinner.   3. Suppose we talk about the good old times.   4. What if we stay home this evening?   5. Suppose we go to the movies. 6. Suppose you tell us about (**raconter**) your trip.   7. I did not know you were back.   8. Most of the passengers didn't know how to swim. 9. Roger thought John was in the jungle in Venezuela.   10. They did not know John was in France.   11. John didn't know they had a son.   12. John wanted to go to see his friends in Paris again.

C. *Répondez en français:*

1. Quel temps faisait-il quand vous avez quitté la maison?   2. Que faisiez-vous hier quand il a commencé à pleuvoir?   3. Qu'avez-vous fait hier quand il a commencé à pleuvoir?   4. Pourquoi êtes-vous resté à la maison hier soir?   5. Pourquoi n'êtes-vous pas allé au cinéma hier soir?   6. Saviez-vous que les Duplessis étaient mariés?   7. Roger savait-il que John était à Paris?   8. Les Duplessis pensaient-ils revoir John ce jour-là?

D. (a) *Remplacez le présent de* venir de *par l'imparfait dans chacune des phrases suivantes:* (Ex.: **Je viens de** finir. — **Je venais de** finir [I had just finished].)

1. Je viens d'arriver ici. 2. Nous venons de déjeuner. 3. Est-ce que John vient d'arriver à Paris? 4. Est-ce que vous venez de jouer au tennis?

(b) *Dites en français:* 1. I had just got home when you telephoned. 2. I had just gone out when it began to snow. 3. John had just arrived in Paris when he went to see his friends. 4. We had just entered the house when we heard the telephone.

E. *Répondez affirmativement et négativement à chacune des questions suivantes:*

1. Avez-vous fait des courses hier? 2. Avez-vous acheté un journal?
3. Avez-vous acheté des journaux? 4. Avez-vous acheté du beurre?
5. Y a-t-il du beurre sur la table? 6. Prenez-vous du café le matin?
7. Est-ce que vous preniez du café quand vous aviez dix ans? 8. Avez-vous reçu des lettres aujourd'hui? 9. Avez-vous reçu une lettre hier?
10. Avez-vous apporté des fruits?

F. *Employez les noms* **le lait** *et* **la bière** *dans chacune des phrases suivantes:*

1. Aimez-vous ____? 2. J'aime ____. 3. Je n'aime pas ____. 4. Voulez-vous ____? 5. Donnez-moi ____. 6. Je bois ____. 7. Je ne bois pas ____. 8. Je bois beaucoup ____. 9. Je ne bois pas beaucoup ____.
10. Je ne bois plus ____. 11. Je ne bois guère ____. 12. Je ne bois que ____.

G. *Dites en français:*

(a) 1. Cats and dogs are animals. 2. Butchers are merchants.
3. Horses are quadrupeds. 4. Apples and pears are fruit (plural).

(b) 1. A lot of things. 2. Many people (**gens**). 3. A kilo of bread. 4. A little bread. 5. A glass of milk. 6. A dozen eggs.

(c) 1. John has friends in Paris. 2. He has good friends. 3. He has other friends in America. 4. I bought some flowers this morning.
5. I bought some beautiful flowers. 6. I am going to buy some more (other) flowers tomorrow.

VII

Le petit Michel

ROGER. —[1]Est-ce que Michel est réveillé, Marie? [2]Voilà bien deux heures qu'il dort.

MARIE. —[3]Je crois l'avoir entendu remuer dans son lit tout à l'heure. [4]Voulez-vous le voir, John?

JOHN. —[5]Certainement. [6]J'ai si souvent entendu parler de lui que je tiens absolument à faire sa connaissance.

(*Dans la chambre de Michel.*)

MARIE. —[7]Je vous présente notre jeune fils Michel.

JOHN. —[8]Quel gentil petit garçon! [9]Regardez ces grands yeux bleus et ce joli sourire!

MARIE. —[10]Il est maintenant de bonne humeur, sans doute parce qu'il a dormi tout l'après-midi. [11]Quand il vient de se réveiller, il est quelquefois de très mauvaise humeur.

JOHN. —[12]J'ai peine à le croire. [13]Quel âge a-t-il, exactement?

MARIE. —[14]Il aura treize mois le premier septembre et il pèse onze kilos.

ROGER. —[1]Is Michel awake, Marie? [2]He has been asleep for two solid hours.

MARIE. —[3]I think I heard him stir in his bed a while ago. [4]Do you want to see him, John?

JOHN. —[5]Certainly. [6]I have heard of him so often that I absolutely insist upon meeting him.

(*In Michel's room.*)

MARIE. —[7]Let me introduce our young son Michel.

JOHN. —[8]What a nice little boy! [9]Look at those big blue eyes and that cute smile.

MARIE. —[10]He is in a good mood (humor) now, because he has slept all afternoon, no doubt. [11]When he has just wakened, he is sometimes in a very bad mood.

JOHN. —[12]I can scarcely believe it. [13]Just how old is he?

MARIE. —[14]He will be thirteen months old on September 1 and he weighs eleven kilos (24.2 pounds, approx.).

[37]

JOHN. —[15]Est-ce qu'il sait marcher?

JOHN. —[15]Can he walk?

ROGER. —[16]Voyons, John, saviez-vous marcher quand vous aviez un an?

ROGER. —[16]Come, John, could you walk when you were one year old?

JOHN. —[17]Franchement, je ne me rappelle pas . . . [18]D'ailleurs, avec une telle mère, ou plutôt avec de tels parents, rien n'est impossible.

JOHN. —[17]Frankly, I don't remember . . . [18]Anyway, with such a mother, or rather with such parents, nothing is impossible.

MARIE. —[19]Oh! voilà bien notre John, qui adore se moquer des gens, [20]tout en leur faisant des compliments.

MARIE. —[19]Oh! Isn't that just like John—who *loves* to kid people [20]while paying them compliments.

JOHN. —[21]Marie, vous me prêtez toute sorte de mauvaises intentions. [22]Malgré tout, nous sommes les meilleurs amis du monde, n'est-ce pas?

JOHN. —[21]Marie, you are attributing all sorts of bad meanings to me. [22]In spite of everything, we are the best friends in the world, aren't we?

A. *Répondez en français:*

1. Comment s'appelle le fils de Roger et de Marie?   2. Qu'est-ce qu'il fait à ce moment-là?   3. Depuis combien de temps dort-il?   4. Pourquoi Marie croit-elle qu'il est réveillé?   5. Est-ce que John a déjà fait sa connaissance?   6. Pourquoi tient-il à faire sa connaissance?   7. Où Roger, John et Marie vont-ils ensemble?   8. Que dit Marie en présentant son fils à John?   9. Comment John trouve-t-il le petit garçon? 10. Qu'est-ce qu'il admire particulièrement?   11. Pourquoi Michel est-il de bonne humeur?   12. Est-il toujours de bonne humeur? 13. Quand est-il de mauvaise humeur?   14. Quel âge a-t-il?   15. Combien pèse-t-il?   16. Est-ce qu'il sait marcher?   17. Saviez-vous marcher quand vous aviez treize mois?   18. Vous rappelez-vous quand vous avez commencé à marcher?   19. Est-ce que Michel sait parler? 20. Quel compliment John fait-il à Marie, à Roger?   21. Est-ce que John aime se moquer des gens tout en leur faisant des compliments? 22. Est-ce que vous aimez vous moquer des gens?   23. Quelle sorte

d'intentions Marie prête-t-elle à John?   24. Est-ce que ce sont de bons amis?

B. *Demandez en français à quelqu'un:*

1. si l'enfant des Duplessis est un garçon ou une fille.   2. comment s'appelle l'enfant.   3. s'il est réveillé.   4. depuis combien de temps il dort.   5. si John a entendu parler de lui.   6. si John a fait sa connaissance.   7. pourquoi il est de bonne humeur.   8. s'il est toujours de bonne humeur.   9. si le petit Michel sait marcher.   10. à quel âge un enfant commence à marcher.   11. quel âge a le petit Michel.   12. combien il pèse.   13. de quelle couleur sont les yeux du petit Michel.   14. si John savait marcher quand il avait un an.   15. si John aime se moquer des gens.

C. *Répondez en français en employant l'expression indiquée:*

(a) **savoir** (*et l'infinitif*)

1. Savez-vous conduire une auto?   2. Savez-vous jouer du piano? 3. Saviez-vous marcher quand vous aviez un an?   4. Saviez-vous parler quand vous aviez deux ans?

(b) **entendre** (*et l'infinitif*)

1. Est-ce que Marie a entendu remuer le petit Michel?   2. John a-t-il entendu parler du petit Michel?   3. Avez-vous entendu parler des châteaux de la Loire?   4. Avez-vous entendu dire que ces châteaux sont très beaux?   5. Avez-vous entendu parler du palais de Versailles?

D. *Dites en français en employant les expressions indiquées:*

(a) **tenir à**

1. I am anxious to meet him.   2. I am anxious to see little Michel. 3. John is anxious to see his friends again.   4. He is anxious to talk about his explorations in the jungle.   5. He is anxious to return to the United States.

(b) **croire avoir entendu, croire entendre**

1. I think I heard him stir in his bed.   2. I think I heard him cry (**pleurer**) a while ago. 3. I think I hear him stirring.   4. I think I

hear him crying.   5. Marie thinks she hears him singing.   6. I think I hear the train.   7. I think I heard a train.   8. I think I heard the train coming (**venir le train**).   9. I think I heard little Michel crying.

(c)   tout en

1. He likes to make fun of people while paying them compliments. 2. They were talking together while walking.   3. We were talking together while walking.   4. He was listening to the radio (**la T.S.F.**) while reading the newspaper.   5. He was reading the paper while listening to the radio.   6. I was looking at his eyes while listening to him.

(d)   du monde, de la ville, etc.

1. We are the best friends in the world.   2. New York is the largest city in the world.   3. There's the best restaurant in town (of the city). 4. John went to one of the best colleges in the United States.   5. That is the biggest hotel in Paris.

E. *Répétez chacune des phrases suivantes en employant* **un tel (une telle, de tels, de telles)** *au lieu de l'expression* **comme ça:**

1. Avec un père comme ça, rien n'est impossible.   2. Avec des parents comme ça, tout est possible.   3. Des amis comme ça sont rares.   4. On ne voit pas souvent des femmes comme ça.

F. *Thème:*

Parents are always proud of their children, and of course the Duplessis love their young son. When Michel was born a year ago, John was still in the Near East. He has often heard of him but he has not yet met him. He is very eager to see him, but little Michel has been asleep for two hours.

Marie thinks she hears him move in his bed. She goes to his room. Michel has just wakened, and because he has slept two hours he is in a good humor. He is (**C'est**) a nice little boy with (**aux**) big blue eyes and the prettiest smile in the world. Roger says he weighs eleven kilos, and that he can almost walk. John answers that with such parents he must (**doit**) be the best baby in the city.

VIII

Adjectifs

23. AGREEMENT OF ADJECTIVES.

Adjectives agree in gender and number with the noun they modify.

24. INTERROGATIVE ADJECTIVE quel? *(what)*.

	SINGULAR	PLURAL
MASCULINE	quel?	quels?
FEMININE	quelle?	quelles?

Ex.: **Quel temps** fait-il? **Quelle heure** est-il? A **quelle heure** dînez-vous? **Quels** sont les mois de l'année?

25. DEMONSTRATIVE ADJECTIVE ce *(this, that, those)*.

	SINGULAR	PLURAL
MASCULINE	**ce (cet)**	ces
FEMININE	**cette**	ces

The masculine form **ce** is used before nouns that begin with a consonant (other than a mute **h**), **cet** before those that begin with a vowel or mute **h**. Ex.: **Ce matin. Ce soir. Cet après-midi. Cet hôtel.**

The suffixes **–ci** and **–là**, which formerly meant *here* and *there,* are sometimes attached to nouns to sharpen the meaning of a preceding demonstrative adjective. Nouns (and demonstrative pronouns) with these suffixes are often used in oppositions: J'aime mieux **cette robe-ci** que **celle-là (cette robe-là).** I like *this dress* better than *that one (that dress).*

Note, however, that these suffixes are not used indiscriminately. The suffix **-là** is used with many expressions of time —

referring either to the past or the future. Ex.: **Ce jour-là** *that day,* **cette année-là** *that year,* **ce matin-là** *that morning,* **cette semaine-là** *that week,* **à ce moment-là** *at that time,* **à cette heure-là** *at that hour,* etc. But on the other hand, the suffix **-ci** is used much less frequently. Ex.: **ce mois-ci** *this month,* **à cette heure-ci** *at this hour,* **ces jours-ci** *these days.* You would not normally use the suffix **-ci** with **cette année, cette semaine, ce matin, en ce moment.** And for *this day* you would of course say **aujourd'hui.**

26. POSSESSIVE ADJECTIVES **mon, ton, son,** etc.

SINGULAR		PLURAL	
MASCULINE	FEMININE	MASCULINE AND FEMININE	
mon	ma (mon)	mes	*my*
ton	ta (ton)	tes	*your*
son	sa (son)	ses	*his, her, its*
notre	notre	nos	*our*
votre	votre	vos	*your*
leur	leur	leurs	*their*

(1) Note particularly that possessive adjectives agree in gender and number *with the noun they modify* — not with the noun to which they refer.

Roger parle de **son père** et de **sa mère** (*his,* singular).
Marie parle de **son père** et de **sa mère** (*her,* singular).
John parle de **ses voyages** (*his,* plural).
Roger et Marie parlent de **leur fils** (*their,* singular).
Ils parlent de **leurs amis** (*their,* plural).

(2) The feminine forms **ma, ta, sa,** are used before feminine nouns that begin with a consonant (other than a mute **h**); **mon, ton, son,** before those that begin with a vowel or a mute **h.**

ma sœur, **ma** petite sœur, **mon** autre sœur
ma nouvelle adresse, **mon** adresse

27. INDEFINITE ADJECTIVES.

	SINGULAR		PLURAL	
MASCULINE	FEMININE	MASCULINE	FEMININE	
un autre	une autre	d'autres	d'autres	*other*
l'autre	l'autre	les autres	les autres	
le même	la même	les mêmes	les mêmes	*same*
quelque	quelque	quelques	quelques	*some, a few*
un tel	une telle	de tels	de telles	*such (a)*
tout le	toute la	tous les	toutes les	*all, all the*
aucun	aucune			*no, not one*
chaque	chaque			*each*
		plusieurs	plusieurs	*several*

Note particularly the following: **quelque temps,** *some time;* **tout le temps,** *all the time;* **tout l'été** *the whole summer;* **toute la journée,** *all day;* **toute l'année,** *all year;* **tous les jours,** *every day;* **tous les soirs,** *every evening;* **tous les ans,** *every year;* **tous les trois ans,** *every three years;* **chaque jour (mois, année),** *each day (month, year).*

28. DESCRIPTIVE ADJECTIVES.

(1) The following normally precede the noun they modify:

	SINGULAR		PLURAL
MASCULINE	FEMININE	MASCULINE	FEMININE
beau (bel)	belle	beaux	belles
bon	bonne	bons	bonnes
mauvais	mauvaise	mauvais	mauvaises
joli	jolie	jolis	jolies
grand	grande	grands	grandes
gros	grosse	gros	grosses
long	longue	longs	longues
petit	petite	petits	petites
jeune	jeune	jeunes	jeunes
vieux (vieil)	vieille	vieux	vieilles
nouveau (nouvel)	nouvelle	nouveaux	nouvelles

The forms **bel, vieil,** and **nouvel** are used before masculine singular nouns that begin with a vowel or mute **h.**

(2) All other descriptive adjectives normally follow the noun they modify.

29. DESCRIPTIVE ADJECTIVES THAT NORMALLY PRECEDE THE NOUN MODIFIED.

The uses and meanings of these adjectives are extremely subtle. Here are a few remarks that will help to clarify this very complicated question:

(1) **Grand-grande** frequently means *large* in the sense of *tall*: **un grand arbre.** But it often has other meanings: **une grande maison,** *a big house;* **de grands yeux,** *big eyes;* **de grands pieds,** *big feet;* **les grandes personnes,** *grown-ups;* **un grand garçon,** *a big boy;* **une grand-mère,** *a grandmother.*

Un grand homme means "a great man" — *not* a tall man. If you want to translate "He's a tall man" into French, you could say: "C'est un homme grand"; but French people would be more likely to say "Il est grand" or "C'est un homme de haute taille."

(2) **Gros-grosse** ordinarily means *big, large* — in the sense of *voluminous.* You would say: **un gros livre, un gros chien, un gros poisson, une grosse voiture, une grosse fortune, une grosse orange, un gros dahlia.** You would *not* use the word **grand** with such nouns as **orange** or **poisson. Un grand dahlia** would refer to the height of the plant rather than to the size of the flower.

(3) **Jeune** usually means *young.* But note the following: **une jeune fille,** *a girl;* **des jeunes filles,** *girls;* **un jeune homme,** *a young man.* The plural of **un jeune homme** is **des jeunes gens;** but **des jeunes gens** also means *young people* in general. Ex.: **Marie était avec deux jeunes gens** (boys). **Marie, Roger, et John sont des jeunes gens** (mixed).

(4) **Petit-petite** means *small*. But note the following: **une petite fille**, *a little girl*, **des petites filles**, *little girls;* **une petite-fille**, *a granddaughter;* **un petit pain**, *a roll;* **des petits pains**, *rolls;* **des petits pois**, *green peas.*

(5) **Bon-bonne**, *good;* **mauvais-mauvaise**, *bad.* These words also mean *right* and *wrong:* **la bonne route, la mauvaise route; la bonne réponse, la mauvaise adresse.**

Bon is also used in the following expressions: **faire bon voyage**, *to have a good trip;* **acheter à bon marché**, *to buy at a favorable (low) price;* **du bon vin**, *wine of good quality;* **du bon beurre**, *butter of good quality;* **si j'ai bonne mémoire**, *if I remember correctly.*

(6) **Vieux-vieille**, *old* — in the sense of *aged;* **Ancien-ancienne**, *old* in the sense of *former.*

Un **vieux** ministre, an old (elderly) cabinet member.

Un **ancien** ministre, a former cabinet member.

But when **ancien** follows the noun modified (as it usually does), it has about the same meaning as **vieux**. Ex.: **un livre ancien**, *an old book;* **un vieux livre**, *an old book.*

(7) **Nouveau-nouvelle**, *new* — in the sense of *recent* or *additional.* Ex.: **Il a écrit un nouveau livre. Neuf-neuve**, new — in the sense of *brand new, unused.*

"Marie a acheté **un chapeau neuf**" and "Marie a acheté **un nouveau chapeau**" have about the same meaning, but the former stresses the fact that the hat is *new.* **Un nouveau livre** is merely *a new book.* But **un livre nouveau** is *a book that has just been published.*

(8) **Pauvre** usually follows the noun and means *poor* — the opposite of rich: C'est **un homme pauvre.** But when **pauvre** precedes the noun it means *unfortunate.*: **Le pauvre homme!** *The unfortunate fellow!*

30. COMPARATIVE OF ADJECTIVES: REGULAR.

(1) *Superiority* is expressed by **plus . . . que.**

Roger est **plus grand que** Marie.
Il fait **plus** chaud en Égypte **qu'**en France.

(2) *Equality* is expressed by **aussi . . . que.**

Marie est **aussi** intelligente **que** Roger.
Il fait **aussi** chaud aujourd'hui **qu'**hier.

(3) *Inferiority* is expressed by **moins . . . que.**

Marie est **moins** grande **que** Roger.
Le Havre est **moins** beau **que** Paris.

31. SUPERLATIVE OF ADJECTIVES: REGULAR.

(1) **le plus (la plus, les plus).**

Paris est **la plus grande** ville de France.

(2) **le moins (la moins, les moins).**

L'hiver est la saison **la moins agréable.**

Note that the superlative forms of adjectives normally stand in the same position in relation to the noun modified as their positive forms.

Le petit garçon. Le plus petit garçon.
Le garçon intelligent. Le garçon le plus intelligent.

32. IRREGULAR COMPARISON OF ADJECTIVES.

POSITIVE	COMPARATIVE	SUPERLATIVE
bon–bonne	meilleur–meilleure	le meilleur–la meilleure
bons–bonnes	meilleurs–meilleures	les meilleurs–les meilleures
mauvais–mauvaise	pire	le pire–la pire
mauvais–mauvaises	pires	les pires–les pires
petit–petite*	moindre	le moindre–la moindre
petits–petites	moindres	les moindres

---

* The regular comparison of **petit** is more common. The irregular forms (**moindre**) are used in set expressions. Ex.: Je n'en ai pas la **moindre idée.** C'est le **moindre de mes soucis.** Il n'a pas la **moindre chance** de réussir.

A. *Répondez en français en employant la forme convenable de l'adjectif possessif:*

1. Où demeurent vos parents?   2. Où habite votre famille?   3. Quel âge a votre père?   4. Votre mère est-elle allée en France?   5. Où habitent les parents du petit Michel?   6. Que fait le père de Michel? 7. Comment s'appelle la mère de Michel?   8. Comment John a-t-il trouvé le dîner de Marie?   9. Est-ce que John a parlé des voyages qu'il a faits?   10. A-t-il assisté au mariage de Marie et de Roger? 11. A-t-il reçu l'annonce du mariage de Marie et de Roger?   12. Est-ce que les Duplessis sont les meilleurs amis de John?

B. *Demandez à quelqu'un:*

1. l'heure qu'il est.   2. son âge.   3. la date de son anniversaire.   4. le nom du fils de Marie et de Roger.   5. la couleur de ses yeux.   6. le temps qu'il fait aujourd'hui.   7. à quelle heure il va dîner.   8. à quel âge il a commencé à parler.

C. *Dites en français en employant les expressions indiquées:*

(a) ce, cet, cette, ces; -ci, -là

1. This morning.   2. This year.   3. That morning.   4. That year. 5. This week.   6. That week.   7. This evening.   8. That evening. 9. This day (Today).   10. That day.   11. These days.   12. At that time.   13. At this time.   14. This tree.   15. These trees.   16. This girl.   17. These girls.

(b) tout, toute, tous, toutes

1. Every morning.   2. Every day.   3. Every year.   4. Every three years.   5. Every summer.   6. Every Thursday.   7. All day long.   8. All summer.   9. All the time.   10. All the afternoon.   11. All week. 12. All year.

(c) chaque

1. Each morning.   2. Each day.   3. Each evening.   4. Each week. 5. Each summer.   6. Each winter.   7. Each time (**fois**).

(*d*) **quelque**

1. I spent a few days in Pittsburgh.   2. A few weeks.   3. A few years.
4. A little time (**quelque temps**).   5. We took a few little pleasure
trips.

D. *Répondez trois fois à chacune des questions suivantes en
employant les expressions indiquées:*

plus . . . que, aussi . . . que, moins . . . que

1. Est-ce que Roger est aussi grand que sa femme?   2. Est-il aussi
gentil?   3. Est-il plus âgé que sa femme?   4. Est-ce qu'il fait plus
chaud au mois d'octobre qu'au mois d'avril?   5. Est-ce que les chiens
sont plus intelligents que les chats?   6. Est-ce que les femmes sont
aussi raisonnables que les hommes?

E. *Répondez en français:*

1. Quelle est la meilleure saison de l'année pour voyager?   2. Quel
est le meilleur moment de la journée pour travailler?   3. Où habite
votre meilleur ami?   4. Où habite votre meilleure amie?   5. D'où
viennent les meilleures oranges?   6. Quel est le meilleur moment de la
journée pour faire des courses?   7. Quel est le moment le moins
favorable pour travailler?   8. (*a*) Quelle est la plus mauvaise saison
de l'année?   (*b*) Quelle est la pire saison de l'année?

F. *Dites en français:*

(*a*) **Un garçon.**   1. He's* a young boy.   2. He's a handsome boy.
3. He's a bad boy.   4. He's a nice looking boy.   5. He's a tall boy.
6. He's a fat boy (**gros**).   7. He's a little boy.   8. He's a bachelor
(**un vieux garçon**).   9. They are young boys (**Ce sont de jeunes
garçons**).

(*b*) **Une jeune fille.**   1. She's a girl.   2. They are girls.   3. She's
a pretty girl.   4. They are pretty girls.   5. They are tall girls.   6. She's
an intelligent girl.

---

* Note on the use of **c'est, il est** (see p. 49).

(*c*) **Un arbre.** 1. It's a young tree. 2. A beautiful tree. 3. A tall tree. 4. An old tree.

(*d*) 1. It's a long trip. 2. It's a long walk. 3. A long story. 4. A new book. 5. A new road. 6. Some new books. 7. New ideas. 8. A long time (**longtemps**, *adv.*).

(*e*) 1. This man is taller than his wife. 2. He is younger than his wife. 3. He is less intelligent than his wife. 4. He is as nice as his wife.

(*f*) 1. She's a nice girl. 2. He is a nice boy. 3. He is nicer than his brother. 4. His brother has a nice little house.

(*g*) 1. The Eiffel Tower is higher than Notre Dame de Paris. 2. Notre Dame is much older than the Eiffel Tower. 3. It is one of the largest monuments in Paris. 4. It is also one of the finest.

(*h*) (**gros**) 1. There is a big dog. 2. He is almost as big as a Saint Bernard. 3. He is much bigger than a bull-dog (**bouledogue**).

(*i*) 1. It's a good dessert. 2. It is better than the salad. 3. It is the best dinner of the week. 4. John is a good student. 5. He is better than his father. 6. He is the best student in the class. 7. Henri is a bad student. 8. He is worse than his father. 9. He is the worst student in the class. 10. George is smaller. 11. Mary is smaller. 12. Hélène is the smallest girl in the class. 13. Being small (**être petite**) is the least of her worries.

---

1. HE IS, SHE IS, IT IS are expressed in French by **c'est** when **est** is followed directly by **le, la, un, une** or a possessive adj. (**mon, son,** etc.) Ex.: **C'est la** voiture de mon père. **C'est une** bonne voiture. **C'est sa** voiture.

2. THEY ARE is expressed in French by **ce sont** when **sont** is followed directly by **les, des (de)** or a possessive adj. (**mes, ses,** etc.) Ex.: **Ce sont les** photos de Marie. **Ce sont de** bonnes photos. **Ce sont ses** photos.

3. HE IS, SHE IS, IT IS are usually expressed in French by **il est, elle est** when **est** is followed directly by a descriptive adjective or an unmodified noun. Ex.: **Il est intelligent. Il est ingénieur. Elle est charmante.**

4. THEY ARE is expressed in French by **ils sont, elles sont** when **sont** is followed directly by a descriptive adjective or by an unmodified noun. Ex.: **Ils sont heureux. Elles sont heureuses. Ils sont Américains.**

IX

CONVERSATION UNIT

Au Louvre

ROGER. —[1]Je vais au Louvre cet après-midi. [2]Je devais y aller hier, mais je n'ai pas eu le temps. [3]Voulez-vous venir avec moi?

JOHN. —[4]Je veux bien. [5]Mais pourquoi cet intérêt soudain dans la peinture et la sculpture?

ROGER. —[6]Hélas, il ne s'agit ni de peinture ni de sculpture. [7]Je dois aller dans les bureaux d'une administration financière m'occuper d'une affaire d'impôts pour mon usine. [8]Ces bureaux sont dans une des ailes du Louvre.

JOHN. —[9]Est-ce qu'il vous faudra longtemps?

ROGER. —[10]Je ne sais pas au juste. [11]La dernière fois que j'y suis allé, il ne m'a fallu que quelques minutes. [12]Mais, comme vous le savez, il faut quelquefois attendre à la porte d'un bureau.

JOHN. —[13]Qu'est-ce que je pourrai bien faire, pendant que vous discutez avec un fonctionnaire les finances de votre usine?

ROGER. —[1]I am going to the Louvre this afternoon. [2]I was supposed to go yesterday, but I didn't have time. [3]Do you want to come with me?

JOHN. —[4]I'll be glad to. [5]But why this sudden interest in painting and sculpture?

ROGER. —[6]Alas, it is not a question of either painting or sculpture. [7]I have to go to the offices of a section of the treasury department to take care of a tax question for my company (factory). [8]Those offices are in one of the wings of the Louvre.

JOHN. —[9]Will it take you long?

ROGER. —[10]I don't know exactly. [11]The last time I went there, it took only a few minutes. [12]But, as you know, you sometimes have to wait at the door of an office.

JOHN. —[13]What can I do, while you are discussing the finances of your company with a government employe?

ROGER. —[14]Vous pouvez visiter le Musée. [15]Ce sera excellent pour votre culture artistique. [16]Je vous retrouverai à quatre heures dans la Grande Galerie, aux pieds de la Joconde.

JOHN. —[17]Aux pieds de la Joconde?

ROGER. —[18]C'est une façon de parler, bien entendu. [19]Vous savez ce que je veux dire.

(*Dans la Grande Galerie, quelques heures plus tard*)

JOHN. —[20]Vous êtes un peu en retard. [21]Voilà plus d'une heure que je vous attends.

ROGER. —[22]J'aurais dû arriver plus tôt, sans doute. [23]Mais il y a des choses qui dépendent de nous et d'autres qui ne dépendent pas de nous.

JOHN. —[24]En tout cas, je n'ai pas perdu mon temps. [25]Ce musée est vraiment étonnant. [26]Il faudrait des journées entières pour le visiter. [27]Voudriez-vous voir quelques salles?

ROGER. —[28]Pas aujourd'hui. [29]On va fermer dans quelques minutes. [30]Il vaut mieux revenir une autre fois.

ROGER. —[14]You can visit the museum. [15]It will be excellent for your artistic culture. [16]I'll meet you at four o'clock in the Grande Galerie, at the feet of the Mona Lisa.

JOHN. —[17]At the feet of the Mona Lisa?

ROGER. —[18]That's just a way of talking, of course. [19]You know what I mean.

(*In the Grande Galerie, a few hours later*)

JOHN. —[20]You are a little late. [21]I have been waiting for you for more than an hour.

ROGER. —[22]I should have got here sooner, of course. [23]But there are things that are under our control and others that are not.

JOHN. —[24]In any case, I have not wasted my time. [25]This museum is really astonishing. [26]It would take (entire) days to go through it. [27]Would you like to see a few rooms?

ROGER. —[28]Not today. [29]They are going to close in a few minutes. [30]It's better to come back another time.

A. *Répondez en français à chacune des questions suivantes:*

1. Où Roger va-t-il cet après-midi?   2. Quand devait-il aller au Louvre?
3. Pourquoi n'y est-il pas allé?   4. Que demande-t-il à John?   5. John

accepte-t-il son invitation? 6. Roger va-t-il au Louvre parce qu'il s'intéresse aux arts? 7. S'agit-il de peinture ou de sculpture? 8. Alors, pourquoi doit-il aller au Louvre? 9. Où se trouvent les bureaux où il doit aller? 10. Lui faudra-t-il longtemps pour s'occuper de son affaire? 11. Combien de temps lui a-t-il fallu la dernière fois? 12. Faut-il souvent attendre à la porte d'un bureau? 13. Que fera John pendant que Roger s'occupe de son affaire? 14. Où John et Roger vont-ils se retrouver? 15. Dans quelle galerie du Louvre se trouve la Joconde? 16. Quand les deux amis se retrouvent-ils? 17. Roger est-il à l'heure (*on time*)? 18. Combien de temps y a-t-il que John l'attend? 19. Que lui dit Roger pour s'excuser? 20. Qu'a fait John pendant son absence? 21. A-t-il visité tout le musée du Louvre? 22. Combien de temps faudrait-il pour le visiter? 23. Qu'est-ce que John propose à Roger? 24. Pourquoi Roger ne peut-il pas visiter le musée aujourd'hui? 25. Quand propose-t-il de revenir?

B. *Demandez en français à quelqu'un:*

1. où Roger doit aller cet après-midi. 2. pourquoi il doit aller au Louvre. 3. quand il devait y aller. 4. s'il s'agit de peinture ou de sculpture. 5. de quoi il s'agit. 6. où se trouvent les bureaux dont il s'agit. 7. de quelle affaire Roger doit s'occuper. 8. s'il sait au juste combien de temps il lui faudra. 9. où John et Roger doivent se retrouver. 10. s'il a jamais entendu parler de la Joconde. 11. comment s'appelle en anglais ce portrait célèbre. 12. où John et Roger se retrouvent quelque temps plus tard. 13. si John a perdu son temps pendant l'absence de Roger. 14. s'il a eu le temps de visiter tout le musée. 15. pourquoi il vaut mieux revenir une autre fois.

C. *Employez une des expressions indiquées dans votre réponse aux questions suivantes:*

(a) y aller

1. Pourquoi Roger va-t-il au Louvre? 2. Est-ce qu'il y va souvent? 3. Y est-il déjà allé? 4. Quand devait-il y aller? 5. Pourquoi n'y est-il pas allé hier? 6. Allez-vous souvent en ville? 7. Y êtes-vous allé hier? 8. Quand avez-vous l'intention d'y aller?

(*b*) **de bonne heure, plus tôt, tard, en retard, à l'heure**

1. A quelle heure êtes-vous rentré hier soir?   2. Êtes-vous rentré de bonne heure? (deux réponses)   3. Roger était-il à l'heure quand il a retrouvé John?   4. Est-ce que Roger devait arriver plus tôt?   5. Est-ce qu'il aurait dû arriver plus tôt?   6. Êtes-vous arrivé à l'heure à la gare? (deux réponses)   7. Quand êtes-vous parti de la maison?   8. Quand avez-vous fini votre travail hier soir?

(*c*) **plus de, plus que**

1. Depuis combien de temps John attend-il Roger? (*More than an hour.*)   2. Combien de temps a-t-il fallu à Roger pour s'occuper de son affaire?   3. Avez-vous plus de responsabilités que votre père?   4. Avez-vous plus de travail que votre frère?   5. L'Asie a-t-elle plus d'habitants que l'Europe?

D. *Dites en français en employant* il s'agit *ou* il s'agissait:

1. It is a question of a tax problem.   2. It is a matter of a few minutes.   3. It was a question of a tax problem.   4. It is about one of your friends.   5. It was a question of one of my friends.   6. It was a question of going to see his friends.   7. It is a question of finding (the) time.   8. It was about a terrible accident.

E. *Faites une seule phrase en groupant les deux propositions qui se suivent et en employant* "ne ... ni ... ni ...."

1. Il ne s'agit pas de peinture. Il ne s'agit pas de sculpture.   2. Il ne fait pas trop chaud. Il ne fait pas trop froid.   3. Je n'ai pas de frères. Je n'ai pas de sœurs.   4. John n'est pas allé en Hollande. Roger n'est pas allé en Hollande. (Ni John ni Roger n'est . . .)   5. John n'a pas de parents en France. John n'a pas de parents en Hollande. (. . . ni en France ni en Hollande)   6. John n'est pas allé en Suisse. John n'est pas allé en Belgique.   7. Il n'a pas visité Florence. Il n'a pas visité Rome.   8. Marie n'a pas vu les Alpes. Roger n'a pas vu les Alpes.

F. *Thème:*

One afternoon, Roger asked John if he would like (wanted) to go with him to the Louvre. John gladly accepted his friend's invitation. He thought of course that they were going to visit the Louvre Museum together. But when they arrived at the Louvre, Roger said that he had a little errand to do, nothing much (**pas grand'chose**), a simple tax question for his company. John waited for his friend a quarter of an hour, half an hour, one hour, more than one hour. He knew that administration is never simple. Yet when Roger returned, he said to his old friend: "Old man, I know that it is not your fault. But I have not come from Arabia to Paris to wait at the door of some official of the Internal Revenue Service (**un fonctionnaire du ministère des finances**).

X

Devoir, Falloir, Pouvoir, Vouloir, Savoir

33. REMARK ABOUT THESE VERBS.

These verbs are irregular both in form and meaning. They are doubly difficult for English-speaking persons because their English equivalents are also irregular and because in both languages some of the forms have two or more entirely different meanings. Therefore the forms and meanings of these verbs must be studied carefully, understood sharply, and practiced systematically.

34. Devoir *(must, should, ought, to be supposed to, etc.).*

(1) The *present tense* of **devoir** is used to express:

(*a*) probability:

Quelle heure est-il? — **Il doit être** au moins 5 heures. (*It must be . . .*)

(*b*) an action which one expects to fulfill:

Je dois aller au Louvre cet après-midi. (*I am supposed to . . .***)**

(*c*) obligation:

Vous devez travailler davantage. (*You must . . .*)

(2) The *imparfait* is most commonly used to express an action that was expected to take place but that (usually) did not take place:

Je devais y aller hier, mais je l'ai complètement oublié. (*I was supposed to . . .*)
Je ne suis pas allé au laboratoire hier, car **je devais aller** au Louvre. (*I was supposed to . . .*)

[55]

(3) The *passé composé* is most commonly used to express probability (in the past) :

Où est votre montre?
J'ai dû la **laisser** à la maison. (*I must have* . . .)

(4) The *conditional* is used to express the speaker's judgment as to the desirability or propriety of an action (present or future) :

Je devrais visiter toutes les salles. (*I should, ought to* . . .)
Vous ne **devriez** pas **perdre** votre temps. (*You shouldn't* . . .)

(5) The *conditional perfect* is used to express the speaker's judgment (disapproval) of:

(*a*) an action that has taken place:

Vous n'**auriez** pas **dû** y aller. (*You shouldn't have gone there.*)

(*b*) the fact that an action did not take place: .

Vous auriez dû venir me voir. (*You should have, ought to have* . . .)

35. Devoir MEANING *"to owe."*

Devoir is normally followed by an infinitive (as in the preceding examples); but it is also used as a transitive verb with the meaning "to owe.":

Qu'est-ce que **je** vous **dois?** What (How much) do *I owe* you?
— **Vous** me **devez** 150 francs. *You owe* me 150 francs.

The forms of **devoir** will be found on pp. 257-258.

36. Falloir *(must, to have to, to be necessary, etc.).*

(1) Meaning of **falloir.**
Most authorities say that **devoir** denotes moral obligation and that **falloir** denotes physical necessity. In present day usage, this distinction is not always observed.

(2) Use of **falloir.**

Falloir may be followed by an infinitive, by a clause in the subjunctive, or by a noun:

FOLLOWED BY AN INFINITIVE

(*a*) Completely impersonal:

Il faut manger pour vivre. (*One must* . . .)
Il faut quelquefois **attendre** dans les bureaux. (*One has to* . . .)

(*b*) Impersonal in form, personal in meaning:

Si vous allez en ville, **il faudra attendre** l'autobus. (*You'll have to* . . .)

Hier, **il a fallu attendre** une demi-heure (*I, we, you, they*—depending on the context—*had to* . . .)

Il faudra faire la queue. (*I, you,* etc., *will have to* . . .)

FOLLOWED BY AN INFINITIVE WITH PERSONAL PRONOUN

Ex.: **Il me faut faire** des courses ce matin. Note that this usage was current in the past but that now it is rather unusual in spoken French. Today you would be more likely to say: Il faut que je fasse des courses (*see below*), Je dois faire des courses, *or, even,* J'ai des courses à faire.

FOLLOWED BY A CLAUSE IN THE SUBJUNCTIVE

Ex.: **Il faut que je fasse** des courses. This pattern is very current and will be taken up in detail in the discussion of the subjunctive.

FOLLOWED BY A NOUN OR AN EXPRESSION OF TIME

Il faudrait beacoup **d'argent.** (*It would take* . . .)
Il faut du courage pour faire cela. (*It takes* . . .)
Il faut vingt **minutes** pour aller à Saint-Cloud. (*It takes* . . .)
Il faudra une heure. (*It will take* . . .)
Il faudrait des journées entières. (*It would take* . . .)
Il ne m'a fallu que quelques **instants.** (*It took me only* . . .)
Est-ce qu'il vous **faudra** longtemps? (*Will it take you* . . . ?)

The forms of **falloir** will be found on p. 261.

37. Pouvoir *(can, may, to be able, etc.).*

(1) The present indicative of **pouvoir** means either *may* or *can**:

> Est-ce que **je peux voir** le bébé? (*May I . . . ?*)
> Est-ce que **je peux** vous **aider?** (*Can I . . .?*)

The future is frequently used in preference to the present when the immediate future is involved:

> Qu'est-ce que **je pourrai** faire? (*What can I do?*)
> **Vous pouvez** (or **pourrez**) visiter le Musée. (*You can . . .*)

(2) The *imparfait,* the *passe composé,* and the conditional all mean *could:*

   (*a*) The *imparfait* means *could* in the sense of *was able to:*

> Comme **je ne pouvais pas aller** voir ma mère, . . . (*Since I couldn't . . .*)

   (*b*) The *passé composé* means *could* in the sense of *I succeeded in:*

> Heureusement, **j'ai pu trouver** un taxi. (*I could get . . .*)
> Par malheur, **je n'ai pas pu trouver** de taxi. (*I couldn't get . . .*)

   (*c*) The conditional means *could* in the sense of *would be able:*

> **Je ne pourrais pas trouver** de taxi à cette heure-ci. (*I couldn't, I wouldn't be able to . . .*)
> **Vous pourriez aller** en ville à pied. (*You could . . .*)

(3) The conditional perfect means *could have* in the sense of *would have been able to:*

> **J'aurais pu attendre** l'autobus. (*I could have waited . . .*)

Note that **pouvoir** is always followed by the *present* infinitive. Although in English we say: I could have *gone,* in French you say **J'aurais pu y aller** (*lit.:* I would have been able to go.)

The forms of **pouvoir** will be found on p. 267.

---

* **Pouvoir** is not used to express *can* in phrases like "Can you play the violin?" "Can you drive a car?" For these expressions, see **savoir.**

38. Vouloir *(to want)*, **vouloir bien** *(to be willing)*.

(1) *Present indicative:*

Voulez-vous venir avec moi au Louvre? (*Do you want to ...?*)

Je veux bien. (*I am willing. Yes, thank you.*)

For a negative answer, you would not say: **Je ne veux pas** (*I won't*), which would be impolite, but: **Non, merci. Je regrette.**

(2) *Imparfait:*

Comme **je voulais** visiter le Louvre, je suis parti de bonne heure. (*I wanted to ...*)

(3) *Passé composé:*

J'ai voulu visiter le musée. (*I wanted to, decided to ...*)

(4) *Conditional:*

Je voudrais voir la Salle d'Apollon. (*I want, would like to ...*)

(5) *Conditional perfect:*

J'aurais voulu voir la Joconde. (*I would have liked to ...*)

The forms of **vouloir** will be found on pp. 275-276.

39. Vouloir dire *(to mean)*.

Qu'est-ce que **ça veut dire?** (*What does that mean?*)

Vous savez ce que **je veux dire.** (*You know what I mean.*)

40. Savoir *(to know, to know how)*.

(1) *Present indicative:*

Savez-vous la date? (*Do you know ...*)

Sait-elle faire la cuisine? (*Does she know how to ...*)

Savez-vous jouer du piano? (*Do you know how to ...*)

(2) *Imparfait:*

Je ne savais pas votre adresse à ce moment-là. (*I didn't know ...*)

(3) *Passé composé:*

Quand **j'ai su** votre adresse ... (*When I learned, found out ...*)

(4) *Future:*

Quand **je saurai** son adresse . . . (*When I find out, learn* . . .)

The forms of **savoir** will be found on pp. 269-270.

41. Distinction between savoir and connaître.

Both verbs are normally translated by the English verb "to know"; but **connaître** means "to know" in the sense of "to be acquainted with." However, as "to be acquainted with" is scarcely ever used in English and as **connaître** is very frequently used in French, it is useful to study carefully the way the two words are used in French.

(1) **Savoir** is used to refer to a fact or a specific piece of information such as: dates, time, happenings, names, age, price, etc.

(*a*) It may have a noun or pronoun as a direct object:

Savez-vous l'heure de départ du train?
Non, **je ne la sais** pas.
John ne **sait** pas l'**âge** du petit Michel.

(*b*) It may introduce clauses beginning with: **que . . . , si . . . , combien . . . , où . . . , quand . . . , quel . . . ,** etc.

Je ne sais pas où habitent les Duplessis.
Savez-vous à quelle heure part le train?
Les Duplessis ne savaient pas que John était à Paris.

(*c*) It may be followed by an infinitive. In this case it means "to know how":

La plupart des passagers **ne savaient pas nager.**
Savez-vous faire la cuisine?

(2) **Connaître** is always used with a noun or pronoun as a direct object and it is chiefly used in speaking of persons, places, literary or artistic works:

Connaissez-vous les Duplessis? — Non, je ne **les connais pas.**
John **connaît Versailles.** Il ne **connaît** pas **Saint-Cloud.**

Connaissez-vous l'*Iliade?* (les *Joueurs de cartes* de Cézanne? le *Cimetière marin* de Valéry?)

Note that **connaître** cannot be used with infinitives or before the words **où, quand, combien,** etc.

(3) *To know by heart* is **savoir par coeur.**

— Connaissez vous le *Cimetière marin?* — Oui, je le **sais par cœur.**

(4) **Savoir** and **connaître** are more or less interchangeable in a few cases:

Je sais le grec.
Je connais le grec.
Savez-vous l'histoire de la prise de Troie?
Connaissez-vous cette histoire?

A. *Répondez en français:*

1. Où Roger doit-il aller cet après-midi? 2. Qu'est-ce qu'il devait faire hier? 3. Doit-il attendre au bureau? 4. Faut-il souvent attendre à la porte d'un bureau? 5. Avez-vous des courses à faire? 6. Est-ce que vous devez les faire aujourd'hui? 7. Deviez-vous les faire hier? 8. Auriez-vous dû les faire la semaine dernière? 9. Voulez-vous les faire maintenant? 10. Faut-il les faire tout de suite? 11. Savez-vous le grec? 12. Connaissez-vous l'*Iliade* d'Homère? 13. Savez-vous la date de la mort d'Homère? 14. Pourriez-vous me dire quand il a écrit l'*Iliade?* 15. Savez-vous l'histoire de la prise de Troie? 16. Connaissez-vous cette histoire? 17. Voudriez-vous entendre cette histoire? 18. Avez-vous pu lire l'*Iliade?*

B. (a) *Répétez chacune des phrases suivantes en remplaçant l'impératif par l'expression* **Il faut** (*ou* **Il ne faut pas**) *et l'infinitif:* (Ex.: N'allez pas trop vite. — **Il ne faut pas aller trop vite.**)

1. Restez calme. 2. Soyez à l'heure. 3. Ne soyez pas en retard. 4. Ne perdez pas votre temps. 5. Allez voir ce film. 6. Partez à temps. 7. Ne courez pas dans la rue. 8. Soyez gentil pour tout le monde.

9. Attendez un instant. 10. Venez me voir. 11. Visitez le musée.
12. Appelez un taxi.

 (*b*) Même exercice avec **Vous devez** (you must).

 (*c*) Même exercice avec **Vous devriez** (you should, you ought to).

 (*d*) Même exercice avec **Vous auriez dû . . . hier** (you should have . . .)

C. *Transposez chacune des phrases suivantes au conditionnel passé:* (Ex.: Il ne faut pas avoir peur. — Il n'aurait pas fallu avoir peur.)

1. John doit aller revoir ses amis. 2. Je peux travailler davantage.
3. Je ne dois pas perdre mon temps. 4. Il faut partir plus tôt. 5. Nous devons être à l'heure. 6. Je veux aller à la campagne pour le week-end. 7. John veut assister au mariage. 8. Peut-il venir au mariage?

D. Verb Drill. *Dites en français:*

1. I must . . . 2. I should . . . 3. I should have . . . 4. I can . . .
5. I can't . . . 6. I could (imparfait) . . . 7. I couldn't (passé composé) . . . 8. I could (conditional) . . . 9. May I . . . ? 10. Will you . . . ? 11. Would you like . . . ? 12. I would like . . . 13. You shouldn't . . . 14. You mustn't . . . 15. I shouldn't have . . .
16. You couldn't have . . . 17. You wouldn't have wanted to . . .
18. You wouldn't have been able to . . .

E. *Thème:*

 "You must see that film."

 "I would like to see it. I couldn't go to the movies yesterday."

 "Could you go (to it) tonight?"

 "No, I can't go (to it) tonight. But I could go (to it) tomorrow."

 "It is too late. You should have seen the film last week."

 "I would have liked to see it. I was free Thursday; I could have seen it that night. You should have told me about it. One should not miss such films. When there are good films, will you please let me know (**me le faire savoir**)?"

 "Yes, I am willing. I should have thought of it sooner."

Portrait de François Ier, par Clouet.

La Renaissance française

Château de Chenonceaux.

Catherine de Médicis.

Château de Chambord.

La Salamandre, emblème de François I.

David et Goliath, d'après un livre ayant appartenu
à Louise de Savoie.

Tapisserie: les vendanges.

FROM "Louise de Savoie et François I" BY R. MAULDE DE LA CLAVIÈRE (Perrin)

A la cour de Louise de Savoie. "La musique à Cognac."

Château de Blois: porc-épic.

Le Grand Escalier du château de Blois.

Le Louvre, vu des jardins du Carrousel.

L'ancien régime

Place Vendôme.

En haut, à gauche — Partie du Louvre construite par François Premier.

En bas, à gauche — Prise de la Bastille, le 14 juillet 1789.

Versailles la nuit.

Portrait de Marie-Antoinette.

Versailles. Jardin de l'Orangerie.

En bas, à droite — Versailles. Intérieur. Période de Louis XIV.

Louis XIV.

Versailles. Le Petit Trianon construit au XVIIIe siècle.

Versailles. La Galerie des Glaces (Hall of Mirrors).

XI

CONVERSATION UNIT

Le pétrole saharien

John est allé aux bureaux de la Société Nationale des Recherches de Pétrole en Algérie voir Bernard Jeannin, dont il a fait la connaissance au cours de son séjour à Paris.

John has gone to the offices of the National Research Co. for Oil in Algeria to see Bernard Jeannin whom he met in the course of his stay in Paris.

JOHN. —[1]La dernière fois que je vous ai vu, [2]vous étiez fort enthousiaste au sujet de la découverte de pétrole dans le Sahara. [3]Où en sont maintenant vos travaux de prospection?

BERNARD. —[4]Ça marche on ne peut pas mieux. [5]Les forages se poursuivent dans la région d'Hassi-Messaoud. [6]La zone des gisements s'étend sur plus de 1000 kilomètres carrés. [7]Nous comptons que dans quelques années d'ici, la production saharienne suffira à nos besoins.

JOHN. —[8]J'ai entendu dire qu'un certain nombre de puits étaient déjà en opération à l'heure actuelle.

BERNARD.—[9]Une quinzaine, si je ne me trompe pas. [10]Nous en sommes encore au commencement. [11]Nous nous occupons actuellement de l'établissement

JOHN. —[1]The last time I saw you, [2]you were very enthusiastic about the discovery of oil in the Sahara. [3]How far along is your work of prospecting?

BERNARD. —[4]It couldn't be going better. [5]Drilling is continuing in the Hassi-Messaoud region. [6]The oil land extends over more than 1000 square kilometers. [7]We expect that within a few years from now, the Saharan yield will suffice for our needs.

JOHN. —[8]I have heard that a certain number of wells were already in operation at present.

BERNARD. —[9]About fifteen, if I am not mistaken. [10]We are just at the beginning. [11]We are busy at present with the laying of pipelines and building an

des pipe-lines et de la construction d'une «route du pétrole» [12]qui aura 700 kilomètres de long et qui ira jusqu'à
la Méditerranée. [13]Cela fait
partie d'un vaste plan de développement agricole et industriel de l'Algérie. [14]Déjà les
populations du pays s'habillent
et se nourrissent mieux qu'auparavant. [15]Peu à peu, Européens et Africains s'habituent à
travailler ensemble, vers un but
commun.

JOHN. —[16]Vous m'avez dit que
vous connaissez la région
d'Hassi-Messaoud, n'est-ce pas?

BERNARD. —[17]Un peu. [18]Il n'y a
d'ailleurs pas grand'chose à
connaître. [19]A part le pétrole,
c'est le paysage saharien tel
qu'on se l'imagine d'ordinaire:
[20]du sable à perte de vue, des
dunes mouvantes, avec ça et là
quelque arbuste qui s'efforce de
pousser.

JOHN. —[21]Hélas! Je ne le connais que trop bien, vous savez,
[22]le désert avec ses journées
brûlantes et ses nuits presque
trop fraîches . . .

"oil road" [12]that will be 700
kilometers long and that will go
all the way to the Mediterranean. [13]That is a part of a huge
plan for the agricultural and
industrial development of Algeria. [14]Already the local population is better dressed and
better fed than before. [15]Little
by little, Europeans and Africans are getting used to working together, towards a common goal.

JOHN. —[16]You told me that you
know the Hassi-Messaoud region, didn't you?

BERNARD. —[17]A little. [18]Anyway
there is not much to know.
[19]Aside from the oil, it is the
Sahara landscape as you usually imagine it: [20]sand as far as
you can see, moving dunes, with
here and there a bush trying
hard to grow.

JOHN.—[21]Alas! I know it only
too well, you know—[22]the desert with its burning days and
its nights that are almost too
cold . . .

A. *Répondez en français:*

1. Où John est-il allé? 2. Pourquoi est-il allé là? 3. Quand a-t-il
fait la connaissance de Bernard? 4. Qu'est-ce qu'on a découvert dans
le Sahara? 5. Dans quelle région se poursuivent les forages? 6. La

zone des gisements est-elle considérable? 7. Sur combien de kilomètres carrés s'étend-elle? 8. Quand la production saharienne suffira-
t-elle aux besoins du pays? 9. Y a-t-il des puits en opération à l'heure
actuelle? 10. Combien de puits sont actuellement en opération?
11. De quoi s'occupe-t-on actuellement? 12. Jusqu'où la route en
construction ira-t-elle? 13. Quelle est la longueur de cette route?
14. De quoi ce projet fait-il partie? 15. Quel est à l'heure actuelle le
résultat du plan de développement agricole et industriel de l'Algérie?
16. Quel est le résultat au point de vue des relations entre Européens
et Africains? 17. Bernard connaît-il la région d'Hassi-Messaoud?
18. Comment s'imagine-t-on d'ordinaire le paysage saharien? 19. La
végétation est-elle très abondante? 20. John connaît-il bien le désert?
21. Pourquoi dit-il qu'il ne le connaît que trop bien? 22. Les journées dans le désert sont-elles très chaudes? 23. Les nuits sont-elles
aussi chaudes que les journées?

B. *Demandez en français à quelqu'un:*

1. s'il a entendu parler de la découverte de pétrole dans le Sahara.
2. si les travaux marchent bien. 3. si la production actuelle suffit aux
besoins du pays. 4. de quoi les ingénieurs s'occupent à l'heure actuelle.
5. jusqu'où ira la route du pétrole. 6. quel est l'objet du plan en opération. 7. comment les populations profitent de ce plan. 8. si Bernard
connaît la région d'Hassi-Messaoud. 9. comment on s'imagine d'ordinaire le paysage saharien. 10. s'il a jamais vu un désert. 11. s'il y a
des montagnes dans le Sahara. 12. s'il y a une grande différence de
température entre le jour et la nuit.

C. *Employez une des expressions indiquées en réponse à chacune des questions suivantes:*

(*a*) suffire (à), il suffit de

1. Quand la production de pétrole suffira-t-elle aux besoins du pays?
2. La production actuelle suffit-elle? 3. Suffit-il d'être riche pour être
heureux?

(*b*) faire partie de

1. De quel plan général la construction d'une route du pétrole fait-elle

partie?   2. Connaissez-vous un autre projet qui fait partie du même plan?   3. Faites-vous partie d'une association sportive?

(c) à l'heure actuelle, actuellement

1. Combien de puits de pétrole sont en opération à l'heure actuelle? 2. De quels travaux s'occupe-t-on actuellement?   3. Où en sont les travaux à l'heure actuelle?   4. Comment va votre travail actuellement?

(d) pas grand'chose

1. Y a-t-il beaucoup à voir dans le désert du Sahara?   2. Avez-vous beaucoup à faire ce soir?   3. Que faites-vous d'habitude le dimanche?

D. *Dites en français:*

(a) **en être (à)**   1. How far along is your prospecting (**travaux de prospection**)?   2. How far along is your work?   3. We are still at the beginning.   4. I am still at the beginning.

(b) **de long, de large, de haut**   1. The road will be 700 kilometers long.   2. The street is ten meters wide.   3. The river was 30 meters wide.   4. The Eiffel Tower is 300 meters high.

(c) **plus de**   1. The road will be over 700 kilometers long.   2. The street was over 20 meters wide.   3. This building will be more than 200 meters high.   4. The oil deposits extend over more than 1000 square kilometers.   5. At the present time, North Africa has more than 20 million inhabitants.

E. *Thème:*

A few years ago, oil was found in the Sahara Desert. The most important strike (discovery) was made in the Hassi-Messaoud region. A certain number of wells are already in operation and they expect (**compter**) the exploitation of the oil deposits in the Sahara will completely change economic conditions in this part of the world.

Transportation (**le transport**) is the main problem. Engineers are now working (**s'occuper**) on the installation of a pipe-line and the construction of a road from Hassi-Messaoud to the sea. A broad plan for the agricultural and industrial development of Algeria is already in operation. Europeans and Africans are getting used to working together and relations between the two groups are better than before (**qu'auparavant**).

XII

XII

GRAMMAR UNIT

Verbes pronominaux

42. FORM OF REFLEXIVE VERBS.

Verbs that are conjugated with a pronoun subject and a pronoun object that refers to the subject are called reflexive verbs *(verbes pronominaux):* **Je me** rappelle; **Il se** moque de nous.

The forms of the reflexive pronoun object are: **me, te, se, nous, vous, se.** The reflexive pronoun object is expressed even with the infinitive (Nous allons **nous occuper** de cela) and the present participle (En **se réveillant,** le bébé a pleuré). All reflexive verbs are conjugated with **être.**

43. MEANING OF REFLEXIVE VERBS.

In English, the few reflexive verbs that are commonly used *(to hurt, kill, delude, kid oneself,* etc.) are clearly reflexive in meaning. But in French, reflexive verbs are much more numerous and they may have a reflexive meaning, an active meaning, or a passive meaning.

REFLEXIVE MEANING

Il s'est accusé.	He accused himself.
Il s'est tué.	He killed himself.

ACTIVE MEANING

Je **me** demande quelle heure il est.	I wonder . . . (NOT: I ask myself.)
On **se** l'imagine.	One imagines it (NOT: one imagines it to himself.)

[67]

PASSIVE MEANING

Je **me** suis trompé.	I was mistaken. (NOT: I have deceived myself.)
Ils **s'**habillent et **se** nourrissent mieux.	They are better clothed and fed. (NOT: They dress themselves and feed themselves better.)

44. USE.

(1) Many ordinary verbs may be used reflexively. The difference in meaning is often obvious:

J'arrête l'auto.	I stop the car.
L'auto **s'arrête.**	The car stops.

But sometimes the difference in meaning is striking:

Je lève la main.	I raise my hand.
Je **me** lève.	I get up.
J'appelle mon frère.	I call my brother.
Je **m'**appelle Jacques.	My name is Jacques.
Je rappelle mon frère.	I call my brother back.
Je **me** rappelle.	I remember.
J'en doute.	I doubt it.
Je **m'en** doute.	I rather think so. I suspect so.

(2) Only a few common verbs are always reflexive:

L'enfant **s'écrie.**	The child cries out.
John **se moque** de nous.	John is kidding us.
Je **me souviens** de ce pays.	I remember that country.
L'arbuste **s'efforce** de pousser.	The shrub is trying to grow.

(3) The reflexive pronoun is also found in a number of common expressions:

Cela **se fait.** Cela ne se fait pas.	That is done. That is not done.
Cela **se dit.**	That is said.
Cela **se peut.**	That is possible.
Cela **se comprend.**	That is comprehensible.
Ce mot **s'écrit** avec deux "c".	That word has two "c's".

45. POSITION OF REFLEXIVE PRONOUNS

(1)   In affirmative forms, both pronouns, subject and object, precede the verb — in the order: subject, object:

Je me lève. **Vous vous** trompez. **Il se** trompe.

In the third person, the subject may be a noun:

Le bébé se réveille.

In compound tenses, both pronouns precede the auxiliary:

Je me suis levé. **Vous vous** êtes trompé. **Il s'est** trompé. **Le bébé s'est** réveillé.

(2)   In the inverted interrogative forms, the pronoun object precedes the verb and the pronoun subject follows it:

Vous trompez-**vous**? **Se** réveille-t-**il**? Le bébé **se** réveille-t-**il**?

In compound tenses, the inverted pronoun subject follows the auxiliary verb — not the participle:

Vous **êtes-vous** trompé? **S'est-il** réveillé? Le bébé **s'est-il** réveillé?

(3)   In negative forms, **ne** precedes the object pronoun and **pas** follows the verb:

Je **ne** me lève **pas**. Vous **ne** vous trompez **pas**. Le bébé **ne** se réveille **pas**.

In compound tenses, **pas** follows the auxiliary verb:

Je ne me suis **pas** levé. Vous ne vous êtes **pas** trompé. Le bébé ne s'est **pas** réveillé.

46. AGREEMENT OF THE PAST PARTICIPLE OF REFLEXIVE VERBS.

This is one of the trickiest details of French grammar. French people often have to stop and think before they are sure. It is particularly difficult for English-speaking persons, because we are likely to think French verbs function just as English verbs do. This is often not the case. In English we say: You ask someone *(dir. obj.)* for something; but in French "**On demande** quelque chose à quelqu'un" *(indirect obj.).* In English: You tell someone something; but in French "On **dit** quelque chose à quelqu'un." Therefore it is necessary to analyze the French verb in question — not its English equivalent.

(1) If the reflexive pronoun is a direct object of the verb, the past participle of course agrees with it:

Elle s'est lev**ée** (*f sing*).	She got up.
Nous nous sommes arrêt**és** (*m pl*).	We stopped.
Ils se sont tromp**és** (*m pl*).	They were mistaken.
Elles se sont assis**es** (*f pl*).	They sat down.
Une centaine de **personnes se** sont noy**ées** (*f pl*).	A hundred persons drowned.

(2) If the reflexive pronoun is the indirect object of the verb, the past participle does not agree with it:

Elle s'est rappel**é** l'histoire.	She remembered the story.
Elle s'est demand**é** quelle heure il était.	She wondered what time it was.
Elle s'est fait des illusions.	She kidded herself.
Elle s'est imagin**é** le paysage saharien.	She imagined the Sahara landscape.

(3) In the case of reciprocal constructions, the object pronoun may be direct or indirect.

Ils se sont battus.	They had a fight.
Ils se sont parl**é**.	They talked to each other.

(4) If the reflexive pronoun is neither direct nor indirect object, the past participle agrees with the subject of the verb:

Elle s'en est all**ée**.	She went away.
Ils se sont enfuis.	They fled.
Elles se sont écri**ées**.	They cried out.

A. *Exercices sur les formes des verbes pronominaux.*

(*a*) *Mettez chacune des phrases suivantes au passé composé:* 1. Je me lève très tôt. 2. Je m'occupe de votre affaire. 3. Je me trompe. 4. Le taxi s'arrête. 5. John se moque de nous. 6. Ils s'efforcent de travailler ensemble. 7. Européens et Africains s'habituent à travailler ensemble. 8. Marie s'habille rapidement.

(*b*) *Posez la question à laquelle répondrait chacune des phrases suivantes:* 1. Je me lève à sept heures. 2. Je m'occupe du bébé. 3. John se trompe. 4. Il s'est trompé. 5. Je me suis occupé du bébé. 6. Je me suis levé à sept heures. 7. John et Roger se sont bien amusés.

(*c*) *Mettez chacune des phrases suivantes à la forme négative:* 1. Je me moque de vous. 2. Vous vous trompez. 3. Je me suis moqué de vous. 4. Vous vous êtes trompé. 5. Le bébé s'est réveillé. 6. Roger s'est occupé de lui.

(*d*) *Mettez chacune des phrases suivantes au pluriel:* 1. Il se trouve en Afrique. 2. Je m'habitue à travailler. 3. Je m'efforce de faire des progrès. 4. Je m'occupe de l'établissement d'un pipeline. 5. Il s'est habitué à voyager. 6. Je me suis efforcé de bien travailler. 7. Il s'est occupé de cela. 8. Je me suis réveillé à huit heures. 9. Je me suis dépêché. 10. Elle s'est blessée. 11. Elle s'est accusée. 12. Je ne me suis pas trompé. 13. Je me suis assis. 14. Elle s'est assise. 15. Le travail se poursuit. 16. Je m'en vais ce soir. 17. Je me couche de bonne heure. 18. Je m'en doute.

B. *Employez l'infinitif dans chacune des phrases suivantes en commençant par* **Nous allons.** (Ex.: Nous nous habituons à cela. — Nous allons nous habituer à cela.)

1. Nous nous réveillons à sept heures. 2. Nous nous dépêchons. 3. Nous nous occupons de tout. 4. Nous nous efforçons de bien travailler. 5. Nous nous habituons à travailler ensemble. 6. Nous nous retrouvons demain. 7. Nous nous levons de bonne heure.

C. *Dites en français en employant le participe présent avec* **en.** (Ex.: En m'occupant du bébé, je ...)

1. By getting up early, we ... 2. On remembering that story, I ... 3. While taking care of the baby, you ... 4. By getting used to that, we ... 5. While trying our best to work well, we ... 6. By stopping at Lyon, I ...

D. *Dites en français:*

(*a*) **tromper, se tromper**

1. He is deceiving us.   2. He is mistaken.   3. You are mistaken.   4. I was mistaken.   5. He deceived me.   6. He was mistaken.

(*b*) **douter (de)** *to doubt,* **se douter (de)** *to suspect*

1. I doubt it.   2. I don't doubt it.   3. I doubted it (imperf.).   4. I didn't doubt it.   5. I suspect so (I rather think so).   6. I rather thought so (I suspected it).

(*c*) **se lever, s'habituer (à), s'habiller**

1. She got up.   2. She got dressed.   3. She got used to working hard. 4. She got used to taking care of the baby.   5. She got used to getting up early.   6. She got used to getting dressed rapidly.

E. *Répondez en français:*

1. A quelle heure vous réveillez-vous d'habitude?   2. A quelle heure vous êtes-vous réveillé ce matin?   3. Vous trompez-vous quelquefois? 4. Vous occupez-vous quelquefois de votre auto?   5. Savez-vous vous occuper d'un cheval?   6. Vous êtes-vous jamais occupé d'un bébé? 7. Vous amusez-vous bien le* samedi soir?   8. Vous êtes-vous bien amusé l'été dernier?   9. Vous rappelez-vous l'histoire de l'accident? 10. Vous souvenez-vous de cette histoire?   11. Est-ce que beaucoup de passagers se sont noyés?   12. Combien de personnes (*f*) se sont noyées?   13. Pourquoi beaucoup de passagers se sont-ils noyés? 14. Se doutaient-ils que leur dernière heure était proche?

F. *Dictée:*

1. Un soir, Roger et Marie ont décidé d'aller au théâtre.   2. Marie s'est habillée avant le dîner.   3. Roger est arrivé en retard et s'est habillé vite.   4. Ils se sont dépêchés.   5. Ils ont été obligés de s'occuper du bébé avant de partir.   6. Ils se sont trompés d'autobus. 7. Ils sont arrivés au théâtre juste au moment où le rideau se levait. 8. Ils se sont bien amusés.

---

* **Le samedi** means: Saturdays, on Saturdays *or* on Saturday. **Samedi** means: next Saturday *or* last Saturday.

Chez l'antiquaire

John profite de son séjour à Paris pour acheter des cadeaux destinés à des personnes qui lui sont chères aux États-Unis. Un jour, dans une petite rue voisine de Saint-Germain-des-Prés, il remarque à la devanture d'un antiquaire un service de table qui lui plaît. Il entre, avec l'intention de l'acheter pour sa sœur, si le prix en est raisonnable.

John is taking advantage of his stay in Paris to buy some presents for his loved ones in the United States. One day, on a little street near Saint-Germain-des-Prés, he notices in the shopwindow of an antique dealer a set of dishes that he likes. He goes in with the idea of buying it for his sister, if the price of it is reasonable.

L'Antiquaire. —¹Vous désirez quelque chose, monsieur?

The Dealer. —¹Something for you, sir?

John. —²Je m'intéresse à ce service qui est à la devanture de votre magasin. ³Pourriez-vous me le montrer?

John. —²I am interested in the set of dishes that is in the window of your store. ³Could you please show it to me?

L'Antiquaire. —⁴Certainement, monsieur. ⁵Je n'en ai mis que quelques échantillons à la vitrine. ⁶Les autres pièces sont ici, dans ce placard. ⁷Je vais vous les faire voir.

The Dealer. —⁴Certainly, sir. ⁵I have put only a few samples in the window. ⁶The other pieces are here in this cupboard. ⁷I will show them to you (make you see them).

John. —⁸Combien y en a-t-il en tout?

John. —⁸How many are there in all?

L'Antiquaire.—⁹Soixante-quinze, monsieur. ¹⁰Le service est complet. ¹¹Il n'y manque pas une

The Dealer. —⁹Seventy-five, sir. ¹⁰The set is complete. ¹¹Not a single piece is missing. ¹²To tell

seule pièce. [12]A vrai dire, lorsque je l'ai acheté, une assiette manquait. [13]Mais, par un hasard heureux, j'ai pu me la procurer chez un antiquaire de Concarneau.

JOHN. —[14]Savez-vous d'où provient ce service?

L'ANTIQUAIRE. —[15]Je l'ai acheté moi-même dans une vente aux enchères en Bretagne. [16]Il faisait partie du mobilier d'un château, qu'on a vendu après décès. [17]C'est de la très belle faïence de Quimper, monsieur. [18]Remarquez la netteté du dessin et l'éclat des couleurs. [19]Et puis, pas un défaut dans la faïence. [20]Au prix indiqué de 650 francs, c'est une occasion magnifique.

JOHN. —[21]Pouvez-vous vous charger de l'expédier en Amérique? [22]C'est un cadeau pour ma sœur.

L'ANTIQUAIRE. —[23]Laissez - moi seulement son adresse. [24]Nous nous chargerons de tout le reste, emballage et frais d'envoi.

JOHN. —[25]Elle le recevra en bon état, n'est-ce pas?

L'ANTIQUAIRE. —[26]Ne craignez rien, monsieur. [27]Nous le lui enverrons dans un bon emballage et nous garantissons tous nos envois.

the truth, when I bought it, one plate was missing. [13]But, by a lucky chance, I succeeded in getting it from an antique dealer in Concarneau.

JOHN. —[14]Do you know where the set comes from?

THE DEALER. —[15]I bought it myself, at an auction sale in Brittany. [16]It was a part of the furnishings of a château which were sold after (the) death (of the owner). [17]It is of the finest Quimper earthenware, sir. [18]Note the clarity of the design and the brilliance of the colors. [19]And besides, not a flaw in the earthenware. [20]At the price of 650 francs, it is a magnificent bargain.

JOHN. —[21]Can you take care of shipping it to America? [22]It is a present for my sister.

THE DEALER. —[23]Just leave me her address. [24]We will take charge of the rest, packing and shipping charges (costs).

JOHN. —[25]She will get it in good condition, won't she?

THE DEALER. —[26]Fear nothing, sir. [27]We will send it to her well packed (in a good packing) and we guarantee all our shipments.

JOHN. —²⁸Entendu. ²⁹Envoyez-le-lui vers le 15 septembre. ³⁰Il ne me reste plus qu'à vous payer, n'est-ce pas?

JOHN. —²⁸All right. ²⁹Send it to her about September 15. ³⁰All I have left to do now is to pay you, isn't it?

A. *Répondez en français:*

1. Pour qui John veut-il acheter des cadeaux? 2. Que remarque-t-il un jour à la devanture d'un antiquaire? 3. Que pense-t-il de ce service de table? 4. Quelle question lui pose l'antiquaire quand il entre dans son magasin? 5. Que demande John à l'antiquaire? 6. Toutes les pièces du service sont-elles à la vitrine? 7. Où l'antiquaire garde-t-il les autres pièces? 8. Combien de pièces y a-t-il en tout? 9. Le service était-il complet quand l'antiquaire l'a acheté? 10. Quelle pièce y manquait? 11. D'où provient le service en question? 12. Pourquoi a-t-il été vendu? 13. Quelle espèce de faïence est-ce? 14. Sur quelles qualités du dessin l'antiquaire attire-t-il l'attention de John? 15. A qui ce service est-il destiné? 16. Qui va se charger de l'envoi? 17. Qu'est-ce que l'antiquaire dit à John de lui laisser? 18. Quand John dit-il à l'antiquaire d'envoyer le service? 19. Qu'est-ce qu'il lui reste à faire?

B. *Demandez en français à quelqu'un:*

1. pour qui John décide d'acheter des cadeaux. 2. où il remarque un service de table. 3. si ce service lui plaît. 4. combien de pièces il y a dans le service. 5. s'il y manque des pièces. 6. s'il y manquait des pièces quand l'antiquaire l'a acheté. 7. où l'antiquaire l'a acheté. 8. d'où provient ce service. 9. où l'antiquaire s'est procuré l'assiette qui manquait. 10. le prix du service en question. 11. où l'antiquaire va expédier le service. 12. qui se chargera de l'emballage. 13. qui va payer les frais d'envoi. 14. si le service arrivera en bon état.

C. *Répondez en français en employant l'expression indiquée:*

(a) remarquer, plaire à

1. Où John a-t-il remarqué un service de table? 2. Qu'est-ce que l'antiquaire lui dit de remarquer à propos de la beauté du service?

3. John remarque-t-il des défauts dans la faïence? 4. Est-ce que le service qu'il a remarqué plaît à John? 5. Pourquoi ce service lui plaît-il? 6. Remarquez-vous souvent des choses qui vous plaisent à la devanture des magasins? 7. Achetez-vous tout ce qui vous plaît?

(b) manquer, se procurer

1. Manque-t-il des pièces au service que John achète? 2. Y manquait-il des pièces quand l'antiquaire l'a acheté? 3. Combien de pièces manquaient? 4. Où l'antiquaire s'est-il procuré les pièces qui manquaient? 5. Où peut-on se procurer des meubles (furniture) anciens? 6. Où peut-on se procurer de vieux livres?

(c) provenir de, faire partie de

1. D'où provient le service que John achète? 2. De quoi ce service faisait-il partie? 3. Combien de pièces faisaient partie du service en question? 4. Savez-vous de quels pays provient le café?

(d) se charger de

1. Qui va se charger d'expédier le service en Amérique? 2. Qui se chargera de l'emballage? 3. Aimez-vous vous charger d'acheter des cadeaux pour d'autres personnes?

D. *Dites en français, en employant* il manque *ou* il reste:

1. There is one plate missing. 2. How many plates are missing? 3. I am missing one plate. 4. There is one table service left. 5. How many plates are left? 6. How many plates have you left?

E. *Thème:*

On a little street near Saint-Germain-des-Prés, John noticed one day some interesting prints (estampes *f*) on display at an antiquarian's shop. He stopped to look at them. They were in color, and showed views of fashionable Paris (mondain) around 1830: men wearing high hats and carrying canes, ladies in long dresses and carrying parasols (ombrelles) to shelter themselves from the sun. John walked into the store. The prints were quite expensive, but the owner was so nice and so convincing that John finally bought them. He had just left the store when he remembered that he could not take them along on his trips. "Well," he thought, "they will make nice presents for my relatives and friends in the U.S."

XIV

GRAMMAR UNIT

Pronoms personnels

47. FORMS OF THE PERSONAL PRONOUNS.

Personal pronouns have two sets of forms: the unstressed forms, which are used with verbs, and the stressed forms, which are used primarily with prepositions. The unstressed forms are sometimes called "conjunctive" pronouns and the stressed forms, "disjunctive" pronouns.

48. UNSTRESSED FORMS OF THE PERSONAL PRONOUNS.

(1) Subject: **je, tu, il (elle, on), nous, vous, ils (elles).**

Allez-**vous** au cinéma ce soir? — Oui, **je** vais au cinéma ce soir.
Où vend-**on** des cartes-postales?
Note that the indefinite personal pronoun **on** is always used with the third person singular form of the verb — even when it means we, you, they, or people.

(2) Object:

(*a*) **Me, te, se, nous, vous** may be used either as direct or indirect object of a verb.

Il **me** voit (*dir. obj.*).
Il **me** dit bonjour (*indir. obj.*).
Je **vous** crois (*dir. obj.*)
Je **vous** demande pardon (*indir. obj.*).

(*b*) **Le, la, les** are used as direct object only. They may refer to persons or things.

Connaissez-vous **Marie** Duplessis? ⎱
Connaissez-vous **la faïence** de Quimper? ⎰ Oui, je **la** connais.
John a-t-il acheté **le service** de table?   Oui, il l'a acheté.
Est-il allé voir **les Duplessis**?   Oui, il est allé **les** voir.

[77]

Note that in French, certain verbs take a direct object although the English equivalents require a preposition:

Attendre (*to wait for*) : J'attends l'autobus. Je l'attends.
Chercher (*to look for*) : Je cherche son adresse. Je la cherche.
Écouter (*to listen to*) : J'écoute l'opéra. Je l'écoute.
Regarder (*to look at*) : John regarde le bébé. Il le regarde.

(*c*) The indirect object forms **lui, leur** and **y**.

1. **Lui, leur** are the indirect object forms that are used to refer to persons. They replace a noun preceded by the preposition **à**.

Avez-vous parlé à **Roger?**	Oui, je **lui** ai parlé.
Avez-vous parlé à **Marie?**	Oui, je **lui** ai parlé.
Écrivez-vous souvent à **vos amis?**	Non, je ne **leur** écris jamais.

Note that in French, certain verbs require the preposition **à** although their English equivalents do not require a preposition:

Plaire à (*to please*) :	Le service de table plaît-il à **John?**
	Oui, il **lui** plaît.
Obéir à (*to obey*) :	Obéissez-vous à **vos parents?**
	Oui, je **leur** obéis.
Ressembler à (*to resemble*) :	Le petit Michel ressemble-t-il à son père?
	Oui, il **lui** ressemble.
Dire à (*to tell, to say to*) :	J'ai dit au revoir à **Marie.**
	Je **lui** ai dit au revoir.
Demander à (*to ask*) :	J'ai demandé l'heure à **John.** Je **lui** ai demandé l'heure.

2. **Y** is the indirect object form that is used to refer to places or things. It replaces a noun preceded by the preposition **à** and sometimes **dans** or **sur**.

Allez-vous souvent **au théâtre?** ⎱	Non, je n'**y** vais pas souvent.
Allez-vous souvent **à la banque?** ⎰	
Obéissez-vous **à la loi?**	Oui, j'**y** obéis.

Répondez-vous toujours **aux let-tres?**	Non, je n'**y** réponds pas toujours.
Pensez-vous souvent **à vos va-cances?**	Oui, j'**y** pense souvent.
Me retrouverez-vous **dans la Grande Galerie?**	Oui, je vous **y** retrouverai.
Serez-vous **sur la terrasse?**	Oui, j'**y** serai.

(d) **En** is used to replace a noun preceded by the preposition **de.**

1. If the noun is used in a partitive sense, **en** may be used to refer to persons or things:

Avez-vous **des assiettes** en faïence?	Oui, j'**en** ai.
Avez-vous **des cousins?**	Oui, j'**en** ai quatre.

2. If the noun to which **en** refers is not used in a partitive sense, it may be used to refer only to places and things:

Avez-vous besoin **d'assiettes?**	Oui, j'**en** ai besoin.
John a-t-il parlé **de son voyage?**	Oui, il **en** a parlé.
Avez-vous peur **des taxis?**	Non, je n'**en** ai pas peur.
Vient-il **du Mexique?** Vient-il **de Paris?** Vient-il **des États-Unis?**	Oui, il **en** vient.

3. **En** is also used in a number of expressions such as:

Il **en** a assez.	He is fed up with it.
Il veut **en** finir.	He wants to be done with it.
Où **en** est-il?	How far along is he (in it)?
Il n'**en** est qu'au début.	He is only at the beginning.
Où **en** sommes-nous?	Where are we (in it)?
Nous **en** sommes à la page 79.	We are on page 79.

(3) Word order.

Personal pronoun objects (unstressed forms) precede the verb and stand in the following order (except for the affirmative imperative):

me	le	lui	en
te	la	leur	
se	les	y	
nous			
vous			

Voulez-vous **me le** montrer?
J'ai pu **me le** procurer.
Je vais **vous les** faire voir.
Nous **le lui** enverrons dans un bon emballage.
Combien **y en** a-t-il?

Of the large number of possible combinations of these pronoun objects, here are the ones that occur most frequently:

> **me le, me la, me les, m'en; vous le, vous la, vous les, vous en; le lui, la lui, les lui, lui en; le leur, la leur, les leur, leur en.**

This word order is of course followed with interrogative and negative forms. In compound tenses, the pronoun objects precede the auxiliary verb.

Marie a donné son adresse à la concierge.
Elle **la lui a** donnée.
Elle ne **la lui a** pas donnée.
La lui a-t-elle donnée?

Roger **s'est** souvenu de l'accident.
Il **s'en** est souvenu.
S'en est-il souvenu?
Il ne **s'en est** pas souvenu.

49. STRESSED FORMS OF THE PERSONAL PRONOUNS.

The stressed forms **moi, toi, lui, elle, nous, vous, eux, elles,** and the indefinite form **soi** may be used alone, as object of a preposition, or with verbs.

(1) As object of a preposition:

> Il est arrivé **avant (après) moi.**

Elle est là, **devant (derrière) vous.**
Ils sont **parmi (près de, loin de, à côté de)** nous.
Il est actuellement **chez (auprès d')** elle.
Cela ne dépend pas **de moi (d'elle, d'eux).**
J'irai au cinéma **avec (sans)** lui.
Je compte **sur vous (sur lui, sur elle).**
On va **chez soi. Chacun pour soi.**
Pensez-vous à Charles? — Oui, je pense **à lui.**

Note that after the preposition **de** the stressed forms are generally used only to refer to persons:

Je parle de Charles **(de lui)**, de Marie **(d'elle)**, des Duplessis **(d'eux).**

(2) With verbs:

(*a*) In addition to, or instead of, an unstressed form — for emphasis:

Moi, je n'en sais rien.
Lui n'en sait rien non plus.
Je l'ai acheté **moi-même.**

Note that all these forms may be used in combination with the word **même: lui-même** (himself), **vous-même** (you, yourself).

(*b*) To specify the persons indicated by a plural form of a personal pronoun:

Elle et **moi** nous avons fait une promenade ensemble.
Lui et **elle** sont partis en voyage.

(*c*) After **c'est, ce sont** (whether expressed or implied):

Qui a pris mes cigarettes? — C'est **moi** (*or* Moi).
Est-ce votre frère? —Non, ce n'est pas **lui.**
Est-ce que ce sont vos cousines? — Oui, ce sont **elles.**

50. USE OF PERSONAL PRONOUNS WITH IMPERATIVES.

(1) Affirmative imperative:

Pronoun objects follow the verb and are joined to it by **a** hyphen.

Voilà des fruits. Regardez-**les.**
Voilà une pomme. Mangez-**la.**
Voulez-vous bien me montrer le service? Montrez-**le-moi.**

When an affirmative imperative has both a direct and an indirect object, the personal pronouns stand in the following order:

le	**moi (m')**	**en**
la	**toi (t')**	
les	**lui**	
	nous	
	vous	
	leur	

Note that **m'** replaces **moi** and **t'** replaces **toi** when followed by **en.**

When used with an imperative form, **lui** means either *to him* or *to her*, and **leur** means *to them* (either masculine or feminine).

Montrez-**le-moi.** Apportez-**la-lui.** Donnez-**les-nous.**
Donnez-**m'en.** Montrez-**nous-en.** Apportez-**lui-en.**
Envoyez-**le-lui.** Envoyez-**les-leur.** Parlez-**lui-en.**

(2) Negative imperative:

Pronoun objects precede the verb and stand in the order of preceding objects in declarative sentences (see paragraph 48, 3).

Ne **me le** montrez pas. Ne **le lui** apportez pas.
Ne **m'en** donnez pas. Ne **lui en** parlez pas.

A. *Répondez en français en remplaçant les noms par les pronoms convenables:*

1. John connaît-il le Musée du Louvre? 2. Où John va-t-il retrouver son ami? 3. Est-ce que Roger a visité les galeries de peinture? 4. Qui a entendu remuer le petit Michel? 5. John a-t-il vu le petit Michel? 6. A-t-il admiré ses beaux yeux? 7. Comment trouve-t-il le petit Michel? 8. Où John a-t-il vu le service de table? 9. Où l'antiquaire a-t-il acheté ce service? 10. Est-ce que l'antiquaire va montrer les assiettes à John? 11. Est-ce que le service plaît à John?

12. Est-ce que John va donner le service à sa soeur? 13. Qui expédiera le service en Amérique? 14. Qui paiera les frais d'envoi? 15. Qui se chargera de l'emballage? 16. Combien de pièces y a-t-il en tout? 17. Est-ce que le prix en est raisonnable? 18. Combien d'assiettes manquent? 19. Est-ce que l'antiquaire garantit ses envois? 20. John a-t-il acheté beaucoup de cadeaux? 21. Est-ce que Roger doit s'occuper d'une affaire d'impôts?

B. *Répondez aux questions suivantes en employant le pronom* y *ou* **en:**

1. Est-ce que Roger doit aller au Louvre? 2. John est-il allé au Vénézuéla? 3. Est-ce qu'il vient du Proche-Orient? 4. A-t-il besoin de repos? 5. Roger a-t-il entendu parler des gisements de pétrole du Sahara? 6. Est-ce qu'on s'occupe actuellement de la construction d'un pipe-line dans le Sahara? 7. Trouve-t-on beaucoup d'arbres dans le Sahara? 8. Y a-t-il déjà un certain nombre de puits de pétrole en opération? 9. John a-t-il parlé de son voyage? 10. A-t-il parlé de ses voyages? 11. Va-t-il bientôt aux États-Unis? 12. Vient-il des États-Unis? 13. Vient-il de Pittsburgh? 14. Comment est-il allé à Saint-Cloud?

C. (Drill on order of two personal pronoun objects.) *Dites en français en employant les formes convenables des pronoms personnels:*

(*a*) **le service de table.** 1. The antique dealer showed it to me. 2. He showed it to you. 3. He showed it to us. 4. He didn't show it to him. 5. He didn't show it to her. 6. He didn't show it to them.

(*b*) **l'assiette** (*f*). 1. He sells it to me. 2. He sells it to you. 3. He sells it to us. 4. He doesn't sell it to him. 5. He doesn't sell it to her. 6. He doesn't sell it to them.

(*c*) **les cadeaux.** 1. He ships them to me. 2. He ships them to you. 3. He ships them to us. 4. He doesn't ship them to him. 5. He doesn't ship them to her. 6. He doesn't ship them to them.

D. *Dites en français en employant les expressions indiquées:*

(*a*) demander quelque chose à quelqu'un

1. I asked Roger for his address.   2. I asked him for it.   3. He asked me for my address.   4. He asked me for it.   5. We asked Marie for her opinion (**son opinion** *f*).   6. We asked her for it.   7. We asked her for the time.   8. We asked her for it.

(*b*) dire quelque chose à quelqu'un

1. I told Marie good-bye.   2. I told her good-bye.   3. I told him to come to see me.   4. I told him to (I told it to him).   5. I told him I was tired.   6. I told him so (I told it to him).   7. I told her so. 8. I didn't tell him so.   9. I didn't tell her so.

(*c*) plaire à

1. I like the Quimper plates.   2. I like them.   3. Do you like them? 4. Does Marie like them?   5. Does she like them?   6. Does Roger like them?   7. Does he like them?   8. He does not like them.

(*d*) ressembler à

1. Little Michel looks like Roger.   2. He looks like him.   3. He does not look like his mother.   4. He does not look like her.   5. Does he look like them?

(*e*) attendre

1. John is waiting for a bus.   2. He is not waiting for it.   3. I am waiting for it.   4. I am waiting for John.   5. I am waiting for him. 6. I am not waiting for him.   7. Are you waiting for him?   8. The Duplessis are not expecting him.   9. I am expecting a letter.   10. I was expecting it yesterday.   11. Marie is expecting a baby.

(*f*) chercher

1. I am looking for a taxi.   2. I am looking for it.   3. John is looking for the apartment of the Duplessis.   4. He is looking for it.   5. He is looking for them.

E. *Répétez les phrases suivantes en remplaçant par les pronoms convenables les noms qui suivent les prépositions:*

1. John est allé chez les Duplessis.   2. Il compte sur Roger.   3. Il compte sur Marie.   4. Il parle du petit Michel.   5. Il va parler avec

le petit Michel.   6. On a dîné sans le petit Michel.   7. John est arrivé
avant Marie.   8. Lui et Roger ont parlé de Marie.   9. On n'a pas
dîné sans Marie.   10. Après le dîner John a parlé avec Marie.
11. Marie s'est occupée du bébé.   12. Ensuite ils ont fait une promenade avec le bébé.

F. *Mettez les phrases suivantes à la forme impérative en
remplaçant les noms par les pronoms convenables:* (Ex.:
Voulez-vous bien me montrer le service? Montrez-le-moi.)

1. Voulez-vous bien le montrer à John?   2. Voulez-vous bien le
montrer à Marie?   3. Voulez-vous bien le montrer aux Duplessis?
4. Voulez-vous bien l'expédier à ma sœur?   5. Voulez-vous bien l'expédier à mes sœurs?   6. Voulez-vous bien me passer le journal?
7. Voulez-vous bien le passer à Marie?   9. Voulez-vous bien le passer
à Roger?   10. Voulez-vous bien venir me voir?   11. Voulez-vous bien
aller voir les Duplessis?   12. Voulez-vous bien aller en ville?   13. Voulez-
vous bien rester à la maison?   14. Voulez-vous bien acheter des
cadeaux?   15. Voulez-vous bien venir chez nous?   16. Voulez-vous
bien prendre du café?

G. *Mettez les phrases suivantes au négatif:*

1. Donnez-le-moi.   2. Envoyez-m'en.   3. Expédiez-les-lui.   4. Achetez-
lui-en.   5. Parlez-lui-en.   6. Pensez-y.   7. Pensez à elle.   8. Allez-y.

XV

CONVERSATION UNIT

Une rencontre

Un jour qu'il traverse la Place de l'Opéra, John se trouve tout à coup face à face avec Helen Frazer et sa mère, qui viennent dans l'autre sens. Ces rencontres inattendues, à Paris ou ailleurs, entre personnes venant de pays éloignés sont d'ailleurs moins rares qu'on ne le penserait.

One day when he is crossing the Opera Square, John is suddenly face to face with Helen Frazer and her mother, who are coming in the opposite direction. These unexpected meetings, in Paris or elsewhere, between people who have come from distant countries are, by the way, not so unusual as you would think.

JOHN. —[1]Mᵐᵉ Frazer! [2]Helen! [3]Quelle surprise! [4]J'ignorais que vous étiez ici!

JOHN. —[1]Mrs. Frazer! [2]Helen! [3]What a surprise! [4]I didn't know you were here!

Mᴹᴱ FRAZER. —[5]Et moi qui vous croyais toujours en Arabie! [6]Henry sera certainement heureux de vous revoir!

MRS. FRAZER. —[5]And *I* thought you were still in Arabia! [6]Henry will certainly be glad to see you again.

JOHN. —[7]Est-ce qu'Henry est aussi à Paris?

JOHN. —[7]Is Henry in Paris too?

HELEN. —[8]Naturellement. [9]Mais vous connaissez mon frère: [10]quand nous lui avons dit que nous irions faire des emplettes cet après-midi, [11]il a déclaré qu'il aimait mieux monter en haut de la Tour Eiffel.

HELEN. —[8]Of course. [9]But you know my brother: [10]when we told him we were going shopping this afternoon, [11]he announced that he preferred to go to the top of the Eiffel Tower.

Mᴹᴱ FRAZER. —[12]Combien de temps comptez-vous rester à Paris, John?

MRS. FRAZER. —[12]How long do you expect to stay in Paris, John?

JOHN. —[13]Je serai encore ici une vingtaine de jours. [14]J'ai retenu passage sur un avion qui partira pour New-York de samedi en quinze.

MME FRAZER. —[15]Nous irons passer le week-end en Touraine. [16]Il y aura une place pour vous dans notre voiture, si vous n'avez rien de mieux à faire. [17]Mais ne vous croyez pas obligé d'accepter l'invitation. [18]Je me rends compte que vous n'avez sans doute pas beaucoup de temps à votre disposition.

JOHN. —[19]Mais si. [20]En ce moment, je suis libre comme l'air, et je serai enchanté de vous accompagner. [21]Quand avez-vous l'intention de partir?

MME FRAZER. —[22]Voyons . . . [23]Il nous faudra à peu près quatre heures de Paris à Orléans, où nous nous arrêterons pour déjeuner. [24]Disons donc que nous nous mettrons en route vers huit heures du matin, vendredi prochain. [25]Dites-nous où vous êtes descendu et nous viendrons vous chercher à sept heures et demie.

JOHN. —[26]Ne vous dérangez pas pour moi.

HELEN. —[27]Aucun dérangement. [28]Donnez seulement votre adresse à maman.

JOHN. —[13]I'll be here about three more weeks. [14]I have reserved space on a plane which will leave for New York two weeks from Saturday.

MRS. FRAZER. —[15]We are going to spend the weekend in Touraine. [16]There will be room for you in our car, if you have nothing better to do. [17]But don't think you have to accept the invitation. [18]I realize that you surely don't have much free time.

JOHN. —[19]Yes I do. [20]Right now I am as free as the air and I shall be delighted to go with you. [21]When do you expect to leave?

MRS. FRAZER. —[22]Let's see . . . [23]It will take (us) about four hours from Paris to Orleans, where we will stop for lunch. [24]Let's say that we will start around eight o'clock (next) Friday morning. [25]Tell us where you are staying and we will come for you at seven thirty.

JOHN. —[26]Don't go out of your way on my account.

HELEN. —[27](It's) no bother. [28]Just give your address to mother.

JOHN. —²⁹Je suis descendu à l'hôtel Meurice. ³⁰Nous nous retrouverons à sept heures et demie, ³¹et je serai tout prêt quand vous arriverez. ³²En attendant, dites bien des choses de ma part à Henry, ³³que je reverrai d'ailleurs sous peu.

JOHN. —²⁹I am staying at the Meurice. ³⁰We will meet at seven thirty, ³¹and I will be all ready when you get there. ³²Meanwhile, say hello to Henry for me. ³³I'll see him soon.

A. *Répondez en français:*

1. Où John rencontre-t-il Helen et sa mère? 2. Savait-il qu'elles étaient à Paris? 3. Où Mᵐᵉ Frazer croyait-elle que John se trouvait à ce moment-là? 4. Qui est Henry? 5. Qu'est-ce qu'il a décidé de faire cet après-midi-là? 6. Combien de temps John compte-t-il rester à Paris? 7. Quand doit-il quitter Paris? 8. Où ira-t-il quand il quittera Paris? 9. A-t-il retenu passage sur un bateau? 10. Combien de temps faut-il pour aller de Paris à New-York en avion? 11. Où Helen et sa mère iront-elles passer le week-end? 12. Comment iront-elles en Touraine? 13. Qu'est-ce que Mᵐᵉ Frazer offre à John? 14. Pourquoi lui dit-elle de ne pas se croire obligé d'accepter son invitation? 15. Pourquoi John sera-t-il enchanté de les accompagner? 16. Combien de temps leur faudra-t-il pour aller de Paris à Orléans? 17. Où s'arrêteront-ils pour déjeuner? 18. Quand se mettront-ils en route? 19. A quelle heure les Frazer viendront-ils chercher John? 20. A quel hôtel est-il descendu? 21. Quand John reverra-t-il Henry? 22. En attendant, qu'est-ce qu'il demande à Helen de dire à son frère?

B. *Demandez en français:*

1. où était John quand il a rencontré Helen et sa mère. 2. s'il comptait les voir. 3. s'il savait qu'elles étaient à Paris. 4. si Henry avait envie de faire des emplettes cet après-midi-là. 5. ce qu'il aimait mieux faire. 6. combien de temps John compte passer encore à Paris. 7. quand partira l'avion sur lequel il a retenu passage. 8. si la Touraine est loin de Paris. 9. s'il connaît bien la Touraine. 10. si Mᵐᵉ Frazer se rend compte que John n'a pas beaucoup de temps à sa disposition. 11. combien de temps il faut pour aller de Paris à Orléans. 12. dans

quelle ville les voyageurs s'arrêteront pour déjeuner. 13. à quelle heure ils se mettront en route. 14. l'adresse de John. 15. le nom de l'hôtel où il est descendu.

C. *Dites en français, en employant l'expression indiquée:*

(a) venir chercher, se retrouver

1. At what time is Mrs. Frazer coming for John? 2. She'll come for him at seven thirty. 3. Where are they going to meet? 4. They are going to meet at the Hotel Meurice. 5. Where shall we meet? 6. We'll meet at the Louvre.

(b) de (ma) part, de la part de

1. Please give my regards to Henry. 2. My parents have asked me to give you their regards. 3. It's nice of him to remember me. 4. It's nice of Mrs. Frazer to invite John to come along with them on their trip.

(c) en ce moment, à ce moment-là, au moment où

1. At the present time, I am completely free. 2. I was in Egypt at that time. 3. At the time I received your invitation, I was in Venezuela. 4. I don't have much to do at present. 5. At that time, no one thought that the boat was going to turn over.

(d) de . . . en huit, en quinze

1. John has passage on a plane which will leave two weeks from Saturday. 2. He'll leave Paris two weeks from today. 3. The Frazers and he will leave for Touraine a week from today. 4. They'll be back in Paris a week from Thursday.

D. *Remplacez les mots en italique par une des expressions indiquées, selon le sens de la phrase:*

(a) ignorer, se douter, se rendre compte

1. *Je ne savais pas* que vous étiez ici. 2. Il y a vingt ans, *personne ne savait* qu'il y avait du pétrole dans le Sahara. 3. *J'imagine* que vous n'avez pas beaucoup de temps à votre disposition. 4. John *ne savait pas* qu'Helen et sa mère étaient à Paris. 5. Avant l'accident, les passagers *n'avaient pas idée* du danger.

(*b*) **une dizaine, une vingtaine, etc.**

1. John passera encore *environ vingt jours* à Paris.   2. Il est arrivé il
y a *à peu près dix jours*.   3. *Environ cent passagers* se sont noyés.
4. Au moment de l'accident, le bateau était *à environ quinze mètres*
de la rive.   5. Il y avait *à peu près cinquante ans* qu'il voyageait sur
le Nil.

E. *Thème:*

One afternoon when he was walking across the Place de l'Opéra,
shortly after his return to Paris, John found himself face to face with
Helen Frazer and her mother. He had not seen them for several
months, and he was very much surprised to meet* them so unexpectedly **(d'une façon si inattendue)**. Since they were planning to
spend the weekend in Touraine, Mrs. Frazer asked John if he would
like to come along.

"It is very nice of you to invite me," said John, "but are you sure
that I won't inconvenience you? There are already the three of
you . . ." **(Vous êtes déjà trois . . .)**

"You won't inconvenience us at all," Mrs. Frazer answered.
"There is plenty of room in the car. We'll be leaving early Friday
morning. What about our coming for you at your hotel at seven
thirty?"

"Fine **(Entendu),**" said John. "I'll be waiting for you when you
come."

---

* Use **rencontrer**, which means to meet unexpectedly, rather than **retrouver**
or **se retrouver** which suggests to meet by appointment.

XVI GRAMMAR UNIT

Futur. Impératif. Adverbes. Nombres cardinaux et ordinaux

51. USE OF THE FUTURE TENSE.

The future tense is used:

(1) To express an action or state of being in the future:

Mon avion **partira** de samedi en quinze.
Nous **irons** passer le week-end en Touraine.
Je **serai** encore ici une vingtaine de jours.

(2) In the result clause of "simple" conditional sentences (i.e. those that express what will happen if a given condition is fulfilled) :

Si **vous nous dites** où vous êtes descendu, **nous viendrons** vous chercher.
Il **y aura** une place pour vous dans notre voiture, si **vous n'avez** rien de mieux à faire.

(3) In temporal clauses introduced by **quand, lorsque, dès que, aussitôt . . . que, tant . . . que,** etc. if the future is implied:

Nous viendrons vous chercher **quand** vous **serez** prêt.
Quand vous **viendrez,** je serai prêt.
Dès que j'arriverai, je vous le ferai savoir.

(4) To express probability:

Voilà une voiture qui vient. Ce **sera** Henri. (It is probably Henri.)
Voilà le téléphone qui sonne. Ce **sera** ma mère.

(5) In a few set expressions that imply futurity:

Faites **comme vous voudrez.** Do as you wish.
Je ferai **ce qui me plaira.** I'll do as I please.

(6) Instead of the imperative, in formal instructions:

Vous partirez tout de suite. **Vous irez** à Londres. **Vous vous présenterez** dès ce soir à cette adresse.
Tu ne **tueras** pas. (Thou shalt not kill.)

52. Imperatives.

The imperative of regular verbs is the same as the second person singular and the first and second persons plural of the present indicative without the subject pronoun.

(1) Regular verbs: **Donne(s), donnons, donnez; finis, finissons, finissez; vends, vendons, vendez.**

Donnez votre adresse à maman.
Finissez vite votre travail.

(2) Auxiliary verbs: **Être: sois, soyons, soyez; Avoir: aie(s), ayons, ayez.**

Soyez tranquille. **Ayez** la bonté d'attendre un instant.

Note that the **s** of the second person singular of first conjugation verbs and of the forms **aie(s), va(s), cueille(s), ouvre(s)** is used only when the form is followed by **y** or **en**:

Donne-moi du café. **Donnes-en** à ton père.
Va à ta chambre. **Vas-y.**

(3) Irregular verbs:

The imperative of most irregular verbs takes its forms from the present indicative. Exceptions: **Sachez que** . . . (I'll have you know . . .), **Veuillez** followed by an infinitive . . . (Please . . .)

Disons que nous nous mettrons en route vers huit heures du matin.
Dites bien des choses de ma part à Henri.

(4) Reflexive verbs.

(*a*) The imperative of reflexive verbs always expresses the personal pronoun object:

Se dépêcher: dépêche-**toi**, dépêchons-**nous**, dépêchez-**vous**.

(*b*) In the negative forms, the object pronoun precedes the verb:

Ne **te dépêche** pas, ne **nous dépêchons** pas, ne **vous dépêchez** pas.
Ne **vous dérangez** pas.
Ne **vous croyez** pas obligé d'accepter l'invitation.

For the order of other personal pronoun objects of imperative forms, see paragraph 50.

53. ADVERBS.

(1) Formation of adverbs:

(*a*) Many adverbs are formed by adding the ending **-ment** to the feminine singular form of an adjective: **facile**-facile**ment**; **fière**-fière**ment**; **vive**-vive**ment**; **malheureuse**-malheureuse**ment**; **courageuse**-courageuse**ment**; and so on. Note, however, that long adverbs are often replaced by a noun and a preposition such as: **par malheur, avec courage, avec patience, à merveille.**

(*b*) Adverbs corresponding to adjectives ending in -ant or -ent usually end in **-amment** or **-emment**, both being pronounced [amã]: **violemment, prudemment, savamment, patiemment.**

(*c*) If the masculine singular form of the adjective ends in a vowel, the adverb is usually formed by adding the ending **-ment** to the masculine singular: **hardi**-hardi**ment**; **joli**-joli**ment**; **aisé**-aisé**ment**. Cf. **gentil**-gentiment.

(*d*) Adjectives are used as adverbs in a few expressions: **sentir bon, sentir mauvais; chanter faux, chanter juste; parler haut, parler bas; coûter cher:**

Parlez plus **haut,** s'il vous plaît.
Ces roses ont coûté **cher.** Elles sentent **bon.**

Note that **vite,** which is little used as an adjective, is very commonly used as an adverb:

C'est **vite fait.** Allez plus **vite.** Vous parlez trop **vite.**

(2) Comparison of adverbs:

(a) Regular comparison: vite, **plus** vite, **le plus** vite.

Marie parle **vite**. Sa soeur parle **plus vite**. Sa mère parle **le plus vite de** toute la famille.

SUPERIORITY: **plus** vite **que** . . .

EQUALITY: **aussi** vite **que** . . .

INFERIORITY: **moins** vite **que** . . .

(b) Irregular comparison:

Bien (*well*), **mieux** (*better*), **le mieux** (*best*).

Mal (*badly*), {**pis** (*worse*), {**le pis** (*the worst*).
{**plus mal**,   {**ie plus mal**.

Peu (*little*), **moins** (*less*), **le moins** (*least*).

NOTE: 1. Don't confuse the adverb **bien** (*well*) with the adjective **bon** (*good*), **meilleur, le meilleur**. 2. Don't confuse the adverb **mal** (*badly*) with the adjective **mauvais** (*bad*). 3. **Pis** and **le pis** are used only in set expressions.

Il a déclaré qu'il **aimait mieux** monter en haut de la Tour Eiffel. Les choses vont **de mal en pis**.

(3) Position of adverbs:

Adverbs may be stressed or unstressed.

(a) The normal (unstressed) position of the adverb is after the verb it modifies:

Donnez seulement votre adresse à maman. (*Just give* . . .)
Je me rends compte que **vous n'avez sans doute pas** beaucoup de temps à votre disposition.
Est-ce qu'Henri **est aussi** à Paris?
Je vous **croyais toujours** en Arabie.
Je **serai encore ici** une vingtaine de jours.
Je le **reverrai d'ailleurs** sous peu.

When verbs are in compound tenses, the adverb usually follows the auxiliary verb:

Roger **est déjà allé** chez les Duplessis.
Il **a bien fait** d'aller les revoir.

Il a beaucoup mangé, beaucoup parlé.
Il n'est peut-être pas encore revenu à Paris.
Henry n'est malheureusement pas venu avec Helen.

(*b*) A few adverbs or adverbial expressions of time such as **demain, hier, aujourd'hui, à huit heures précises,** and **ici** and **là** are normally somewhat stressed and usually come at the end of the phrase:

Nous viendrons vous chercher **demain** matin à sept heures et demie.
Il est revenu **hier.**

54. Cardinal numbers (*one, two, three, etc.*).

1	un, une	6	six	11	onze	16	seize
2	deux	7	sept	12	douze	17	dix-sept
3	trois	8	huit	13	treize	18	dix-huit
4	quatre	9	neuf	14	quatorze	19	dix-neuf
5	cinq	10	dix	15	quinze	20	vingt

21	vingt et un	63	soixante-trois
22	vingt-deux	70	soixante-dix
23	vingt-trois	71	soixante et onze
30	trente	72	soixante-douze
31	trente et un	73	soixante-treize
32	trente-deux	80	quatre-vingts
33	trente-trois	81	quatre-vingt-un
40	quarante	82	quatre-vingt-deux
41	quarante et un	83	quatre-vingt-trois
42	quarante-deux	90	quatre-vingt-dix
43	quarante-trois	91	quatre-vingt-onze
50	cinquante	92	quatre-vingt-douze
51	cinquante et un	100	cent
52	cinquante-deux	101	cent un
53	cinquante-trois	102	cent deux
60	soixante	103	cent trois
61	soixante et un	200	deux cents
62	soixante-deux	300	trois cents

1000	mille*	2000	deux mille*†
1100	onze cents	2100	deux mille cent
1200	douze cents	2110	deux mille cent **dix**
1300	treize cents	20.000	vingt mille*
1400	quatorze cents	100.000	cent mille
1900	dix-neuf cents	1.000.000	un million

NOTE: 1. **et** is used only in the following numbers: 21, 31, 41, 51, 61, 71. 2. These numbers are never written with hyphens: soixante **et** onze. 3. Other numbers below 100 that consist of two or more units are always written with hyphens: **soixante-dix, soixante-douze.**

55. PRONUNCIATION OF THE FINAL CONSONANTS OF NUMBERS.

(1) The final consonant of numbers is ordinarily silent when the word immediately following the number begins with a consonant. Ex.: **cinq** jours; **six** francs; **huit** semaines; **dix** mois; **vingt** francs.

(2) The final consonant of numbers is pronounced (linked) when the word immediately following the number begins with a vowel or a mute **h.** Ex.: **trois‿heures; cinq‿ans; six‿enfants; sept‿hommes; huit‿heures;** etc.

(3) The final consonant of **cinq, six, sept, huit, neuf,** and **dix** is pronounced when the numbers are used alone, in counting, or at the end of a phrase or sentence. Ex.: Combien de cousins avez-vous? — J'en ai **cinq.**

(4) See also the phonetic transcription of numbers, p. 204.

---

* From 1100 to 1900 you may also say: mille cent, mille deux cents, etc., though onze cents, douze cents, etc., are more commonly used.

† Beginning with 2.000, you always count in thousands in French. In English you may say: twenty-one hundred, twenty-two hundred, etc., but in French you may say only: deux mille cent, deux mille deux cents, etc.

56. ORDINAL NUMBERS *(first, second, third, etc.)*.

premier, première	huitième
second, seconde; deuxième	neuvième
troisième	dixième
quatrième	onzième
cinquième	douzième
sixième	vingtième
septième	vingt et unième

NOTE: 1. Only **premier** and **second** have feminine forms. 2. The word **an** *(year)* is used with cardinal numbers but **année** is used with ordinals. Ex.: **cinq ans** *(five years)* ; **la cinquième année** *(the fifth year)* .

57. FRACTIONS.

Ordinal numbers are used in fractions *except for* **la moitié** (1/2) , **le tiers** (1/3) , **le quart** (1/4) .

Thus you say: **un cinquième** (1/5) , **un vingtième** (1/20) , etc. Ex.: 2/3 + 1/12 = 9/12 (3/4) is read: **deux tiers** plus **un douzième** égalent **neuf douzièmes** *(ou* **trois quarts**) .

58. COLLECTIVE NUMBERS ENDING IN -aine.

The suffix –aine indicates an approximate quantity. **Une douzaine** means *twelve;* but the larger numbers are approximate: **une centaine,** *about a hundred.* Others are: **une dizaine, une quinzaine, une vingtaine, une trentaine, une quarantaine, une cinquantaine, une soixantaine.**

Je serai ici encore **une vingtaine** de jours.

59. DATES.

(1) The ordinal number **premier** is used for the first day of the month but the cardinal numbers are used for the other days.

C'est aujourd'hui **le premier février.**
Le deux février, le dix mars, le trente juin.
The same is true for rulers:
François Premier, Henri Quatre, Louis Quinze.

(2) In English we say: eighteen twenty-two, eighteen hundred twenty-two, or eighteen hundred and twenty-two. In French, 1822 can be read in only two ways: **dix-huit cent vingt-deux** or **mille huit cent vingt-deux.** The word **cent** may not be omitted in dates.

> Louis Pasteur est né en 1822 (dix-huit cent vingt-deux). Il est mort en 1895 (dix-huit cent quatre-vingt-quinze).

(3) *In 1822* is **en dix-huit cent vingt-deux.** *In the 19th century* is **au dix-neuvième siècle.**

(4) You say **en avril;** *but* **au mois d'avril.**

(5) Names of the days of the week or the months of the year are not capitalized.

60. TIME OF DAY.

(1) Official time:

The twenty-four hour system is used in all official announcements: railroads, planes, banks, theaters, offices, army, navy, etc.

In this system, fractions of an hour are always expressed in terms of minutes after the hour.

zéro heure vingt (0 h. 20)	12:20 A.M.
douze heures vingt (12 h. 20)	12:20 P.M.
une heure trente (1 h. 30)	1:30 A.M.
treize heures trente (13 h. 30)	1:30 P.M.
six heures cinquante (6 h. 50)	6:50 A.M.
dix-huit heures cinquante (18 h. 50)	6:50 P.M.
huit heures quarante-cinq (8 h. 45)	8:45 A.M.
vingt heures quarante-cinq (20 h. 45)	8:45 P.M.

(2) In conversation:

(*a*) To express the quarter-hours, you say **et quart, et** demie, moins le quart. Ex.: **huit heures et quart** (8:15), **neuf heures et demie** (9:30), **onze heures moins le quart** (10:45).

(*b*) To express minutes between the hour and the half hour following, you say **quatre heures cinq** (4:05), **quatre heures vingt-cinq** (4:25) etc.

But to express minutes between the half hour and the following hour, you measure back from the next hour. Thus: 4:35 is **cinq heures moins vingt-cinq;** 4:50 is **cinq heures moins dix.**

(*c*) Instead of A.M. and P.M., you say: **du matin, de l'après-midi,** or **du soir.** Ex.: **Neuf heures du matin** (9:00 A.M.), **trois heures de l'après-midi** (3:00 P.M.), **dix heures du soir** (10:00 P.M.).

61. MEASUREMENT.

(1) Distance.

The standard unit of linear measure in the metric system is **le mètre** (39.37 inches, approx.). A **kilomètre** is **1000 mètres** (.62 mile, approx.).

> A quelle distance le bateau était-il de la rive? (*How far . . . ?*)
> Il était **à quelques mètres de** la rive.
> Versailles est **à 18 kilomètres de** Paris.
> Quelle est la longueur de la Seine? (*How long . . . ?*)
> La Seine a **800 kilomètres** de long.
> Quelle est la largeur de la Seine à Paris? (*How wide . . . ?*)
> A Paris la Seine a **une centaine de mètres** de large.

(2) Weight.

Le gramme is the standard unit of weight in the metric system. **Un kilogramme = 1,000 grammes** (2.2 pounds, approx.). **Une livre = (½ kilo) = 500 grammes. ½ livre = 250 grammes.**

> Combien pèse le petit Michel? Il pèse **11 kilos.**
> Donnez-moi **une livre de** café.

(3) Volume.

Le litre is the standard unit of volume in the metric system.
Un litre = 1,000 centimètres cubes (.9 quart, approx.).

Donnez-moi **dix litres** d'essence.
Il a bu **un demi-litre d**'eau fraîche.

A. *Répondez en français:*

1. Où irez-vous passer le week-end? 2. Quand partirez-vous? 3. Combien de temps serez-vous encore ici? 3. Si vous avez le temps, viendrez-vous me voir dimanche? 4. Y aura-t-il une place dans la voiture des Frazer si John veut aller en Touraine? 5. Est-ce que Madame Frazer viendra le chercher s'il lui donne son adresse? 6. Sera-t-il prêt quand les Frazer viendront le chercher? 7. Montera-t-il dans leur voiture dès qu'ils arriveront à son hôtel? 8. Si vous allez à Paris, visiterez-vous les galeries de peinture du Louvre? 9. Quand vous irez à Paris, monterez-vous en haut de la Tour Eiffel? 10. Ferez-vous beaucoup d'emplettes quand vous serez en France? 11. Ferez-vous comme vous voudrez? 12. Connaissez-vous la pièce de Shakespeare qui s'appelle en français *Comme il vous plaira?*

B. *Mettez les phrases suivantes à l'impératif:*

1. Vous vous lèverez de bonne heure demain matin. 2. Vous vous habillerez tout de suite. 3. Vous prendrez vite votre petit déjeuner. 4. Ensuite vous lirez le journal. 5. Vous irez à la bibliothèque à huit heures précises. 6. Vous passerez la matinée entière à travailler. 7. Vous rentrerez à midi. 8. Vous déjeunerez comme d'habitude. 9. Vous irez au laboratoire et vous ferez patiemment l'expérience indiquée. 10. Vous prendrez un peu d'exercice et vous vous reposerez un peu avant le dîner. 11. Après le dîner, vous ne perdrez pas votre temps. 12. Vous travaillerez bien jusqu'à dix heures et vous vous mettrez au lit de bonne heure. 13. Vous serez bien sage. 14. Vous aurez de la patience. 15. Vous apprendrez ainsi à travailler assidûment.

C. *Répétez les phrases suivantes en employant chacune des expressions indiquées:*

1. John est à Paris. (**Toujours, encore, de retour, aussi, actuellement.**)

2. Il est allé à Saint-Cloud. (**Sans doute, probablement; hier, aujourd'hui, la semaine dernière.**)

3. Il n'a pas encore acheté de cadeaux. (**Sans doute, sûrement, évidemment, malheureusement.**)

4. Les Frazer ne partiront pas avant neuf heures. (**Certainement, probablement, sans doute.**)

D. *Lisez en français:*

1. Le 1ᵉʳ mai, le 15 juin, le 5 janvier, le 29 juillet, le 17 avril, le 13 mars, le 1ᵉʳ août, le 2 février.

2. Louis XII, Napoléon Iᵉʳ, Henri IV, Louis XIV, François Iᵉʳ, Napoléon III, Charles X, Louis XVI.

3. 1815, 1850, 1875, 1895; 1795, 1775, 1765; 1665, 1650, 1645; 1745, 1845, 1945; 1955, 1965, 1975, 1985, 1990, 1995, 2000.

4. 10 h. 20, 12 h. 52, 14 h. 30, 20 h. 45, 23 h. 59, 0 h. 10, 1 h. 27.

5. 1, 11; 2, 12, 20, 22; 3, 13, 30, 33; 4, 14, 40, 44; 5, 15, 50, 55; 6, 16, 60, 66, 76; 7, 17, 70, 77, 67; 8, 18, 80, 88, 84, 44, 24; 9, 19, 90, 99, 89, 49, 79; 100, 101, 105, 150, 155; 160, 165, 175, 180, 185, 195.

E. *Dites en français:*

1. In May. 2. In the month of May. 3. In 1850. 4. In the 19th century. 5. In 1970. 6. In the 20th century 7. This year (**cette année**). 8. Next year. 9. Last year (*two ways*). 10. Two years.

XVII CONVERSATION UNIT

A Chenonceaux

John et ses amis passent la jour-
née à Chenonceaux. Ils viennent
de visiter l'intérieur du château,
construit au XVIe siècle et qui
est un des monuments les plus
élégants de la Renaissance fran-
çaise. En sortant, ils échangent
leurs impressions.

HELEN. —[1]J'adore ce château!
[2]Si j'avais à choisir entre tous
ceux que nous avons vus, je
choisirais celui-ci. [3]Ce qui me
plaît surtout, c'est qu'il est encore habitable.

HENRY. —[4]Voudrais-tu y habiter?

HELEN. —[5]Cela dépend. [6]Si j'a-
vais tout ce qu'il faut, je serais
très heureuse ici. [7]Bien entendu, il faudrait avoir de nombreux serviteurs: cuisiniers, jar-
diniers, etc., recevoir quantité
d'invités . . .

JOHN. —[8]Comme Henri II et sa
cour, par exemple . . . [9]En un
mot, Helen, vous voudriez mener un genre de vie qui, je le
crains, n'existe plus.

HELEN. —[10]Pourtant, le château

John and his friends spend the
day at Chenonceaux. They have
just gone through the château,
built in the sixteenth century, and
one of the most elegant monu-
ments of the French Renaissance.
As they come out, they exchange
their impressions.

HELEN. —[1]I am crazy about this
château! [2]If I had to choose
between all those we have seen,
I would choose this one. [3]What
pleases me especially is that it
is still livable.

HENRY. —[4]Would you like to live
in it?

HELEN. —[5]That depends. [6]If I
had everything that is needed,
I should be very happy here.
[7]Of course you would have to
have numerous servants, cooks,
gardeners, and so on, have lots
of guests . . .

JOHN. —[8]Like Henri II and his
court, for example . . . [9]In a
word, Helen, you would like to
lead a life which, I fear, no
longer exists.

HELEN. —[10]However, the châ-

a été habité jusqu'à une date récente, n'est-ce pas?

JOHN. —[11]Mais oui, par les Menier, qui en sont toujours propriétaires. [12]C'est pour cela que le château de Chenonceaux est en meilleur état que celui de Chambord, [13]qui depuis des siècles reste plus ou moins vide.

HENRY. —[14]Personnellement, je n'échangerais pas Chambord pour Chenonceaux. [15]Vue à distance, la façade de Chambord est inoubliable. [16]On se croirait au *Pays des Merveilles*.

MME FRAZER. —[17]Voyons, mes enfants, il ne s'agit pas d'échanger un château pour un autre. [18]Ni l'un ni l'autre ne vous appartient.

HELEN. —[19]Quelque chose m'intrigue: [20]pourquoi a-t-on construit une partie du château au milieu d'une rivière?

JOHN. —[21]Rien de plus simple: [22]Catherine de Médicis a décidé que si elle faisait construire cette galerie à deux étages audessus de la rivière, [23]elle pourrait passer de l'autre côté sans sortir de chez elle.

HELEN. —[24]Tiens, c'est une idée! [25]Je n'aurais jamais pensé à cela!

teau was lived in until recently, wasn't it?

JOHN. —[11]Oh yes, by the Menier family (the Meniers), who still own it. [12]That is why the château of Chenonceaux is in better condition than (the one of) Chambord, [13]which has remained more or less empty for centuries.

HENRY. —[14]Personally, I would not exchange Chambord for Chenonceaux. [15]Seen from a distance, the façade of Chambord is unforgettable. [16]You would think you were in Wonderland.

MRS. FRAZER. —[17]Come, children, it is not a question of exchanging one château for another. [18]Neither of them belongs to you.

HELEN. —[19]Something intrigues me: [20]why did they build a part of the château in the middle of a river?

JOHN. —[21]Nothing (is) easier: [22]Catherine de Medici decided that if she had that two-story wing built over the river, [23]she could cross the river without leaving the house.

HELEN. —[24]Well! That's an idea. [25]I would never have thought of that!

A. *Répondez en français:*

1. Quel château John et ses amis viennent-ils de visiter? 2. Quand ce château a-t-il été construit? 3. Quelle est l'époque de la Renaissance française? 4. Qu'est-ce que Marie pense du château? 5. Lequel des châteaux qu'elle a vus choisirait-elle? 6. Pourquoi Chenonceaux lui plaît-il surtout? 7. Voudrait-elle y habiter? 8. Serait-elle heureuse si elle y habitait? 9. De quoi aurait-elle besoin? 10. Quand le château a-t-il été habité? 11. Qui en sont actuellement les propriétaires? 12. Connaissez-vous un autre château de la Renaissance? 13. Pourquoi le château de Chambord n'est-il pas en aussi bon état que celui de Chenonceaux? 14. Lequel des deux châteaux Henry préfère-t-il? 15. Échangerait-il Chambord pour Chenonceaux? 16. Quelle est la partie la plus remarquable du château de Chambord? 17. Où se croirait-on en voyant Chambord? 18. Pourquoi Mme Frazer leur dit-elle qu'il ne s'agit pas d'échanger un château pour un autre? 19. Qu'est-ce qui intrigue Helen? 20. Combien d'étages a la galerie au-dessus de la rivière? 21. Qui a fait construire cette galerie? 22. Pourquoi Catherine de Médicis l'a-t-elle fait construire? 23. Que dit Helen à propos de l'idée qu'a eue Catherine de Médicis?

B. *Demandez en français:*

1. quand le château de Chenonceaux a été construit. 2. qui l'a fait construire. 3. où se trouve Chenonceaux. 4. ce qu'Helen pense du château. 5. si ce château lui plaît. 6. si elle voudrait y habiter. 7. à quelle condition elle voudrait y habiter. 8. s'il y a longtemps que le château a été habité. 9. à qui il appartient à l'heure actuelle. 10. pourquoi le château de Chenonceaux est en meilleur état que celui de Chambord. 11. si Henry aime mieux Chenonceaux que Chambord. 12. quelle vue du château de Chambord lui plaît surtout. 13. où se trouve la galerie du château. 14. combien d'étages a cette galerie. 15. pourquoi elle a été construite.

C. *Dites en français, en employant l'expression indiquée:*

(*a*) jour, journée; an, année

1. John and his friends are spending the day in Chenonceaux. 2. They left Paris two days ago. 3. John has been working for an American

oil company for several years. 4. He would like to go back to the
United States once a year. 5. He has not seen his father for several
years. 6. He was in Egypt last year, and in Venezuela the year
before (**d'avant**). 7. He is going to America this year. 8. Next year,
he'll probably be in another part of the world.

(*b*) **passer . . . à . . .**

1. John and his friends are spending the afternoon visiting Chenonceaux. 2. Last year, John spent six months in Arabia looking for oil.
3. He finds (it) much more pleasant to spend his time visiting castles
in France than looking for oil in the desert.

D. *Remplacez le verbe en italique par la forme appropriée
de* **faire** *suivi de l'infinitif.* (Ex.: Savez-vous qui *a construit*
le château? Savez-vous **qui a fait construire** le château?)

1. Pourquoi Catherine de Médicis *a-t-elle ajouté* une galerie au
château? 2. Elle *a dessiné* les jardins. 3. Elle y *a planté* toutes
sortes de fleurs. 4. Marie *m'a dit* qu'elle ne sortirait pas aujourd'hui
parce qu'elle était malade. 5. Je lui *ai envoyé* des fleurs.

E. *Répondez à chacune des questions suivantes en employant l'expression* **ni l'un ni l'autre:**

1. Connaissez-vous le château de Chambord et celui de Chenonceaux?
2. Ces deux châteaux sont-ils habités à l'heure actuelle? 3. Voudriez-
vous être propriétaire de Chambord ou de Chenonceaux? 4. S'il
s'agissait de choisir entre les deux, lequel choisiriez-vous?

F. *Thème:*

The château of Chenonceaux was built in the first part of the
XVIth century, not by a king or prince as it is generally believed, but
by a rich financier. Later, it belonged to Diane de Poitiers, the beautiful lady who was so often praised (**célébrée si souvent**) by the artists
and poets of the French Renaissance. She had a bridge built over the
river Cher to be able to cross it easily when she wanted to go hunting.

After the death of king Henri II, his widow Catherine de Médicis, who liked neither the château of Chaumont where she lived nor Diane de Poitiers, forced the latter **(celle-ci)** to exchange Chenonceaux for Chaumont. The queen had beautiful gardens designed, and a double gallery built on the bridge. The splendid festivities **(fêtes)** she gave at Chenonceaux have remained famous to our day **(jusqu'à nos jours.)**

XVIII GRAMMAR UNIT

Conditionnel. Infinitif. Participe présent

62. USES OF THE CONDITIONAL.

(1) The conditional tense is used in the result clause of conditional sentences which describe what *would* happen if a given condition *were* fulfilled. The if-clause in this type of conditional sentence is always in the *imparfait* and the result is in the conditional.

Si j'avais à choisir, **je choisirais** Chenonceaux.
Si j'avais tout ce qu'il faut, **je serais** très heureuse ici.

(2) It is also used in contexts in which an if-clause in the *imparfait* is implied:

Bien entendu, **il faudrait** avoir de nombreux serviteurs.
En un mot, **vous voudriez** mener un genre de vie qui n'existe plus.
Je n'échangerais pas Chambord pour Chenonceaux.
On se croirait *au Pays des Merveilles.*

(3) In indirect discourse that depends upon a verb in a past tense, the conditional is used to express future action.

Nous lui avons dit que **nous irions** faire des emplettes cet après-midi.
Roger m'a dit qu'**il irait** au Louvre demain.

Note that this is parallel to English usage. What Roger said was: I shall go to the Louvre tomorrow. This could be reported in direct or in indirect discourse.

DIRECT: Roger m'a dit: "J'irai au Louvre demain." (*I shall go . . .*)
INDIRECT: Roger m'a dit qu'il irait au Louvre demain. (*. . . that he would go . . .*)

(4) The conditional is sometimes used instead of the present tense simply for politeness.

[107]

Pourrais-je vous demander l'heure?
Pourriez-vous me prêter votre voiture?
Je voudrais vous demander un conseil.
Je ne **dirais** pas qu'il a tort.

(5) The conditional is sometimes used to report a rumor or a conjecture:

D'après ce que j'ai entendu dire, les Duplessis **seraient** à la campagne.

Il y a longtemps que je n'ai pas vu Roger. **Serait-il** malade? (*Is he perhaps sick?*)

63. VERBS: + de + INFINITIVE; + à + INFINITIVE; + INFINITIVE ALONE.

(1) The commonest verbs and verbal expressions which may be followed by the preposition **de** and an infinitive are:

achever de, *to finish;* **cesser de,** *to cease, stop;* **se charger de,** *to take charge of;* **conseiller de,** *to advise;* **décider de,** *to decide;* **défendre de,** *to forbid;* **demander de,** *to ask;* **dire de,** *to tell;* **s'efforcer de,** *to try hard;* **empêcher de,** *to prevent;* **essayer de,** *to try;* **s'excuser de,** *to apologize;* **faire bien de,** *to be right;* **finir de,** *to finish;* **forcer de,** *to force;* **se garder de,** *to avoid;* **juger bon de,** *to see fit to;* **manquer de,** *to fail to;* **oublier de,** *to forget;* **permettre de,** *to permit, make possible;* **prier de,** *to request, beg;* **promettre de,** *to promise;* **proposer de,** *to propose, suggest;* **refuser de,** *to refuse;* **regretter de,** *to regret, be sorry;* **remercier de,** *to thank;* **risquer de,** *to risk;* **suffire de,** *to suffice;* **tâcher de,** *to try.*

Madame Frazer **a décidé d'inviter** John.
Il a bien fait d'accepter l'invitation.
Il regretterait de les **déranger.**
Il se gardera bien **d'être** en retard.
Asseyez-vous, **je vous en prie** (*please*).

(2) The commonest verbs and verbal expressions which may be followed by the preposition **à** and an infinitive are:

aider à, *to help;* **apprendre à,** *to learn;* **s'attendre à,** *to expect;* **avoir à,** *to have to;* **avoir de la peine à,** *to have trouble in;* **chercher à,**

to try; commencer à, *to begin;* consentir à, *to consent, agree;* continuer à, *to continue;* enseigner à, *to teach;* s'habituer à, *to get used to;* hésiter à, *to hesitate;* inviter à, *to invite;* parvenir à, *to succeed in;* renoncer à, *to give up;* réussir à, *to succeed in;* tenir à, *to insist upon, to feel urged to.*

> Madame Frazer **a invité** John **à aller** en Touraine.
> Il n'hésite pas **à accepter.**
> Il **tient à revoir** les châteaux de la Loire.
> Il ne s'attendait pas **à les revoir.**
> Il n'a pas grand'chose **à faire.**
> Il **s'est habitué à voyager.**

(3) The commonest verbs and verbal expressions which may take an infinitive without a preposition are:

aimer, *to like;* aimer mieux, *to prefer;* aller, *to go;* avoir beau, *to . . . in vain;* compter, *to count on;* croire, *to think;* désirer, *to want;* devoir, *to have to;* espérer, *to hope;* être censé, *to be supposed to;* faillir, *to be on the point of* — in the past; laisser, *to allow, let;* oser, *to dare;* penser, *to expect;* pouvoir, *to be able;* préférer, *to prefer;* savoir, *to know how;* sembler, *to seem;* il vaut autant, *it is just as well;* il vaut mieux, *it is better;* venir, *to come;* vouloir, *to want to.*

> Il **aimait mieux monter** en haut de la Tour Eiffel.
> Combien de temps **comptez-vous rester** à Paris?
> Nous **viendrons** vous **chercher** à votre hôtel.
> Il **vaut mieux partir** de bonne heure.

The verbs **entendre,** *to hear;* **envoyer,** *to send;* **faire,** *to have something done;* **voir,** *to see,* which also take an infinitive without a preposition, should be studied carefully:

> J'ai **entendu dire** cela. (I have heard that *said.*)
> J'ai **entendu remuer** le bébé. (I heard the baby *stir.*)
> Il a **fait construire** ce château. (He had that château *built.*)
> Je vais vous **faire voir** le service. (I am going to *show* you the set.)
> Nous avons **envoyé chercher** les journaux. (We *sent for* the papers.)
> Nous avons **vu passer** l'auto des Frazer. (*Note the word order.*)

64. Use of prepositions (other than **de** and **à**) with infinitives.

(1) The present infinitive is frequently used after: **par, pour, sans;** and such expressions as: **avant de, afin de** (*in order to*), **loin de, à condition de, de peur de, au lieu de, de manière à.**

> Madame Frazer et Hélène sont venues en ville **pour faire** des emplettes.
> Elles ont commencé **par acheter** des parfums.
> **Avant de finir** leurs courses, elles ont rencontré John.
> Madame Frazer l'a invité à aller avec elle en Touraine.
> Il a accepté **sans hésiter.** **Loin d'être** trop occupé, il est libre comme l'air.

(2) The perfect infinitive may be used after: **après, pour, sans, loin de, au lieu de.**

(*a*) Forms.

Regular verbs: **avoir donné,** *to have given,** having given;* **avoir fini,** *having finished;* **avoir vendu,** *having sold.*

Auxiliary verbs: **avoir eu,** *having had;* **avoir été,** *having been.*

Verbs conjugated with **être**: **être allé,** *having gone.*

Reflexive verbs: **s'être dépêché,** *having hurried;* **s'être couché,** *having gone to bed.*

(*b*) Examples.

> Je regrette **d'avoir oublié** notre rendez-vous.
> Je vous remercie **d'être venu.**
> **Après avoir passé** quelques mois au Vénézuéla, John est parti pour le Soudan.
> **Loin d'avoir fait** de longs voyages, Marie et Roger sont restés sagement à la maison.

---

* Note that the perfect infinitive in English is "to have given," "to have finished," etc.; but we use the perfect participle (having given, having finished, etc.) after prepositions.

65. PRESENT PARTICIPLE WITH PREPOSITION **en.**

(1) Forms.

The present participle of verbs may be found by adding the ending –**ant** to the stem of the first person plural of the present indicative (nous **all** — **ons: all** — **ant;** nous **finiss** — **ons: finiss** — **ant**) except for the verbs **avoir, être,** and **savoir** whose present participles are, respectively, **ayant, étant,** and **sachant.**

(2) Examples.

> **En sortant,** ils échangent leurs impressions. (*On going out, As they go out, In going out, While going out, . . .*)
> Il est difficile de les distinguer même **en** les **examinant** de près. (*even on examining them, even if you examine them . . .*)
> **En quittant** Paris, je suis retourné à Pittsburgh.
> **En attendant** le retour de Marie, nos deux amis parlent de ce qu'ils ont fait au cours des deux dernières années.

A. *Répondez en français par une phrase complète à chacune des questions suivantes:*

1. Seriez-vous content d'habiter dans un grand château? 2. Si vous aviez à choisir, choisiriez-vous Chambord ou Chenonceaux? 3. Si Chenonceaux était à vous, l'échangeriez-vous pour Chambord? 4. Si on habitait dans un château de la Renaissance, qu'est-ce qu'il faudrait avoir? 5. Si vous aviez une grosse fortune, achèteriez-vous une grande maison à la campagne? 6. Si vous aviez une grande maison, voudriez-vous recevoir quantité d'invités? 7. Voudriez-vous mener le genre de vie des gens riches qui vivaient au seizième siècle? 8. Aimeriez-vous faire construire une maison au milieu d'une rivière? 9. Si vous alliez en France, iriez-vous visiter tous les châteaux de la Touraine? 10. Suffirait-il de visiter quelques châteaux? 11. Diriez-vous que ces châteaux sont trop grands pour la vie moderne? 12. Aimeriez-vous voyager *au Pays des Merveilles?* 13. Pourriez-vous me dire où se trouve *le Pays des Merveilles?* 14. D'après ce que vous avez entendu dire, y aurait-il toujours beaucoup de vieux châteaux en Touraine?

B. *Employez chacune des expressions indiquées, avec ou sans préposition, devant les phrases suivantes:*

1. . . . passer le week-end à visiter des châteaux. **(J'ai proposé, J'ai refusé, J'ai jugé bon, Je me garderais bien, J'ai promis.)**

2. . . . regarder sa collection de timbres. **(Il m'a demandé, Il m'a défendu, Il m'a dit, Il m'a conseillé, Il m'a prié, Il m'a permis.)**

3. . . . répondre aux lettres de ses amis. **(Elle a essayé, Elle a cessé, Elle a oublié, Elle a tâché.)**

4. . . . s'occuper du petit Michel. **(Marie a appris, Elle a commencé, Elle s'habitue, Elle réussit, Roger tient, Il a de la peine, Il hésite, Il renonce.)**

5. . . . acheter des cadeaux pour ses amis. **(John compte, Il doit, Il pense, Il est censé, Il espère, Il aime.)**

6. . . . monter en haut de la Tour Eiffel. **(Henri tient, Il décide, Il s'efforce, Il essaie, Il s'attend, Il n'hésite pas, Il ne renonce pas, Il voudrait, Il préfère, Il a réussi, Il a oublié; Madame Frazer ne veut pas, Elle refuse, Elle se garderait bien, Elle hésiterait, Elle regretterait, Elle n'a pas promis, Elle ne propose pas.)**

C. *Dites en français:*

1. Without seeing Chenonceaux. 2. Without going to Chenonceaux. 3. Without going to visit Chenonceaux. 4. Without trying to visit Blois. 5. Instead of going to Touraine. 6. In order to visit Chambord. 7. They began by going to Tours. 8. After having visited Chenonceaux, they went to Chambord. 9. On leaving Chambord, they went to Blois. 10. Before leaving Paris, the Frazers went downtown to make some purchases. 11. While crossing the Place de l'Opéra, John finds himself face to face with the Frazers. 12. While talking of their trips, Mrs. Frazer invited John to go with them to Touraine. 13. Far from refusing their invitation, he accepted it without hesitating. 14. As he left them, he gave Mrs. Frazer his address. 15. After spending two weeks in Paris, John bought some presents for his friends. 16. After having bought the Quimper set of dishes for his sister, he went to look for a silver cup **(une timbale en argent)** for little Michel.

D. *Changez les phrases suivantes de l'expression directe à l'expression indirecte, en remplaçant le futur par le conditionnel.* (Ex.: Il a dit: «J'aurai le temps.» Il a dit qu'il aurait le temps.)

1. Mme Frazer a dit: "Nous irons passer le week-end en Touraine."
2. Elle a dit: "Il y aura une place pour John dans leur voiture."
3. John a répondu: "Mon avion partira pour New-York de samedi en quinze." 4. Il a dit: "Je serai content de revoir les châteaux de la Loire. 5. Il a dit: "Je ne manquerai pas d'être prêt à sept heures et demie. 6. Mme Frazer a dit: "Il faudra à peu près quatre heures de Paris à Orléans."

XIX

CONVERSATION UNIT

Au château de Blois

Le Guide. —[1]Nous sommes maintenant, messieurs dames, dans le cabinet de Catherine de Médicis.* [2]Remarquez la décoration en bois sculpté. [3]Ce panneau-ci cache plusieurs armoires secrètes, où la reine conservait des papiers, des bijoux, même des poisons, dit-on. [4]Il y avait plus de deux cents panneaux, et quatre seulement d'entre eux étaient mobiles. [5]Ceux-ci ressemblaient tellement à ceux-là qu'il était impossible de les distinguer, [6]même en les examinant de très près . . .

(*Le guide et les visiteurs quittent le cabinet de la reine.*)

Henry. —[7]Qu'est-ce qu'elle faisait des poisons qu'elle conservait dans son armoire?

Helen. —[8]C'était peut-être pour les gens qu'elle n'aimait pas!

MME Frazer. —[9]Ne dites pas trop de mal de Catherine de Médicis. [10]J'ai entendu dire qu'elle valait mieux que sa réputation . . .

The Guide. —[1]We are now, ladies and gentlemen, in the office of Catherine de Medici. [2]Note the decoration in carved wood. [3]This panel conceals several secret cupboards in which the queen kept papers, jewels, even poisons, they say. [4]There were more than two hundred panels and only four of them would open (were movable). [5]The latter were so much like the stationary ones (the former) that it was impossible to tell them apart, [6]even when you examine them closely . . .

(*The guide and the visitors leave the office of the queen.*)

Henry. —[7]What did she do with the poisons she kept in her cupboard?

Helen. —[8]They were perhaps for the people she didn't like!

Mrs. Frazer. —[9]Don't criticize (Don't speak too much evil about) Catherine de Medici too much. [10]I have heard that she was better than her reputation . . .

* Femme de Henri II, roi de France de 1547 à 1559.

[114]

HELEN. —[11]La plupart des châteaux que nous avons visités sont vides. [12]Autrefois, ils devaient être meublés. [13]Que sont devenus les meubles?

JOHN. —[14]Même autrefois, les châteaux n'avaient pas beaucoup de meubles, [15]sauf ceux qui servaient de résidence habituelle à quelque grand personnage. [16]Quelques-uns de ceux que nous avons vus—[17]Chambord et celui-ci par exemple—n'ont guère été habités depuis le XVIe siècle. [18]Les meubles qui restaient ont disparu pendant la Révolution.

HELEN. —[19]Je voudrais bien prendre une photo de ces vitres ornées de salamandres..† [20]Mais j'ai oublié mon appareil. [21]Voulez-vous bien me prêter le vôtre?

JOHN. —[22]Mais oui. [23]Le mien ne vaut sans doute pas le vôtre. [24]Mais il fera l'affaire.

HELEN. —[25]Je ne sais pas comment m'en servir.

JOHN. —[26]Rien de plus simple. [27]Il suffit de presser sur le bouton.

HELEN. —[11]Most of the châteaux we have gone through (visited) are empty. [12]They must have been furnished formerly. [13]What has happened to (became of) the furniture?

JOHN. —[14]Even formerly, the châteaux didn't have much furniture, [15]except those that were used as the habitual residence of some important personage. [16]Some of those that we have seen—[17]Chambord and this one, for example—have scarcely been lived in since the XVIth century. [18]The furniture that was left disappeared during the French Revolution.

HELEN. —[19]I would certainly like to take a picture of those windows that are decorated (ornamented) with salamanders. [20]But I forgot my camera. [21]Will you lend me yours?

JOHN. —[22]Why yes. [23]Mine is not as good as yours, no doubt. [24]But it will serve the purpose (do the job).

HELEN. —[25]I don't know how to use it.

JOHN. —[26]Nothing (is) simpler. [27]All you have to do is to press (on) the button.

† La salamandre était l'emblème de François Ier, roi de 1515 à 1547, et le porc-épic était celui de Louis XII (1498-1515).

A. *Répondez en français:*

1. Où sont le guide et les visiteurs du château?   2. Qu'est-ce que le guide fait remarquer aux visiteurs?   3. Que cache le panneau du cabinet?   4. Qui était Catherine de Médicis?   5. Que conservait-elle dans ses armoires secrètes?   6. Combien de panneaux étaient mobiles? 7. Combien d'autres ne l'étaient pas?   8. Était-il possible de distinguer les uns des autres?   9. Que ·demande Henry au sujet des poisons que la reine conservait dans ses armoires secrètes?   10. Est-ce que Catherine de Médicis a une bonne réputation?   11. Que dit Mme Frazer au sujet de cette réputation?   12. La plupart des châteaux sont-ils meublés?   13. Y avait-il autrefois des meubles dans tous les châteaux? 14. Les châteaux ont-ils toujours été habités depuis leur construction? 15. Que sont devenus les meubles à l'époque de la Révolution?   16. De quoi Helen veut-elle prendre une photo?   17. De quel roi la salamandre était-elle l'emblème?   18. Quel était l'emblème de Louis XII? 19. Pourquoi Helen demande-t-elle à John de lui prêter son appareil? 20. John croit-il que son appareil est aussi bon que celui d'Helen? 21. Est-ce qu'Helen sait se servir de cet appareil?   22. Est-il difficile de s'en servir?   23. Que suffit-il de faire?

B. *Demandez en français à quelqu'un:*

1. où le guide accompagné les visiteurs.   2. ce qu'il leur fait remarquer. 3. combien de panneaux il y avait dans le cabinet.   4. combien d'entre eux étaient mobiles.   5. s'il était facile de distinguer ceux qui l'étaient de ceux qui ne l'étaient pas.   6. s'il a entendu parler de Catherine de Médicis.   7. s'il a entendu dire qu'elle a habité à Blois.   8. si la plupart des châteaux sont meublés à l'heure actuelle.   9. s'il reste beaucoup de meubles dans le château de Blois.   10. ce que sont devenus les meubles.   11. quel était l'emblème de François Premier. 12. quel était celui de Louis XII.   13. s'il est difficile de se servir d'un appareil photographique.   14. ce qu'il faut faire pour prendre une photo.

C. *Dites en français, en employant les expressions indiquées:*

(*a*) **servir de, se servir de**

1. Some of these châteaux were used as residences by the French kings.

2. Several of the panels were used as doors to (à) secret cupboards.
3. May I use your camera? 4. Tell me how to use it. 5. One of these châteaux was used as a prison. 6. Helen does not know how to use John's camera.

(b) il reste, rester

1. There is one table service left. 2. How many plates are left?
3. How many plates have you left? 4. I have one dozen left. 5. The furniture which was left was lost during the French Revolution.
6. All the plates which were left were sold at auction.

(c) remarquer

1. Notice the carved wood decoration. 2. Did you notice the staircase (l'escalier)? 3. Yes, I noticed it. 4. I also noticed the salamanders which decorate it.

(d) devenir

1. What became of the furniture? 2. What became of them? 3. What became of him? 4. What became of the château during the French Revolution?

(e) de près, de loin

1. One cannot see them, even looking (at them) closely. 2. Seen from a distance, the château of Chambord is unforgettable. 3. I saw him from a distance. 4. Look closely.

D. *Répondez en français à chacune des questions suivantes:*

1. Avez-vous entendu parler des châteaux de la Loire? 2. Avez-vous entendu dire que le château de Chenonceaux a été construit pour un financier? 3. Avez-vous entendu parler de Diane de Poitiers? 4. Avez-vous entendu dire que Chambord servait de pavillon de chasse (*hunting lodge*) à François Ier?

E. *Remplacez les mots en italique par l'expression* d'entre *et le pronom personnel approprié dans chacune des phrases suivantes:*

1. Beaucoup *des châteaux* datent de l'époque de la Renaissance. 2. La

plupart *de ces châteaux* sont maintenant inhabités.　3. Cependant, des particuliers (private families) habitent dans quelques-uns *des châteaux*. 4. Il y a un château dans plusieurs *des villes de la région.*　5. Deux *de ces villes* sont Blois et Amboise.

F. *Thème:*

Like several châteaux of the French Renaissance, Blois was used as a royal residence. The oldest part was built by king Louis XII. It is a charming construction of rose bricks and white stones, with a high roof and richly decorated windows. Above the doors, one may see the royal emblem, the porcupine. The part added by king Francis the First is famous for its beautiful circular staircase. It is in this part of the château that a well-known event took place in 1588, the assassination of the Duke of Guise by order of king Henri III. The guide always shows the visitors the spot where the duke fell dead, and always quotes **(cite)** the words **(paroles)** of the king when he saw his dead rival: "He is even bigger **(plus grand)** dead than alive!"

XX

Pronoms démonstratifs, possessifs et indéfinis

66. DEMONSTRATIVE PRONOUNS.

In English, the forms *this, that, these,* and *those* are used both as demonstrative adjectives and as demonstrative pronouns; but in French, there is one set of forms for the demonstrative adjective (see paragraph 25) and four sets of forms of demonstrative pronouns. Each of the four sets of forms has a clearly prescribed use.

(1)   The forms of **celui** plus **-ci** and **-là**:

SINGULAR		PLURAL	
celui-ci m ⎱ *this one*		**ceux-ci** m ⎱ *these*	
celle-ci f ⎰		**celles-ci** f ⎰	
celui-là m ⎱ *that one*		**ceux-là** m ⎱ *those*	
celle-là f ⎰		**celles-là** f ⎰	

These forms are used to distinguish between persons or things within a group. They agree in gender and number with the noun to which they refer.

> Remarquez la décoration en bois sculpté. **Celle-ci** cache plusieurs armoires secrètes.
>
> **(Les panneaux.) Ceux-ci** ressemblent tellement à **ceux-là** qu'il est impossible de les distinguer.

Note that while **ceux-ci** means *the latter* and **ceux-là** *the former,* the opposition between the two is not so clear in French as it is in English. For oppositions, **les uns, . . . les autres** is much more commonly used (see paragraph 69, 6.).

(For other uses of the suffixes **-ci** and **-là,** see paragraph 25.)

[119]

(2) **Celui, celle, ceux, celles** (without the suffix **-ci** or **-là**). These forms are always followed by a relative clause or a prepositional phrase.

(Les châteaux) **Ceux qui** servaient de résidence habituelle **. . .**
Ceux que nous avons vus hier **. . .**
Ceux dont le guide nous a parlé **. . .**
Celui de Catherine de Médicis **. . .**
(Les chambres) **Celles que** nous avons visitées **. . .**
Celle de la reine **. . .**
Celles où nous avons remarqué les salamandres **. . .**

(For **l'un** (*the one*) see paragraph 69, 6)

(3) **Ceci,** *this;* cela, ça, *that.*

Cela (or **ça**) is used to refer (*a*) to something that has been said or done, or (*b*) to an undetermined object:

(*a*) **Cela** dépend.	It (or that) depends.
Cela m'intéresse beaucoup.	That, it, interests me a great deal.
Ça ne fait rien.	It makes no difference.
Ça m'est égal.	It's all the same to me.
C'est ça.	That's it.
Comment **ça?**	How's that?
(*b*) Qu'est-ce que c'est que **ça?**	What's that?
Regardez-moi **ça.**	Just look at that.
Où avez-vous acheté **ça?**	Where did you buy that?

Ceci is used chiefly in oppositions: Donnez-moi **ceci** et gardez **cela.** (Note that the pronoun **il** cannot be used in phrases of this type — even though we say "it" in English.)

(4) **Ce,** *this, that, it.*

This form is used:

(*a*) As subject of the verb **être** if the verb is followed by a personal pronoun, a person's name or a noun that is preceded by an article or possessive adjective:

C'est mon père. (*That's* my father. *He's* my father. *It's* my father.)

C'est moi. C'est moi qui ai parlé. C'est une bonne idée. C'est un diplomate célèbre. C'est un beau château. C'est le château de Blois. Ce sont des artistes.
C'est vous que je cherchais. (*You are the one* I was looking for.)
C'est Roger, C'est Madame Frazer.

(*b*) Instead of cela (see above) :

C'est bien. C'est vrai. C'est impossible. C'est peu de chose. Ce n'est rien. Ce n'est pas la peine.

67. POSSESSIVE PRONOUNS.

A possessive pronoun is used to replace a possessive adjective and the noun it modifies. (For possessive adjectives, see paragraph 26.) «J'ai oublié **mon appareil.** Voulez-vous bien me prêter **le vôtre?**» **Le vôtre** takes the place of **votre appareil.** «**Le mien** ne vaut sans doute pas **le vôtre**» *stands for:* Mon appareil ne vaut sans doute pas votre appareil.

(1) The forms of the possessive pronouns are:

SINGULAR		PLURAL	
MASCULINE	FEMININE	MASCULINE	FEMININE
le mien	la mienne	les miens	les miennes (*mine*)
le tien	la tienne	les tiens	les tiennes (*yours*)
le sien	la sienne	les siens	les siennes (*his, hers, its*)
le nôtre	la nôtre	les nôtres	les nôtres (*ours*)
le vôtre	la vôtre	les vôtres	les vôtres (*yours*)
le leur	la leur	les leurs	les leurs (*theirs*)

Possessive pronouns agree in gender and number with the things possessed. Ex.: In answer to the question: «— Avez-vous pris **des photos?**» either Roger or Marie could answer «— Oui, mais **les miennes** ne sont pas aussi bonnes que **les vôtres.**»

(2) The definite articles of the possessive pronouns naturally have contracted forms when used with the prepositions **à** or **de:**

du mien, de la mienne, des miens, des miennes, etc.

au mien, à la mienne, aux miens, aux miennes, etc.

(un appareil) Je sais me servir **du mien,** mais je ne sais pas me servir **du vôtre.**

68. USE OF PREPOSITION à TO EXPRESS POSSESSION.

If the subject of the verb **être** is a noun or a personal pronoun, you normally express possession by using **à** with another noun or personal pronoun (stressed form) after the verb.

Cet appareil est **à moi.** Il est **à moi.**

Cette photo est-elle **à vous?** Non, elle est **à Marie.**

If the subject of **est** is **ce** (**c'**), either the possessive pronoun or **à** with a personal pronoun may be used:

C'est à moi. C'est le mien. C'est la mienne.

69. INDEFINITE PRONOUNS.

The word "indefinite" when applied to pronouns means that the pronoun concerned does not define or determine the person or thing to which it refers. The corresponding indefinite pronouns in English are: each one, every one, several, all, the same, others, and so on.

(1) **Tout, toute, tous, toutes,** *all; everything, everyone.*

Note that the **s** of the *pronoun* **tous** is always pronounced although it is silent in the *adjective* **tous.**

Ils sont **tous** (*touss*) venus. (PRONOUN)

Tous les jours, *every day;* **Tous** les deux, *both.* (ADJECTIVE)

(2) **Plusieurs,** *several.*

Avez-vous pris des photos? Oui, j'en ai pris **plusieurs.**

(3) **On, l'on,*** *one, someone, you, we, people, they.*

On est venu vous voir. En France, **on** parle français.

---

* L'on is used only after **où** and **si.** Ex.: . . . "un pays où **l'on** parle français." Both forms are used with the third person singular of verbs.

(4) **Quelqu'un, (quelqu'une), quelques-uns, quelques-unes** *someone; some, a few.* The feminine singular is practically never used.

> **Quelqu'un** est venu vous voir.
> **Quelques-uns** de ceux que nous avons vus . . .

(5) **Chacun, chacune,** *each one.*

> **Chacune** de ces assiettes est en bon état.

(6) **L'un, l'une, les uns, les unes** *the one, the ones;* **l'autre, les autres** *the other, the others.*

> J'admire **l'un et l'autre.** (*both*)
> Je n'admire **ni l'un ni l'autre.** (*neither*)
> **Ni l'un ni l'autre** ne vous appartient. (*neither*)

(7) **Le même, la même, les mêmes,** *the same one, the same ones.*

> Cet emblème est **le même** que nous avons vu.

(8) **aucun, aucune** (used with **ne**), *none, not a one.*

> **Aucune** des assiettes **n'**a le moindre défaut.

(9) **personne** (used with **ne**) *no one, nobody.*

> Je **n'**ai trouvé **personne.**
> **Personne ne** m'a dit que vous étiez ici.

(10) **rien** (used with **ne**) *nothing, not a thing.*

> Il **n'**y a **rien** de plus simple. **Rien** de plus simple.
> **Rien n'**est plus simple.

(11) Note also the following "indefinite" expressions which are not pronouns: **Quelque chose,** *something;* **autre chose,** *something else;* **pas grand'chose,** *nothing much;* **peu de chose,** *practically nothing.*

> Avez-vous **quelque chose** à faire ce soir? — Je n'ai pas **grand'chose** à faire.

Note also that after **rien** and **quelque chose** an adjective is preceded by the preposition **de.**

> **Quelque chose d'**intéressant. **Rien d'**extraordinaire.

(12) **Ne** is omitted when **rien, personne,** or **aucun** is used without a verb.

Qu'est-ce que vous faites? — **Rien.**
Qui est venu? — **Personne.**

A. *Répondez en français en employant un pronom démonstratif:*

1. Voilà deux châteaux. Lequel préférez-vous?   2. John et Henry portent des chandails (*sweaters*). De quelle couleur est celui de John? 3. De quelle couleur est celui d'Henry?   4. Henry en a deux. Aimez-vous mieux celui qu'il porte aujourd'hui que celui qu'il portait hier? 5. Il a plusieurs cravates. De quelle couleur est celle qu'il porte aujourd'hui?   6. De quelle couleur est celle qu'il portait hier?   7. Marie a plusieurs paires de gants. Est-ce que ceux qu'elle porte aujourd'hui sont blancs?   8. Avez-vous lu les romans de Balzac et ceux de Stendhal? 9. Lesquels préférez-vous?   10. Connaissez-vous les oeuvres de Cézanne et celles de Renoir?   11. Lesquelles aimez-vous le mieux?   12. Voilà deux livres. Est-ce que celui-ci est aussi gros que celui-là?

B. *Répétez chacune des phrases suivantes en remplaçant le nom en italique par le pronom démonstratif convenable:*

1. Regardez ces panneaux. Que pensez-vous de *ce panneau?*   2. *Les panneaux* que nous avons vus à Blois sont remarquables.   3. L'emblème de Louis XII est le porc-épic; *l'emblème* de François Premier est la salamandre.   4. Helen préfère *l'emblème* de François Premier. 5. Henry préfère *l'emblème* de Louis XII.   6. Mme Frazer préfère *l'emblème* de Louise de Savoie.   7. L'emblème *de Louise de Savoie* était un cygne (swan).   8. Est-ce que *les emblèmes* des rois de France vous intéressent?

C. *Dites en français:*

1. Do you prefer the château of Chenonceaux or the one of Blois? 2. I prefer the one that Catherine de Medici had built in the middle of the Cher river.   3. François Premier's (the one of François Ier) is

perhaps larger and more famous.   4. Catherine de Medici's is more
romantic.   5. It is the one we visited the other day.   6. The one
where we saw the salamanders and the porcupines pleases Henry.
7. Helen would like to live in the one where there is furniture of the
Renaissance.   8. Would you prefer this one or that one?   9. The story
of the murder of the Duke de Guise was horrible. That interested
Henry very much.   10. Oh! What's that?   11. That's the emblem of
Louis XII.   12. Don't you know porcupines? — I don't recognize that
one.   13. Have you ever seen a salamander? — No, but this one is
charming.   14. I like François Premier's emblem better than Louis
XII's (that of).   15. François Premier's emblem is gayer than
Louis XII's.   16. His château is bigger than Catherine de Medici's.

D. *Répondez en français en remplaçant les noms en italique par les pronoms convenables:*

1. Voilà mon appareil. Où est *votre appareil?*   2. J'ai trouvé vos
photos très bien. Que pensez-vous *de mes photos?*   3. Est-ce que *vos
photos* sont meilleures que *les photos* d'Henry?   4. Est-ce que *votre
appareil* est aussi bon que *l'appareil* d'Henry?   5. Est-ce que *l'appareil*
de John est aussi bon que *l'appareil* de Mme Frazer?   6. Helen
préfère-t-elle *son appareil* à *l'appareil* de John?   7. A qui est *cet
appareil-ci?*   8. Où est *votre appareil?*   9. Où sont *vos photos?*
10. Où avez-vous pris *vos photos?*   11. (*En montrant une lettre*)
Qu'est-ce que c'est que ça?   A qui est *cette lettre?*   12. Est-ce que
cette lettre est à John?   13. Et *ce livre* est-il à John?   14. A qui est
ce livre-là?

E. *Donnez plusieurs réponses différentes à chacune des questions suivantes:*

1. Connaissez-vous les châteaux de la Touraine?   (*a*) I know
several. (*b*) I know them all. (*c*) I don't know any of them. (*d*) I
don't know a single one of them.
2. Connaissez-vous les cathédrales gothiques(*f*)?   (*Mêmes réponses.*)
3. Connaissez-vous Degas et Cézanne?   (*a*) I know both. (*b*) I

do not know either (neither the one nor the other). (*c*) I have seen the pictures **(tableaux)** of both of them (of the one and of the other). (*d*) I have seen a few of them. (*e*) I have seen several.

4. Est-ce qu'on est venu me voir? (*a*) Yes, someone came. (*b*) No, no one came. (*c*) I didn't see anyone. (*e*) I didn't hear anyone. (*f*) I didn't hear anything. (*g*) Some persons came. (*h*) There were several of them.

5. Qu'est-ce qui est arrivé? (*a*) Nothing happened. (*b*) Nothing much. (*c*) Something interesting. (*d*) Nothing unusual. (*e*) Practically nothing. (*f*) Something else.

6. Que fait John ce soir? (*a*) He has nothing to do. (*b*) He hasn't much to do. (*c*) He has practically nothing to do. (*d*) He has nothing interesting to do. (*e*) He has something interesting to do.

La Tour Eiffel, construite en 1889.

La France au dix-neuvième siècle

A droite — L'Opéra au dix-neuvième siècle.

Paris mondain en 1830. Foyer de l'Opéra.

Fontainebleau. Salon de musique.

Paris romantique. Boulevard des Italiens.

Daumier. L'Amateur d'estampes (Collector of Prints).

Affiche de Toulouse-Lautrec: La Vache enragée.

Au bord de la mer, vers 1870. Monet.

Seurat. Un Dimanche d'été.

Cézanne. Paysage.

Renoir. La Fillette au ruban rouge.

Inauguration du Canal de Suez, en 1869.

Fête du 14 juillet vers la fin du XIXᵉ siècle.

Danseuses de Degas.

XXI CONVERSATION UNIT

Sur la route

HENRY (*qui conduit*). —[1]Voilà des heures qu'il pleut sans arrêt. [2]Il faisait beau quand nous sommes partis; [3]il s'est mis à pleuvoir une demi-heure plus tard, [4]et maintenant on voit à peine à travers le pare-brise. [5]Écoutez la pluie sur le toit de la voiture.

JOHN (*récitant*). —
  [6]O bruit doux de la pluie
  Par terre et sur les toits!

[7]Pour un cœur qui s'ennuie

  O le chant de la pluie!
[8]Dans l'esprit du poète, [9]il s'agissait d'un autre genre de toit, bien entendu.

HENRY. —[10]Ne dites pas des choses comme ça sans me prévenir! [11]J'ai été si surpris que j'ai failli quitter la route.

HELEN. —[12]Cette pluie ne me déplaît pas du tout. [13]Elle me donne au contraire un sentiment de confort, de bien-être.

HENRY. —[14]Je crains, ma chère sœur, que ton bien-être ne soit de courte durée. [15]J'ai l'im-

HENRY (*who is driving*). —[1]It's been raining steadily for hours. [2]The weather was fine when we started, [3]it began to rain a half hour later, [4]and now you can scarcely see through the windshield. [5]Listen to the rain on the roof of the car.

JOHN (*reciting*). —
  [6]Oh gentle noise of the rain
  On the ground and on the roofs!

[7]For a heart that is desperately sad

  Oh the song of the rain!
[8]In the mind of the poet, [9]it was a question of another sort of roof, of course.

HENRY. —[10]Don't say such things without warning me! [11]I was so surprised that I almost ran off the road.

HELEN. —[12]This rain doesn't bother me at all. [13]On the contrary it gives me a feeling of comfort, of well-being.

HENRY. —[14]I am afraid, my dear sister, that your well-being may be short-lived (of short dura-

pression que nous nous sommes trompés de route.

JOHN. —[16]J'aperçois là-bas un poteau-indicateur. [17]Lisez ce qu'il dit.

HENRY. —[18]Je ne peux rien voir à cause de la pluie.

JOHN. —[19]Arrêtez-vous un instant et ouvrez la portière.

HENRY (*lisant*). —[20]Il dit: G-I-E-N, 65 kilomètres.

HELEN. —[21]Comment prononcez-vous G-I-E-N?

JOHN. —[22]Je crois que GIEN rime avec CHIEN.

HELEN. —[23]Je ne sais jamais comment on prononce les noms propres. [24]On écrit REIMS et on dit RINCE, [25]LAON et on dit LENT, [26]CAEN et on dit QUAND; [27]le nom de la rivière LA SAÔNE rime avec BEAUNE. [28]Je n'y comprends rien.

HENRY. —[29]Vraiment, ce n'est pas le moment de chercher à comprendre. [30]Au lieu de discuter la prononciation des noms propres, [31]tu ferais mieux de me dire quelle route je dois suivre!

HELEN (*piquée*). —[32]Qui sait? [33]Pas moi. [34]Je ne connais pas très bien la France.

tion). [15]I have the impression that we have taken the wrong road.

JOHN. —[16]I see a signpost up ahead. [17]Read what it says.

HENRY. —[18]I can't see a thing because of the rain.

JOHN. —[19]Stop a moment and open the door.

HENRY (*reading*). —[20]It says: G-I-E-N, 65 kilometers.

HELEN. —[21]How do you pronounce G-I-E-N?

JOHN. —[22]I think Gien rhymes with *chien*.

HELEN. —[23]I never know how you pronounce proper names. [24]You write REIMS and you say *rince*, [25]LAON and you say *lent*, [26]CAEN and you say *quand;* [27]the name of the river LA SAÔNE rhymes with BEAUNE. [28]I don't get it (understand it at all).

HENRY. —[29]Really, this is not the time to try (seek) to understand. [30]Instead of discussing the pronunciation of proper names, [31]you would do better to tell me what road to follow.

HELEN (*annoyed*). —[32]Who knows? [33]Not I. [34]I don't know France very well.

JOHN. —[35]Si je me permets de vous donner mon avis, vous n'avez guère le choix. [36]Suivez celle-ci jusqu'au prochain village. [37]Là, nous verrons bien quelle route il faut prendre.

JOHN. —[35]If I may take the liberty of giving you my opinion, you scarcely have any choice. [36]Follow this one as far as the next village. [37]There we will certainly see what road we must take.

A. *Répondez en français:*

1. Où sont John et ses amis? 2. Qui conduit l'auto? 3. Quel temps fait-il? 4. Quand s'est-il mis à pleuvoir? 5. Où peut-on entendre la pluie? 6. Quels vers John récite-t-il? 7. Qui a écrit ces vers? (Verlaine.) 8. Qu'est-ce qu'Henry pense des vers que John récite? 9. Qu'est-ce qu'Henry a failli faire quand il a entendu John? 10. Est-ce que la pluie déplaît à Helen? 11. Pourquoi la pluie lui plaît-elle? 12. Que craint Henry? 13. Est-ce qu'il est sur la bonne route? 14. Qu'est-ce qu'il aperçoit là-bas? 15. Pourquoi ne peut-il pas lire l'inscription tout d'abord? 16. Qu'est-ce que John lui dit de faire? 17. Que dit l'inscription? 18. Marie sait-elle toujours comment prononcer les noms propres? 19. Savez-vous où sont les villes que cite Marie? 20. Que dit Henry à sa sœur qui discute la prononciation des noms propres? 21. Que lui répond-elle? 22. Quel conseil John donne-t-il à son ami? 23. Pourquoi lui dit-il d'aller jusqu'au prochain village?

B. *Demandez en français:*

1. s'il fait beau quand John et ses amis sont sur la route. 2. s'il pleut depuis longtemps. 3. s'il faisait beau quand ils sont partis. 4. quand il a commencé à pleuvoir. 5. si Henry peut voir à travers le pare-brise. 6. pourquoi il ne peut pas voir. 7. si Henry a été surpris. 8. ce qu'il a failli faire. 9. ce qu'Helen pense de la pluie. 10. quel sentiment la pluie lui donne. 11. ce que craint Henry. 12. s'il s'est trompé de route. 13. ce qu'Henry aperçoit. 14. s'il peut lire ce qui est écrit sur le poteau-indicateur. 15. si Helen comprend quelque chose à la prononciation des noms propres. 16. ce qu'Henry lui dit de faire au lieu de discuter la prononciation des noms propres. 17. ce

qu'Helen répond à son frère. 18. pourquoi elle ne peut pas lui dire quelle route il doit suivre. 19. où Henry pourra demander quelle route il doit suivre.

C. *Dites en français, en employant les expressions indiquées:*

(*a*) **se mettre à, se mettre en route**

1. It started to rain half an hour later. 2. What time was it when the rain started? 3. When did you begin working last night? 4. I began working around 9 o'clock. 5. What time did you start on your way? 6. We started out at eight. 7. Next time (**la prochaine fois**) we'll start out earlier.

(*b*) **faillir**

1. I almost left the road. 2. The car almost left the road. 3. We almost had an accident. 4. One day when (**que**) his carriage was late, Louis XIV said: "I almost had to wait! (I almost waited!)"

(*c*) **se tromper (de)**

1. I feel that we have taken the wrong road. 2. I went to the wrong door. 3. Don't go to the wrong house. 4. Aren't you mistaken? 5. I made a mistake. 6. Don't make a mistake.

(*d*) **le moment (de)**

1. It's time to leave. 2. It's not the proper time to do it. 3. He came at the right time. 4. He came at dinner time.

(*e*) **chercher à**

1. This is not the time to try to understand. 2. Don't try to understand! 3. I tried to speak to him, but I couldn't find him.

D. *Remplacez* **faire bien** *par* **faire mieux** *dans chacune des phrases suivantes:*

1. Tu ferais bien de me dire quelle route je dois suivre. 2. Est-ce que nous ne ferions pas bien de partir plus tôt? 3. Vous feriez bien de partir à sept heures et demie au lieu de huit heures. 4. Vous feriez bien de me prévenir quand vous dites ces choses-là. 5. Il aurait bien fait de m'avertir.

E. *Thème:*

The pronunciation of proper names, especially names of small cities, is not always evident to French people (**les Français**). Whereas common nouns are used everywhere, proper names sometimes have a local pronunciation with which people elsewhere are not always familiar. And the names of the inhabitants of some of these cities are even worse. Of course everybody knows that the inhabitants of Paris are called "Parisiens," and those of Marseille "Marseillais." But sometimes the name of an inhabitant is very different from that of the city in which he lives. You perhaps have heard of the old city of Aix-en-Provence, near Marseille. But you probably don't know that its inhabitants are called "Aquisextains," and that Victor Hugo was a "Bizontin" since he was born in Besançon. As the French themselves say: "One never knows."

XXII

GRAMMAR UNIT

Verbes irréguliers

70. A QUICK LOOK AT IRREGULAR VERBS.

The best way to learn irregular verbs is to practice using them orally in exercises such as those suggested below. However, it is useful to look at them in groups and to understand how they differ from regular verbs. You can see almost at a glance that most of the forms of many of them are perfectly regular. The following observations may help you recognize the chief ways in which they are irregular.

(1) The present indicative is the only tense of irregular verbs that is practically always irregular.

(*a*) Instead of having one stem throughout like regular verbs (see paragraph 4), irregular verbs usually have two stems, one for the first and second persons plural and another for the other four persons. Ex.: **venir:** je **vien**s — nous **ven**ons; **mettre:** je **met**s — nous **mett**ons.

(*b*) Endings. Practically all irregular verbs have the present indicative endings **-s, -s, -t, -ons, -ez, -ent.** A few have those of the first conjugation: **-e, -es- -e,** etc.

(2) *Imparfait.* Except for **être,** the *imparfait* of all irregular verbs follows the pattern of regular verbs: the endings are always regular and the stem is always the same as the stem of the first person plural of the present indicative.

(3) Future. Of the 30 irregular verbs mentioned in this lesson, less than a third have an irregular future. For verbs that do have an irregular future (and conditional), it should be noted that the endings are always regular and that a single stem is always used throughout the two tenses.

(4) Past participle. Verbs ending in -er always have a past participle in -é. Verbs in -ir have a past participle in -i, -u, or -ert. Verbs in -re have a past participle in -u, -is, it, or -aint (-eint, -oint). Those in -oir have a past participle in -u. Those following the same pattern are grouped together below.

(5) The forms of the subjunctive and the *passé simple* will be studied in Units 26 and 30.

71. IRREGULAR VERBS ENDING IN -er.

There are only two verbs in this group: **aller,** and **envoyer,** *to send.*

(1) **Aller,** *to go.*

— Où **allez-vous,** Monsieur? — **Je vais** à Saint-Cloud.

PRÉSENT: **Je vais, tu vas, il va, nous allons, vous allez, ils vont.**
IMPARFAIT: **J'allais.**
PASSÉ COMPOSÉ: **Je suis allé(e).**
FUTUR: **J'irai.**

Note that **s'en aller,** *to leave, to go away* has practically the same use and meaning as **partir** except that **s'en aller** is rarely used in compound tenses.

(2) **Envoyer,** *to send.*

On m'a envoyé au Vénézuéla.
On m'envoie maintenant en Amérique.

PRÉSENT: **J'envoie, tu envoies, il envoie, nous envoyons, vous envoyez, ils envoient.**
IMPARFAIT: **J'envoyais.**
PASSÉ COMPOSÉ: **J'ai envoyé.**
FUTUR: **J'enverrai.**

Renvoyer, *to send back, to send away* is of course conjugated like **envoyer.**

72. FIRST GROUP OF IRREGULAR VERBS IN **-ir: partir, sortir, sentir, servir, dormir,** etc.

These verbs have two stems in the present indicative: par—part—, ser—serv—, dor—dorm—, etc.; and the past participle of all these verbs ends in –i.

(1) **Partir,** *to leave.*

Il faisait beau quand **nous sommes partis.**

PRÉSENT: **Je pars, tu pars, il part, nous partons, vous partez, ils partent.**

IMPARFAIT: **Je partais.**

PASSÉ COMPOSÉ: **Je suis parti(e).**

FUTUR: **Je partirai.**

(2) **Sortir,** *to go out* (intransitive), *to take out* (transitive).

Il faisait beau quand **nous sommes sortis.**

J'ai sorti mon portefeuille.

PRÉSENT: **Je sors, tu sors, il sort, nous sortons, vous sortez, ils sortent.**

IMPARFAIT: **Je sortais.**

PASSÉ COMPOSÉ: **Je suis sorti(e)** (*intrans.*), **J'ai sorti** (*trans.*).

FUTUR: **Je sortirai.**

(3) **Sentir,** *to smell;* **se sentir,** *to feel.*

Ces roses **sentent** bon.

Je ne me sens pas très bien.

PRÉSENT: **Je sens, tu sens, il sent, nous sentons, vous sentez, ils sentent.**

IMPARFAIT: **Je sentais.**

PASSÉ COMPOSÉ: **J'ai senti.**

FUTUR: **Je sentirai.**

(4) **Servir,** *to serve;* **se servir de,** *to use, to help oneself;* **servir à,** *to be of use;* **servir de,** *to serve as, to be used as.*

Marie **sert** le dîner.

Hélène **se sert de** l'appareil de Jean.

Cela ne **sert à** rien. (That is useless.)

Le château de Loches **a servi de** prison.

PRÉSENT: Je sers, tu sers, il sert, nous servons, vous servez, ils servent.
IMPARFAIT: Je servais.
PASSÉ COMPOSÉ: J'ai servi.
FUTUR: Je servirai.

(5) **Dormir,** *to sleep;* **s'endormir,** *to fall asleep.*

Le petit Michel a dormi tout l'après-midi.
Il **dort** bien la nuit.
Il **s'endort** de bonne heure.

PRÉSENT: Je **dors,** tu **dors,** il **dort,** nous **dormons,** vous **dormez,** ils **dorment.**
IMPARFAIT: Je **dormais.**
PASSÉ COMPOSÉ: J'ai **dormi.**
FUTUR: Je **dormirai.**

Compounds of these verbs follow the same pattern of conjugation. Ex.: **sentir — consentir,** *to consent;* **partir — repartir,** *to set out again.*

73. SECOND GROUP OF IRREGULAR VERBS IN **-ir: venir, tenir.**

These verbs have two stems for the present indicative (**viens — venons**), an irregular future (**viendrai**) and a past participle in **–u.**

(1) **Venir,** *to come;* **venir de** (with infinitive) *to have just.*
D'où **venez-vous,** John?
Je **viens** de France.
Est-ce que **vous venez d'**arriver en France?

PRÉSENT: Je **viens,** tu **viens,** il **vient,** nous **venons,** vous **venez,** ils **viennent.**
IMPARFAIT: Je **venais.**
PASSÉ COMPOSÉ: Je suis **venu (e).**
FUTUR: Je **viendrai.**

Revenir, *to come back;* **devenir,** *to become;* **prévenir,** *to warn;* **se souvenir (de),** *to remember;* **convenir,** *to be suitable, to agree,* are conjugated like **venir.**

(2) **Tenir,** *to hold, to keep;* **tenir à,** *to insist upon, to be eager to.*

Henri **tient** à monter en haut de la Tour Eiffel.

PRÉSENT: **Je tiens, tu tiens, il tient, nous tenons, vous tenez, ils tiennent.**

IMPARFAIT: **Je tenais.**

PASSÉ COMPOSÉ: **J'ai tenu.**

FUTUR: **Je tiendrai.**

Retenir, *to retain, to reserve;* **appartenir (à),** *to belong to* are conjugated like **tenir.**

74. THIRD GROUP OF IRREGULAR VERBS IN -ir: **ouvrir,** *to open,* **couvrir,** *to cover;* **souffrir,** *to suffer.*

Ouvrez la portière.

Roger **a ouvert** la lettre.

PRÉSENT: **J'ouvre, tu ouvres, il ouvre, nous ouvrons, vous ouvrez, ils ouvrent.**

IMPARFAIT: **J'ouvrais.**

PASSÉ COMPOSÉ: **J'ai ouvert.**

FUTUR: **J'ouvrirai.**

75. FIRST GROUP OF VERBS ENDING IN -re: **connaître, croire, boire, lire.**

The past participle of these verbs ends in **-u: connaître —connu, croire — cru, boire — bu, lire — lu.**

(1) **Connaître,** *to know, to be acquainted with.*

Connaissez-vous les Duplessis?

Je ne **connais** pas très bien la France.

PRÉSENT: **Je connais, tu connais, il connaît, nous connaissons, vous connaissez, ils connaissent.**

IMPARFAIT: **Je connaissais.**

PASSÉ COMPOSÉ: **J'ai connu.**

FUTUR: **Je connaîtrai.**

(2) **Croire,** *to believe; to think.*

Je **crois** que Gien rime avec chien.

Croyez-vous cette histoire?

PRÉSENT: **Je crois, tu crois, il croit, nous croyons, vous croyez, ils croient.**

IMPARFAIT: **Je croyais.**

PASSÉ COMPOSÉ: **J'ai cru.**

FUTUR: **Je croirai.**

(3) **Boire,** *to drink.*

Buvez-vous du café? — Oui, j'en **bois** tous les matins.

Il **a bu** un demi-litre d'eau fraîche.

PRÉSENT: **Je bois, tu bois, il boit, nous buvons, vous buvez, ils boivent.**

IMPARFAIT: **Je buvais.**

PASSÉ COMPOSÉ: **J'ai bu.**

FUTUR: **Je boirai.**

(4) **Lire,** *to read.*

Voilà un poteau-indicateur. **Lisez** ce qu'il dit.

Lisant: Il dit: Gien, 65 kilomètres.

PRÉSENT: **Je lis, tu lis, il lit, nous lisons, vous lisez, ils lisent.**

IMPARFAIT: **Je lisais.**

PASSÉ COMPOSÉ: **J'ai lu.**

76. SECOND GROUP OF IRREGULAR VERBS IN **-re.**

(1) Past participle in **-is: mettre — mis, prendre — pris.**

(*a*) **Mettre,** *to put, to put on;* **se mettre à,** *to begin.*

Je **mets** mon imperméable quand il pleut.

Il s'est **mis** à pleuvoir. J'ai **mis** mon imperméable.

Si **je me permets** de vous donner mon avis, vous n'avez guère **le** choix.

PRÉSENT: **Je mets, tu mets, il met, nous mettons, vous mettez, ils mettent.**

IMPARFAIT: **Je mettais.**

PASSÉ COMPOSÉ: **J'ai mis.**

FUTUR: **Je mettrai.**

Permettre, *to permit,* **promettre,** *to promise,* **remettre,** *to deliver; to put back,* and other compounds of **mettre** are conjugated like **mettre.**

(*b*) **Prendre,** *to take.*

Vous ne **comprenez** pas? — Non, je n'y **comprends** rien.
J'ai été si **surpris** que j'ai failli quitter la route.

PRÉSENT: **Je prends, tu prends, il prend, nous prenons, vous prenez, ils prennent.**
IMPARFAIT: **Je prenais.**
PASSÉ COMPOSÉ: **J'ai pris.**
FUTUR: **Je prendrai.**

Comprendre, *to understand,* **surprendre,** *to surprise,* **apprendre,** *to learn,* and other compounds of **prendre** are conjugated like **prendre.**

(2) Past participle in **-it:** dire, écrire, conduire.

(*a*) **Dire,** *to say, to tell.*

On écrit *Laon* et on **dit** *lent.*
Ne **dites** pas ces choses-là sans me prévenir.

PRÉSENT: **Je dis, tu dis, il dit, nous disons, vous dites, ils disent.**
IMPARFAIT: **Je disais.**
PASSÉ COMPOSÉ: **J'ai dit.**
FUTUR: **Je dirai.**

(*b*) **Écrire,** *to write.*

On écrit *Caen* et on dit *quand.*

PRÉSENT: **J'écris, tu écris, il écrit, nous écrivons, vous écrivez, ils écrivent.**
IMPARFAIT: **J'écrivais.**
PASSÉ COMPOSÉ: **J'ai écrit.**
FUTUR: **J'écrirai.**

Décrire, *to describe,* is conjugated like **écrire.**

(*c*) **Conduire,** *to drive; to conduct.*

Henri **conduit** l'auto.
Il **a conduit** toute la journée.

PRÉSENT: **Je conduis, tu conduis, il conduit, nous conduisons, vous conduisez, ils conduisent.**

IMPARFAIT: **Je conduisais.**

PASSÉ COMPOSÉ: **J'ai conduit.**

FUTUR: **Je conduirai.**

Produire, *to produce,* and **construire,** *to build* are conjugated like **conduire.**

(3) Past participle in -i: suivre, suffire.

(*a*) **Suivre,** *to follow; to take* (a course).

Suivez cette route jusqu'au prochain village.

Je la **suis** depuis une heure. (I have been following it for an hour.)

PRÉSENT: **Je suis, tu suis, il suit, nous suivons, vous suivez, ils suivent.**

IMPARFAIT: **Je suivais.**

PASSÉ COMPOSÉ: **J'ai suivi.**

FUTUR: **Je suivrai.**

(*b*) **Suffire,** *to suffice, to be sufficient,* etc. This verb is used mostly as an impersonal verb.

Il **suffit** de presser sur le bouton. (All you need do . . .)

PRÉSENT: **Il suffit.**

IMPARFAIT: **Il suffisait.**

PASSÉ COMPOSÉ: **Il a suffi.**

FUTUR: **Il suffira.**

77. VERBS ENDING IN -indre: **plaindre,** *to pity,* **se plaindre,** *to complain;* **craindre,** *to fear;* **atteindre,** *to reach, to attain;* **éteindre,** *to extinguish;* **peindre,** *to paint,* **rejoindre,** *to meet, to catch up with.*

The present tense of this group of verbs has two stems. In all cases the plural stem ends in -gn-: Je **crains** — nous **craignons.**

The past participle of these verbs ends in -int and is identical with the third person singular of the present tense: **il craint,** il a **craint; il atteint,** il a **atteint; il peint,** il a **peint; il rejoint,** il a **rejoint.**

Craindre, *to fear.*

Je crains que votre bien-être ne soit de courte durée.
Ne craignez rien, Monsieur.
Henri se plaint de la pluie.

PRÉSENT: **Je crains, tu crains, il craint, nous craignons, vous craignez, ils craignent.**
IMPARFAIT: **Je craignais.**
PASSÉ COMPOSÉ: **J'ai craint.**
FUTUR: **Je craindrai.**

Note that the verbs ending in **-eindre** and **-oindre** have **-e-** or **-o-** in their stem throughout: il peint, elle nous rejoint.

78. Faire, *to make, to do.*

Il faisait beau quand nous sommes partis.
Mon appareil fera l'affaire.
Tu ferais mieux de me dire quelle route il faut prendre.

PRÉSENT: **Je fais, tu fais, il fait, nous faisons, vous faites, ils font.**
IMPARFAIT: **Je faisais.**
PASSÉ COMPOSÉ: **J'ai fait.**
FUTUR: **Je ferai.**

79. Voir, *to see;* apercevoir, *to perceive, to see;* recevoir, *to receive.*

These verbs have a past participle in **-u**, two stems in the present tense, and an irregular future.

J'aperçois là-bas un poteau-indicateur. (Je vois ...)
Je l'ai aperçu de loin. (J'ai vu ...)

PRÉSENT: **Je vois, tu vois, il voit, nous voyons, vous voyez, ils voient.**
IMPARFAIT: **Je voyais.**
PASSÉ COMPOSÉ: **J'ai vu.**
FUTUR: **Je verrai.**

Apercevoir

PRÉSENT: **J'aperçois, tu aperçois, il aperçoit, nous apercevons, vous apercevez, ils aperçoivent.**

IMPARFAIT: J'apercevais.
PASSÉ COMPOSÉ: J'ai aperçu.
FUTUR: J'apercevrai.

The conjugation of **recevoir** is like that of **apercevoir**.

A. *Répondez en français par une phrase complète à chacune des questions suivantes:*

1. Où allez-vous dîner ce soir?   2. Êtes-vous allé en ville hier? 3. Irez-vous en Touraine pour le week-end?   4. Où a-t-on envoyé John?   5. Est-ce qu'on l'enverra en Afrique cet été?   6. Est-ce qu'il part cette semaine?   7. Est-ce que vous sortez tous les soirs?   8. Est-ce que vos parents sortent tous les soirs?   9. Est-ce que le petit Michel dort bien la nuit?   10. A quelle heure s'endort-il?   11. A-t-il dormi hier après-midi?   12. Ses parents dorment-ils bien?   13. Marie a-t-elle servi le café?   14. Est-ce que vous servez le café chez vous?   15. Savez-vous vous servir d'un appareil?

16. Vous servez-vous de votre appareil tous les jours?   17. Prenez-vous beaucoup de photos?   18. Avez-vous pris des photos l'hiver dernier?   19. En prendrez-vous l'année prochaine?   20. Est-ce que John vient d'arriver à Paris?   21. D'où vient-il?   22. Les Duplessis viennent-ils dîner avec John?   23. Les Frazer viendront-ils le chercher à son hôtel?   24. Mme Frazer tient-elle à monter en haut de la Tour Eiffel? 25. Y tenez-vous?   26. Est-ce qu'Henri y tient?   27. Les Frazer ont-ils retenu des chambres à Orléans?   28. Comment les Duplessis ont-ils reçu John? (à bras ouverts)   29. Est-ce que la terre est couverte de neige aujourd'hui?   30. Connaissez-vous les Frazer?

31. John les connaît-il?   32. Lisez-vous le journal tous les jours? 33. L'avez-vous lu ce matin?   34. Le lirez-vous ce soir?   35. Buvez-vous beaucoup de café?   36. En avez-vous bu ce matin?   37. Est-ce que vous mettez votre imperméable quand il fait beau?   38. Est-ce qu'il s'est mis à pleuvoir ce matin de bonne heure?   39. Qui conduit l'auto des Frazer?   40. Aimez-vous conduire?   41. Conduisez-vous souvent?   42. Vos parents conduisent-ils souvent?   43. Craignez-vous la pluie?   44. Vos parents la craignent-ils?   45. Vous plaignez-vous quand il pleut?   46. Henri se plaint-il de la pluie?   47. John aperçoit-il

un poteau-indicateur? 48. Est-ce que les Frazer l'aperçoivent aussi?
49. Qui l'a aperçu le premier? 50. Est-ce que vous recevez beaucoup
de lettres? 51. Vos parents en reçoivent-ils beaucoup? 52. En avez-
vous reçu ce matin? 53. Espérez-vous que vous en recevrez ce soir?

B. *Mettez les phrases suivantes au pluriel:*

1. Je dors bien la nuit. 2. Je prends de bonnes photos. 3. Il prend
de bonnes photos. 4. Je me suis mis à travailler sérieusement. 5. Je
me suis permis de vous donner des conseils. 6. Il craint les chauffeurs
de taxi. 7. Il rejoint ses amis tout à l'heure. 8. J'ai rejoint ma
famille pour les vacances. 9. Je ne me plains pas du mauvais temps.
10. Il s'est plaint du mauvais temps. 11. J'aperçois un taxi là-bas.
12. J'ai aperçu un taxi. 13. J'ai reçu des cartes-postales. 14. Elle
reçoit ses amis.

C. *Mettez chacune des phrases suivantes au passé composé:*

1. Mme Frazer va en France. 2. Elle rejoint Henri. 3. Un jour, en
traversant la Place de l'Opéra elle aperçoit John Hughes. 4. Elle le
voit de loin. 5. John l'invite à prendre quelque chose à la terrasse
du Café de la Paix. 6. Mme Frazer prend un café crème. 7. Soudain
elle se sent mal. 8. Elle se plaint d'avoir mal au cœur. 9. Elle souffre
pendant quelques instants. 10. Elle se remet bientôt. 11. Elle se met
à sourire de nouveau. 12. Cette crise est de courte durée. 13. John
offre de la reconduire à son hôtel. 14. Elle ne veut pas le déranger.
15. Il se permet de la reconduire tout de même. 16. Elle le remercie
vivement.

D. *Thème:* **Si j'avais une grosse fortune.**

1. I would buy a big house. 2. I would have lots of guests (I would
receive quantity of guests). 3. I would not fear anything. 4. I would
lead a kind of life that is entirely extraordinary. 5. I would paint.
6. I would drive big cars. 7. I would have several houses built. 8. I
would not complain of taxes. 9. I would not take the liberty (se **permettre**) of giving advice to everybody. 10. I would sleep late every
morning. 11. I would do whatever I wanted to (all that would please
me). 12. I would be royally bored.

Les gendarmes

HENRY. —[1]Qu'est-ce que c'est que ça, là-bas, au milieu de la route?

JOHN. —[2]Vous ne voyez pas ce que c'est? [3]Regardez leurs pèlerines. [4]Ce sont des gendarmes.*

HENRY. —[5]Qu'est-ce qui se passe?

JOHN. —[6]Je n'en sais rien. [7]Peut-être qu'un crime a été commis.

HENRY. —[8]Que faut-il faire? faire demi-tour?

JOHN. —[9]Ah! maintenant je sais ce que c'est! [10]Un crime a été commis et c'est vous qui êtes le criminel! [11]Naturellement, vous essayez d'échapper à la police, qui vous poursuit.

HENRY. —[12]Ce que vous dites n'est pas exact. [13]La police ne me poursuit pas. [14]Elle m'attend.

HELEN. —[15]Soyez sérieux et ralentissez. [16]Je ne sais pas ce

HENRY. —[1]What's that, up ahead, in the middle of the road?

JOHN. —[2]Don't you see what it is? [3]Look at their capes. [4]It's troopers.

HENRY. —[5]What's going on?

JOHN. —[6]I have no idea. [7]Perhaps a crime has been committed.

HENRY. —[8]What must we do? Turn around?

JOHN. —[9]Now I know what it is. [10]A crime has been committed and you are the criminal! [11]Obviously, you are trying to escape the police and they are trailing (pursuing) you.

HENRY. —[12]What you say is not exactly true (exact). [13]The police are not trailing me. [14]They are waiting for me.

HELEN. —[15]Don't be silly, and slow down. [16]I don't know

---

* The "gendarmes" are national police. Their duties correspond roughly to those of our State Troopers and our sheriffs. City policemen are *not* "gendarmes" but "agents de police" or "sergents de ville."

qu'ils veulent, [17]mais il est certain que ces braves gendarmes ont quelque chose à nous dire. [18]Voyons de quoi il s'agit.

(*Henry s'arrête. Les gendarmes s'approchent.*)

UN DES GENDARMES (*à Henry*). —[19]Veuillez me montrer vos papiers, monsieur.

HENRY. —[20]Lesquels voulez-vous?

LE GENDARME. —[21]Votre passeport, votre permis de conduire et votre police d'assurance. (*Après avoir examiné les papiers*) [22]Tout est en règle. [23]Vous pouvez continuer.

MME FRAZER. —[24]Pourquoi ne demandes-tu pas à monsieur les renseignements dont tu as besoin?

HENRY. —[25]Tiens, c'est une idée! [26]A quoi est-ce que je pensais? (*Au gendarme*) [27]Nous voulons aller à Orléans. [28]Laquelle des deux routes est la plus courte, [29]celle sur laquelle nous sommes ou celle qui passe par Romorantin? [30]Qu'en pensez-vous?

LE GENDARME. —[31]Il n'y a pas grande différence, monsieur. [32]Si j'étais à votre place, je ne changerais pas de route.

what they want, [17]but it is certain that those worthy policemen have something to say to us. [18]Let's see what's up.

(*Henry stops. The policemen come to the car (approach).*)

ONE OF THE POLICEMEN (*to Henry*). —[19]Please show me your papers, sir.

HENRY. —[20]Which ones do you want?

THE POLICEMAN. —[21]Your passport, your driver's license, and your insurance policy. (*After examining the papers*) [22]Everything is in order. [23]You can go ahead.

MRS. FRAZER. —[24]Why don't you ask the gentleman for the information you need?

HENRY. —[25]Well! That's an idea. [26]What was I thinking about? (*To the policeman*) [27]We want to go to Orléans. [28]Which of the two roads is the shorter, [29]the one we are on or the one that goes through Romorantin? [30]What do you think (of it)?

THE POLICEMAN. —[31]There is not much difference, sir. [32]If I were you (If I were in your place), I would not change roads.

HENRY. —³³Merci beaucoup. (*Ils s'en vont.*)

HENRY. —³³Thank you very much. (*They leave.*)

HELEN. —³⁴Ce qui me gêne, c'est que nous ne saurons jamais pourquoi ces gendarmes nous ont arrêtés.†

HELEN. —³⁴What bothers me is that we will never know why those policemen stopped us.

HENRY. —³⁵Qu'est-ce que ça fait? ³⁶Il nous ont remis en liberté, et c'est tout ce qui importe.

HENRY. —³⁵What difference does it make? ³⁶They set us free and that is the only thing that matters.

A. *Répondez en français:*

1. Henry voit-il quelque chose sur la route? 2. Sait-il ce que c'est? 3. A quoi John reconnaît-il que ce sont des gendarmes? 4. Que demande Henry lorsqu'il les voit? 5. Comment John explique-t-il leur présence? 6. Qu'est-ce qu'Henry propose de faire? 7. De quoi John l'accuse-t-il? 8. Est-ce que la police poursuit Henry? 9. Quel conseil Helen donne-t-elle à son frère? 10. Pourquoi lui dit-elle de s'arrêter? 11. Savent-ils de quoi il s'agit? 12. Que font les gendarmes quand l'auto s'arrête? 13. Qu'est-ce qu'un des gendarmes demande à Henry de lui montrer? 14. Henry sait-il de quels papiers il s'agit? 15. Quels papiers le gendarme veut-il examiner? 16. Qu'est-ce qu'il dit à Henry après avoir examiné ses papiers? 17. Qu'est-ce que Mᵐᵉ Frazer dit à Henry de demander au gendarme? 18. Henry y avait-il pensé? 19. Où veut-il aller? 20. Combien de routes peut-il prendre pour aller à Orléans? 21. Qu'est-ce qu'il veut savoir au sujet de ces deux routes? 22. Y a-t-il une grande différence entre les deux? 23. Que ferait le gendarme s'il était à la place d'Henry? 24. Que fait Henry après avoir parlé au gendarme? 25. Qu'est-ce qui gêne Marie? 26. Henry pense-t-il que cela importe beaucoup? 27. Qu'est-ce qui importe, à son avis?

---

† **arrêter** means both *to stop* and *to arrest*. Helen used it to mean *stop* and Henry makes a *jeu de mots* by implying that she meant *arrest*.

B. *Demandez en français à quelqu'un:*

1. ce qu'Henry voit sur la route.   2. comment il reconnaît que ce sont des gendarmes.   3. ce que c'est qu'un gendarme.   4. si John sait ce qui se passe.   5. de quoi il s'agit.   6. ce que les gendarmes demandent à Henry.   7. quels papiers ils veulent voir.   8. ce que c'est qu'un passeport.   9. qui a besoin d'un passeport.   10. s'il faut un passeport pour voyager en Europe.   11. à qui Mme Frazer dit à son fils de demander des renseignements.   12. laquelle des deux routes est la plus courte.   13. ce qu'il ferait s'il était à votre place.   14. ce qui gêne Helen.   15. si cela importe beaucoup.   16. ce qui importe.

C. *Dites en français, en employant les expressions indiquées:*

(*a*) se passer, arriver*

1. What's going on?   2. What happened?   3. What happened to your pictures?   4. I don't know what happened to them.   5. When did it happen?   6. It happened two years ago.   7. Let's forget what happened.   8. I cannot forget what happened to us.

(*b*) à la place (de)

1. If I were you, I wouldn't take the other road.   2. Put yourself in my place.   3. I don't know what I would do if I were in your place. 4. If I were Henry, I would slow down and stop.

(*c*) avoir besoin de

1. You need a driver's license to drive a car.   2. What do you need to travel?   3. What you need is a car, of course, and you also need money.   4. I have a car, but I do not have the money I need (use **dont**).

(*d*) penser à, penser de

1. What are you thinking about?   2. I am thinking of our trip to Touraine.   3. What do you think of it?   4. When I think of it, I think of the rain.   5. Don't you also think of the two gendarmes who stopped us?   6. Naturally. I think of them all the time.

---

* **Arriver** and **se passer** both mean *to happen*. Note, however, that if the verb has an indirect object, **arriver** must be used.

D. *Dites en français à quelqu'un:*

1. de ralentir. 2. d'ouvrir la portière. 3. de regarder le poteau-indicateur. 4. de faire demi-tour. 5. que vous croyez voir des gendarmes. 6. qu'ils ont l'air de vous attendre. 7. que vous vous doutez de ce qu'ils veulent. 8. qu'ils veulent sans doute regarder vos papiers. 9. que vous avez failli vous tromper de route. 10. que vous finirez bien par arriver à Orléans.

E. *Thème:*

As he was driving along a narrow road between Bourges and Orléans, Henry thought he saw two men standing on each side of a bridge over a small river. John told him to notice their capes. Henry immediately realized that these two gentlemen were gendarmes. "What's going on? What do they want? I haven't done anything . . . ," he thought, for it seems that you (**on**) are always a little afraid when you are stopped by the police. There was really no reason to be afraid. Sometimes the police stop passing cars, just to make sure (**s'assurer**) that everything is O.K., for instance, to make sure that the car has not been stolen or that the driver has not committed some crime. After looking at Henry's papers, at his passport and driver's license, the gendarmes let him continue (**on**) his trip.

XXIV GRAMMAR UNIT

Pronoms relatifs et interrogatifs

80. INTERROGATIVE PRONOUNS: SHORT FORMS.

(1) Persons.
Qui? *Who? whom?*
This form is used either as a subject or object of a verb or as object of a preposition.

> **Qui** est allé à Saint-Cloud?
> **Qui** John est-il allé voir?
> **Chez qui** est-il allé?

(2) Things.
(*a*) **Que?** (unstressed) *what?*
This form is used primarily as object of a verb. **Que** faut-il faire? **Que** dites-vous?

(*b*) **Quoi?** (stressed) *what?*
This form is used either alone: **Quoi? Que** dites-vous? or after prepositions:

> **De quoi** parlez-vous?
> **A quoi** pensez-vous?

Note also that it is used in the word **pourquoi?** and in the expressions: **Quoi** de nouveau? **Quoi** de neuf? *What's new?*

81. INTERROGATIVE PRONOUNS: LONG FORMS.

(1) Persons.
Qui est-ce qui? *Who?* (subject form)
Qui est-ce que? *Whom?* (object form)

Qui est-ce qui a demandé des renseignements?
A qui est-ce que Roger a parlé?
Chez qui est-ce que John a dîné?

(2) Things.

Qu'est-ce qui? *What?* (subject form).
Qu'est-ce que? *What?* (object form).

Qu'est-ce qui se passe?	*What's happening?*
Qu'est-ce que ça peut faire?	*What difference does that make?*
De quoi est-ce que vous avez besoin?	*What do you need?*
A quoi est-ce qu'il pensait?	*What was he thinking about?*

(3) To ask for a definition or a description, the form that is commonly used is: **Qu'est-ce que c'est que . . . ?**

Qu'est-ce que c'est que ça?	*What's that?*
Qu'est-ce que c'est que ce livre?	*What's that book?*

In formal writing, the form **Qu'est-ce que . . .?** is used: **Qu'est-ce que** le classicisme?

82. THE INTERROGATIVE PRONOUN **lequel**.

Lequel? Laquelle? Lesquels? Lesquelles? *which? which one? which ones?* are used to distinguish between persons or things within a group. They may be used as subject or object of a verb or as object of a preposition.

Laquelle des deux routes est la plus courte?
Lequel de ces châteaux préférez-vous?

In combination with the prepositions **à** or **de,** the usual contractions are found: **auquel, auxquels, duquel, desquels,** etc.

Duquel de ces châteaux avez-vous pris des photos?

83. THE RELATIVE PRONOUN **qui**.

(1) The relative pronoun **qui,** meaning *who, which, that* is used as the subject of a verb and may refer to persons or things.

C'est vous qui êtes le criminel.
La route qui passe par Romorantin . . .

(2) It is also used after prepositions **à, de, avec, chez, pour** to refer to persons only.

> Les gendarmes **à qui** nous avons parlé . . .

84. THE RELATIVE PRONOUNS que, quoi.

(1) The relative pronoun **que**, meaning *whom, which, that,* is used as the direct object of a verb and may refer either to persons or things.

> Le château **que** nous avons vu hier . . .
> Les gendarmes **que** nous avons vus hier . . .

In these phrases, **que** must be expressed although in English we often say: *The château we saw.*

(2) The relative pronoun **quoi** *(what)* is used after prepositions.

> Je ne sais pas à **quoi** je pensais.
> Je ne sais pas de **quoi** vous avez besoin.

85. THE RELATIVE PRONOUN dont.

This form, meaning *of whom, of which, about whom, whose,* etc. is equivalent to the preposition **de** and **qui, quoi,** or the forms **duquel, desquels,** etc. (See paragraph 87). It may refer to persons or things.

> Pourquoi ne demandes-tu pas les renseignements **dont** tu as besoin?
> Le bébé **dont** on a parlé s'appelle Michel.
> Le château **dont** nous avons vu la façade . . .
> Celui **dont** nous avons vu l'intérieur . . .

86. THE RELATIVE PRONOUN WITH ce.

Ce qui, ce que, ce dont, *what, that which,* etc.

> SUBJECT: **Ce qui** me gêne, c'est que nous ne saurons jamais . . .
>   C'est tout **ce qui** importe.
> OBJECT: **Ce que** vous dites n'est pas exact.
>   **Ce dont** j'ai besoin, c'est d'un bon appareil.

Compare the similar use of **ce qui** and **ce que** in indirect questions, in paragraph 89.

87. THE RELATIVE PRONOUN **lequel, laquelle, lesquels, lesquelles.**

These forms, which correspond to **qui, que**, etc., are used primarily after prepositions to refer to things.

La route **sur laquelle** nous sommes . . .
Voilà l'appareil **avec lequel** j'ai pris ces photos.

Note that these forms are sometimes used to refer to persons in a sentence where there are two possible antecedents:

Le père de ma femme, **lequel** . . . (to refer to **père**)
Le père de ma femme, **laquelle** . . . (to refer to **femme**)

88. Où, *in which, when, where.*

This form is used instead of expressions like **dans lequel**, etc.

Le jour **où** ils sont arrivés à Orléans . . .
La maison **où** habitent les Duplessis . . .

89. INDIRECT QUESTIONS.

After expressions like **Savez-vous . . .? Je ne sais pas . . .,
Dites-moi . . . , Voyons . . .** etc., **qui, lequel,** and **quoi,** are used just as they are in direct questions:

DIRECT: **Qui** est venu? INDIRECT: Savez-vous **qui** est venu?
DIRECT: **De qui** parlez-vous? INDIRECT: Je ne sais pas **de qui** vous parlez.
DIRECT: **De quoi** s'agit-il? INDIRECT: Voyons **de quoi** il s'agit.

On the other hand, instead of **Que?, Qu'est-ce qui?,** and **Qu'est-ce que?** the forms **ce qui** and **ce que** are used in indirect questions:

DIRECT: **Qu'est-ce qui** se passe? INDIRECT: Voyez-vous **ce qui** se passe?
DIRECT: **Qu'est-ce que** c'est? INDIRECT: Je ne sais pas **ce que** c'est.
DIRECT: **Qu'est-ce qu'ils** veulent? INDIRECT: Je ne sais pas **ce qu'ils** veulent.

A. *Demandez à quelqu'un:*

1. qui a invité John à aller en Touraine.   2. ce qu'il a répondu.
3. qui conduit l'auto de Mme Frazer.   4. chez qui John est allé à son
retour à Paris.   5. de quoi John et Roger ont parlé.   6. ce qui se
passe sur la route.   7. qui a arrêté l'auto des Frazer.   8. ce que les
gendarmes ont demandé.   9. de quels renseignements Henry a besoin.
10. à quoi pensait Henry.   11. lequel des châteaux de Touraine il
préfère.   12. ce qui gêne Henry.   13. ce que c'est qu'un passeport.
14. ce que c'est qu'un permis de conduire.   15. ce que c'est qu'un
gendarme.   16. ce qu'il faut faire.   17. quelle route il faut prendre.
18. ce que veulent les gendarmes.

B. *Posez les questions suivantes par l'expression indirecte en commençant par* **Savez-vous . . .** *?* Ex.: Qu'est-ce qui se passe? Savez-vous ce qui se passe?

1. Qui est venu me voir?   2. Qu'est-ce qu'il a dit?   3. Qui est-ce qui
est venu avec lui?   4. Qu'est-ce qu'il voulait?   5. De quoi a-t-il parlé?
6. De quoi s'agissait-il?   7. Qu'est-ce qui arrivera?   8. Qu'est-ce qui
s'est passé?   9. Qu'est-ce que c'est qu'une police d'assurance?

C. *Combinez deux phrases en une seule en employant un pronom relatif ou l'adverbe* **où.** (Ex.: John va voir les Duplessis. Il est de passage à Paris. John, qui est de passage à Paris, va voir les Duplessis.)

1. John va voir les Duplessis. Ils habitent à Saint-Cloud.   2. John va
voir les Duplessis. Il les connaît depuis longtemps.   3. Il admire le
petit Michel. Il le voit pour la première fois.   4. Le bébé est de bonne
humeur. Il a dormi tout l'après-midi.   5. Mme Frazer invite John à
aller en Touraine. En Touraine il y a beaucoup de châteaux de la
Renaissance.   6. Henry aime bien conduire. C'est le fils de Mme
Frazer.   7. Henry est monté en haut de la Tour Eiffel. Nous avons
entendu parler de lui.   8. Henry demande à Helen de lire ce qu'il y a
sur le poteau-indicateur. Il ne peut pas le voir.   9. Il demande des
renseignements. Il en a besoin.   10. Les gendarmes lui ont donné des

renseignements. Ils l'ont arrêté. 11. John montre des photos à Helen. Il les a prises en Touraine. 12. Les Frazer et John ont déjeuné à Orléans. Ils ont quitté Paris de bonne heure. 13. Ils ont acheté de l'essence. Ils en avaient besoin. 14. Ils ont visité plusieurs châteaux. Ils en avaient entendu parler.

D. *Dites en français:*

1. What interests me is the emblem of François Premier. 2. What bothers me is that I am hungry. 3. What we need is a good dinner. 4. What we ate at lunch was excellent; but what I want now is some cool water. 5. Which of those châteaux is the most beautiful? 6. With which of those cameras did you take these pictures? 7. Which of these photos do you like best? 8. What's that? 9. Don't you know what it is? 10. I know it is a signpost but I don't know what it says. 11. Read what it says. 12. The day (when) (où) we left it rained. 13. The day (when) we took the wrong road, it rained all day long. 14. John recited a poem of Verlaine in which it was a question of rain on the roof.

E. *Posez la question à laquelle chacune des phrases suivantes répondrait, en employant des pronoms interrogatifs:*

1. Ce sont des gendarmes. 2. Ils portent des pèlerines. 3. Ils demandent les papiers d'Henry. 4. Henry demande des renseignements. 5. Il préfère le château de Chenonceaux. 6. Il admire l'emblème de Louis XII. 7. Mme Frazer préfère celui de Louise de Savoie. 8. Il y a quelque chose là-bas au milieu de la route. 9. Il faut s'arrêter. 10. Henry parle de la pluie. 11. La pluie l'ennuie. 12. La poésie le gêne.

XXV CONVERSATION UNIT

Le cultivateur

Les Frazer se sont arrêtés dans un village de la Beauce* pour envoyer une dépêche. A la poste, John parle à un cultivateur de l'endroit.

JOHN. —¹Voilà un bien vilain temps pour les récoltes!

LE CULTIVATEUR. —²Ah, monsieur, il vaut mieux ne pas en parler! ³Il y a de quoi désespérer. ⁴L'année dernière, c'était la sécheresse, et cette année, c'est la pluie. ⁵Les avoines sont en train de germer dans les champs. ⁶C'est la fin de tout.

JOHN. —⁷Je ne crois pas qu'il faille désespérer. ⁸Le temps finira par s'arranger.

LE CULTIVATEUR. —⁹Je me dis ça tous les jours. ¹⁰Je souhaite que la pluie s'arrête et qu'il fasse beau, ¹¹mais j'ai peur que mes souhaits ne servent pas à grand'chose . . . ¹²Si au moins nos produits se vendaient bien. ¹³Mais bien que nous soyons obligés de dépenser plus qu'autrefois, ¹⁴la culture rapporte de moins en moins.

The Frazers have stopped in a village of La Beauce to send a telegram. At the post office, John is talking with a local farmer.

JOHN. —¹This is very bad weather for the crops!

THE FARMER. —²Oh, sir, it's too awful for words. ³It's enough to make you give up (despair). ⁴Last year, it was the drought and this year it's the rain. ⁵The oats are already sprouting in the fields. ⁶This is the last straw (the end of everything).

JOHN. —⁷I don't think one should give up. ⁸The weather will clear up (get better) in time.

THE FARMER. —⁹I tell myself that every day. ¹⁰I wish the rain would stop and that the weather would be fine, ¹¹but I am afraid my wishes are not going to help much. ¹²If only (at least) our products sold well! ¹³But although we have to spend more than in the past, ¹⁴farming brings in less and less.

---

* La Beauce is a rich agricultural region southwest of Paris.

JOHN. —[15]Je croyais que le gouvernement fixait les prix . . .

LE CULTIVATEUR. —[16]Oui, mais à moins qu'il établisse des prix plus élevés pour les produits agricoles, [17]les cultivateurs n'arriveront bientôt plus à joindre les deux bouts. [18]Il faut que nous payions plus cher tout ce que nous achetons, [19]les semences, les engrais, sans compter les machines.

JOHN. —[20]Il me semble en effet qu'on voit dans les champs bien plus de machines qu'autrefois.

LE CULTIVATEUR. —[21]Il y a vingt ans, monsieur, on voyait partout des chevaux. [22]Maintenant, à moins que vous n'alliez dans des coins perdus, vous ne verrez plus de chevaux: [23]rien que des tracteurs, des **moissonneuses-batteuses**, et toutes sortes de machines. [24]Ici, il n'y a pas un seul cultivateur qui n'ait son tracteur. [25]Il suffit que l'un d'eux en ait un pour que son voisin veuille aussi avoir le sien . . . [26]Voulez-vous que je vous dise ce que j'en pense? [27]Le gouvernement est en train de ruiner le cultivateur!

JOHN. —[28]Dans mon pays, nous avons un peu les mêmes pro-

JOHN. —[15]I thought the government was fixing prices.

THE FARMER. —[16]Yes, but unless it sets higher prices for farm products, [17]the farmers will soon not be able to make both ends meet any longer. [18]We have to pay more for everything we buy, [19]seed, fertilizer, not to mention (counting) farm machinery.

JOHN. —[20]It does seem to me, as a matter of fact, (It seems to me, indeed), that you see far more machines in the fields than in the past.

THE FARMER. —[21]Twenty years ago, sir, you saw horses everywhere. [22]Now, unless you go to out-of-the-way places, you won't see any horses any more: [23]nothing but tractors, combines, and all sorts of machines. [24]Here, there isn't a single farmer who hasn't his tractor. [25]If *one* has one, it is enough to make his neighbor want to have one too (*his*) . . . [26]Do you want me to tell you what I think (about it)? [27]The government is gradually bankrupting the farmers.

JOHN. —[28]In my country, we have somewhat the same prob-

blèmes. ²⁹La situation de l'agriculture restera difficile jusqu'à ce qu'on les ait résolus. ³⁰Mais j'espère bien qu'on arrivera un jour à les résoudre.

lems. ²⁹The situation of farming will remain difficult until they have been solved. ³⁰But I certainly hope that some day they will succeed in solving them.

A. *Répondez en français:*

1. Où les Frazer se sont-ils arrêtés? 2. Pourquoi se sont-ils arrêtés? 3. A qui John parle-t-il? 4. De quoi parle-t-il? 5. Qu'est-ce que le cultivateur lui répond lorsque John lui parle du temps? 6. Quel temps a-t-il fait l'année dernière? 7. Quel temps fait-il cette année? 8. Quel est l'effet de la pluie sur les avoines? 9. Que lui dit John pour le consoler? 10. Est-ce que le cultivateur croit que ses souhaits servent à quelque chose? 11. Pense-t-il que la culture rapporte beaucoup? 12. Par qui les prix sont-ils fixés? 13. Est-ce que le cultivateur croit que ces prix sont assez élevés? 14. Que doivent acheter les cultivateurs? 15. Quel changement John remarque-t-il en ce qui concerne l'agriculture? 16. Voyait-on beaucoup de chevaux il y a vingt ans? 17. En voit-on beaucoup maintenant? 18. Qu'est-ce qui a remplacé les chevaux? 19. Est-ce que la plupart des cultivateurs ont un tracteur? 20. Qu'est-ce que l'homme à qui parle John pense du gouvernement? 21. Les problèmes agricoles existent-ils seulement en France? 22. Jusqu'à quel moment la situation de l'agriculture restera-t-elle difficile? 23. Qu'est-ce que John espère?

B. *Demandez en français à quelqu'un:*

1. où sont les Frazer. 2. ce que c'est que la Beauce. 3. ce que le cultivateur pense du temps. 4. s'il pense que le temps va s'arranger. 5. si la culture coûte plus qu'autrefois. 6. si elle rapporte davantage. 7. si les prix fixés par le gouvernement sont assez élevés. 8. ce qui arrivera si le gouvernement n'augmente pas les prix. 9. ce que les cultivateurs ont besoin d'acheter. 10. s'il y a maintenant beaucoup de chevaux dans la culture. 11. ce qu'il y a à leur place. 12. pourquoi le cultivateur se plaint du gouvernement. 13. combien de temps

la situation des cultivateurs restera difficile.   14. si le problème agricole
sera un jour résolu.

C. *Dites en français, en employant les expressions indiquées:*

(a) **il vaut mieux**

1. It's better not to talk about it.   2. It's better to stop.   3. We had
better stop.   4. Wouldn't it be better to turn around?   5. It's better
to wait for good weather.

(b) **de quoi**

1. It's enough to make you give up.   2. He has enough to live on.
3. Soon farmers won't have enough to live on.   4. There is no reason
to give up.   5. You are welcome (**Il n'y a pas de quoi**).

(c) **arriver à**

1. Soon farmers will no longer succeed in making ends meet.   2. Some
day, they'll succeed in solving this problem.   3. But they have not
succeeded yet (in it).   4. Do you think I will succeed in finding a
shorter road?   5. No, I don't think you will succeed (in it).

(d) **servir à** *

1. I am afraid my wishes aren't of much use.   2. What's the use of
this secret cupboard?   3. Its not used for anything now.   4. But it was
used to keep papers, jewels, and even poisons, they say.

D. *Employez les expressions indiquées dans chacune des phrases suivantes:*

(a) **en train de**

1. Le gouvernement ruine les cultivateurs.   2. Les avoines germent
dans les champs.   3. On cherche une solution au problème agricole.
4. Pendant que John parlait à un cultivateur, Mme Frazer envoyait
une dépêche.

(b) **de plus en plus, de moins en moins**

1. Nous payons plus cher tout ce que nous achetons.   2. Les machines
coûtent plus cher.   3. Mais la culture rapporte moins.   4. Nos

---

* Cf. **servir** and **se servir de** in Unit XIX.

produits se vendent moins bien.   5. Moins de cultivateurs arrivent à joindre les deux bouts.

E. *Thème:*

At the post office of a village in La Beauce where they had stopped because Mrs. Frazer wanted to send a telegram, John spoke to a local farmer. They talked about the weather and the crops, and the farmer complained of both. Even if farmers everywhere are seldom quite satisfied, it seems that this man had good reason to complain. In France as in the U.S., farmers have to pay higher and higher prices for what they buy, and they receive less and less for what they sell.

Centuries ago, John thought, people often did not have enough bread to eat. Even at the beginning of the last century, white bread was still a luxury **(un luxe)**. Now France grows **(récolte)** too much wheat, and the French people do not eat as much bread as (they did) in the past. Other countries still do not have enough. I am afraid the world has some very difficult problems to solve.

XXVI GRAMMAR UNIT

Subjonctif: présent et passé composé

90. FORMATION OF THE PRESENT SUBJUNCTIVE.

(1) The endings of the present subjunctive of all verbs (except **être** and **avoir**) are: **-e, -es, -e, -ions, -iez, -ent;**

(2) The stem of the present subjunctive of regular verbs is the same as that of the first person plural of the present indicative. Ex.: *Pres. Ind.*: Nous **donn**ons, nous **finiss**ons, nous **vend**ons; *Pres. Subjunctive:* je **donn**e, je **finiss**e, je **vend**e.

(3) Forms of the present subjunctive of **être** and **avoir** and of regular verbs:

(*a*) **être:** je sois, tu sois, il soit, nous soyons, vous soyez, ils soient.

(*b*) **avoir:** j'aie, tu aies, il ait, nous ayons, vous ayez, ils aient.

Note that the stem of the present subjunctive of **avoir** is pronounced [ɛ] like the **è** in **près**, thus: [ɛ, ɛ, ɛ, ɛjõ, ɛje, ɛ.]

(*c*) **donner:** je donne, tu donnes, il donne, nous donnions, vous donniez, ils donnent.

(*d*) **finir:** je finisse, tu finisses, il finisse, nous finissions, vous finissiez, ils finissent.

(*e*) **vendre:** je vende, tu vendes, il vende, nous vendions, vous vendiez, ils vendent.

91. USE AND MEANING OF THE PRESENT SUBJUNCTIVE.

MEANING

For all practical purposes there is no difference between the meaning of the indicative and the subjunctive.

USE

(1) The subjunctive is used in subordinate clauses introduced by **que** and depending upon certain verbs that express wishing, wanting, desiring; joy, sorrow, happiness, regret, fear; approval or disapproval, etc. Among the verbs of this group which may take the subjunctive, the following are the most frequently used: **vouloir, désirer; aimer mieux, préférer; souhaiter,** *to wish;* **craindre,** *to fear;* **être content, être heureux; regretter; être fâché; avoir peur,** and a number of impersonal expressions such as **il faut que . . ., il vaut mieux que . . ., il suffit que . . . ,** etc.

> **Il faut** que **nous payions** plus cher tout ce que nous achetons.
> **Voulez-vous** que **je** vous **dise** ce que j'en pense?
> **Je souhaite** que la pluie s'arrête et qu'**il fasse** beau.
> **J'ai peur** que mes souhaits ne **servent** pas à grand'chose.
> **Il suffit** que l'un d'eux en **ait** un pour que son voisin veuille avoir le sien.

Espérer, which means *to hope* in the sense of *to expect* does *not* take a subjunctive:

> J'espère qu'**il fera** beau.

As these verbs may also be followed by infinitives (see paragraph 63, 3), it is necessary to note:

(*a*) If the main verb and dependent verb both have the same subject, the infinitive is always used.

> **Je** voudrais vous dire . . . (infinitive); BUT:
> **Voulez-vous** que **je** vous dise . . . ? (subjunctive).

(*b*) If the verb depending upon **Il faut que** (or other impersonal expressions) has an expressed subject, the subjunctive must be used in the subordinate clause; but if the dependent verb has no expressed subject, the infinitive is used.

> Il faut que **nous** payions . . . (subjunctive). *We* must pay . . .
> Il faut **payer** à la caisse. (infinitive). *One* must pay . . .

(2) **Croire** and **penser** do *not* always take the subjunctive.

(a) Verbs depending upon affirmative forms of **croire** and **penser** are in the indicative. Ex.: **Je crois** qu'il va pleuvoir.

(b) Verbs depending upon interrogative or negative forms of these verbs may be in the indicative or the subjunctive. The subjunctive, in such cases, implies a greater degree of uncertainty.

> **Croyez-vous** qu'il **pleuve** ce soir? *or* **Croyez-vous** qu'il **pleuvra** ce soir?
>
> **Je ne crois pas** qu'il **faille** désespérer. *or* Je ne crois pas qu' il **faut** désespérer.

(3) The subjunctive is normally used in subordinate clauses depending upon expressions that express possibility but not probability such as: **Il est possible que, Il se peut que, Il est peu probable, Il n'est pas sûr que.**

> **Il est possible** qu'il **pleuve** encore demain.

But note that after expressions that suggest probability or certainty, the indicative is normal.

> Je suis **sûr** qu'il **pleuvra.**
> Il est **certain** qu'il **neigera.**
> Il est **probable** que **nous serons** en retard.

(4) The subjunctive must be used in clauses introduced by certain conjunctive expressions of which the following are the most frequently used: **à moins que,*** *unless;* **avant que,*** *before;* **bien que, quoique,** *although;* **jusqu'à ce que,** *until;* **quoi que,** *whatever;* **pour que,** *so that;* **de peur que,** *for fear that.*

> **A moins que vous n'alliez** dans les coins perdus, . . .
> **A moins qu'il établisse** des prix plus élevés pour les produits agricoles, . . .
> **Bien que nous soyons** obligés de dépenser plus qu'autrefois, . . .
> **Quoi qu'ils fassent,** les cultivateurs n'arriveront bientôt plus à joindre les deux bouts.

(5) The subjunctive is used in relative clauses whose ante-

---

* After **avant que** and **moins que** the use of the pleonastic **ne** is optional.

cedent is indefinite or is modified by the word **seul** or by a superlative:

> Voilà **le plus beau** château que **j'aie** jamais vu.
> Ici, il n'y a **pas un seul** cultivateur qui n'**ait** son tracteur.
> Je ne connais **personne qui puisse** résoudre ce problème.

92. VERBS THAT ARE IRREGULAR IN THE SUBJUNCTIVE.

(1) Commonest irregular verbs whose present subjunctive has two stems:

apercevoir: aperçoive, aperçoives, aperçoive, **apercevions, aperceviez,** aperçoivent.
aller: aille, ailles, aille, **allions, alliez,** aillent.
boire: boive, boives, boive, **buvions, buviez,** boivent.
croire: croie, croies, croie, **croyions, croyiez,** croient.
devoir: doive, doives, doive, **devions, deviez,** doivent.
envoyer: envoie, envoies, envoie, **envoyions, envoyiez,** envoient.
mourir: meure, meures, meure, **mourions, mouriez,** meurent.
prendre: prenne, prennes, prenne, **prenions, preniez,** prennent.
recevoir: reçoive, reçoives, reçoive, **recevions, receviez,** reçoivent.
tenir: tienne, tiennes, tienne, **tenions, teniez,** tiennent.
venir: vienne, viennes, vienne, **venions, veniez,** viennent.
voir: voie, voies, voie, **voyions, voyiez,** voient.
vouloir: veuille, veuilles, veuille, **voulions, vouliez,** veuillent.

(2) Commonest irregular verbs whose present subjunctive has only one stem:

faire: fasse, fasses, fasse, fassions, fassiez, fassent.
pouvoir: puisse, puisses, puisse, puissions, puissiez, puissent.
savoir: sache, saches, sache, sachions, sachiez, sachent.

(3) Commonest irregular verbs whose present subjunctives follow the pattern of regular verbs and can be derived from the first person plural of the present indicative (see paragraph 90):
connaître, conduire, construire, courir, cueillir (accueillir), dire, dormir, écrire, lire, mettre, partir, plaire, plaindre, pleuvoir, suivre, vivre.

93. FORMATION AND USE OF THE *passé composé* OF THE SUBJUNCTIVE.

(1) Formation. The *passé composé* of the subjunctive is composed of the present subjunctive of the auxiliary verb and the past participle of the verb.

être: j'aie été, tu aies été, il ait été, nous ayons été, vous ayez été, ils aient été.

avoir: j'aie eu, tu aies eu, etc.

donner: j'aie donné, tu aies donné, etc.

aller: je sois allé, tu sois allé, il soit allé, nous soyons allés, vous soyez allé(s), ils soient allés.

prendre: j'aie pris, tu aies pris, etc.

(2) Generally speaking, the *passé composé* of the subjunctive is used like the present subjunctive except that it expresses completed action — past or future.

> La situation de l'agriculture restera difficile jusqu'à ce qu'on **ait résolu** ce problème.
> Voilà le plus beau château que **j'aie** jamais **vu.**
> J'ai peur qu'**il se soit trompé** de route.
> Je ne crois pas qu'**il ait plu** cette nuit.
> Bien qu'**ils soient allés** en Touraine, ils n'ont pas vu tous les châteaux.

A. *Dites en français chacune des phrases suivantes en employant l'expression* **Il faut que . . . :**

1. Je déjeune tout de suite. 2. Nous déjeunons à Orléans. 3. Je choisis la meilleure route. 4. Vous choisissez la meilleure route. 5. Henry répond au téléphone. 6. Nous répondons aux lettres. 7. Je suis à l'heure. 8. Vous êtes à l'heure. 9. Je serai prêt à partir à sept heures. 10. Nous serons prêts à partir à huit heures. 11. J'ai de la patience. 12. Nous avons de la patience. 13. Nous nous levons de bonne heure. 14. Vous vous levez de bonne heure. 15. John va chez les Duplessis. 16. Nous allons en ville. 17. John prend un taxi. 18. Il fait signe au chauffeur. 19. Nous faisons des emplettes.

20. Nous achetons des cadeaux. 21. Le chauffeur sait l'adresse des Duplessis. 22. John envoie une dépêche. 23. Il met une lettre à la poste. 24. Il dit ce qu'il pense. 25. Nous disons toujours ce que nous pensons.

B. *Dites les phrases suivantes en français en employant chacune des expressions indiquées:*

(*a*) **Il vaut mieux que**

1. Nous partons tout de suite. 2. Vous venez avec nous. 3. Nous prenons la bonne route. 4. Nous regardons les poteaux-indicateurs. 5. Nous lisons ce que disent les poteaux-indicateurs. 6. Nous demandons des renseignements. 7. Les gendarmes examinent nos passeports. 8. Ils regardent notre police d'assurance. 9. Ils savent que nous sommes Américains. 10. Ils portent des imperméables.

(*b*) **Je souhaite que . . . ; J'espère que . . .**

1. Vous viendrez nous voir. 2. Vous resterez prendre le thé. 3. Vous me parlerez de votre voyage. 4. Vous me direz votre avis. 5. Vous me permettrez de vous donner un conseil. 6. Vous ne serez pas fâché.

(*c*) **Il est possible que . . .**

1. Nous aurons encore de la pluie. 2. Nous payerons plus cher tout ce que nous achetons. 3. Nous n'arriverons plus à joindre les deux bouts. 4. On établira des prix plus élevés pour les produits agricoles. 5. Le temps finira par s'arranger. 6. On ne verra plus de chevaux dans les champs.

(*d*) **Je ne suis pas sûr que . . .; Il me semble que . . .**

1. John est à Paris. 2. Il est allé visiter le Louvre. 3. Il a rencontré Mme Frazer. 4. Il part demain. 5. Il a donné son adresse à Henry. 6. Henry est monté en haut de la Tour Eiffel. 7. Il s'est levé de bonne heure. 8. Il viendra prendre John à son hôtel.

(*e*) **Je ne crois pas que . . . ; Je crois que . . .**

1. Vous dormez. 2. Vous serez ici à sept heures du matin. 3. Vous conduisez trop vite. 4. Vous vous plairez ici. 5. Nous aurons le temps de déjeuner à Orléans. 6. Nous recevrons quantité d'invités.

(f) **Je regrette que . . .**

1. John n'a pas pu assister au mariage. 2. Il est allé en Égypte en été. 3. Il a oublié d'envoyer un cadeau de mariage. 4. Il lui a fallu passer plusieurs mois dans la jungle du Vénézuéla. 5. Il n'a pas regardé les poteaux-indicateurs. 6. Henry s'est trompé de route. 7. Les gendarmes n'ont pas mis leur imperméable.* 8. Il a plu toute la journée.

C. *Combinez deux phrases en une seule en employant les expressions indiquées.* (Ex.: Je suis en France depuis deux mois. Je ne suis pas encore allé voir Versailles. [**Bien que**] Bien que je sois en France depuis deux mois, je ne suis pas encore allé voir Versailles.)

1. Il fait froid. Nous allons faire une promenade. (**A moins que, quoique**)

2. Allons vite au Louvre. La nuit tombe. (**Avant que**)

3. Vous allez au Louvre. Vous ne verrez pas *la Joconde*. (**A moins que**)

4. Je sais chanter. Je ne chanterai pas à l'Opéra ce soir. (**Bien que.**)

5. Vous êtes riche. Vous n'êtes pas heureux. (**Quoique.**)

6. Je fais tout ce que je peux. Je n'arrive pas à joindre les deux bouts. (**Bien que.**)

D. *Répondez affirmativement, puis négativement en français à chacune des questions suivantes:*

1. Croyez-vous qu'il y ait une place pour John dans l'auto des Frazer?

2. Croyez-vous que John sera prêt à partir à sept heures et demie?

3. Pensez-vous qu'Henry vienne le chercher à sept heures et demie?

4. Est-ce qu'il vous semble que les Frazer déjeuneront à Orléans?

5. Mme Frazer espère-t-elle qu'ils arriveront à midi à Orléans? 6. Est-elle sûre qu'ils puissent voir tous les châteaux de la Renaissance?

---

* Compare this use of the singular noun with: **Ils sont entrés le chapeau sur la tête.**

E. *Dites en français:*

1. Unless we leave early . . .   2. Unless we arrive at noon . . .   3. In order that we may arrive on time . . .   4. For fear that we will be late . . .   5. Before we leave . . .   6. Before they come . . .   7. We will wait for you until you get here.   8. We will wait until you have finished having lunch.

F. *Répondez en français en employant* Il se peut que . . . :

1. Irez-vous en Touraine l'été prochain?   2. Est-ce que vous faites des emplettes ce soir?   3. Sortez-vous demain soir?   4. Saurez-vous parler français couramment à la fin de l'année?   5. Aurons-nous le temps de visiter toutes les salles du Musée?   6. Serez-vous prêt à partir à sept heures du matin?   7. Vous couchez-vous de bonne heure ce soir? 8. Écrirez-vous des lettres dimanche après-midi?   9. Pouvez-vous venir nous voir dimanche prochain?

G. *Dites en français:*

1. That's the most beautiful château I have visited.   2. That's the most interesting book I have read this year.   3. Roger is not the only Frenchman I know.   4. Do you know some Parisians to whom you can write?   5. Do you know anyone who knows Greek?   6. I do not know anyone who can do my work.

XXVII CONVERSATION UNIT

Lettres

La fin du séjour de John en France approche. Le lendemain de son retour à Paris, après son excursion avec les Frazer dans la région de la Loire, il s'occupe de sa correspondance. Voici ce qu'il écrit à Mme Frazer: *

> Hôtel Meurice
> Paris, le 24 août

Chère Madame,

Avant de quitter Paris, je tiens à vous remercier encore de votre aimable invitation à vous accompagner en Touraine. J'étais déjà allé dans cette jolie région, mais je ne l'avais jamais parcourue en si agréable compagnie. Je regrette un peu, comme vous, que le "Jardin de la France" ait été si copieusement arrosé au cours de notre voyage. Mais la pluie fait pousser les fleurs, et je n'oublierai jamais les fleurs, surtout les énormes dahlias, qui semblent pousser partout en Touraine.

D'après ce que m'a dit Henry, vous avez l'intention de rentrer aux États-Unis à la fin du mois prochain. Nous nous reverrons donc sous peu, ce qui sera pour moi un grand plaisir.

D'ici là, chère Madame, je vous prie de faire mes amitiés à Helen et à Henry, et d'agréer mes hommages respectueux.

> John

Il envoie aussi un mot à l'antiquaire pour faire expédier le service de table destiné à sa soeur:

---

* The English prompt script for these letters will be found in the Appendix, pp. 217-218.

Monsieur,

Vous trouverez ci-inclus un mandat-poste de 165 frs en paiement du reliquat dû sur votre facture No. 2.226, datée du 19 courant.

Je crois vous avoir dit, au moment de l'achat, d'envoyer le service de table de façon à ce qu'il arrive à l'adresse indiquée vers le milieu du mois de septembre. Toutefois, comme je n'aurai pas encore atteint San Francisco à cette époque, je désire maintenant que l'envoi arrive à sa destination une quinzaine de jours plus tard. Je vous prie donc de fixer la date d'expédition qui convient le mieux, en tenant compte des délais imposés par le transport et par les formalités de douane.

Veuillez agréer, Monsieur, mes salutations empressées.

John Hughes

Enfin, pendant son absence de Paris, John a reçu de Mme Lucien Ferry une invitation à dîner, qu'il est obligé de décliner pour la raison qu'il indique:

Chère Madame,

Rien ne m'aurait donné plus de plaisir que d'accepter votre aimable invitation à dîner mardi prochain. Malheureusement, je ne serai plus à Paris à cette date. J'aurai quitté la France la veille, et je serai sans doute déjà arrivé à Philadelphie.

Je regrette vivement de ne pas pouvoir être des vôtres. J'aurais été heureux de me retrouver chez vous avec des amis communs, au souvenir de qui je vous prie de me rappeler.

Je vous prie, chère Madame, d'agréer mes respectueux hommages.

John Hughes

NOTE. In English, it is unusual to go beyond such formulas as "Dear Mr. Blank" and "Sincerely yours" or "Yours very truly"; but in French, the formulas are a little more elaborate.

In a business letter, you begin: *Monsieur* and end: *Veuillez agréer, Monsieur, mes salutations empressées.* (Please accept...)

In a letter to a married woman — Mrs. Frazer, for example — you begin — *Chère Madame* — and end: *Je vous prie, chère Madame, d'agréer mes hommages respectueux.* You don't use an imperative — even *Veuillez* — in addressing a woman.

In a letter to a high administrative official, you begin: *Monsieur,* or, if you know him personally, *Cher Monsieur;* and you end: *Veuillez agréer, Monsieur,* (or *cher Monsieur*) *l'expression de mes meilleurs sentiments.*
It is more flattering to say: *Je vous prie, Monsieur, d'agréer . . .*

Young people writing to each other often use a less formal complimentary close such as: *Votre bien dévoué(e)* or *Ton vieil ami,* etc.

Many people include in the complimentary close such phrases as: *Veuillez agréer l'expression de mes sentiments les plus distingués,* or *Veuillez agréer l'expression de ma plus haute considération,* or *Veuillez croire à mes sentiments respectueux et les meilleurs,* etc.; but it is better to use a simple complimentary close than a fancy one. They all just mean *Sincerely yours* anyway.

A. *Répondez en français:*

1. John doit-il bientôt quitter la France?   2. Que fait-il le lendemain de son retour à Paris?   3. Pourquoi écrit-il à Mme Frazer?   4. Avait-il déjà parcouru la Touraine?   5. Comment appelle-t-on quelquefois la Touraine?   6. Quelle espèce de fleurs a-t-il vue pendant son voyage? 7. Que dit-il au sujet de la pluie?   8. Quand les Frazer ont-ils l'intention de rentrer aux États-Unis?   9. Quand John compte-t-il les revoir?   10. Pourquoi John envoie-t-il un mot à l'antiquaire? 11. Qu'est-ce qu'il a inclus dans sa lettre?   12. Quand a-t-il reçu la facture de l'antiquaire?   13. Quand lui avait-il dit d'envoyer le service de table?   14. Pourquoi veut-il maintenant que l'envoi arrive quinze jours plus tard?   15. Qui fixera la date de l'expédition?   16. De quoi l'antiquaire devra-t-il tenir compte quand il fixera cette date? 17. Quelle invitation John a-t-il reçue pendant qu'il était en Touraine?

18. Pourquoi ne peut-il pas l'accepter? 19. Où sera-t-il au moment
du dîner auquel il est invité? 20. Quand aura-t-il quitté la France?
21. D'après ce qu'il dit dans sa lettre, connaît-il quelques-uns des autres
invités? 22. Au souvenir de qui demande-t-il à Mme Ferry de le
rappeler? 23. Comment termine-t-il sa lettre?

B. *Demandez en français à quelqu'un:*

1. si John va rester encore longtemps en France. 2. de quoi il s'occupe
avant son départ. 3. ce qu'il tient à faire avant de quitter Paris.
4. si John connaissait déjà la Touraine. 5. si les fleurs poussent bien
en Touraine. 6. ce qui les fait pousser. 7. si les Frazer quitteront
bientôt la France. 8. où John compte les revoir. 9. ce que c'est qu'un
mandat-poste. 10. si John sera à San Francisco au milieu d'octobre.
11. s'il aurait été heureux d'accepter l'invitation qu'il a reçue pendant
son absence. 12. pourquoi il lui est impossible de l'accepter. 13. avec
qui il aurait été heureux de se retrouver. 14. à qui il demande à
Mme Ferry de le rappeler.

C. *Dites en français, en employant les expressions indiquées:*

(a) le lendemain, la veille — hier, demain

1. The day after he returned to Paris, John took care of his correspondence. 2. Yesterday, he spent the whole day writing letters.
3. He received an invitation for the day after he left **(son départ).**
4. He could have gone the day before he leaves. 5. But the day after,
he expects to be in Philadelphia. 6. Tomorrow, he is supposed to go
to Air-France to take care of his passage.

(b) d'après

1. According to what Henry told me, you will be back in the United
States next month. 2. According to him, you will be leaving two
weeks from today. 3. According to the information I have, it takes
only seven hours to fly (go by plane) from Paris to New York.

(c) convenir (à)

1. Please set the most suitable shipping date. 2. Does the middle of
September suit you? 3. Yes, this date suits me perfectly.

(*d*) s'occuper de

1. John is taking care of his correspondence. 2. Will you take care of sending the table service? 3. Yes, I will take care of it. 4. I am going to take care of it today.

(*e*) tenir compte de

1. Don't forget to take into account the time it takes to go through customs (pour accomplir les formalités de douane). 2. I'll take it into account. 3. He didn't pay any attention to what I told him. 4. He should have taken it into account.

D. *Employez l'expression indiquée après chacune des phrases suivantes pour dire à la personne à qui vous écrivez:*

1. que vous voulez la remercier de son aimable invitation (Je tiens à).

2. que vous comptez la revoir bientôt (sous peu).

3. que vous auriez été heureux d'être un de ses invités (des vôtres).

4. que vous la priez de présenter vos amitiés à ses parents (rappeler au bon souvenir de).

5. d'agréer vos salutations empressées (Veuillez).

E. *Thème:*

Before leaving for the United States, John wrote several letters.

First of all, he wrote to Mrs. Frazer to thank her for her kind invitation, and to tell her that in spite of the bad weather, he had greatly enjoyed (apprécié) the trip they had taken together to the Loire region.

Then he wrote to the dealer in antiques from whom (chez qui) he had bought a Quimper earthenware table service to tell him to ship it. He added that the dealer knew better than he how long it takes such a shipment to reach its destination, and he asked him to set the most appropriate date.

Finally, he wrote to a lady who had invited him to dinner. He was very sorry not to be able to accept her invitation, but by (à) the date set for the dinner, he would be on his way (en route pour) to America.

Temps composés. Voix passive

94. PLUPERFECT INDICATIVE.

(1) Formation.

The pluperfect tense is composed of the past participle of the verb and the *imparfait* of the auxiliary verb.

(*a*) Verbs conjugated with **avoir:**

J'avais acheté, etc.	I had bought, etc.
J'avais fini	I had finished
J'avais vendu	I had sold
J'avais été	I had been
J'avais eu	I had had

(*b*) Verbs conjugated with **être** (see paragraph 10):

J'étais allé(e)	I had gone
J'étais parti(e)	I had left
J'étais venu(e)	I had come
Je m'étais levé(e)	I had got up
Je m'étais mis(e) à	I had started

(2) Use.

As in English, the pluperfect tense expresses a past action that took place completely before another past action took place.

J'avais **fixé** la date de mon départ, quand j'ai reçu votre invitation.

J'étais déjà **allé** dans cette jolie région, mais **je ne** l'**avais jamais parcourue** en si aimable compagnie.

95. FUTURE PERFECT INDICATIVE.

(1) Formation.

The future perfect is formed like the pluperfect except that the future of the auxiliary is used:

(*a*) Verbs conjugated with **avoir:**

J'aurai fini	I shall have finished
J'aurai été	I shall have been
J'aurai eu	I shall have had

(*b*) Verbs conjugated with **être:**

Je serai parti(e)	I shall have left
Il sera parti	He will have gone (away)
Je me serai levé(e)	I shall have got up

(2) Use.

As in English, the future perfect tense is used to express an action that will take place in the future before another future action takes place. Note that in French, the second future action is expressed by the future tense whereas in English it is expressed by the present tense.

J'aurai fini mon travail quand vous arriverez.

The future perfect is often used to express an action that will have taken place in the future before a specified date.

Je n'aurai pas encore atteint San Francisco à cette époque.
Je serai parti avant son arrivée.

96. THE CONDITIONAL PERFECT.

(1) Formation.

The conditional perfect is formed like the future perfect except that the conditional of the auxiliary is used:

(*a*) Verbs conjugated with **avoir:**

J'aurais acheté	I would have bought
J'aurais fini	I would have finished
J'aurais été	I would have been
J'aurais eu	I would have had

(*b*) Verbs conjugated with **être:**

Je serais allé(e)	I would have gone
Je serais parti(e)	I would have left
Je me serais couché(e)	I would have gone to bed

(2) Use.

This tense is most commonly used in conditional sentences in which the verb in the if-clause is in the pluperfect. It expresses an action that would have taken place, if another action had taken place (compare paragraph 62). Note, however, that the if-clause is very often implied rather than expressed.

> Henri ne se serait pas trompé de route s'il avait fait attention aux poteaux-indicateurs.
>
> J'aurais été heureux de me retrouver chez vous . . .
>
> Rien ne m'aurait donné plus de plaisir que d'accepter votre aimable invitation . . .

97. THE PASSIVE VOICE.

(1) Distinction between the active and the passive voice.

The active voice comprises the forms of a verb that express an action made *by the subject* of the verb: **J'ai accompagné** mon père.

The passive voice comprises the forms that express an action that is made *upon the subject:* **Je suis accompagné** par mon père.

(2) Formation of the passive voice.

The passive conjugation of a verb consists of the different tenses of the auxiliary **être** and the past participle of the verb.:

PRESENT INDICATIVE: **Je suis accompagné(e)**
IMPARFAIT: **J'étais accompagné(e)**
PASSÉ COMPOSÉ: **J'ai été accompagné(e)**
FUTUR: **Je serai accompagné(e)**, etc.

Only transitive verbs have a passive voice.

(3) Examples of the use of the passive voice.

> Le château **a été habité** jusqu'à une date récente.
>
> Chenonceaux **a été construit** au milieu de la rivière.
>
> Versailles **a été construit** par Louis XIV.
>
> Henri IV **a été assassiné** par Ravaillac.

NOTE: (a) the passive voice of the following verbs is often followed by **de: être aimé, accompagné, craint, détesté, estimé, honoré, escorté, précédé, respecté, suivi.**

Elle est **aimée de** tout le monde.
Quand il est entré, il **était suivi de** quelques agents de police.

(b) the adjectives **couvert** and **entouré** are also followed by **de:**

Les murs étaient **couverts de** belles tapisseries.
Le château de Chenonceaux est **entouré d'**eau.
La terre est **couverte de** neige.

(4) Reflexive verbs (see paragraph 43) and active verbs with the indefinite pronoun **on** are often used when the passive voice would be used in English.

Je me suis trompé.   I was mistaken.
On m'a donné une pomme.   I was given an apple.

A. *Mettez chacune des phrases suivantes au plus-que-parfait en ajoutant la proposition:* **quand vous avez téléphoné.** (Ex.: Je suis allé chez le voisin. J'étais allé chez le voisin quand vous avez téléphoné.)

1. Je suis sorti.   2. Je ne suis pas rentré.   3. J'ai commencé à travailler.   4. J'ai retenu passage sur l'avion.   5. J'ai accepté l'invitation des Frazer.   6. Je me suis couché.   7. Nous nous sommes mis à table. 8. J'ai lu la nouvelle dans le journal.   9. J'ai mis la lettre à la poste. 10. J'ai envoyé le télégramme.

B. *Mettez chacune des phrases suivantes au futur antérieur* (future perfect) *en ajoutant la proposition:* **quand vous arriverez.** (Ex.: Je finirai mon travail. J'aurai fini mon travail quand vous arriverez.)

1. Je partirai.   2. Je déjeunerai.   3. J'écrirai cette lettre.   4. Je me lèverai.   5. Je ferai mes bagages.   6. J'achèterai les billets.   7. J'aurai le temps de finir ce livre.   8. J'irai à la banque.   9. Je me réveillerai.

C. *Mettez les phrases suivantes aux temps composés.* (Ex.: S'il pleuvait, je mettrais mon imperméable. S'il avait plu, j'aurais mis mon imperméable.)

1. Si John vous invitait à dîner, accepteriez-vous son invitation? 2. Si vous aviez le temps, iriez-vous en Touraine? 3. Si nous pouvions le faire, nous irions voir ce match. 4. Si John était à Paris, il assisterait au mariage de ses amis. 5. Si le petit Michel dormait bien, il serait de bonne humeur. 6. Si Marie savait l'adresse de John, elle l'inviterait à dîner. 7. Si nous allions à Paris, nous ne manquerions pas de visiter les musées. 8. Si j'étais à votre place, je regarderais les poteaux-indicateurs.

D. *Combinez deux phrases en une seule en employant un plus-que-parfait et l'expression indiquée.* (Ex.: (où) Roger a retrouvé John dans la Grande Galerie. Il a promis de le rejoindre là. Roger a retrouvé John dans la Grande Galerie où il avait promis de le rejoindre.)

(a) **où**

1. Il est allé en Touraine. Il y est déjà allé il y a deux ans. 2. Il est revenu en France. Il y a passé deux ans avant son voyage en Afrique.

(b) **car**

1. Nous sommes partis de bonne heure. Nous avons décidé d'arriver à Orléans avant midi. 2. La route était glissante. Il a plu toute la journée. 3. Je suis rentré chez moi. J'ai oublié mon portefeuille. 4. Je n'ai pas pu vous écrire pendant les vacances. J'ai perdu votre adresse. 5. Je suis allé à l'hôpital. J'ai pris rendez-vous avec le docteur. 6. J'ai passé l'après-midi en ville. J'ai promis de faire des courses pour ma mère.

E. *Dites en français:*

1. Mrs. Frazer is loved by everyone. 2. She is respected by her children. 3. She is honored by her neighbors. 4. She is always surrounded by her friends. 5. She has a fine house that was built two

years ago by a famous architect. 6. Her house is filled with beautiful furniture. 7. The walls are covered with old tapestries. 8. When Mrs. Frazer went to Touraine, she was accompanied by her children and John. 9. When she was at Chenonceaux, the ground was covered with leaves. 10. One day Henry took the wrong road (was mistaken about the road). 11. It was raining so hard **(tant)** that visibility was very poor (one could scarcely see the signs). 12. He stopped when he saw some policemen. 13. When he asked for information, he was told ("they" told him) to continue on the same road. 14. When you **(on)** are not paying attention, you often miss the road.

XXIX CONVERSATION UNIT

Des nouvelles de John

*Quatre mois après que John eut quitté la France, les Duplessis reçurent de lui la lettre suivante: ** *

Des rives de l'Apure, le 25 novembre

Mes chers amis,

Lorsque je quittai la France en septembre dernier, je m'attendais à vous revoir à la fin de mon congé. Le sort me fut bien cruel, qui m'envoya sur les rives inhospitalières de l'Apure. Mais vous ne savez pas ce que c'est que l'Apure, et plût au ciel que moi-même je n'en eusse jamais entendu parler! L'Apure est une rivière du Vénézuéla, un affluent de l'Orénoque. Bref, je suis une fois de plus dans la jungle, à un endroit qui n'est guère accessible que par hélicoptère.

Ce n'est pas, quoi que vous puissiez croire, un lieu de déportation pour les indésirables, bien qu'il y en ait quelques-uns — vous vous en rendrez compte tout à l'heure. Je dirige un camp de prospecteurs dans des régions presque inexplorées du Vénézuéla et de la Colombie. Tous les matins, mes hommes se rendent par hélicoptère en divers endroits, où ils font exploser des charges de dynamite, de façon à déterminer la configuration du sol. Ce qui arriva hier à une de nos équipes vous donnera une idée de la vie que nous menons ici.

Pourtant, la journée commença comme d'habitude. L'hélicoptère vint chercher nos trois hommes le matin, et il les déposa dans une clairière au milieu de la jungle. Là, ils se mirent au travail. Tout alla bien jusqu'à midi. A ce moment des Indiens arrivèrent, et menaçant les intrus des armes les plus hétéroclites, ils s'emparèrent de tout ce qu'ils possédaient, argent, montres, outils, et les dépouillèrent

---

* The English prompt script for this letter will be found in the Appendix, pp. 220-221.

de leurs vêtements. Quand l'hélicoptère revint les chercher le soir, le
pilote trouva nos trois hommes qui l'attendaient avec une impatience
facile à comprendre. Se douterait-on jamais qu'une telle aventure
pût arriver, de nos jours, à d'honnêtes prospecteurs?

Je ne sais pas combien de temps je resterai ici. Je me dis parfois
que vous êtes beaucoup plus sages que moi. Vous rappelez-vous,
Roger, ce que vous me disiez un jour: "Ma vie a été bien tranquille
comparé à la vôtre"? Surtout, ne faites pas du petit Michel un
ingénieur, ou tout au moins, qu'il laisse le pétrole tranquille! Et
pourtant . . .

J'espère malgré tout vous revoir un de ces jours. En attendant,
mes chers amis, puisque ma lettre vous arrivera sans doute vers le
Nouvel An, je vous souhaite à tous les trois une joyeuse année et toute
sorte de prospérité.

Bien cordialement,

John

A. *Répondez en français:*

1. Depuis combien de temps John avait-il quitté la France quand les
Duplessis ont reçu de ses nouvelles?   2. De quand sa lettre était-elle
datée?   3. Dans quel pays était-il quand il l'a écrite?   4. Qu'est-ce
que c'est que l'Apure?   5. En avez-vous jamais entendu parler?   6. De
quel fleuve l'Apure est-il un affluent?   7. L'endroit où se trouve John
est-il facilement accessible?   8. Quel est le meilleur moyen de l'atteindre?   9. Qu'est-ce que John fait à cet endroit?   10. Pourquoi les
prospecteurs font-ils exploser des charges de dynamite?   11. Pourquoi
John raconte-t-il à ses amis ce qui est arrivé la veille?   12. Quand
l'hélicoptère vint-il chercher les trois hommes?   13. Où les déposa-t-il?
14. Que firent-ils après cela?   15. Qu'est-ce qui se passa à midi?
16. De quoi les Indiens s'emparèrent-ils?   17. Quand l'hélicoptère
revint-il chercher les trois hommes?   18. Les prospecteurs étaient-ils
heureux de revoir le pilote?   19. John sait-il combien de temps il
restera au Vénézuéla?   20. Qu'est-ce que Roger lui a dit un jour?
21. Quel conseil John donne-t-il aux parents du petit Michel?
22. Croit-il vraiment ce qu'il dit?   23. Que souhaite-t-il aux Duplessis
en attendant de les revoir?   24. Pourquoi leur adresse-t-il ses souhaits?

B. *Demandez en français à quelqu'un:*

1. de qui les Duplessis reçoivent des nouvelles.   2. la date de la lettre
de John.   3. l'endroit où est John au moment où il écrit sa lettre.
4. ce qu'il pense de l'endroit où il se trouve.   5. quelle est la meilleure
façon d'y arriver.   6. si John se plaît beaucoup là où il est.   7. de
quoi il s'occupe.   8. comment voyagent les équipes de prospecteurs.
9. ce que font les prospecteurs pour déterminer la configuration du sol.
10. ce qui s'est passé le matin.   11. ce qui est arrivé à midi.   12. comment les Indiens s'emparèrent de ce que possédaient les prospecteurs.
13. si la vie de Roger est plus tranquille que celle de John.   14. à
quel moment John croit que sa lettre atteindra sa destination.

C. *Dites en français, en employant les expressions indiquées:*

(*a*) s'attendre à (ce que)

1. I was expecting to see you (again) at the end of my leave.   2. Did
you expect to receive a letter from Venezuela?   3. No, I was not expecting it.   4. I expected that you would return here at the end of
your leave.   5. The Duplessis did not expect to hear (to learn) that
John was in the jungle once more.

(*b*) recevoir des nouvelles (de)

1. They did not expect to hear from him at that time.   2. They had
not heard from him for three months.   3. The last time they heard
from him, he had just left Paris.   4. I have not heard from my
parents for two weeks.

(*c*) se rendre compte (de, que)

1. You will realize it in a while.   2. Do you realize that prospecting
sometimes is a dangerous occupation?   3. Yes, I realize it, after what
happened to John's prospectors.   4. Did you realize that the latter use
dynamite to determine the configuration of the soil?   5. No, I didn't
realize it.

(*d*) se douter (de, que)

1. Would one ever suspect that such a thing might happen?   2. The
prospectors never suspected that Indians would take everything they

had. 3. The Duplessis did not suspect that John had once more been sent to Venezuela. 4. I suspect what happened. 5. There were Indians near them, but the prospectors did not suspect it.

D. *Thème:*

Poor John did not expect to be sent back to Venezuela, but he knows that in his profession, one must expect anything. Once more he finds himself in the jungle, with the monkeys, the parrots and the mosquitoes. To amuse himself, he can perhaps go fishing for piranhas. I don't know if you have heard of these little fish. They travel together and are so fierce that they can devour a whole cow in half an hour . . . At any rate, John will one of these days be a member of the executive council (conseil d'administration) of a large petroleum company, and he will sit behind a big desk in one of New York's skyscrapers. In the meantime, he is young and strong, and he is used to (il a l'habitude de) life in the jungle. We all wish him luck.

XXX

Passé simple. Imparfait et plus-que-parfait du subjonctif

98. MEANING AND USE OF THE *passé simple*.

The names *passé simple* (simple past) and *passé composé* (compound past) are used to distinguish two past tenses which, generally speaking, have the same meaning: both tenses are used to express simple past actions. The *passé composé* is the normal past tense in spoken French (see paragraph 5) ; the *passé simple* is used in literary narrative style and occasionally in formal speech. The *imparfait* is used with the *passé simple* in the same ways that it is used with the *passé composé* (see paragraphs 15 and 16).

99. FORMATION OF THE *passé simple*.

REGULAR VERBS

(1) The stem of the *passé simple* of verbs of the first conjugation is found by dropping the **-er** ending: **aimer — aim-;** and the endings are: **-ai, -as, -a, -âmes, -âtes, -èrent.**

(2) The stem of the *passé simple* of verbs of the second and third conjugations is found by dropping the **-ir** or **-re** ending; the endings for both conjugations are: **-is, -is, -it, -îmes, -îtes, -irent.**

(3) Forms:

aimer: j'aimai, tu aimas, il aima, nous aimâmes, vous aimâtes, ils aimèrent.

finir: je finis, tu finis, il finit, nous finîmes, vous finîtes, ils finirent.

vendre: je vendis, tu vendis, il vendit, nous vendîmes, vous vendîtes, ils vendirent.

être AND avoir

être: je fus, tu fus, il fut, nous fûmes, vous fûtes, ils furent.
avoir: j'eus, tu eus, il eut, nous eûmes, vous eûtes, ils eurent.

OTHER IRREGULAR VERBS

The *passé simple* of irregular verbs cannot be mastered at a glance, but at least one can quickly see which forms need to be studied.

As the *passé simple* is used mostly in the third person, only this person will be listed in this place.

(1) The *passé simple* of all verbs ending in **-er** is regular.

(2) The *passé simple* of nearly all irregular verbs ending in **-ir** is regular. Notable exceptions are:

(*a*) **tenir** and **venir:**

il tint [il tɛ̃], **ils tinrent** [il tɛ̃ʀ]
il vint [il vɛ̃], **ils vinrent** [il vɛ̃ʀ]

(*b*) **courir** and **mourir**

il courut, ils coururent
il mourut, ils moururent

(3) The *passé simple* of verbs ending in **-re** often has an irregular stem:

(*a*)

conduire: il conduisit, ils conduisirent
dire: il dit, ils dirent
écrire: il écrivit, ils écrivirent
faire: il fit, ils firent
mettre: il mit, ils mirent
naître: il naquit, ils naquirent
prendre: il prit, ils prirent
suivre: il suivit, ils suivirent
vaincre: il vainquit, ils vainquirent

(*b*)

atteindre: **il atteignit, ils atteignirent**
craindre: **il craignit, ils craignirent**
peindre: **il peignit, ils peignirent**
plaindre: **il plaignit, ils plaignirent**
rejoindre: **il rejoignit, ils rejoignirent**

Note that the stem of verbs in group (*b*) is like the stem of the first person plural of the present indicative.

(*c*)

conclure: **il conclut, ils conclurent**
connaître: **il connut, ils connurent**
lire: **il lut, ils lurent**
vivre: **il vécut, ils vécurent**

(4) The *passé simple* of verbs in **-oir** has an irregular stem which ends in **-u.**

apercevoir: **il aperçut, ils aperçurent**
boire: **il but, ils burent**
croire: **il crut, ils crurent**
devoir: **il dut, ils durent**
falloir: **il fallut** (impersonal)
pleuvoir: **il plut** (impersonal)
pouvoir: **il put, ils purent**
recevoir: **il reçut, ils reçurent**
savoir: **il sut, ils surent**
valoir: **il valut, ils valurent**
     Exceptions:
s'asseoir: **il s'assit, ils s'assirent**
voir: **il vit, ils virent**

100. EXAMPLES OF USE OF THE *passé simple* IN NARRATIVE STYLE.

Lorsque je **quittai** la France, je m'attendais à vous revoir à la fin de mon congé. Le sort me **fut** bien cruel, qui m'**envoya** sur les rives de l'Apure . . .

La journée **commença** comme d'habitude. L'hélicoptère **vint** chercher nos trois hommes et les **déposa** dans une clairière au milieu de la jungle. Là, ils **se mirent** à travailler. Tout **alla** bien jusqu'à midi. A ce moment des Indiens **arrivèrent,** . . . ils **s'emparèrent** de tout ce qu'ils possédaient, argent, montres, outils, et les **dépouillèrent** de leurs vêtements. Quand l'hélicoptère **revint** le soir, le pilote **trouva** nos trois hommes qui l'attendaient avec une impatience facile à comprendre.

Compare:

> Bonaparte **mena** en Italie une armée qui était victorieuse (which was already victorious — that is, a victorious army).
>
> Bonaparte **mena** en Italie une armée qui **fut** victorieuse (which, after he got there, was victorious).

101. IMPERFECT SUBJUNCTIVE.

(1) The imperfect subjunctive forms of all verbs can be inferred from the *passé simple* as follows: drop the last letter of the first person singular and add the endings **-sse, -sses, -ˆt, -ssions, -ssiez, -ssent.** The third singular of the imperfect subjunctive always has a circumflex accent on the vowel of the ending and ends in a **t.**

(2) Regular verbs:

aimer: *passé simple,* tu **aimas;** *imperfect subjunctive:*
aimasse, aimasses, aimât, aimassions, aimassiez, aimassent.
finir: *passé simple,* tu **finis;** *imperfect subjunctive:*
finisse, finisses, finît, finissions, finissiez, finissent.
vendre: *passé simple,* tu **vendis;** *imperfect subjunctive:*
vendisse, vendisses, vendît, vendissions, vendissiez, vendissent.

(3) Auxiliary verbs:

être: *passé simple:* tu **fus;** *imperfect subjunctive:*
fusse, fusses, fût, fussions, fussiez, fussent.
avoir: *passé simple:* tu **eus;** *imperfect subjunctive:*
eusse, eusses, eût, eussions, eussiez, eussent [ys, ys, y, ysjõ, ysje, ys].

(4) The imperfect subjunctive of a few irregular verbs:

As this tense is used chiefly in the third person, only this person will be given here:

tenir: *passé simple:* il **tint**; *imp. subj.:* il **tînt**, ils **tinssent**
venir: *passé simple:* il **vint**; *imp. subj.:* il **vînt**, ils **vinssent**
faire: *passé simple:* il **fit**; *imp. subj.:* il **fît**, ils **fissent**
craindre: *passé simple:* il **craignit**; *imp. subj.:* il **craignît**, ils **craignissent**.
pouvoir: *passé simple:* il **put**; *imp. subj.:* il **pût**, ils **pussent.**
savoir: *passé simple:* il **sut**; *imp. subj.:* il **sût**, ils **sussent**

102. PLUPERFECT SUBJUNCTIVE.

This tense is made of the past participle of a verb and the imperfect subjunctive of the auxiliary.

Verbs conjugated with **avoir:**
> j'eusse aimé, j'eusse fini, j'eusse vendu

Verbs conjugated with **être:**
> je fusse parti, je fusse venu, etc.

103. USES OF TENSES IN THE SUBJUNCTIVE.

(1) When the verb of the main clause is in the present or future,

(*a*) an action or a state of being in the present or in the future is expressed by the present subjunctive in the subordinate clause.

> Il **vaut** mieux que **vous veniez** tout de suite.
> Il **faudra** qu'il **vienne** me voir.

(*b*) an action or state in the past is expressed by the *passé composé* of the subjunctive in subordinate clauses:

> Je doute qu'**il soit arrivé** à sept heures du matin.
> Je ne crois pas qu'**il ait été** très malade.

(2) When the verb of the main clause is in a past tense,

(*a*) the verb of the subordinate clause is put in the imperfect subjunctive to express an action that is present or future in relation to the verb of the main clause:

> Se **douterait**-on jamais qu'une telle aventure **pût** arriver?
> **Je craignais** qu'il **partît**. (*would leave*)
> **J'ai demandé** qu'il **répondît** immédiatement.
> **Je voulais** qu'il **vînt** dîner chez nous demain.

(*b*) the verb of the subordinate clause is put in the pluperfect subjunctive to express an action that was past in relation to the verb of the main clause:

> Plût au ciel que moi-même **je** n'en **eusse** jamais **entendu** parler.
> (**Plût** is imp. subj. of **plaire:** "Might it please heaven that . . . ")
> Je craignais qu'**il fût parti** avant mon arrivée. (*had left*)
> Je ne croyais pas qu'**il eût quitté** l'hôpital.

Except for the third person singular, the imperfect and pluperfect subjunctives are now used sparingly even in writing. They are even rarer in conversational French.

A. *Mettez les phrases suivantes au pluriel:*

1. Il arriva.   2. Il trouva.   3. Il se reposa.   4. Il s'en occupa.   5. Il finit.   6. Il répondit.   7. Il réussit.   8. Il se mit à parler.   9. Il reçut. 10. Il s'en aperçut.   11. Il eut.   12. Il fut.   13. Il but de l'eau fraîche. 14. Il apprit la nouvelle.   15. Il reconnut.   16. Il sut.   17. J'arrivai. 18. J'allai.   19. Je trouvai.   20. Je montai.   21. J'aperçus.   22. Je m'aperçus.   23. Je fus.   24. Je répondis.

B. *Remplacez le passé composé par le passé simple dans les phrases suivantes:*

1. John est arrivé à Paris le 18 août.   2. Il est descendu à l'hôtel Meurice.   3. Le lendemain il a décidé d'aller voir les Duplessis.   4. Il a pris un taxi qu'il a attendu quelque temps.   5. Roger l'a reçu à bras ouverts.   6. Il l'a invité à dîner.   7. John a vu pour la première fois le fils des Duplessis.   8. Il a été très heureux de revoir ses amis.   9. Un jour qu'il traversait la Place de l'Opéra, John a rencontré Mme Frazer et Helen.

10. Il a été très étonné de les voir, car il ne savait pas qu'elles étaient à Paris.   11. Mme Frazer a eu l'amabilité de l'inviter à les accompagner en Touraine.   12. Le vendredi suivant, ils ont quitté Paris.   13. Henry est venu chercher John à son hôtel à sept heures et demie.   14. Ils se sont mis en route à huit heures.   15. Il leur a fallu quatre heures pour aller de Paris à Orléans où ils ont déjeuné.   16. Le lendemain ils sont allés à Chenonceaux où ils ont visité le château. 17. Le temps a été désagréable pendant une bonne partie de leur séjour en Touraine.   18. Malgré cela, John a trouvé le voyage fort agréable.

C. *Remplacez* **même si** *par* **bien que** *et le subjonctif dans les phrases suivantes:*

1. Même s'il a plu beaucoup, nos amis ont visité plusieurs beaux châteaux.   2. Même si John avait beaucoup à faire, il a accepté l'invitation de Mme Frazer.   3. Même si Henry s'est trompé de route, ils sont arrivés sans trop de retard.   4. Même si John a acheté plusieurs cadeaux, il doit en acheter d'autres avant son départ.   5. Même s'il avait déjà vu la plupart des châteaux, il a été content d'aller en Touraine.

D. *Dites les phrases suivantes en commençant par la phrase indiquée et en employant l'imparfait du subjonctif.* (Ex.: Louis XIV voulait . . . Molière est allé à la cour. Louis XIV voulait que Molière allât à la cour.)

(*a*) **Louis XIV voulait**

1. Molière a joué une nouvelle comédie.   2. On a construit Versailles. 3. Le Nôtre a dessiné les jardins.   4. Molière est venu souvent à Versailles.

(*b*) **Le roi ne voulait pas**

1. Ses ministres eurent trop d'influence.   2. On le fit attendre.   3. On écrivit contre lui.   4. La noblesse gouverna l'État.

E. *Thème.*

Racine was born at la Ferté-Milon in 1639. He became an orphan early and was reared by his grandmother. He entered the school of Port-Royal, where he received an excellent education. He had for teachers **(maîtres)** some of the great scholars of the time. He learned Latin and Greek and read most of the Greek and Latin classics. To the great annoyance **(mécontentement)** of his masters, he began to write for the theatre. They wanted him to become a lawyer **(avocat)** but he didn't want to.

Later, they sent him to Uzès to study theology. He read Saint Thomas but he continued to write poetry **(faire des vers)**.

He came back to Paris in 1663. He made the acquaintance of Boileau, La Fontaine, and others. In the course of his career as a dramatic author, which lasted about ten years, he wrote several fine tragedies. In 1677 he gave up **(abandonner)** the theatre, got married and, eventually, had five sons and five daughters. For a long time, he lead a family life and he took care of his children's education with great care **(soin)**.

At the request **(la prière)** of Mme de Maintenon he composed two religious tragedies, *Esther* and *Athalie,* which were performed at the school of Saint-Cyr. He died in 1699.

Racine was perhaps the greatest French dramatic poet.

Rue de Montmartre, par Utrillo.

La France actuelle

LA FRANCE ARTISTIQUE

Utrillo. Paris sous la neige.

Maurice, Utrillo, V,
1934,

Dufy: *Le Paddock à Deauville.*

Palais de Chaillot.

Chapelle de Matisse, à Vence.

En haut, à droite — *Église moderne par Le Corbusier.*

En bas, à droite — *L'Immeuble "Le Corbusier" à Marseille.*

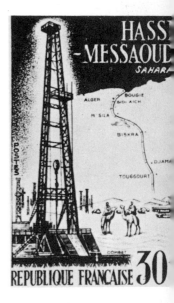

Émission de timbres illustrant industries et techniques modernes.

Puits de pétrole à Hassi-Messaoud.

LA FRANCE INDUSTRIELLE

Machine agricole.

Le Cheval et le tracteur.

Barrage en Dordogne.

Aéroport d'Orly.

Avions à réaction "Caravelle."

L'Atar volant, engin Sol Air expérimental (the flying Atar, an experimental ground-to-air vehicle).

Fusée Véronique (Guided missile).

Vue des Usines Renault à Billancourt (Paris). Au fond, le **Pont** de Saint-Cloud.

Récupération de soufre (Refining sulfur) *à Lacq.*

Utilisation de l'énergie solaire, Centre de Mont Louis.

REFERENCE MATERIALS

Table of Sounds of the French Language
As Represented by Symbols of the International Phonetic Alphabet

CONSONANTS

	Bi-labial	Labio-dental	Dental and Alveolar	Palato-alveolar	Palatal	Velar	Uvular
Plosive	p b		t d			k g	
Nasal	m		n		ɲ		
Lateral			l				
Rolled			r*				ʀ
Fricative		f v	s z	ʃ ʒ			
Semi-vowels	w ɥ				j (ɥ)	(w)	

VOWELS

	Front	Central	Back
Close	i y		u
Half-close	e ø	ə	o õ
Half-open	ɛ œ ɛ̃ œ̃		ɔ
Open	a	a	ɑ ɑ̃

* The symbols [ʀ] and [r] represent two ways of producing "r" in French. The [ʀ] is produced between the back of the tongue and the soft palate, the [r] with the tip of the tongue against the teeth or gums. Only the [ʀ] is used in the phonetic transcriptions in this book, but the alveolar [r] is quite commonly used in many parts of France.

Improving your accent

For the table of sounds, see the opposite page.

104. STRESS.

In English — and in most other languages, certain syllables are strongly accented and others are given a very weak utterance. In French, on the contrary, words do not have accented syllables and consequently every pronounced syllable receives an equal amount of emphasis. If you observe a French person who speaks English with a heavy accent, you think he is just accenting the wrong syllables; but in reality he is giving equal stress to each syllable as he would when speaking French. Instead of saying "Where's the rest'rant?" (in four syllables) with a strong accent on "where" and "rest-" — as we would, our French person would be likely to say something like: "Wear eez zee res-tau-rant?" in six clear syllables of equal stress.

EXERCISES.

(1) Contrast the pronunciation of the following pairs of words, making it a point to stress the accented syllables in the English words and trying to give equal stress to each syllable in the French words:

Eng. an′-uh-mul, *Fr.* **a-ni-mal;** *Eng.* min′-uh-rul, *Fr.* **mi-né-ral;** *Eng.* national (nash-un-ul) , *Fr.* **na-tio-nal** [na-sjɔ-nal].*

Note, meanwhile, that in French, syllables tend to begin with a consonant and to end with a vowel sound (see paragraph 111) .

(2) In order to get the pattern of rhythm of French words clearly in mind, say rapidly: tóc-tóc-tóc-, **a-ni-mal;** tóc-tóc-tóc,

---

* The key to pronunciation indicated between square brackets is the International Phonetic Alphabet, which is used for the transcription of all the conversations (see pp. 206-220). This will be studied later; for the time being, the principal objective is to get the habit of giving equal stress to each pronounced syllable of each phrase.

mi-né-ral; tóc-tóc-tóc, **na-tio-nal** [nas-jɔ-nal]; tóc-tóc-tóc-tóc-tóc, **in-ter-na-tio-nal** [ɛ̃-tɛʀ-na-sjɔ-nal].

After learning to say a few words and groups of words with equal stress on all syllables, you will be able to pronounce words and phrases without establishing the rhythm in advance with the syllable "tóc"; but whenever you find it difficult to catch the rhythm of a phrase, it is helpful to tap the number of syllables of the phrase on a table with a coin or some other hard object. This of course takes time; but you can't expect to overcome the speech habits of a lifetime in five minutes.

(3) Examples from Conversation I.

Sentence 1 (6 syllables) : Où allez-vous monsieur? [u-a-le-vu-mə-sjø?]
Sentence 2 (Three groups: 1, 5, and 3 syllables) :

| Treize, | avenue du Palais | à Saint-Cloud. |
| [tʀɛz, | av-ny dy pa-lɛ | a sɛ̃-klu.] |

Repeat each group several times and then repeat the entire sentence in nine equal syllables.

Sentence 3 (Three groups: 6, 3, and 5 syllables) :

6   C'est près du pont de Saint-Cloud [sɛ pʀɛ dy põd sɛ̃-klu]
3   à l'entrée de [a lɑ̃ tʀed]
5   l'autoroute de l'Ouest. [lɔ-to-ʀut də lwɛst.]

Repeat each group several times and then repeat the entire sentence in fourteen equal syllables.

Sentence 4 (3 syllables) : Entendu. [ɑ̃-tɑ̃-dy]
Sentence 5 (5 syllables) : Montez, s'il vous plaît. [mõ-te sil vu plɛ.]

(4) It is a good idea to listen to the voices on the tapes, to note consciously the rhythm of phrases, and to keep trying to imitate the voices until you can utter a string of syllables evenly and effortlessly. It may take a little time; but it is well worth the effort, for once you develop this skill, it is much easier to make the sounds of the language sound right.

105. ACCENT.

As a result of our way of accenting some syllables and slighting others, in English we tend to pronounce both the consonants and the vowels that are in an accented syllable differently from the way we pronounce them when they are in other positions. Compare the initial and the final "t" in *temperate, talent, ticket:* the initial "t" is uttered with a puff of air (aspiration) and the second "t" (in final position phonetically) is scarcely heard at all. In French the [t], as well as other pronounced consonants, is completely articulated in practically all positions: **tante, tenter.**

Note also that in the accented syllable in the words *animal, mineral,* and *national* the vowel in the first syllable is clearly pronounced and that the other vowels — whether written **i, e, a,** or **o** — sound more or less like **uh.** In French, however, pronounced vowels must be given their proper value in all positions.

106. POSITION OF THE TONGUE.

As the organs of speech other than the tongue are used in English very much as they are used in French, it is not necessary to study their functioning in order to speak French well. But as the tongue is used very differently in the two languages, it is absolutely essential that you learn to use it in new ways if you want to speak French with "a good accent." For example, in English the tip of the tongue is turned up when we pronounce the consonants **t, d, s, z, n, l, r, ch, zh, y,** and some of the vowels; but in French the tip of the tongue *is never turned up.* Another essential difference between the two languages is that initial consonants are uttered with much greater expenditure of breath in English than in French.

107. CONSONANTS.

(1) Explanation and exercises for consonants that are produced with the tongue toward the front of the mouth: [t, d, s, z, n, l, ʃ, ʒ].

Observe carefully the difference between English and French pronunciation of these sounds and contrast the pairs of words in English and French. (*a*) Place the tip of the tongue firmly against the front teeth consciously for each French word and use as little breath as possible. In this way the upper surface of the tongue (not the tip) will be against or near the alveolar ridge (the ridge just behind the upper front teeth) for the French words.

[t] as in	tout.	Contrast Eng. two with Fr. tout.
[d] as in	décide.	Contrast Eng. day with Fr. décide.
[n] as in une banane.		Contrast Eng. banana with Fr. une banane.
[l] as in	le lit.	Contrast Eng. will with Fr. s'il vous plaît.
[s] as in	je sais.	Contrast Eng. say with Fr. Je sais.
[z] as in	vous‿avez.	Contrast Eng. zebra with Fr. zèbre.
[ʃ] as in	le chauffeur.	Contrast Eng. show with Fr. le chauffeur.
[ʒ] as in	jamais.	Contrast Eng. pleasure with Fr. jamais.

Repeat these pairs of words several times, using the tip of the tongue consciously for each English word and moving the tongue forward consciously for each French word. Make the French sounds sound different from the English ones!

(*b*) Repeat the following French words and phrases, making it a point to keep the tip of the tongue against the front teeth and to use as little breath as possible:

du tabac [dytaba], du thé [dyte], la table, la date, des dates, il décide, le taxi, l'hôtel, les hôtels, le petit hôtel, entendu, des tomates, le château, s'il vous plaît, du lait, je joue, jamais, janvier, gentil, jeune, joli, juste, la chaise, la chambre, la chance, changer, je change, le chèque, des bananes, Suzanne, la neige.

(2) Explanation and exercises for the consonants that are pronounced with the tongue in the back of the mouth: [k, g, ɲ, ʀ].

[k] and [g] are pronounced approximately as most people pronounce them in English except that when at the beginning

of a word they are uttered with a greater expenditure of breath in English.

(*a*) Place the tip of the tongue against the lower front teeth (so that the vowels will be pronounced properly) and use as little breath as possible in pronouncing the French words.

[k] as in le café.   Contrast Eng. coffee with Fr. le café.
[g] as in le gaz.   Contrast Eng. gas with Fr. le gaz.

Repeat the following:

la carte, la cause, combien, comment, je connais, qui, que, quel, les quais, les courses;

la galerie, le gardien, grave, le guide, le garage, le garçon, la gorge, les gants.

(*b*) The sound [ɲ] as in "un signe" is the one usually pronounced in English "Swingyour partner." It is pronounced further back in the mouth than the somewhat similar sound in Eng. onion.

Repeat the following words, making it a point to produce the sound [ɲ] in the back of the mouth — if possible:

un signe, le champagne, la Bretagne, l'agneau, le peigne, le règne, nous craignons, Que craignez-vous?

(*c*) The sound [ʀ] as in "après" has no counterpart in English. To produce the French "uvular R", the back of the tongue is placed close to the soft palate as if to gargle. In order to avoid saying an American "r" unintentionally, the tip of the tongue should be placed more firmly than ever face down against the lower front teeth and held there. With the tongue in this position: (*a*) Pronounce "ugh" as in English *mug*. (*b*) Repeat and prolong the "gh": ugh-gh-gh-gh. (*c*) With the tongue still in position, try to repeat this sound without actually pronouncing the [g]. (*d*) Without moving the tongue, make the sound [ʀ] gently. Do not gargle it. Note that when French is spoken with elegance, you scarcely hear the [ʀ] at all. (*e*)

Repeat, using as little breath as possible. (*f*) Pronounce the following words gently, carefully, and repeatedly:

l'art [laʀ], rare [ʀɑʀ], or [ɔʀ], l'orange [lɔʀɑ̃ʒ], l'aurore [lɔʀɔʀ], horreur [ɔʀœʀ], heureux [øʀø], Paris [paʀi], Marie [maʀi], la mairie [lameʀi], Américain [ameʀikɛ̃], après [apʀɛ], très [tʀɛ], frais [fʀɛ], un frère [œ̃ fʀɛʀ], gros [gʀo], gras [gʀa], grec [gʀɛk], gris [gʀi], j'ai appris [ʒe apʀi], avril, péril, rire, etc.

Repeat this exercise daily until you can pronounce the French [ʀ] easily and correctly without thinking about it.

(3) Explanation and exercises for the consonants that are pronounced with the lips or lips and teeth without use of the tongue: [p], [b], [f], [v], [m].

These sounds are produced as in English except that they are uttered when initial with much more breath in English than in French. Hold a strip of paper before your lips and pronounce Eng. *paper* and French **le papier,** using as little breath as possible for the French word. The paper should not move for the French word!

[p] as in le **papier.**	Contrast Eng. paper with Fr. le papier.
[b] as in **beaucoup.**	Contrast Eng. boat with Fr. beaucoup.
[f] as in la **fleur.**	Contrast Eng. flower with Fr. la fleur.
[v] as in **vous** êtes.	Compare Eng. vow and Fr. vous.
[m] as in **madame.**	Compare Eng. madam and Fr. madame.

The difference between initial **p, b,** and **f** in English and French is striking. The difference between **v** and **m** in the two languages is less noticeable.

(*a*) Pronounce each of the following words with a strip of paper in front of your lips until you can say them all without causing the paper to move:

1. papa, le papier, un peu, mon père, je ne peux pas partir avec Pierre, la petite poupée en papier;

2. une banane, là-bas, le beurre, beau, bon, la bouche, des bonbons, un beau bouquet, beaucoup de bananes;

3. l'enfant, la famille, la fleur, la feuille, février, des pommes frites, des fraises, mon frère.

(*b*) If you have difficulty pronouncing these consonants at the beginning of words, try putting them at the end of the previous word: la fleur [laf-lœʀ], le papier [lǝp-ap-je], la poupée [lap-up-e] so as to reduce the initial puff of air.

108. VOWELS.

In pronouncing vowels in accented syllables in English, most of us tend to make them into diphthongs — that is, to insert a short ĭ or ŭ before or after the vowel: *day* (dāĭ), *die* (dĭĭ), *doe* (dōŭ), *do* (dŭu) or (dĭu). But in French, the vowels are pronounced without any diphthongization whatever. Generally speaking, the vowels in French are always short; although some French persons tend to lengthen any vowel that is followed by final [m, n, ʀ, ʒ, j, v, z, vʀ] this practice seems justifiable only if the lengthened syllable is at the end of a phrase. You could lengthen the [ɛ] in **père** in the phrase "Où est votre père?" but not in "Mon père est parti."

It is fairly easy to pronounce the French vowels correctly if (1) they are pronounced quickly and without stress, and (2) if the tongue does not move out of position while the vowel is being pronounced.

A glance at the vowels on the Table of Sounds of the French Language (p. 192) shows that most of the vowels are in pairs. It is useful to consult this table frequently until you have a clear picture of the way the vowels are produced.

(1) [i] as in "vite" and [y] as in "une minute" are pronounced with the tongue placed forward in the mouth (tip against the lower front teeth) with the mouth almost closed. The difference between the two sounds is that the lips are retracted for the [i] and slightly rounded for the [y]. The tongue position is the same for the two sounds.

Pronounce each of the following pairs of sounds and syllables several times, moving only the lips and holding the tip
of the tongue firmly against the lower front teeth:

[i], [y]; [pi], [py]; [bi], [by]; [fi], [fy]; [vi], [vy]; [ni],
[ny]; [ʀi], [ʀy].

Pronounce the following words and syllables:

y, eu; pie, pu; bi-, bu; fit, fut; vie, vue; nid, nu; riz, rue.

Repeat this exercise until you can pronounce the symbols and
the words just alike.

(2) [e] as in "été" and [ø] as in "je peux" are pronounced
with the tip of the tongue against the lower front teeth and
the mouth opened a trifle wider than for [i] and [y]. The difference between the two sounds is that the lips are retracted for
the [e] and slightly rounded for the [ø]. The tongue position
is the same for the two sounds.

Pronounce each of the following pairs of sounds and syllables several times, moving only the lips:

[e], [ø]; [pe], [pø]; [be], [bø]; [fe], [fø]; [ke], [kø]; [ne],
[nø]; [se], [sø].

Pronounce the following words and syllables:

ai, œufs; pé-, peu; bé-, bœufs; fé-, feu; quai, queue; né, nœud;
cé-, ceux.

(3) [ɛ] as in "il est," [œ] as in "neuf," [ɛ̃] as in "la fin,"
[œ̃] as in "un lit," and [ɔ] as in "la poste" are all pronounced
with the mouth half-open.

(a) The difference between [ɛ] and [œ] is that the lips are
slightly rounded and the tongue is slightly farther back for
the latter.

Pronounce each of the following pairs of sounds several
times:

[ɛ], [œ]; celle, seul; serre, sœur; père, peur; mère, meurt.

(b) The difference between [ɛ] and [ɛ̃] is that the latter is pronounced by allowing a part of the air to go into the nasal cavity.

[ɛ], [ɛ̃]; fait, fin; laid, lin; mais, main; paix, pain; c'est, sain.

(c) The difference between [œ] and [œ̃] is that the latter is produced by allowing a part of the air to enter the nasal cavity.

[œ], [œ̃]; un œuf, un bœuf; la peur, le parfum [lə paʀfœ̃].

(d) The difference between [œ] and [ɔ] is that the tongue is still farther back for the latter.

[œ], [ɔ]; heure, or; peur, port; beurre, bord; sœur, sort.

(4) [a] as in "la table" [ɑ] as in "pas encore" and [ɑ̃] as in "en France" are pronounced with the mouth well open.

(a) The difference between [a] and [ɑ] is that the tongue is slightly farther back in the mouth for the latter.

[a], [ɑ]; il n'a pas; là-bas, il a passé.

(b) The difference between [ɑ] and [ɑ̃] is that the latter is produced by allowing a part of the air to enter the nasal cavity.

[ɑ], [ɑ̃]; pas, enfant; pas en France; pas encore; là-bas en mer.

(5) [o] as in "l'hôtel" and [õ] as in "bon" are pronounced with the mouth half-closed.

[o], [õ]; beau, bon; faux, fond; l'eau, long; mot, mon.

(6) [u] as in "vous" is pronounced with the mouth practically closed, with the lips rounded and the tongue in the back of the mouth.

[u]; nous, vous, bout, cou, doux, fou, goût, houx, loup, mou.

Pronounce the following pairs of words, making it a point to move the tongue forward for [y] and back for [u]. The lips remain rounded but the tongue makes the distinction between the sounds.

[y], [u]; nu, nous; fut, fou; bu, bout; du, doux; eu [y], houx [u]; lu, loup; mu, mou; pu, poux; rue, roux; su, sou; tu, tout. Pas du tout. Les galeries du Louvre.

(7) The mute [ə]. (a) In addition to the open [ɛ] as in "vous êtes" and the close [e] as in "l'été," there is also the mute "e" which, as its name implies, is usually silent (as in **avenue** [avny]). Although it is usually silent, it sometimes has the sound [ə] as in "une demi-heure." [yn dəmiœʀ].

Repeat the following phrases, noting that most of the mute "e's" are completely silent:

1. Je décide d'aller revoir Marie. 2. Je monte dans le taxi. 3. Les Duplessis demeurent avenue de Longchamps. 4. Si ça ne vous fait rien. 5. De retour.

Repeat the following, noting that some of the mute "e's" are pronounced:

1. Est-ce que nous sommes à Saint-Cloud? 2. Une demi-heure. 3. Montez Monsieur [məsjø]. 4. Le chauffeur. 5. Venez nous voir. 6. Revenez bientôt.

(b) There is no easy and dependable rule for sounding or omitting the mute "e's", but the following suggestions may be helpful.

1. Although mute "e's" were normally pronounced a few hundred years ago, they have now practically disappeared from the spoken language. Generally speaking, (a) mute "e's" are not sounded in phrases which can be easily pronounced without them; (b) if mute "e's" occur initially in two successive syllables (as in Je ne parle pas anglais), the first one is pronounced [ə] and the second one is not sounded. Ex.: le cheval, le repas, le petit déjeuner. But **ce que** is pronounced [skə].

2. It is customary to sound the [ə] of the article **le** in pronouncing individual words (especially in giving a *dictée*) or at the beginning of a sentence. Ex.: le château est sur la place. But French people tend to omit the mute "e's" even in initial syllables: le château, le chauffeur; remarquez; regardez; retournez-vous. This looks difficult but it is easier than it looks.

3. As the rules for writing poetry were developed long ago, when mute "e's" were commonly pronounced, the [ə] preceding a consonant is commonly sounded in reading poetry or in singing. Ex.: **toute ma vie,** which would have three syllables [tut ma vi] in conversation, would have five in an operatic aria [tu tɔ ma vi ə].

4. When in doubt as to the pronunciation of mute "e's" in this book, one can always consult the phonetic transcriptions of the Conversations (pages 206-220.)

109. SEMI-VOWELS.
[w], [j], and [ɥ].

(1) [w] as in "**voilà**" is pronounced with the lips — approximately as in English.

moi, une poire, la boîte, une fois; oui, Louis, soyez, loyer, voyons.

(2) [j] as in **bien** [bjɛ̃] is pronounced with the tip of the tongue against the lower front teeth.

bien, rien, tiens, la fille, gentille, la famille, travailler, vieux [vjø], vieille [vjɛj].

(3) [ɥ] as in "**la nuit**" [lanɥi] is produced by saying [y] and [i] in rapid succession. The tip of the tongue should of course be against the lower front teeth and care should be taken not to make the sound [w].

Repeat the following:

[y] [i], [y] [i], [y] [i], [ɥ], [ɥ], [ɥ].

Repeat this exercise until you can say [ɥ] without a trace of the sound of [w].

Repeat the following pairs of words and syllables with the same precaution:

nid, nuit; lit, luit; qui, cuit; frit, fruit; si, suis; Brie, bruit; vite, huit; fit, fuit; bi-, buis; j'y, juillet; chien, juin; cite, suite; nage, nuage; tel, actuel; avance, nuance; cède, Suède; cette, cacahuète.

Phonetic Transcriptions

110. CARDINAL NUMBERS AND CONVERSATIONS.

CARDINAL NUMBERS

DATES, NUMBERS, COUNTING.

(1) In dates, street numbers, telephone numbers, in count-ing, etc. the cardinal numbers are pronounced as follows:

1. œ̃	11. õz	21. vɛ̃teœ̃
2. dø	12. duz	22. vɛ̃tdø
3. tʀwɑ	13. tʀɛz	23. vɛ̃ttʀwɑ
4. katʀ	14. katɔrz	24. vɛ̃tkatʀ
5. sɛ̃k	15. kɛ̃z	25. vɛ̃tsɛ̃k
6. sis	16. sɛz	26. vɛ̃tsis
7. sɛt	17. dissɛt	27. vɛ̃tsɛt
8. ɥit	18. dizɥit	28. vɛ̃tɥit
9. nœf	19. diznœf	29. vɛ̃tnœf
10. dis	20. vɛ̃	

30. tʀɑ̃t	31. tʀɑ̃teœ̃	32. tʀɑ̃tdø, etc.
40. kaʀɑ̃t	41. kaʀɑ̃teœ̃	42. kaʀɑ̃tdø, etc.
50. sɛ̃kɑ̃t	51. sɛ̃kɑ̃teœ̃	52. sɛ̃kɑ̃tdø, etc.
60. swasɑ̃t	61. swastɑ̃eœ̃	62. swasɑ̃tdø, etc.
70. swasɑ̃tdis	71. swasɑ̃teõz	72. swasɑ̃tduz, etc.

80. katʀəvɛ̃	81. katʀəvɛ̃eœ̃, etc.
90. katʀəvɛ̃dis	91. katʀəvɛ̃eõz, etc.
100. sɑ̃	101. sɑ̃ œ̃ 102. sɑ̃ dø, etc.
500. sɛ̃sɑ̃	501. sɛ̃sɑ̃ œ̃, etc.
600. sisɑ̃	601. sisɑ̃ œ̃, etc.
700. sɛtsɑ̃	701. sɛtsɑ̃ œ̃, etc.
800. ɥisɑ̃	801. ɥisɑ̃ œ̃, etc.
900. nœfsɑ̃	901. nœfsɑ̃ œ̃

1000. mil, 1001. mil œ̃, etc.	5000. sɛ̃mil
1100. õzsɑ̃ *or* milsɑ̃	6000. simil
1200. duzsɑ̃ *or* mildøsɑ̃	7000. sɛtmil

1300. trɛzsɑ̃ *or* miltʀwɑsɑ̃, etc.	**8000.** ɥimil
2000. dø mil	**9000.** nœfmil
2100. dømil sɑ̃	**10.000.** dimil
2200. dømildøsɑ̃	**500.000.** sɛ̃sɑ̃mil
2300. dømiltʀwɑsɑ̃, etc.	**1.000.000.** œ̃miljõ

(2) When cardinal numbers are used purely as adjectives and are immediately followed by the nouns they modify,

(*a*) their final consonants are linked to a word beginning with a vowel:

1.	un enfant	œ̃nɑ̃fɑ̃
2.	deux enfants	døzɑ̃fɑ̃
3.	trois enfants	trwazɑ̃fɑ̃
5.	cinq enfants	sɛ̃kɑ̃fɑ̃
6.	six enfants	sizɑ̃fɑ̃
7.	sept enfants	sɛtɑ̃fɑ̃
8.	huit enfants	ɥitɑ̃fɑ̃
9.	neuf* enfants	nœfɑ̃fɑ̃
10.	dix enfants	dizɑ̃fɑ̃

(*b*) the final consonant of 2, 3, 5, 6, 8, 10, is silent before a word beginning with a consonant:

2.	deux francs	døfʀɑ̃
3.	trois francs	tʀwɑfʀɑ̃
5.	cinq francs	sɛ̃fʀɑ̃
6.	six francs	sifʀɑ̃
8.	huit francs	ɥifʀɑ̃
10.	dix francs	difʀɑ̃

(*c*) the pronunciation of the final consonant of 7 and 9 before a word beginning with a consonant is optional:

7.	sept francs	sɛtfʀɑ̃ *or* sɛfʀɑ̃
	dix-sept francs	dissɛtfʀɑ̃ *or* dissɛfʀɑ̃
9.	neuf francs	nœffʀɑ̃
	dix-neuf francs	diznœffʀɑ̃

---

* Note that in **neuf ans** and **neuf heures**, the f is pronounced **v.**

CONVERSATIONS

Unit I

rətur a paʀi.

də pasaʒ a paʀi apʀɛ zyn lõgapsãs, ʒã yg desid dale ʀvwaʀ sɛzami paʀizjẽ ʀɔʒe e maʀi dyplɛsi, mẽtnã maʀje e kidmœʀ dəpүi kɛlkə tã a sẽklu. il vjẽd fɛʀsiɲ acẽ ʃofœʀdətaksi. lə taksi saʀɛt.

lə ʃofœʀ. —[1]ualevu, məsjø?

ʒã. —[2]tʀɛz, avny dy palɛ a sẽklu. [3]sɛ pʀɛ dy põd sẽklu, a lãtʀed lɔtoʀut də lwɛst.

lə ʃofœʀ. —[4]ãtãdy. mõte silvuplɛ.

ʒã. —[5]vɔlõtje. ilja diminyt kə ʒatãz cẽtaksi. (ʒã mõt dãltaksi.)

lə ʃofœʀ. —[6]si sanvufɛʀjẽ, ʒəvɛ pʀãdʀ le ke. [7]sɛpətɛtʀcẽ pø ply lõ, mɛzõ pɛʀ mwẽdtã.

ʒã. —[8]kɔmã sa?

lə ʃofœʀ. —[9]lə lõde ke, tut le vwatyʀ võ dãlmɛm sãs. [10]sava boku plyvit.

ʒã. —[11]kõbjẽd tã fotil puʀale a sẽklu?

lə ʃofœʀ. —[12]ilfo ãviʀõ yn dəmiœʀ, tutoply.

ʒã (cẽpøplytaʀ). —[13]sɔmnudeʒa a sẽklu?

lə ʃofœʀ. —[14]nõməsjø. vuzɛt tuʒuʀ apaʀi. [15]õnsɛʒamɛ u paʀi kɔmãs e u ilfini.

Unit III

ʃe lɛ dyplɛsi.

ʀɔʒe aʀsy ʒã a bʀazuvɛr, e ʒã a ete tʀɛzøʀød ʀətruve sõnami. maløʀøzmã, mari etɛ sɔrti o mɔmãd laʀivedʒã. ãnatãdã sõʀtur, nodøzami paʀl dəskilzõfe okuʀ dɛdø dɛʀnjɛʀzane.

ʀɔʒe. —[1]vunave pamal vwajaʒe dəpүivɔtʀədepaʀ ilja døzã, nɛspa?

ʒã. [2]—ekɔmã! [3]kɔmvulsave, ãkitã paʀi, ʒə sүiʀtuʀne a filadɛlfi. [4]dəla ʒ(ə) sүizale a pitsbœʀg, u ʒe pɑse kɛlkəmwɑ dã lɛ labɔʀatwaʀ dyn kõpaɲid petʀɔl. [5]pүiõma ãvwaje o venezүela.

ʀɔʒe. —[6]vuzɛtzale osi dãl pʀɔʃɔʀjã, nɛspa?

ʒã. —[7]atãde! ʒne pɑzãkɔʀ finid paʀled mɛvwajaʒ . . . [8]dy venezүela ʒ(ə)sүi paʀti puʀ lə sudã. [9]ʒe kitel sudã puʀ leʒipt, leʒipt puʀ laʀabi saudit. [10]õmᾶvwa mε̃tnᾶ ozetazyni, paseœ̃kõ3ed tʀwɑ mwɑ kə 3nepɑ vɔle.

ʀɔ3e. —[11]kõpaʀe alavotʀ mavi a ete bjε̃ tʀᾶkil. [12]dəpʮinɔtʀə maʀja3, maʀi e mwa nu sɔm ʀεste bjε̃ sa3mᾶ alamεzõ, [13]sɔf bjε̃nᾶtᾶdy kεlkəpti vwaja3 dagʀemᾶ.

3ᾶ. —[14]3eʀsy lε̃vitasjõ a vɔtʀ maʀja3 kᾶ 3etε dᾶ la 3õgl venezʮeljεn. [15]3ne papyvniʀ asiste alaseremɔni. sεtεtʀɔ lwε̃.

ʀɔ3e. —[16]ᾶ tukɑ, ʀεste dine avεk nu səswaʀ. [17]maʀisʀa ᾶʃᾶted vuʀvwaʀ, e nuʀpaʀlʀõ dy bõvjətᾶ.

Unit V

kõvεʀsasjõ a tabl.

3ᾶ. —[1]maʀi, vɔtʀ dine etε delisjø. [2]3ənsavε padytu, iljadøzᾶ, kə vuzetje sibɔnkʮizinjεʀ.

maʀi. —[3]3apʀesi vivmᾶ vɔtʀə kõplimᾶ. [4]mε ditnuœ̃pø skəvuzavefε okuʀdsedødεʀnjεʀzane.

3ᾶ. —[5]lanedεʀnjεʀ asεtdat, 3etεzᾶne3ipt. [6]vusuvnevu dytεʀiblaksidᾶ kiayljø syʀ lə nil?

ʀɔ3c. —[7]3əmsuvjε̃dəkεlkəʃoz—[8]œ̃ bato ki tʀᾶspɔʀtε de pasa3e syʀ lə nil, nεspa?

3ᾶ. —[9]3etε dᾶlvwazina3 omɔmᾶd laksidᾶ. [10]lə lᾶdmε̃, 3e akõpaɲe œ̃dmεzami kivulε pʀᾶdʀ defɔto puʀœ̃ 3uʀnal.

ʀɔ3e. —[11]kεski εtaʀive, εgzaktəmᾶ?

3ᾶ. [12]setε œ̃tʀε vjøbato. [13]dəpʮi swasᾶtdizᾶ, il tʀᾶspɔʀtε de pasa3e syʀ lə nil. [14]iljavεdlaplas puʀ ynswasᾶtεn də pasa3e. [15]lə3uʀ də laksidᾶ, õnᾶna ᾶbaʀke plydsᾶsε̃kᾶt. [16]lə batovnεtapεn dəkite laʀiv, lɔrskə lo a kəmᾶse a ᾶtʀe a lε̃teʀjœʀ.

maʀi. —[17]purkwal kapitεn nεtilpɑ ʀtuʀne obɔʀ?

3ᾶ. —[18]ilaesεje. [19]lə bato etε akεlkəmεtʀ dybɔʀ kᾶ laksidᾶ a y ljø. [20]iletε mεm si pʀεdybɔʀ [21]kõnalᾶse dekɔʀd a de3ᾶ syʀlaʀiv dyflœv. [22]natyʀεlmᾶ, plyzil tiʀε syʀlekɔʀd, plylbato sε̃klinε. [23]ilafini paʀʃaviʀε. [24]ynsᾶtεndəpεʀsɔn səsõ nwaje. [25]la plypaʀ depasa3en savε pana3e.

maʀi. —[26]setᾶ veʀite yn bjε̃ tʀististwaʀ. [27]kᾶtilsõ mõte dᾶlbato, sε povrə3ᾶn savεpak lœr dεʀnjεʀœʀ etε pʀɔʃ.

ʀɔ3e. —[28]O! tεlεlavi! . . . [29]sinuzaljõ pʀadʀləkafe osalõ.

Unit VII

ləpti miʃɛl.

ʀɔʒe. —[1]ɛskəmiʃɛl ɛʀevɛje, maʀi? [2]vwala bjẽ døʒœʀ kil dɔʀ.

maʀi. —[3]ʒkʀwa lavwaʀ ãtãdy ʀəmɥe dãsõli tutalœʀ. [4]vulevulvwaʀ, ʒã?

ʒã. —[5]sɛʀtɛnmã. [6]ʒe sisuvã ãtãdy paʀledlɥi kəʒtjẽzapsɔlymã a fɛʀ sakɔnɛsãs.

(dãlaʃãbʀ dəmiʃɛl.)

maʀi. —[7]ʒvupʀezãt nɔtʀ ʒœnfis miʃɛl.

ʒã. —[8]kɛl ʒãtipti gaʀsõ! [9]ʀəgaʀde se gʀãzjø blø e sə ʒɔli suʀiʀ!

maʀi. —[10]ilɛ mẽtnãd bɔnymœʀ, sãdut paʀskil a dɔʀmi tulapʀemidi. [11]kãtil vjẽd səʀevɛje, ilɛkɛlkəfwa dətʀɛ mɔvɛzymœʀ.

ʒã. —[12]ʒepɛnaləkʀwaʀ . . . [13]kɛlaʒ atil, ɛgzaktəmã?

maʀi. —[14]ilɔʀa tʀɛzmwal pʀəmje sɛptãbʀ e ilpɛz õzkilo.

ʒã. —[15]ɛskil sɛmaʀʃe?

maʀi. —[16]vwajõ, ʒã, savjevu maʀʃe kãvuzavjeẽnã?

ʒã. —[17]fʀãʃmã, ʒənməʀapɛlpɑ . . . [18]dajœʀ, avɛkyntɛlmɛʀ, u plyto avɛk dətɛl paʀã, ʀjẽ nɛtẽpɔsibl.

maʀi. —[19]o vwala bjẽ nɔtʀ ʒã, kiadɔʀs mɔkedeʒã, [20]tutã lœʀ fəzã dekõplimã.

ʒã. —[21]maʀi, vum pʀɛte tutsɔʀt də mɔvɛz ẽtãsjõ. [22]malgʀetu, nusɔm lemejœʀzamidymõd, nɛspɑ?

Unit IX

o luvʀ.

ʀɔʒe. —[1]ʒvɛzoluvʀ sɛtapʀemidi. [2]ʒədvɛziale jɛʀ, meʒnepɑzyl tã. [3]vulevuvniʀ avɛkmwa?

ʒã. —[4]ʒvøbjẽ. [5]mɛpuʀkwa sɛtẽteʀesudẽ dãlapẽtyʀ elaskyltyʀ?

ʀɔʒe. —[6]elɑs, il nəsaʒi nidpẽtyʀ nid skyltyʀ. [7]ʒdwazale dãlebyʀo dynadministʀasjõ finãsjɛʀ mɔkype dynafɛʀ dẽpo puʀmõnyzin. [8]sebyʀo sõdãz yn dezɛl dy luvʀ.

ʒã. —[9]ɛskilvu fodʀa lõtã?

ʀɔʒe. —[10]ʒənsɛpɑzoʒyst. [11]ladɛʀnjɛʀfwak ʒisɥizale, ilnəmafalykəkɛlkə minyt. [12]mɛ, kɔmvulsave, ilfo kɛlkəfwa atɑ̃dʀ alapɔʀt dœ̃byʀo.

ʒɑ̃. —[13]kɛskəʒpuʀe bjɛ̃fɛʀ, pɑ̃dɑ̃k vudiskytezavɛk œ̃ fõksjɔnɛʀ lefinɑ̃s dəvɔtʀyzin?

ʀɔʒe. —[14]vupuve vizitel myze. [15]səsʀa ɛksɛlɑ̃ pur vɔtʀ kyltyʀaʀtistik.
[16]ʒvuʀtʀuvʀe akatʀœʀ dɑ̃lagʀɑ̃dgalʀi, opjed laʒɔkõd.

ʒɑ̃. —[17]opjed laʒɔkõd?

ʀɔʒe. —[18]sɛtynfasõd paʀle, bjɛnɑ̃tɑ̃dy. [19]vusaveskəʒvødiʀ.
(dɑ̃ lagʀɑ̃d galʀi, kɛlkəzœʀ plytaʀ)

ʒɑ̃. —[20]vuzɛtzœ̃pø ɑ̃ʀtaʀ. [21]vwala plydynœʀ kəʒvuzatɑ̃.

ʀɔʒe. —[22]ʒɔʀɛ dy aʀive plyto, sɑ̃dut. [23]mɛziljadeʃoz ki depɑ̃d dənu e dotʀ kin depɑ̃dpad nu.

ʒɑ̃. —[24]ɑ̃tukɑ, ʒnepapɛʀdy mõtɑ̃. [25]sə myze ɛvʀɛmɑ̃tetɔnɑ̃. [26]ilfodʀɛ deʒuʀnez ɑ̃tjɛʀ pur ləvizite. [27]vudʀievu vwaʀ kɛlkəsal?

ʀɔʒe. —[28]pazɔʒuʀdɥi. [29]õvafɛʀme dɑ̃ kɛlkəminyt. [30]ilvomjø ʀəvniʀ ynotʀəfwa.

UNIT XI

lə petʀɔl saaʀjɛ̃.

ʒɑ̃ ɛtale obyʀod la sɔsjete nasjɔnal deʀʃɛʀʃ dəpetʀɔlɑ̃nalʒeʀi vwaʀ bɛʀnaʀ ʒanɛ̃, dõtilafe la kɔnɛsɑ̃s okuʀd sõ seʒuʀapaʀi.

ʒɑ̃. —[1]ladɛʀnjɛʀ fwakəʒvuzevy, [2]vuzetje fɔʀtɑ̃tuzjast osyʒe dladeku- vɛʀt də petʀɔl dɑ̃l saaʀa. [3]u ɑ̃sõ mɛtnɑ̃ votʀavod pʀɔspɛksjõ?

bɛʀnaʀ. —[4]samaʀʃ õnpøpamjø. [5]lefɔʀaʒ səpuʀsɥiv dɑ̃ laʀeʒjõ dasi- mɛsaud. [6]la zon de ʒizmɑ̃ setɑ̃ syʀ plyd mil kilɔmɛtʀ kaʀe. [7]nu kõtõ kədɑ̃ kɛlkəzane disi, la pʀɔdyksjõ saaʀjen syfiʀʀa a no bəzwɛ̃.

ʒɑ̃. —[8]ʒe ɑ̃tɑ̃dydiʀ kœ̃ sɛʀtɛ̃ nõbʀ dəpɥi ete deʒa ɑ̃nɔpeʀasjõ a lœʀ- aktɥel.

bɛʀnaʀ. —[9]yn kɛ̃zen, si ʒən mətʀõp pɑ. [10]nuzɑ̃sɔmzɑ̃kɔʀ o kɔmɑ̃smɑ̃. [11]nu nuzɔkypõ aktɥelmɑ̃ dəletablismɑ̃ de piplin ed la kõstʀyksjõ dyn ʀut dy petʀɔl [12]ki ɔʀa sɛt sɑ̃ kilɔmɛtʀ də lõ e ki iʀa ʒyska la meditɛʀane. [13]sla fɛ paʀti dœ̃ vastə plɑ̃d devlɔpmɑ̃ agʀikɔl e ɛ̃dystʀiɛl də lalʒeʀi. [14]deʒa le pɔpylasjõ dypɛi sabij es nuʀis mjø kopaʀavɑ̃. [15]pø a pø, œʀɔpeɛ̃ e afʀikɛ̃ sabity a tʀavaje ɑ̃sɑ̃bl, vɛʀ œ̃by kɔmœ̃.

ʒɑ̃. —¹⁶vumavedik vu kɔnɛse laʀeʒjõ dasi-mɛsaud, nɛspɑ?

bɛʀnaʀ. —¹⁷œ̃pø. ¹⁸il nja dajœʀ pɑgʀɑ̃ʃoza kɔnɛtʀ. ¹⁹a paʀ lə petʀɔl, sɛl pɛizaʒ saaʀjẽ tɛl kõs limaʒin dɔʀdinɛʀ: ²⁰dysɑbl a pɛʀt dəvy, de dyn muvɑ̃t, avɛk sa e la kɛlkaʀbyst ki sefɔʀs də puse.

ʒɑ̃. —²¹elɑs! ʒənəl kɔnɛ kətʀɔ bjẽ, vusave, ²²lədezɛʀ avɛk se ʒuʀne bʀylɑ̃t ese nɥi pʀɛskə tʀɔ fʀɛʃ.

Unit XIII

ʃe lɑ̃tikɛʀ.

ʒɑ̃ pʀɔfit dəsõseʒuʀapaʀi puʀaʃtedekado dɛstine adepɛʀsɔn kilɥisõ̃ʃɛʀ ozetazyni. œ̃ʒuʀ, dɑ̃zynpətit ʀy vwazin də sẽʒɛʀmẽdepʀe, ilʀəmaʀk aladvɑ̃tyʀ dœ̃nɑ̃tikɛʀ œ̃seʀvis də tabl kilɥiplɛ. ilɑ̃tʀ, avɛk lẽtɑ̃sjõd laʃte puʀsasœʀ, silpʀi ɑ̃nɛʀezɔnabl.

lɑ̃tikɛʀ. —¹vudezire kɛlkəʃoz, məsjø?

ʒɑ̃. —²ʒmẽteʀɛs asəseʀvis ki ɛtaladvɑ̃tyʀ də vɔtʀ magazẽ. ³puʀjevu məlmõtʀe?

lɑ̃tikɛʀ. —⁴sɛʀtɛnmɑ̃, məsjø. ⁵ʒnɑ̃nemi kə kɛlkəzeʃɑ̃tijõ alavitʀin. ⁶lezotʀ pjɛs sõtisi dɑ̃splakaʀ. ⁷ʒve vulefɛʀwaʀ.

ʒɑ̃. —⁸kõbjẽ jɑ̃natil ɑ̃tu?

lɑ̃tikɛʀ. —⁹swasɑ̃tkẽz, məsjø. ¹⁰lə sɛʀvis ɛ kõplɛ. ¹¹ilnimɑ̃kpazynsœlpjɛs. ¹²avʀediʀ, lɔʀskəʒleaʃte, ynasjɛt mɑ̃kɛ. ¹³mɛ, paʀœ̃azaʀøʀø, ʒepym lapʀɔkyʀe ʃezœ̃nɑ̃tikɛʀ dəkõkaʀno.

ʒɑ̃. —¹⁴savevu dupʀɔvjẽ sə sɛʀvis?

lɑ̃tikɛʀ. —¹⁵ʒleaʃtemwamɛm, dɑ̃zynvɑ̃t ozɑ̃ʃɛʀ ɑ̃bʀətaɲ. ¹⁶ilfəze paʀti dy mɔbilje dœ̃ʃato, kõnavɑ̃dy apʀedese. ¹⁷sɛdlatʀebɛlfajɑ̃s dəkẽpɛʀ, məsjø. ¹⁸ʀəmaʀke lanɛtte dydesẽ e lekladekulœʀ. ¹⁹epɥi, pazœ̃defodɑ̃lafajɑ̃s. ²⁰opʀi ẽdike dəsisɑ̃sẽkɑ̃t fʀɑ̃, set ynɔkazjõ maɲifik.

ʒɑ̃. —²¹puvevu vuʃaʀʒed lɛkspedje ɑ̃nameʀik? ²²sɛtœ̃kado puʀmasœʀ.

lɑ̃tikɛʀ. —²³lɛsemwa sœlmɑ̃ sõnadʀɛs. ²⁴nunuʃaʀʒʀõ də tulʀɛst, ɑ̃balaʒ e fʀe dɑ̃vwa.

ʒɑ̃. —²⁵ɛl ləʀsəvʀa ɑ̃bɔneta nɛspɑ?

lɑtikɛʀ. —²⁶nəkʀeɲe ʀjẽ, məsjø. ²⁷nu lə lɥi ɑ̃veʀõ dɑ̃zœ̃bɔnɑ̃balaʒ enugaʀɑ̃tisõ tunozɑ̃vwa.

ʒɑ̃. —²⁸ɑ̃tɑ̃dy. ²⁹ɑ̃vwaje lə lɥi vɛʀ ləkẽz sɛptɑ̃bʀ. ³⁰ilnəm ʀɛst ply kavupɛje, nɛspɑ?

Unit XV

yn ʀɑ̃kõtʀ.

õ̃ʒuʀ kiltʀavɛʀs laplas dǝlɔpeʀa, ʒɑ̃ sǝtʀuv tutaku fasafas avɛk ɛlɛn fʌeⁱzɚ esamɛʀ, kivjɛn dɑ̃ lotʀǝsɑ̃s. seʀɑ̃kõtʀǝzinatɑ̃dy apaʀi u ajœʀ, ɑ̃tʀǝ pɛʀsɔn vǝnɑ̃d pɛizelwaɲe sõ dajœʀ mwɛ̃ ʀɑʀ kõ nǝl pɑ̃sʀɛ. ʒɑ̃. —¹madam fʌeⁱzɚ! ²ɛlɛn! ³kɛl syʀpʀiz! ⁴ʒiɲɔʀɛ kǝvuzetje isi! madam fʌeⁱzɚ. —ᵉe mwa ki vu kʀwajɛ tuʒuʀ ɑ̃naʀabi. ⁶ɑ̃ʀi sʀa sɛʀtɛnmɑ̃ øʀød vuʀvwaʀ. ʒɑ̃. —⁷ɛskɑ̃ʀi ɛtosi apaʀi? ɛlɛn. —⁸natyʀɛlmɑ̃. ⁹mɛ vukɔnese mõfʀɛʀ: ¹⁰kɑ̃ nulɥi avõdik nuziʀjõ fɛʀdezɑ̃plɛt sɛtapʀɛmidi, ¹¹iladeklaʀe kilɛmɛ mjø mõte ɑ̃ odla-tuʀefɛl. madam fʌeⁱzɚ. —¹²kõbjɛ̃dtɑ̃ kõtevu ʀɛste apaʀi, ʒɑ̃? ʒɑ̃. —¹³ʒǝ sre ɑ̃kɔʀisi yn vɛ̃tɛn dǝʒuʀ. ¹⁴ʒɛʀtǝny pasaʒ syʀõ̃navjõ kipaʀtiʀa puʀ nju jɔʀk dǝ samdi ɑ̃kɛz. madam fʌeⁱzɚ. —¹⁵nuziʀõ pasel wikɛnd ɑ̃tuʀɛn. ¹⁶iljɔʀa ynplaspuʀvu dɑ̃ nɔtʀ vwatyʀ, sivunave ʀjɛ̃dmjø afɛʀ. ¹⁷mɛ nǝvukʀwaje pazɔbliʒe daksɛpte lɛ̃vitasjõ. ¹⁸ʒǝmʀɑ̃kõt kǝ vunavesɑ̃dutpa bokudtɑ̃ avɔtʀ dispozisjõ. ʒɑ̃. —¹⁹mɛsi. ²⁰ɑ̃smɔmɑ̃, ʒǝsɥi libʀ kɔmlɛʀ, eʒǝsʀe ɑ̃ʃɑ̃ted vuzakõpaɲe. ²¹kɑ̃ avevu lɛ̃tɑ̃sjõd paʀtiʀ? madam fʌeⁱzɚ. —²²vwajõ . . . ²³ilnufodra apøpʀe katʀœʀ dǝ paʀi a ɔʀleɑ̃, ununuz aʀɛtʀõ puʀdeʒœne. ²⁴dizõ dõk kǝ nunumɛtʀõzɑ̃-ʀut vɛʀ ɥitœʀ dymatɛ̃ vɑ̃dʀǝdi pʀɔʃɛ. ²⁵ditnu uvuzɛt desɑ̃dy, e nuvjɛ̃dʀõ vu ʃɛʀʃe a sɛtœʀedmi. ʒɑ̃. —²⁶nǝvudeʀɑ̃ʒepa puʀmwa. ɛlɛn. —²⁷okõ̃ deʀɑ̃ʒmɑ̃. ²⁸dɔne sœlmɑ̃ vɔtʀadʀɛsa mamɑ̃. ʒɑ̃. —²⁹ʒǝsɥidesɑ̃dyalotɛl mœʀis. ³⁰nunuʀtʀuvʀõ asɛtœʀedmi, ³¹e ʒǝsʀetupʀe kɑ̃vuzaʀivʀe. ³²ɑ̃natɑ̃dɑ̃, dit bjɛ̃ de ʃoz dǝmapaʀ a ɑ̃ʀi, ³³kǝʒǝʀvɛʀe dajœʀ supø.

Unit XVII

a ʃǝnõso.

ʒɑ̃ e sɛzami paslaʒuʀne a ʃǝnõso. il vjɛn dǝ vizite lɛ̃teʀjœʀ dy ʃato, kõstʀɥi o sɛzjɛm sjɛkl, e ki ɛtõ̃ de mɔnymɑ̃ le plyzelegɑ̃d laʀǝnǝ-sɑ̃s fʀɑ̃sɛz. ɑ̃ sɔʀtɑ̃, ilzeʃɑ̃ʒlœʀz ɛ̃pʀɛsjõ.

ɛlɛn. —[1]ʒadɔʀ səʃato! [2]si ʒavɛ za ʃwaziʀ ɑ̃tʀ tusøk nuzavõvy, ʒə
ʃwaziʀɛ səlɥi si. [3]skim plɛ syʀtu, sɛ kil ɛt ɑ̃kɔʀabitabl.

ɑ̃ʀi. —[4]vudʀɛty iabite?

ɛlɛn. — [5]sladepɑ̃. [6]si ʒavɛtuskilfo, ʒəsʀɛ tʀɛzøʀøzisi. [7]bjẽ nɑ̃tɑ̃dy, il
fodʀɛtavwaʀ dənõbʀø sɛʀvitœʀ, kɥizinje, ʒaʀdinje, ɛtsɛteʀa,
ʀəsəvwaʀ kɑ̃tited ẽvite . . .

ʒɑ̃. —[8]kɔm ɑ̃ʀi dø e sakuʀ, paʀɛgzɑ̃pl . . . [9]ɑ̃nœ̃mo, ɛlɛn, vuvudʀie
məneœ̃ ʒɑ̃ʀ dəvi ki, ʒəlkʀẽ, nɛgzistə ply.

ɛlɛn. —[10]puʀtɑ̃, lə ʃato a ete abite ʒyska yn dat ʀɛsɑ̃t, nɛspɑ?

ʒɑ̃. —[11]mɛwi, paʀ le mənje, ki ɑ̃sõ tuʒuʀ pʀɔpʀieteʀ. [12]sɛ puʀ sla
kəl ʃatod ʃənõso ɛtɑ̃ mejœ̃ʀ eta kə səlɥid ʃɑ̃bɔʀ, [13]ki dəpɥi de
sjɛkl ʀɛstplyzumwẽvid.

ɑ̃ʀi. —[14]pɛʀsɔnɛlmɑ̃, ʒneʃɑ̃ʒʀɛ pɑ ʃɑ̃bɔʀ puʀ ʃənõso. [15]vy a distɑ̃s,
lafasad də ʃɑ̃bɔʀ ɛtinubliabl. [16]õskʀwaʀɛto pɛi de mɛʀvɛj.

madam f.ʀeⁱzᵊᵛ. —[17]vwajõ, mezɑ̃fɑ̃, il nə saʒi pɑ deʃɑ̃ʒe œ̃ ʃato puʀœ̃
notʀ. [18]nilœ̃ ni lotʀənə vuzapaʀtjẽ.

ɛlɛn. —[19]kɛlkəʃoz mẽtʀig: [20]puʀkwa atõ kõstʀɥi ynpaʀti dy ʃato o
miljø dyn ʀivjɛʀ?

ʒɑ̃. —[21]ʀjẽd plysɛpl: [22]katʀin dəmedisis* a deside kə si ɛlfəze kõstʀɥiʀ
sɛt galʀi a døzetaʒ odsyd la ʀivjɛʀ, [23]ɛl puʀɛ pɑsed lotʀəkote sɑ̃
sɔʀtird ʃezɛl.

ɛlɛn. —[24]tjẽ, sɛtynide! [25]ʒnɔʀɛ ʒamɛ pɑ̃se a sla!

UNIT XIX

o ʃatod blwa.

lə gid. —[1]nusɔm mẽtnɑ̃, mesjø dam, dɑ̃l kabinɛd katʀin də medisis.*
[2]ʀəmaʀke la dekɔʀasjõ ɑ̃bwaskylte. [3]səpanosi kaʃ plyzjœʀzaʀm-
waʀ səkʀɛt, u laʀɛn kõsɛʀve de papje, de biʒu, mɛm de pwazõ,
ditõ. [4]iljave plyddøsɑ̃pano e katʀsœlmɑ̃ dɑ̃tʀøetemɔbil. [5]søsiʀə-
sɑ̃blɛ tɛlmɑ̃ asøla kiletɛtẽpɔsiblədle distẽge, [6]mɛmɑ̃lezɛgzaminɑ̃-
dtʀɛpʀɛ.

(lə gid e le vizitœʀ kit lə kabinɛdlaʀɛn.)

ɑ̃ʀi. —[7]kɛskɛl ʃəze depwazõ kɛl kõsɛʀve dɑ̃sõnaʀmwaʀ?

ɛlɛn. —[8]sɛtɛ pøtɛtʀəpuʀ leʒɑ̃ kɛlnɛmɛpɑ!

madam f.ʀeⁱzᵊᵛ. —[9]nə dit pɑ tʀɔdmal də katʀin də medisis. [10]ʒe
ɑ̃tɑ̃dydir kɛl valɛ mjøk saʀepytasjõ . . .

ɛlɛn. —¹¹la plypaʀ de ʃatok nuzavõ vizite sõ vid. ¹²otʀəfwa, il
dəvetɛʀə mœble. ¹³kə sõ dəvny le mœbl?

ʒã. —¹⁴mɛmotʀəfwa, le ʃato navɛ pɑ bokud mœbl, ¹⁵sɔf sø ki sɛʀvɛd
ʀezidãs abityɛl a kɛlkəgʀã pɛʀsɔnaʒ. ¹⁶kɛlkəzœ̃dəsøk nuzavõvy—
¹⁷ʃabɔʀ e səlyisi paʀ ɛgzãpl—nõgɛ̃ʀ ete abite dəpyil sɛzjɛm sjɛkl.
¹⁸lemœbləkiʀɛste õ dispaʀy pãdã laʀevɔlysjõ.

ɛlɛn. —¹⁹ʒvudʀɛbjɛ̃ pʀãdʀynʃɔlɔd sevitʀ ɔʀned salamãdʀ.¹ ⁸⁰mɛ ʒe
ublie mõnapaʀej. ²¹vulevu bjɛ̃m pʀɛtel votʀ?

ʒã. —²²mɛ wi. ²³ləmjɛ̃n vo sãdut pɑlvotʀ. ²⁴mɛzilfʀa lafɛʀ.

ɛlɛn. —²⁵ʒənsɛpɑ kɔmã mã sɛʀviʀ.

ʒã. —²⁶ʀjɛ̃d ply sɛpl. ²⁷ilsyfid pʀɛse syrlbutõ.

* fam də ãridø, rwad fʀãs də kɛ̃z sã kaʀãtset a kɛ̃z sã sɛ̃kãtnœf.

† la salamãdʀ ete lãblɛm də fʀãswa pʀəmje ʀwadə kɛ̃z sã kɛ̃z a
kɛ̃z sã kaʀãt set el pɔʀkepiketɛ səlyidə lwi duz (katɔʀz sã katʀə vɛ̃
dizyit a kɛ̃z sã kɛ̃z).

UNIT XXI

syʀ la ʀut.

ãʀi (ki kõdyi). —¹vwala dezœʀ kil plø sãzaʀɛ. ²il fɔze bo kã nu
sɔm paʀti, ³il sɛ miza plœvwaʀ yn dəmiœʀ ply taʀ, ⁴e mɛtnã õ
vwatapɛn a tʀavɛʀ lə paʀbʀiz. ⁵ekute la plyi syʀ lə twad la
vwatyʀ.

ʒã (ʀesitã).
—⁶o bʀyi du də la plyi
paʀ tɛʀ e syʀ lɛ twa!
⁷pur œ̃ kœʀ ki sãnyi
o lə ʃã də la plyi!

⁸dã lɛspʀi dy pɔet, ⁹il saʒise dœ̃notʀəʒãʀ də twa, bjɛ̃nãtãdy.

ãʀi. —¹⁰nə dit pɑ de ʃoz kɔm sa sãm pʀevniʀ! ¹¹ʒe ete si syʀpʀi kə
ʒe faji kite la ʀut.

ɛlɛn. —¹²sɛt plyi nəm deplɛ pɑ dytu. ¹³ɛl mədon o kõtʀɛʀ œ̃ sãtimãd
kõfɔʀ, də bjɛ̃nɛtʀ.

ãʀi. —¹⁴ʒkʀɛ̃, ma ʃɛʀ sœʀ, kə tõ bjɛ̃nɛtʀ nə swad kuʀtə dyre. ¹⁵ʒe
lɛpʀɛsjõ kə nunu sɔm tʀõped ʀut.

ʒã.—¹⁶ʒapɛʀswa labɑ̃œ̃pɔto-ɛ̃dikatœʀ. ¹⁷lizeskildi.

ãʀi. —¹⁸ʒənpø ʀjɛ̃ vwaʀ a koz də la plyi.

ʒɑ̃. —¹⁹aʀɛtevu œ̃nɛ̃stɑ̃ e uvʀe la pɔʀtjɛʀ.

ɑ̃ʀi (lizɑ̃). —²⁰il di: ʒe-i-ə-ɛn swasɑ̃t sɛ̃ kilɔmɛtʀ.

ɛlɛn. —²¹kɔmɑ̃ pʀɔnõse vu ʒe-i-ə-ɛn?

ʒɑ̃. —²²ʒkʀwakə ʒjɛ̃ ʀimavɛk ʃjɛ̃.

ɛlɛn. —²³ʒənsɛ ʒamɛ kɔmɑ̃ õ pʀɔnõs le nõ pʀɔpʀ. ²⁴õnekʀi ɛʀ-ə-i-ɛm-ɛs e õ di: ʀɛ̃s, ²⁵ɛl-a-o-ɛn et õ di lɑ̃; ²⁶se-a-ə-ɛn e õ di kɑ̃; ²⁷lənõd la ʀivjɛʀ la son rim avɛk bon. ²⁸ʒnikõpʀɑ̃ ʀjɛ̃.

ɑ̃ʀi. —²⁹vʀɛmɑ̃, snɛpɑl mɔmɑ̃d ʃɛʀʃe a kõpʀɑ̃dʀ. ³⁰o ljød diskyte la pʀɔnõsjɑsjõ de nõ pʀɔpʀ, ³¹ty fʀɛ mjød mə diʀ kɛl ʀut ʒə dwa sɥivʀ.

ɛlɛn (pike). —³²ki sɛ? ³³pɑmwa. ³⁴ʒən kɔnɛ pɑ tʀɛbjɛ̃ la fʀɑ̃s.

ʒɑ̃. —³⁵si ʒəm pɛʀmɛd vu dɔne mõnavi, vu nave gɛʀ ləʃwa. ³⁶sɥive sɛlsi ʒysko pʀɔʃɛ̃ vilaʒ. ³⁷la, nu vɛʀo bjɛ̃ kɛl ʀut ilfo pʀɑ̃dʀ.

UNIT XXIII

le ʒɑ̃daʀm.

ɑ̃ʀi. —¹kɛskə sɛksa, la bɑ, o miljød la ʀut?

ʒɑ̃. —²vunvwaje pɑskəsɛ? ³ʀəgaʀde lœʀ pɛlʀin. ⁴sə sõ de ʒɑ̃daʀm.

ɑ̃ʀi. —⁵kɛskis pɑs?

ʒɑ̃. —⁶ʒnɑ̃ sɛ ʀjɛ̃. ⁷pətɛtʀ kœ̃ kʀim a ete kɔmi.

ɑ̃ʀi. —⁸kə fotil fɛʀ? fɛr dəmituʀ?

ʒɑ̃. —⁹a! mɛ̃tnɑ̃ ʒəsɛskəse. ¹⁰œ̃ kʀim a ete kɔmi, e sɛ vu kiɛt ləkʀiminɛl. ¹¹natyʀɛlmɑ̃, vuzɛseje deʃape a la pɔlis, ki vu puʀsɥi.

ɑ̃ʀi. —¹²skə vudit nɛ pɑz ɛgzakt. ¹³la pɔlis nəm puʀsɥi pɑ. ¹⁴ɛl matɑ̃.

ɛlɛn. —¹⁵swaje sɛʀjø e ralɑ̃tise. ¹⁶ʒən sɛpɑs kil vœl, ¹⁷mezilɛ sɛʀtɛ̃ kəsebʀav ʒɑ̃daʀm õ kɛlkə ʃoz a nu dir. ¹⁸vwajõ də kwa il saʒi.

(ɑ̃ʀi saʀɛt. le ʒɑ̃daʀm sapʀɔʃ.)

œ̃ de ʒɑ̃daʀm (a ɑ̃ʀi). —¹⁹vœje mə mõtʀe vo papje, məsjø.

ɑ̃ʀi. —²⁰lekɛl vulevu?

lə ʒɑ̃daʀm. —²¹vɔtʀ pɑspɔʀ, vɔtʀə pɛʀmid kõdɥiʀ e vɔtʀ pɔlis dasyʀɑ̃s. (apʀɛzavwaʀ ɛgzamine le papje) ²²tut ɛtɑ̃ʀɛgl. ²³vu puve kõtinɥe.

madam fʀɛⁱzɚ. —²⁴puʀkwa nədmɑ̃dəty pɑ(z)a məsjø le ʀɑ̃sɛɲmɑ̃ dõ ty a bəzwɛ̃?

ɑ̃ʀi. —²⁵tjɛ̃, sɛt yn ide! ²⁶a kwa ɛskəʒ pɑ̃se.

(o ʒɑ̃daʀm) ²⁷nu vulõzale a ɔʀleɑ̃. ²⁸lakɛl de dø ʀut ɛ la ply kuʀt,

²⁹sɛl syʀ lakɛl nu sɔm u sɛl ki pɑs paʀ ʀɔmɔʀɑ̃tɛ̃? ³⁰kɑ̃ pɑ̃se vu?
lə ʒɑ̃daʀm. —³¹il nja pɑ gʀɑ̃d difɛʀɑ̃s, məsjø. ³²si ʒetɛza vɔtrə plas,
ʒən ʃɑ̃ʒʀɛ pɑd ʀut.
ɑ̃ʀi. —³³mɛʀsi boku. (il sɑ̃ võ.)
ɛlɛn. —³⁴skim ʒɛn, sɛk nun sɔʀõ ʒamɛ puʀkwa se ʒɑ̃daʀm nuzõtaʀɛte.
ɑ̃ʀi. —³⁵kɛskə sa fɛ? ³⁶il nuzõʀmi ɑ̃ libɛʀte, e sɛ tus ki ɛ̃pɔʀt.

Unit XXV

lə kyltivatœʀ.

le fʀeⁱzɚ sə sõtaʀɛte dɑ̃zœ̃ vilaʒ də la bos puʀ ɑ̃vwaje yn depɛʃ.
a la pɔst, ʒɑ̃ paʀl a œ̃ kyltivatœʀ də lɑ̃dʀwa.
ʒɑ̃. —¹vwala œ̃ bjɛ̃ vilɛ̃ tɑ̃ puʀ le ʀekɔlt.
lə kyltivatœʀ. —²a, məsjø, il vo mjøn pɑzɑ̃paʀle. ³il jadkwa dezɛspeʀe.
⁴lane dɛʀnjɛʀ, setɛ la sɛʃʀɛs, e sɛt ane sɛ la plɥi. ⁵lezavwan
sõtɑ̃tʀɛ̃d ʒɛʀme dɑ̃ le ʃɑ̃. ⁶sɛ la fɛ̃ dətu.
ʒɑ̃. —⁷ʒənkʀwapɑ kil faj dezɛspeʀe. ⁸lə tɑ̃ finiʀa paʀ saʀɑ̃ʒe.
lə kyltivatœʀ. —⁹ʒəm di sa tuleʒuʀ. ¹⁰ʒəswɛt kə la plɥi saʀɛt e kil
fas bo, ¹¹mɛ ʒe pœʀ kə me swɛn sɛʀv pɑzagʀɑ̃ʃoz . . . ¹²si o
mwɛ̃ no pʀɔdɥis vɑ̃dɛ bjɛ̃! ¹³mɛ bjɛ̃ kə nu swajõ ɔbliʒed depɑ̃se
ply kotʀəfwa, ¹⁴lakyltyʀ ʀapɔʀt də mwɛ̃zɑ̃mwɛ̃.
ʒɑ̃. —¹⁵ʒkʀwajɛ kəlguvɛʀnəmɑ̃ fikse lepʀi.
lə kyltivatœʀ. —¹⁶wi, mɛza mwɛ̃ kil etablis de pʀi plyzelve puʀ le
pʀɔdɥizagʀikɔl, ¹⁷le kyltivatœʀ naʀivʀõ bjɛ̃to ply a ʒwɛ̃dʀə le dø
bu. ¹⁸il fo kə nu pɛjõ ply ʃɛʀ tuskə nuzaʃtõ, ¹⁹le səmɑ̃s, le zɑ̃gʀɛ,
sɑ̃ kõte le maʃin.
ʒɑ̃. —²⁰ilmə sɑ̃bl ɑ̃nefɛ kõvwa dɑ̃ leʃɑ̃ bjɛ̃ plyd maʃin kotʀəfwa.
lə kyltivatœʀ. —²¹il ja vɛtɑ̃, məsjø, õ vwajɛ paʀtu deʃvo. ²²mɛ̃tnɑ̃, a
mwɛ̃k vu nalje dɑ̃ de kwɛ̃ pɛʀdy, vun vɛʀe plyd ʃəvo: ²³ʀjɛ̃ kə
de tʀaktœʀ, de mwasɔnøz-batøz, e tut sɔʀt də maʃin. ²⁴isi, il nja
pɑs œ̃ sœl kyltivatœʀ ki nɛ sõ tʀaktœʀ. ²⁵il sufi kə lœ̃ dø ɑ̃ nɛ tœ̃
puʀkə sõ vwazɛ̃ vœj osi avwaʀ lə sjɛ̃. ²⁶vulevu kəʒvu diz skə ʒɑ̃
pɑ̃s? ²⁷lə guvɛʀnəmɑ̃ ɛtɑ̃tʀɛ̃d ʀɥinel kyltivatœʀ.
ʒɑ̃. —²⁸dɑ̃ mõ pɛi, nuzavõ œ̃ pø le mɛm pʀɔblɛm. ²⁹la sitɥasjõ də
lagʀikyltyʀ ʀɛstʀa difisil ʒyskas kõ leze ʀezɔly. ³⁰me ʒɛspɛʀ bjɛ̃
kõnaʀivʀa œ̃ ʒuʀ a le ʀezudʀ.

Unit XXVII

lɛtʀ.

la fɛ̃ dy seʒuʀ də ʒɑ̃ ɑ̃ fʀɑ̃s apʀɔʃ. lə lɑ̃dmɛ̃ də sõʀtuʀ a paʀi, apʀɛ sõnɛkskyʀsjõ avɛk le fʁeⁱzᵊ dɑ̃ la ʀeʒjõd la lwaʀ, il sɔkyp də sakɔʀɛspõdɑ̃s. vwasi skil ekʀit a madam fʁeⁱzᵊ :

> ɔtɛl mœʀis
> paʀi, lə vɛ̃t katʀ u

ʃɛʀ madam:

avɑ̃dkite paʀi, ʒə tjɛ̃za vu ʀmɛʀsje ɑ̃kɔʀ də vɔtʀ ɛmabl ɛ̃vitasjõ a vuzakõpaɲe ɑ̃ tuʀɛn. ʒete deʒa ale dɑ̃ sɛt ʒɔli ʀeʒjõ, mɛʒən lavɛ ʒamɛ paʀkuʀy ɑ̃ si agʀeabl kõpaɲi. ʒə ʀgʀɛt œ̃ pø, kɔm vu, kəl ʒaʀdɛ̃d la fʀɑ̃s ɛtete si kɔpjøzmɑ̃taʀoze o kuʀ də nɔtʀəvwajaʒ. mɛ la plɥi fɛ puse le flœʀ eʒ(ə)nubliʀe ʒamɛ le flœʀ, syʀtu lezenɔʀm dalja, ki sɑ̃bl puse paʀtu ɑ̃ tuʀɛn.

dapʀɛs kə ma di ɑ̃ʀi, vuzave lɛ̃tɑ̃sjõd ʀɑ̃tre ozetazyni alafɛ̃dy mwɑ pʀɔʃɛ̃. nu nu ʀəveʀõdõk supø, ski sʀa puʀ mwa œ̃ gʀɑ̃ plɛziʀ.

disi la, ʃɛʀ madam, ʒə vupʀid fɛʀ mɛzamitje a ɛlɛn e a ɑ̃ʀi e dagʀee mɛzɔmaʒ ʀɛspɛktɥø.

> ʒɑ̃

ilɑ̃vwa osi œ̃ mo a lɑ̃tikɛʀ puʀ fɛʀ ɛkspedje lə sɛʀvis də tablə dɛstine a sa sœʀ.

məsjø,

vu tʀuvʀe si ɛ̃kly œ̃ mɑ̃da-pɔst də sɑ̃ swasɑ̃tsɛ̃ fʀɑ̃ ɑ̃ pɛmɑ̃ dy ʀəlika dy syʀ vɔtʀə faktyʀ nymeʀo dəmil døsɑ̃ vɛ̃t sis, date dy diz nœf kuʀɑ̃.

ʒkʀwa vuzavwaʀ di, o mɔmɑ̃d laʃa, dɑ̃vwajel sɛʀvis də tabl də faʃõ askil aʀiv a ladʀɛs ɛ̃dike vɛʀ lə miljø dy mwɑd sɛptɑ̃bʀ. tutfwa, kɔm ʒə nɔʀe pazɑ̃kɔʀ atɛ̃ sɑ̃fʀɑ̃sisko a sɛt epɔk, ʒə deziʀ mɛtnɑ̃ kə lɑ̃vwa aʀiv a sa dɛstinasjõ yn kɛ̃zɛn dəʒuʀ plytaʀ. ʒvu pʀi dõk də fikse la dat dɛkspedisjõ ki kõvjɛ̃ ləmjø, ɑ̃ tənɑ̃ kõt de delɛ ɛ̃poze paʀ lə tʀɑ̃spɔʀ e paʀ le fɔʀmalite də dwan.

vœejezagʀee, məsjø, me salytɑsjõzɑ̃pʀɛse.

> ʒɑ̃ yg

ɑ̃fɛ̃, pɑ̃dɑ̃ sɔ̃napsɑ̃s də paʀi, ʒɑ̃ aʀsy də madam lysjɛ̃ feʀi yn ɛ̃vitasjɔ̃ a dine, kil ɛtɔbliʒedə dekline puʀ la ʀɛzɔ̃ kil ɛ̃dik: ʃɛʀ madam:

ʀjɛ̃ nə mɔʀɛ dɔne plyd plɛziʀ kə daksɛpte vɔtʀɛmabl ɛ̃vitɑsjɔ̃ adine maʀdi pʀɔʃɛ̃. maløʀøzmɑ̃, ʒɑ̃n səʀe plyzapaʀi a sɛt dat. ʒɔʀe kite lafʀɑs la vɛj, e ʒəsʀe sɑ̃dut deʒa aʀive a filadɛlfi.

ʒə ʀgʀɛt vivmɑ̃dən pɑ puvwaʀ ɛtʀə de votʀ. ʒɔʀɛzete øʀø də maʀtʀuve ʃe vu avɛk dezami kɔmɑ̃, o suvniʀ də ki ʒə vu pʀid mə ʀaple.

ʒə vu pʀi, ʃɛʀ madam, dagʀee me ʀɛspɛktɥø zɔmaʒ.

ʒɑ̃ yg

PROMPT SCRIPT — UNIT XXVII

Letters

The end of John's stay in France is drawing near. The day after his return to Paris, after his trip with the Frazers to the Loire region, he is taking care of his correspondence. This is what he writes to Mrs. Frazer.

Hôtel Meurice
Paris
August 24

Dear Mrs. Frazer:

Before leaving Paris, I *must* thank you again for your kind invitation to go with you to Touraine. I had already been to that lovely part of the country, but I had never traveled through it in such pleasant company. I am a little sorry, as you are, that the "Garden of France" was so copiously sprinkled during our trip. But rain makes flowers grow, and I'll never forget the flowers, especially the huge dahlias, that seem to grow everywhere in Touraine.

According to what Henry told me, you are planning to go back to the United States at the end of next month. So we will meet again soon, and that will be a great pleasure for me.

In the meantime, please say hello to Helen and Henry for me.

Sincerely yours,
John

He also sends a short letter to the antique shop dealer to take care of shipping the set of china for his sister.

Dear Sir:

You will find herewith a money order for 165 francs in payment of the balance due on your bill No. 2,226, dated the 19th of this month.

I think I told you when I bought the set of china to ship it so it would arrive at the address I gave you towards the middle of September. However, as I will not (yet) have reached San Francisco at that time, I now want the shipment to reach its destination about two weeks later. So will you please choose the most suitable shipping date, bearing in mind the time required for transportation and getting it through customs.

Sincerely yours,

John Hughes

Lastly, during his absence from Paris, John got a dinner invitation from Mrs. Lucien Ferry which he has to decline for the reason he gives.

Dear Mrs. Ferry:

Nothing would have given me more pleasure than to accept your kind invitation to dinner next Tuesday. Unfortunately I will no longer be in Paris on that date. I will have left France the day before and I will no doubt have arrived in Philadelphia.

I am very sorry indeed that I can't be among your guests. I would have been happy to be at your house again with mutual friends. Will you please remember me to them?

Sincerely yours,

John Hughes

Unit XXIX

de nuvɛl də ʒɑ̃.

katrə mwɑ aprɛkə ʒɑ̃ y kite la fʀɑ̃s, le dyplɛsi ʀəsyʀ də lɥi la lɛtʀ sɥivɑ̃t.

de ʀiv də lapyʀ, lə vɛ̃tsɛk nɔvɑ̃bʀ.

me ʃɛʀzami:

lɔʀskəʒ kitɛ la fʀɑ̃s ɑ̃ sɛptɑ̃bʀə dɛʀnje, ʒmatɑ̃dɛza vu ʀvwaʀ a la fɛ̃d mõ kõʒe. lə sɔʀ mə fy bjɛ̃ kʀyɛl, ki mɑ̃vwaja syʀ le ʀivz inɔspitaljɛʀ də lapyʀ. mɛ vun save pɑskə sɛ kə lapyʀ, e plyto sjɛl kə mwamɛm ʒnɑ̃nys ʒamez ɑ̃tɑ̃dy paʀle! lapyʀ ɛtyn ʀivjɛʀ dy venezɥela, œ̃naflyɑ̃ də lɔʀenɔk. bʀɛf, ʒsɥizyn fwad ply dɑ̃ la ʒõgl, a œ̃nɑ̃dʀwa ki nɛ gɛʀ aksɛsiblə kə paʀ elikɔptɛʀ.

snɛpɑ, kwakə vu pɥisje kʀwaʀ, œ̃ ljø də depɔʀtasjõ puʀ lezɛ̃desiʀabl, bjɛ̃ kil jɑ̃nɛ kɛlkəzœ̃—vu vuzɑ̃ ʀɑ̃dʀe kõt tutalœʀ. ʒədiʀiʒ œ̃ kɑ̃ də pʀɔspɛktœʀ dɑ̃ de ʀeʒõ pʀɛskinɛksplɔʀe dy venezɥela ed la kɔlõbi. tu le matɛ̃, mezɔm sə ʀɑ̃d paʀ elikɔptɛʀ ɑ̃ divɛʀzɑ̃dʀwa, u il fõtɛksploze de ʃaʀʒ də dinamit, də fasõ a detɛʀmine la kõfigyʀasjõ dy sɔl. ski aʀiva jɛʀ a yn də noz ekip vu dɔnʀa yn ided la vi kə nu mənõz isi.

puʀtɑ̃, la ʒuʀne kɔmɑsa kɔm dabityd. lelikɔptɛʀ vɛ̃ ʃɛʀʃe no tʀwazɔm lə matɛ̃, e il ledepoza dɑ̃zyn klɛʀjɛʀ o miljødla ʒõgl. la il səmiʀto tʀavaj. tutala bjɛ̃ ʒyska midi. as mɔmɑ̃ dezɛ̃djɛ̃ aʀivɛʀ, e mənasɑ̃ lezɛ̃tʀy dezaʀm le plyzeteʀɔklit, il sɑ̃paʀɛʀ də tu skil pɔsedɛ, aʀʒɑ̃, mõtʀ, uti, e le depujɛʀ də lœʀ vɛtmɑ̃. kɑ̃ lelikɔptɛʀ ʀəvɛ̃ le ʃɛʀʃe lə swaʀ, lə pilɔt tʀuva no tʀwaz ɔm ki latɑ̃dɛtavɛk yn ɛ̃pasjɑ̃s fasila kõpʀɑ̃dʀ. sə dutʀetõ ʒamɛ kyn tɛl avɑ̃tyʀ pytaʀived no ʒuʀ a dɔnɛt pʀɔspɛktœʀ?

ʒɔn sɛ pɑ kõbjɛ̃d tɑ̃ ʒə ʀɛstʀe isi. ʒɔm di paʀfwa kə vuzɛt boku ply saʒ kəmwa. vuʀaple vu, ʀɔʒe, skə vum dizje œ̃ ʒuʀ: «ma vi a ete bjɛ̃ tʀɑ̃kil kõpaʀe a la votʀ»? syʀtu nə fɛt pɑ dypti miʃɛl œ̃nɛ̃ʒenjœʀ, u tutomwɛ̃, kil lɛs lə petʀɔl tʀɑ̃kil! e puʀtɑ̃ . . .

ʒɛspɛʀ malgʀe tu vuʀvwaʀ œ̃dseʒuʀ. ãnatãdã, me ʃɛʀzami, pɥiskə
ma lɛtʀ vuzaʀivʀa sã dut vɛʀ lə nuvɛl ã, ʒvu swɛt a tu le tʀwɑ yn
bɔnane e tut sɔʀt də pʀɔspeʀite.

bjɛ̃ kɔʀdjalmã,

ʒã

PROMPT SCRIPT — UNIT XXIX

News from John.

Four months after John had left France, the Duplessis received the
following letter from him:

From the banks of the Apure,
November 25

Dear Friends:

When I left France last September, I expected to see you again at
the end of my vacation. Fate, which sent me to the inhospitable banks
of the Apure, was very cruel. But you do not know what the Apure is,
and I wish to heaven (might it be pleasing to heaven) that *I* had never
heard of it! The Apure is a river of Venezuela, a tributary of the
Orinoco. In a word, I am once more in the jungle, in a place that is
scarcely accessible except by helicopter.

Whatever you might think, it is not a place for deportation of
undesirables, although there are a few of them — you shall see in a
moment. I am in charge of a camp of prospectors in some almost
unexplored regions of Venezuela and Colombia. Every morning, my
men go by helicopter to various places where they explode charges of
dynamite so as to determine the configuration of the ground (lay of
the land). What happened yesterday to one of our crews will give
you an idea of the life that we lead here.

And yet, the day began as usual. The helicopter came to pick up
our three men in the morning and it put them down in a clearing in
the midst of the jungle. There, they started to work. All went well
until noon. At that moment some Indians arrived, and, threatening
the intruders with the most unusual weapons, they seized everything
they had: money, watches, tools, and they stripped them of their

clothes. When the helicopter came back for them in the evening, the pilot found our three men waiting for him with easily comprehensible impatience. Would one ever suspect that such an adventure could happen these days to honest prospectors?

I don't know how long I'll stay here. I sometimes tell myself that you are much wiser than I am. Do you remember, Roger, what you were telling me one day: "My life has been very calm compared to yours?" Above all, don't make an engineer of little Michel, or, at least, let him leave oil alone! And yet . . .

I hope to see you again one of these days in spite of everything. Meanwhile, since my letter will reach you probably around New Years, I wish all three of you a happy New Year and all sorts of prosperity.

Sincerely yours,
John

Syllabication

111. Division of words into syllables.

In dividing French words into syllables, in so far as possible each syllable should begin with a consonant and end in a vowel.

(1) When a single consonant stands between two vowels, the consonant goes with the vowel which follows it: bu-reau, ta-bac. hô-tel, ga-re, vou-lez.

(2) When a double consonant (**tt, dd, pp,** etc.) stands between two vowels:

(*a*) in most cases it represents a single sound and stands in the following syllable: do**nn**ez [dɔne], a**ll**ez [ale], exce**ll**ent [ɛkselɑ̃], a**dd**ition [adisjõ];

(*b*) in some cases it represents two consonants, one of which is pronounced with the previous vowel and one with the following one: a**cc**ident [aksidɑ̃], su**gg**érer [sygʒeʀe].

(3) When two or more different consonants stand between vowels:

(*a*) one consonant may go with the vowel which precedes and one with the one which follows: mer-ci, par-lez, res-taurant, ob-ser-vatoire;

(*b*) two consonants may form a consonant cluster* and stand together at the beginning of the following syllable: ta-ble, li-bre, a-près, qua-tre;

(*c*) one consonant may go with the preceding vowel and a consonant cluster* may stand together at the beginning of the next syllable: en-ten-dre, or-ches-tre, mal-gré, em-ploi.

The digraphs **ch, ph, th, gn** (each of which of course represents a single sound) always stand with the vowel which follows.

---

*The following are the consonant clusters which occur commonly: **bl, cl, fl, gl, pl; br, cr, dr, gr, pr, tr, vr.**

It is very important to know how French words are divided into syllables, because certain letters are pronounced one way when they are final in a syllable and in a different way when they are followed in the syllable by a pronounced consonant or by a vowel. For example: in the word **un,** the vowel **u** is followed in the same syllable by the letter **n** and is therefore nasalized, i.e. the word is pronounced [œ̃]; in the word **u-ne,** the vowel **u** is final in the syllable and is not nasalized, i.e. the word is pronounced [yn]. Likewise, **faim** is pronounced [fɛ̃], but **j'ai-me** is pronounced [ʒɛm]. **In-telligent** is pronounced [ɛ̃tɛliʒɑ̃], but **i-nutile** is pronounced [inytil].

Linking

112. Principles of linking.

You have learned to say "les hôtels," "les Américains," and so on — giving the "s" the sound [z]. When a final consonant which is normally silent is pronounced with the initial vowel of the following word, it is said to be linked. **La liaison** means binding together. When linking takes place, two words are bound together: you say [lezotɛl] as if it were one word rather than [le zotɛl] as if it were two. A consonant that is linked should always be pronounced lightly.*

Linking takes place only between words that are closely related syntactically and which naturally fall into rhythmic groups (such as a noun and its modifiers).

EXERCISES

1. With Linking.

Repeat the following, making the linking properly (without exaggeration):

(1) BETWEEN A NOUN AND ITS MODIFIERS: (*a*) *Article and noun:* Les enfants. Les hôtels. Les églises. Les heures. Les Américains. Les étudiants. Les Anglais. (*b*) *Adjective and noun:* Un bon hôtel. Les bons hôtels. Les petits enfants. Trois heures. Six heures. Neuf heures [nœvœʀ]. Les États-Unis. Les Champs-Élysées. (*c*) *Article and adjective:* Les autres restaurants.

(2) BETWEEN PERSONAL PRONOUN AND VERB: (*a*) *Normal order:* Nous avons. Vous avez. Ils ont. Vous êtes. Vous allez. Ils entrent. Ils arrivent. Ils habitent. (*b*) INVERTED ORDER: Est-il? Sont-ils? Ont-ils? (*c*) Note that the tendency to bind verb

---

* Some authorities say that in linking the letter is "carried over" to the next word; but we avoid this term because it suggests to English speaking students that the letter should be given the importance of an initial consonant.

forms together is so strong that if the third person singular of a verb does not end in a "t", a "t" is inserted between the verb and inverted pronoun anyway: A-t-il? Parle-t-il? Étudie-t-il?

(*3*) BETWEEN THE WORD **pas** AND AN ADVERB OR ADJECTIVE: Pas‿encore. Pas‿ici. Pas‿Américain.

2. Without Linking.

Repeat the following WITHOUT linking and note that linking DOES NOT take place:

(*1*) Between a noun subject and verb: John appelle un taxi. Le train arrive. Les trains arrivent. Les Anglais aiment les sports.

(*2*) Before words beginning with an aspirate "h": des hors-d'œuvre.

(*3*) After the word **et**: Roger et elle. Vingt‿et un. (The "t" of **et** is NEVER pronounced under any circumstances.)

3. Optional Linking.

In some cases, linking is optional. When in doubt, you can always consult the phonetic transcriptions of the Conversations. When linking is optional, the present trend in France is not to link.

Elision

113. WHEN ELISION TAKES PLACE.

When a vowel is dropped out before a word beginning with a vowel or mute **h,** *elision* (élision) is said to take place. Elision is possible only in the following words: The **e** in: **je, me, te, se, ce, de, le, ne, que;** the **a** in **la;** and the **i** in the word **si** when it is followed by **il, ils.**

Elision is incorrect before a word beginning with an aspirate **h** or before the word **onze:** le/huit octobre, le/onze mars.

Diacritical Signs

114. THE DIFFERENT DIACRITICAL SIGNS.

The following typographical signs are used (*a*) to distinguish between two or more possible pronunciations of a letter, or (*b*) to distinguish between two words which are pronounced alike, and, except for the diacritical marks, are spelled alike. *In no case do these signs indicate that a syllable should be stressed.*

(1) The acute accent (′) (accent aigu) is used only on the vowel **e**: l'été, espérer. The **é** is practically always pronounced [e].

(2) The grave accent (`) (accent grave) is used mostly on **e** followed by a final **s** or **-re**: très, près, après-midi; père, frère, j'espère, ils allèrent. The **è** is always pronounced [ɛ].

This accent is also used on the **a** in the preposition **à,** *to,* to distinguish it from the third person singular of the present indicative of **avoir.** Likewise it is used on the **a** of the adverb **là,** *there,* to distinguish it from the article **la,** *the,* as well as on the **u** of the adverb **où,** *where,* to distinguish it from the conjunction **ou,** *or.*

(3) The circumflex accent (^) (accent circonflexe) is found on all the vowels except **y**: âme, même, île, hôtel, sûr. An **â** is usually pronounced [ɑ], **ê** [ɛ], **î** [i], **ô** [o], **û** [y].

(4) The cedilla (¸) (cédille) under **c** indicates that the letter is pronounced [s].

(5) When a diaeresis (¨) (tréma) is placed over the second of two vowels, it indicates that the vowel so marked begins a new syllable. **Noël, naïf.** Note, however, that the name **Saint-Saëns** is pronounced [sɛ̃ sɑ̃s].

Relation between spelling and pronunciation

115. Consonants.

LETTER	PRONUNCIATION	
b	[b]	in practically all cases: une banane, le bébé.
	[p]	when followed by **t** or **s**: absurde, absent, absolument, obtenir.
		Silent when final: les soldats de plomb.
c	[k]	when followed by **a, o, u,** or **l, r**: le café, le corps, la curiosité, je crois.
	[s]	when followed by **e, i, y**: c'est, certainement, ici, la bicyclette.
	[k]	usually when final: avec, le sac.
		Silent in: le tabac, franc, blanc, le porc.
	[g]	in second, secondaire, anecdote.
ç	[s]	Used only before **a, o, u**: le français, le garçon, j'ai reçu.
cc	[k]	except when followed by **e, i, y**: accorder.
	[ks]	when followed by **e, i, y**: accepter, accident.
ch	[ʃ]	usually: chercher, le chimiste, chez, Charles.
	[k]	sometimes: un orchestre, le chœur.
d	[d]	in practically all cases: dans, l'addition, madame, le sud.
		Usually silent when final: le pied, le nid, le hasard, le nord.
	[t]	in: tout de suite, le médecin, quand il ...
f	[f]	in practically all cases: franc, le café.
	[f]	usually when final: le chef, neuf, le rosbif, un œuf.
		Silent in: les œufs, les bœufs, la clef.
	[v]	in: neuf heures, neuf ans.
g	[g]	when followed by **a, o, u,** or **l, r**: la gare, grand.
	[ʒ]	when followed by **e, i, y**: gentil, les gens, la girafe, le gymnase.

LETTER	PRONUNCIATION	
gg	[gʒ]	when followed by **e, i, y**: suggérer.
gn	[ɲ]	la campagne, la Bretagne, la vigne.
gu	[g]	in: la guerre, le guide.
	[gɥ]	in: aiguille.
	[gy]	in: aigu.
h		Always silent: l'homme, l'hôtel, les hors-d'œuvre.
j	[ʒ]	janvier, je déjeune.
k	[k]	le kilo.
l	[l]	usually pronounced even when final: l'hôtel, le cheval.
		Silent in: gentil, le fusil, le fils, le pouls.
	[j]	when preceded by **ai** or **ei**: le travail, le soleil, vieil, etc.
ll	[j]	when preceded by **ai, ei, ui**: travailler, vieille.
	[j]	usually when preceded by **i**: la fille, gentille, juillet, la famille.
	[l]	in: ville, village, mille, tranquille, illustrer, etc.
m	[m]	at the beginning of a syllable: aimer, madame, calme. When final in a syllable, **m** causes the preceding vowel to be nasalized but is not otherwise pronounced: faim [fɛ̃], chambre [ʃɑ̃bʀ], ensemble [ɑ̃sɑ̃bl], important [ɛ̃pɔʀtɑ̃].
mm	[m]	l'homme, comme, comment.
n	[n]	at the beginning of a syllable; nous, une, inutile. When final in a syllable or when followed by a consonant, **n** nasalizes a preceding vowel but is not otherwise pronounced: bon [bõ], vingt [vɛ̃], enfant [ɑ̃fɑ̃], intelligent [ɛ̃tɛliʒɑ̃], la France [lafʀɑ̃s]. Silent in **-ent** verb endings.
nn	[n]	bonne, sonner, donnez, l'année.
p	[p]	in practically all cases: le papier, le départ, l'aptitude, le pneu, la psychologie, le psaume. Usually silent when final: trop, beaucoup. Silent in: le temps, compter, la sculpture, etc.

LETTER	PRONUNCIATION	
q, qu	[k]	in practically all cases: qui, que, quel, le coq.
qu	[kw]	in: une aquarelle, un aquarium.
r	[ʀ]	in practically all cases: la rue, très, l'art, vers.
		Pronounced when final in: le fer, la mer, fier, cher, car, pour, l'hiver, etc.
		Silent in infinitive ending **-er,** and in: boucher, boulanger, charcutier, épicier, monsieur, léger, premier, volontiers, etc.
s	[s]	at beginning of a word or when preceded or followed by a consonant: absent, sang, aspect, etc.
	[z]	when between vowels: la raison, la maison, les roses.
	[z]	when linked: vous‿avez.
		Usually silent when final: les, tables, lesquels.
	[s]	in: le fils, mars, le sens, tous (*pronoun*), omnibus, autobus, Reims, Saint-Saëns, etc.
sc	[sk]	when followed by **a, o, u,** or **l, r:** la sculpture, scolaire.
	[s]	when followed by **e, i, y:** la science, le scénario.
ss	[s]	assez, aussi, essayer.
t	[t]	at beginning of a syllable: le temps, l'été, l'amitié.
		Silent when final in verb forms (except in linking) and in most nouns and adjectives: le lit, le restaurant, élégant, différent, cent, vingt, excellent, tout, etc.
	[t]	in: l'est, l'ouest, net, dot, Brest, tact, intact, exact.
th	[t]	le thé, le théâtre.
ti	[s]	in **-tion** ending, and in: démocratie, initial, patience, etc.
v	[v]	in all cases: voulez-vous? avez-vous?
w	[v]	in: le wagon, Waterloo.
	[w]	in: le tramway, le sandwich.
x	[ks]	in: excellent, le luxe, l'index.
	[gz]	in: exact, exemple, examen.
	[s]	in: soixante; and in dix, six when final in a phrase.

LETTER   PRONUNCIATION

[z]   in: dix, six when linked: dix‿enfants.
        Silent in: dix, six, when followed by a word beginning
        with a pronounced consonant: dix francs; and in: la
        paix, la voix, etc.

z   [z]   le zéro, le gaz, zut!
        Silent in -ez verb ending and in: chez (except in
        linking).

116. VOWELS.

LETTER	PRONUNCIATION
a, à	[a] in most cases: la gare, l'accident, la table, à Paris.
	[ɑ] in: pas, phrase, vase, etc.
â	[ɑ] in most cases: âge, âme, pâle, château.
ai	[ɛ] except when final: j'avais, il avait, il fait, ils avaient.
	[ə] in: nous faisons, je faisais, tu faisais, etc.
	[e] when final: j'ai, j'irai.
au	[o] in most cases: au Canada, haut, il faut, chaud.
	[ɔ] in: j'aurai, le restaurant, Paul.
ay	[ɛj] in: essayer, payer, ayez.
	[ei] in: le pays.
	[aj] in: La Fayette.
è, ê	[ɛ] je me lève, le père, la tête, vous êtes.
é	[e] l'été, espérer, allé.
e	[ɛ] when followed by two consonants or in final syllable when followed by a single pronounced consonant: rester, verte, avec, mettre; and in: il est.
	[e] in final syllable when followed by silent **d, f, r, z**: pied, la clef, le boucher, allez; and in: et, and les, mes, etc.
	[ə] in the words je, me, te, se, ce, le, de, ne, que; and in the first syllable of many words such as: venir, demander, demain, cheval, etc. This [ə] is usually omitted in conversation if the phrase is easily pronounced without that vowel. Silent in words of more than one syllable when final or when followed by silent **s** or **nt:** ville, robes, parle, parles, parlent.
eau	[o] le bureau, l'eau, le veau.
ei	[ɛ] la neige, la peine.

LETTER	PRONUNCIATION	
ey	[ɛj]	asseyez-vous.
eu	[œ]	in most cases when followed in the same word by a pronounced consonant: neuf, leur, jeune, Europe.
	[ø]	when final, or when followed by the sound [z] or a silent final consonant: un peu, deux, il veut, les yeux, heureuse.
	[y]	in passé simple, imperfect subjunctive, and past participle of avoir: j'eus, etc.; il eût, etc.; il a eu, etc.
i	[i]	ici.
o	[ɔ]	except when followed by a silent final consonant or the sound [z] or [sj]: notre, joli, l'école, objet, hors-d'œuvre, les pommes, la note, la dot, la robe.
	[o]	when followed by a silent final consonant or the sound [z] or [sj]: mot, dos, nos, gros, la rose, poser, position, motion.
ô	[o]	le nôtre, table d'hôte, ôter.
œu	[œ]	when followed in the same word by a pronounced consonant: la sœur, hors-d'œuvre, un œuf, le bœuf.
	[ø]	in the plural forms œufs [ø], bœufs [bø].
oi	[wa]	moi, une poire, la boîte, une fois.
	[wɑ]	trois, le mois, le bois, les pois, le roi, froid.
ou, où	[u]	nous, voulez-vous? toujours, où? ou.
oui	[wi]	Louis, oui.
oy	[waj]	loyer, soyons, voyons.
u	[y]	sur, plus, une, la rue, du café.
ua	[ɥa]	nuage.
ue	[ɥɛ]	actuel, actuellement.
ui	[ɥi]	puis, huit, je suis, la nuit, lui, le bruit, juillet.
uy	[yj]	gruyère.
	[ɥij]	fuyez, ennuyer, appuyer.

117. NASAL VOWELS.

(a) Generally speaking, when vowels are followed in the same syllable by **m, n,** the vowel is nasalized and the **m** or **n** is not pronounced.

LETTER	PRONUNCIATION	
a	[ɑ̃]	quand, sans, grand, l'anglais, la chambre, allemand.
ae	[ɑ̃]	Caen, Saint-Saëns.
ai	[ɛ̃]	le pain, le bain, la faim, la main.
ao	[ɑ̃]	Laon, le paon.
e	[ɑ̃]	en, ensemble, le temps, le membre, la dent, vendre, emmener [ɑ̃mne], l'ennui, évident.
	[a]	évidemment, solennel, la femme.
	[ɛ̃]	examen, européen, le citoyen.
i	[ɛ̃]	la fin, le vin, vingt, impossible.
ie	[jɛ̃]	bien, rien, le chien, ancien, il tient, vous viendrez, etc.
	[i]	in: ils étudient.
	[jɑ̃]	in: patience, orient, science.
o	[õ]	on, bon, non, sont, onze, l'oncle, le nom, le nombre, compter.
	[ə]	in: monsieur.
oi	[wɛ̃]	loin, moins, le coin, le point.
u	[œ̃]	un, chacun, lundi, le parfum.
	[ɔ]	in a few Latin words: album, postscriptum, maximum.
ui	[ɥɛ̃]	juin.

(b) Vowels followed by **mm, nn** are usually not nasalized.

a	[a]	année, constamment, élégamment.
e	[ɛ]	ennemi, prennent, tiennent, viennent.
o	[ɔ]	comme, comment, bonne, sonner, l'homme, nommer, le sommeil, Sorbonne, la monnaie.

VERB FORMS
A. Regular Verbs

118. Formation of regular verbs from key forms.

All the forms of regular verbs can be derived from the following key forms: the present infinitive, the present indicative, the past participle, and the *passé simple*. The following paragraphs explain how the various forms can be derived.

119. Forms which can be derived from the infinitive.

(1) To form the present indicative, you drop the infinitive ending **-er, -ir,** or **-re** and add the following endings:

> Verbs ending in **-er:** **-e, -es, -e, -ons, -ez, -ent.**
> Verbs ending in **-ir:** **-is, -is, -it, -issons, -issez, -issent.**
> Verbs ending in **-re:** **-s, -s, —, -ons, -ez, -ent.**

(2) To form the future tense, add to the infinitive* the endings: **-ai, -as, -a, -ons, -ez, -ont.** Examples:

donner	je donnerai	*I shall give*
finir	je finirai	*I shall finish*
vendre	je vendrai	*I shall sell*

(3) To form the present conditional, add to the infinitive* the endings: **-ais- ais, -ait,- ions, -iez, -aient.** Examples:

donner	je donnerais	*I should* or *would give*
finir	je finirais	*I should* or *would finish*
vendre	je vendrais	*I should* or *would sell*

120. Forms derived from the present indicative.

(1) To form the present participle, drop the **-ons** of the first person plural of the present indicative and add the ending **-ant.** Examples:

---

* For infinitives of the third conjugation, the **-e** of the **-re** ending is omitted. Ex.: je vendrai, je répondrai, etc.

nous donnons	donnant	*giving*
nous finissons	finissant	*finishing*
nous vendons	vendant	*selling*

(2) To form the imperfect indicative, drop the **-ons** of the first person plural of the present indicative and add the endings: **-ais, -ais, -ait, -ions, -iez, -aient.** Examples:

nous donnons	je donnais	*I was giving, etc.*
nous finissons	je finissais	*I was finishing, etc.*
nous vendons	je vendais	*I was selling, etc.*

(3) To form the imperative, use the following forms of the present indicative without the pronoun subject: the second person singular, the first person plural, and the second person plural. Examples:

tu donnes	**donne(s)***	*give*
tu finis	**finis**	*finish*
tu vends	**vends**	*sell*
nous donnons	**donnons**	*let's give*
nous finissons	**finissons**	*let's finish*
nous vendons	**vendons**	*let's sell*
vous donnez	**donnez**	*give*
vous finissez	**finissez**	*finish*
vous vendez	**vendez**	*sell*

(4) To form the present subjunctive drop the **-ons** of the first person plural of the present indicative and add the endings: **-e, -es, -e, -ions, -iez, -ent.** Examples:

nous donnons	je donne	*I give†*
nous finissons	je finisse	*I finish*
nous vendons	je vende	*I sell*

---

* In verbs of the first conjugation, the s of the second singular ending is used only when followed by the word **y** or **en.**

† The subjunctive forms are translated in several different ways, depending upon the context.

121. FORMS IN WHICH THE PAST PARTICIPLE* IS USED.

(A) The past participle is used in conjunction with the different tenses of the auxiliary verb **avoir** (in a few cases **être**, see paragraph 10) to form the compound tenses of verbs.

(1) To form the *passé composé,* use the present tense of the auxiliary verb with the past participle of the verb. Examples:

j'ai donné   *I gave, I have given*
je suis arrivé   *I arrived, I have arrived*

(2) To form the pluperfect, use the imperfect tense of the auxiliary verb with the past participle of the verb. Examples:

j'avais donné   *I had given*
j'étais arrivé   *I had arrived*

(3) To form the past anterior (a literary tense which is approximately equivalent to the pluperfect), use the *passé simple* of the auxiliary verb with the past participle of the verb. Examples:

j'eus donné   *I had given*
je fus arrivé   *I had arrived*

(4) To form the future perfect, use the future tense of the auxiliary verb with the past participle of the verb. Examples:

j'aurai donné   *I shall have given*
je serai arrivé   *I shall have arrived*

(5) To form the conditional perfect, use the present conditional of the auxiliary verb with the past participle of the verb. Examples:

j'aurais donné   *I should* or *would have given*
je serais arrivé   *I should* or *would have arrived*

---

* For the formation of the past participle, see p. 133.

(6) To form the *passé composé* of the subjunctive, use the present subjunctive of the auxiliary verb with the past participle of the verb. Examples:

j'aie donné   *I have given, etc.*
je sois arrivé   *I have arrived, etc.*

(7) To form the pluperfect of the subjunctive, use the imperfect subjunctive of the auxiliary verb with the past participle of the verb, Examples:

j'eusse donné   *I had given, etc.*
je fusse arrivé   *I had arrived, etc.*

(8) To form the perfect infinitive, use the present infinitive of the auxiliary verb and the past participle of the verb. Examples:

avoir donné   *to have given*
être arrivé   *to have arrived*

(B) The past participle is used in conjunction with the different tenses of the auxiliary verb **être** to form the tenses of the passive voice of transitive verbs (i.e. of verbs normally conjugated with **avoir**). Examples:

PRESENT INDIC.	**je suis** flatté	*I am flattered*
IMPERFECT	**j'étais** flatté	*I was flattered*
FUTURE	**je serai** flatté	*I shall or will be flattered*
CONDITIONAL	**je serais** flatté	*I should or would be flattered*
PASSÉ COMPOSÉ	**j'ai été** flatté	*I was or have been flattered*
PLUPERFECT	**j'avais été** flatté	*I had been flattered*
PAST ANTERIOR	**j'eus été** flatté	*I had been flattered*

Although some of the forms of the passive voice look very complicated, they present no real difficulty either from the point of view of form or meaning. When broken down into their component parts and translated literally into English,

they practically always make good sense *and good English.*
Examples:

    Il avait été tué.   He   had   been killed.
    Vous auriez été étonné.   You would have been surprised.

The English passive voice is by no means always rendered in French by the passive voice. (See *use of faire with an infinitive* 63 (3).)

122. FORMS WHICH CAN BE DERIVED FROM THE PASSÉ SIMPLE.*

To form the imperfect subjunctive, drop the last letter of the first person singular of the *passé simple,* and add the endings: -sse, -sses, -ˆt, -ssions, -ssiez, -ssent.

PASSÉ SIMPLE		IMPERFECT SUBJ.
je donnai	*I gave*	je donnasse
je finis	*I finished*	je finisse
je vendis	*I sold*	je vendisse

The vowel preceding the **t** of the third person singular of the imperfect subjunctive always has a circumflex accent. Ex.: donnât, finît, vendît, eût, fût, etc.

123. REGULAR CONJUGATIONS.

(A) Infinitive and tenses formed on **it:**

FUTURE

I	II	III
donner	**finir**	**vendre**
je donnerai	je finirai	je vendrai
tu donneras	tu finiras	tu vendras
il donnera	il finira	il vendra
nous donnerons	nous finirons	nous vendrons
vous donnerez	vous finirez	vous vendrez
ils donneront	ils finiront	ils vendront

---

* For the formation of the *passé simple,* see paragraph 99, pp. 182-183.

CONDITIONAL

je donnerais	je finirais	je vendrais
tu donnerais	tu finirais	tu vendrais
il donnerait	il finirait	il vendrait
nous donnerions	nous finirions	nous vendrions
vous donneriez	vous finiriez	vous vendriez
ils donneraient	ils finiraient	ils vendraient

(B) Present indicative and tenses which can be formed from it:

PRESENT INDIC.

je donne	je finis	je vends
tu donnes	tu finis	tu vends
il donne	il finit	il vend
nous **donnons**	nous **finissons**	nous **vendons**
vous donnez	vous finissez	vous vendez
ils donnent	ils finissent	ils vendent

IMPERATIVE

donne(s)	finis	vends
donnons	finissons	vendons
donnez	finissez	vendez

PRESENT PART.

donnant	finissant	vendant

IMPERFECT

je donnais	je finissais	je vendais
tu donnais	tu finissais	tu vendais
il donnait	il finissait	il vendait
nous donnions	nous finissions	nous vendions
vous donniez	vous finissiez	vous vendiez
ils donnaient	ils finissaient	ils vendaient

PRESENT SUBJUNCTIVE

je donne	je finisse	je vende
tu donnes	tu finisses	tu vendes
il donne	il finisse	il vende

nous donnions	nous finissions	nous vendions
vous donniez	vous finissiez	vous vendiez
ils donnent	ils finissent	ils vendent

(C) Past participle and tenses in which past participle appears:

(1) Verbs conjugated with **avoir**:

PAST PARTICIPLE

| **donné** | **fini** | **vendu** |

PASSÉ COMPOSÉ

| j'ai donné, etc. | j'ai fini, etc. | j'ai vendu, etc. |

PLUPERFECT

| j'avais donné, etc. | j'avais fini, etc. | j'avais vendu, etc. |

PAST ANTERIOR

| j'eus donné, etc. | j'eus fini, etc. | j'eus vendu, etc. |

FUTURE PERFECT

| j'aurai donné, etc. | j'aurai fini, etc. | j'aurai vendu, etc. |

CONDITIONAL PERFECT

| j'aurais donné, etc. | j'aurais fini, etc. | j'aurais vendu, etc. |

PASSÉ COMPOSÉ SUBJUNCTIVE

| j'aie donné, etc. | j'aie fini, etc. | j'aie vendu, etc. |

PLUPERFECT SUBJUNCTIVE

| j'eusse donné, etc. | j'eusse fini, etc. | j'eusse vendu, etc. |

PERFECT INFINITIVE

| avoir donné | avoir fini | avoir vendu |

PERFECT PARTICIPLE

| ayant donné | ayant fini | ayant vendu |

(2) Verbs conjugated with **être**:

PAST PARTICIPLE	**arrivé** (*from* arriver)
PASSÉ COMPOSÉ	je suis arrivé(e), etc.
PLUPERFECT	j'étais arrivé(e), etc.
PAST ANTERIOR	je fus arrivé(e), etc.
FUTURE PERFECT	je serai arrivé(e), etc.
CONDITIONAL PERFECT	je serais arrivé(e), etc.
PASSÉ COMPOSÉ SUBJUNCTIVE	je sois arrivé(e), etc.
PLUPERFECT SUBJUNCTIVE	je fusse arrivé(e), etc.
PERFECT INFINITIVE	être arrivé(e) (s)
PERFECT PARTICIPLE	étant arrivé(e) (s)

(D) Passé simple and imperfect subjunctive:

PASSÉ SIMPLE

je donnai	je finis	je vendis
tu donnas	tu finis	tu vendis
il donna	il finit	il vendit
nous donnâmes	nous finîmes	nous vendîmes
vous donnâtes	vous finîtes	vous vendîtes
ils donnèrent	ils finirent	ils vendirent

IMPERFECT SUBJUNCTIVE

je donnasse	je finisse	je vendisse
tu donnasses	tu finisses	tu vendisses
il donnât	il finît	il vendît
nous donnassions	nous finissions	nous vendissions
vous donnassiez	vous finissiez	vous vendissiez
ils donnassent	ils finissent	ils vendissent

**124. VERBS OF THE FIRST CONJUGATION WHICH ARE REGU-
LAR EXCEPT FOR A SLIGHT VARIATION IN THEIR STEM.**

(A) Verbs whose stem vowel is a mute **e** (acheter, appeler)
have two stems.

(1) Whenever in conjugation the mute **e** of the stem
vowel is followed by a syllable containing a mute **e**, the **e** of

the stem vowel is pronounced [ε]. This occurs in the following forms: the first, second, and third person singular and the third person plural of the present indicative and the present subjunctive (**-e, -es, -e, -ent**); the second person singular of the imperative (**-e** or **-es**); and the six forms of both the future and conditional (**-erai**, etc., **-erais**, etc.)

(2) Whenever the mute **e** of the stem vowel is followed by a syllable containing any vowel other than a mute **e**, it is pronounced [ə] as in the infinitive. This phenomenon is reflected in the spelling as follows:

(*a*) In **acheter**, *to buy;* **geler**, *to freeze;* **lever**, *to raise;* **mener**, *to lead;* **peser**, *to weigh;* and a few other verbs, the stem vowel is written **è** when followed by a syllable containing a mute **e**. Ex.: PRESENT: J'**achète**, tu **achètes**, il **achète**, nous achetons, vous achetez, ils **achètent**; FUTURE: **j'achèterai**, etc.; CONDITIONAL: **j'achèterais**, etc.

(b) In **appeler**, *to call;* **jeter**, *to throw;* and a few other verbs ending in **-eler, -eter**, the final **l** or **t** of the stem is doubled when followed by a mute syllable. Ex.: PRESENT: J'**appelle**, tu **appelles**, il **appelle**, nous appelons, vous appelez, ils **appellent**; FUTUR: j'**appellerai**, etc.

(B) In **espérer**, *to hope;* **céder**, *to yield;* **préférer**, *to prefer* and a few other verbs whose stem vowel is **é**, the stem vowel is written **è** and pronounced [ε] in the present indicative (and present subjunctive) when followed by a mute syllable. Ex.: PRESENT: J'**espère**, tu **espères**, il **espère**, nous espérons, vous espérez, ils **espèrent**. (In the future and conditional, however, the stem vowel of these verbs is written **é**. Ex.: J'espérerai.)

(C) Verbs ending in **-cer, -ger, -yer** show a slight variation in the spelling of the stem *but not in its pronunciation.*

(1) In **commencer, avancer**, etc., the final **c** of the stem is written **ç** whenever in conjugation it is followed by an **a**

or **o.** Ex.: PRESENT: Je commence, tu commences, il commence, nous **commençons,** vous commencez, ils commencent; PRESENT PART.: **commençant;** IMPERFECT: je **commençais,** tu **commençais,** il **commençait,** nous commencions, vous commenciez, ils **commençaient;** PASSÉ SIMPLE: je **commençai,** etc.

(2) In **manger,** *to eat,* and other verbs ending in **-ger,** you write **ge** instead of **g** whenever the following vowel is **a** or **o.** Ex.. PRESENT: je mange, tu manges, il mange, nous **mangeons,** vous mangez, ils mangent; IMPERFECT: je **mangeais,** etc.; PASSÉ SIMPLE: je **mangeai,** etc.

(3) In **ennuyer,** *to bother,* and other verbs ending in **-oyer, -uyer,** you write **i** instead of **y** whenever the following letter is a mute **e.** Ex.: il **ennuie,** *but* nous **ennuyons.**

(4) In **payer,** *to pay,* and other verbs ending in **-ayer, -eyer,** you may write **y** throughout the verb, or, if you prefer, you may write **i** instead of **y** whenever the following letter is a mute **e.** Ex.: Je paye *or* je paie, *but* nous payons.

B. Auxiliary Verbs

125. CONJUGATION OF AUXILIARY VERBS **être** AND **avoir.**

SIMPLE TENSES

INFINITIVE

être, *to be*   avoir, *to have*

PRESENT INDICATIVE

je suis, *I am*   j'ai, *I have*
tu es   tu as
il est   il a
nous sommes   nous avons
vous êtes   vous avez
ils sont   ils ont

IMPERFECT

j'étais, *I was*   j'avais, *I had*
tu étais   tu avais
il était   il avait
nous étions   nous avions
vous étiez   vous aviez
ils étaient   ils avaient

PASSÉ SIMPLE

je fus, *I was*   j'eus, *I had*
tu fus   tu eus
il fut   il eut
nous fûmes   nous eûmes
vous fûtes   vous eûtes
ils furent   ils eurent

FUTURE

je serai, *I shall* or *will be*   j'aurai, *I shall* or *will have*
tu seras   tu auras
il sera   il aura
nous serons   nous aurons
vous serez   vous aurez
ils seront   ils auront

CONDITIONAL

je serais, *I should* or *would be*   j'aurais, *I should* or *would have*
tu serais   tu aurais
il serait   il aurait
nous serions   nous aurions
vous seriez   vous auriez
ils seraient   ils auraient

PRESENT SUBJUNCTIVE

je sois, *I am,* etc.   j'aie, *I have,* etc.
tu sois   tu aies
il soit   il ait
nous soyons   nous ayons
vous soyez   vous ayez
ils soient   ils aient

IMPERFECT SUBJUNCTIVE

je fusse, *I was,* etc.   j'eusse, *I had,* etc.
tu fusses   tu eusses
il fût   il eût
nous fussions   nous eussions
vous fussiez   vous eussiez
ils fussent   ils eussent

IMPERATIVE

sois, *be*   aie, *have*
soyons   ayons
soyez   ayez

Present Participle
étant   ayant

COMPOUND TENSES

Past Participle
été   **eu**

Passé Composé
j'ai été, *I was, I have been*, etc.   j'ai eu, *I had, I have had*, etc.

Pluperfect
j'avais été, *I had been*, etc.   j'avais eu, *I had had*, etc.

Past Anterior
j'eus été, *I had been*, etc.   j'eus eu, *I had had*, etc.

Future Perfect
j'aurai été, *I shall have been*, etc.   j'aurai eu, *I shall have had*, etc.

Conditional Perfect
j'aurais été, *I should* or *would*   j'aurais eu, *I should* or *would*
   have been, etc.   *have had*, etc.

Passé Composé Subjunctive
j'aie été, *I have been*, etc.   j'aie eu, *I have had*, etc.

Pluperfect Subjunctive
j'eusse été, *I had been*, etc.   j'eusse eu, *I had had*, etc.

Perfect Infinitive
avoir été, *to have been*   avoir eu, *to have had*

Perfect Participle
ayant été, *having been*   ayant eu, *having had*

C. Irregular Verbs

126. FORMATION OF IRREGULAR VERBS.

Although the rules for deriving the forms of regular verbs (see paragraphs 118-122) do not apply strictly to all irregular verbs, they do apply to a substantial proportion of their forms (see paragraphs 70-79).

127. REFERENCE LIST OF COMMONEST IRREGULAR VERBS.

abattre	*see* battre	131	conduire			134
s'abstenir	*see* tenir	167	connaître			135
abstraire	*see* traire	168	conquérir	*see* acquérir	128
accourir	*see* courir	137	consentir	*see* dormir	144
accueillir	*see* cueillir	141	construire	*see* conduire	134
acquérir		128	contenir	*see* tenir	167
admettre	*see* mettre	152	contraindre	*see* craindre	138
aller		129	contredire	*see* dire	143
apercevoir	*see* recevoir	161	contrefaire	*see* faire	147
apparaître	*see* connaître	135	convaincre	*see* vaincre	169
appartenir	*see* tenir	167	convenir	*see* venir	171
apprendre	*see* prendre	160	coudre			136
assaillir	*see* cueillir	141	courir			137
s'asseoir		130	couvrir	*see* ouvrir	156
astreindre	*see* craindre	138	craindre			138
atteindre	*see* craindre	138	croire			139
avoir		125	croître			140
battre		131	cueillir			141
boire		132	se débattre	*see* battre	131
bouillir	*see* dormir	144	décevoir	*see* recevoir	161
combattre	*see* battre	131	découvrir	*see* ouvrir	156
commettre	*see* mettre	152	décrire	*see* écrire	145
comprendre	*see* prendre	160	se dédire	*see* dire	143
compromettre	*see* mettre	152	déduire	*see* conduire	134
concevoir	*see* recevoir	161	défaire	*see* faire	147
conclure		133	démentir	*see* dormir	144

dépeindre	*see* craindre	138	inscrire	*see* écrire	145
déplaire	*see* plaire	157	interdire	*see* dire	143
déteindre	*see* craindre	138	intervenir	*see* venir	171
détenir	*see* tenir	167	introduire	*see* conduire	134
détruire	*see* conduire	134	joindre	*see* craindre	138
devenir	*see* venir	171	lire		151
devoir		142	maintenir	*see* tenir	167
dire		143	maudire	*see* dire	143
discourir	*see* courir	137	médire	*see* dire	143
disparaître	*see* connaître	135	mentir	*see* dormir	144
distraire	*see* traire	168	mettre		152
dormir		144	mourir		153
écrire		145	mouvoir		154
élire	*see* lire	151	naître		155
émettre	*see* mettre	152	obtenir	*see* tenir	167
émouvoir	*see* mouvoir	154	offrir	*see* ouvrir	156
endormir	*see* dormir	144	omettre	*see* mettre	152
s'endormir	*see* dormir	144	ouvrir		156
enfreindre	*see* craindre	138	paraître	*see* connaître	135
s'enfuir	*see* fuir	149	parcourir	*see* courir	137
entreprendre	*see* prendre	160	partir	*see* dormir	144
entretenir	*see* tenir	167	parvenir	*see* venir	171
entrevoir	*see* voir	174	peindre	*see* craindre	138
entr'ouvrir	*see* ouvrir	156	percevoir	*see* recevoir	161
envoyer		146	permettre	*see* mettre	152
éteindre	*see* craindre	138	plaindre	*see* craindre	138
être		125	se plaindre	*see* craindre	138
exclure	*see* conclure	133	plaire		157
extraire	*see* traire	168	pleuvoir		158
faire		147	poursuivre	*see* suivre	166
falloir		148	pourvoir	*see* voir	174
feindre	*see* craindre	138	pouvoir		159
fuir		149	prédire	see *dire*	143
geindre	*see* craindre	138	prendre		160
haïr		150	prescrire	*see* écrire	145
inclure	*see* conclure	133	pressentir	*see* dormir	144

prévenir	*see* venir	171	servir	*see* dormir	144
prévoir	*see* voir	174	se servir de	*see* dormir	144
produire	*see* conduire	134	sortir	*see* dormir	144
promettre	*see* mettre	152	souffrir	*see* ouvrir	156
proscrire	*see* écrire	145	soumettre	*see* mettre	152
provenir	*see* venir	171	sourire	*see* rire	163
recevoir		161	souscrire	*see* écrire	145
reconduire	*see* conduire	134	soustraire	*see* traire	168
reconnaître	*see* connaître	135	soutenir	*see* tenir	167
recueillir	*see* cueillir	141	se souvenir	*see* venir	171
réduire	*see* conduire	134	suffire		165
rejoindre	*see* craindre	138	suivre		166
remettre	*see* mettre	152	surprendre	*see* prendre	160
renvoyer	*see* envoyer	146	taire	*see* plaire	157
repartir	*see* dormir	144	se taire	*see* plaire	157
se repentir	*see* dormir	144	teindre	*see* craindre	138
reprendre	*see* prendre	160	tenir		167
résoudre		162	traduire	*see* conduire	134
ressentir	*see* dormir	144	traire		168
restreindre	*see* craindre	138	transmettre	*see* mettre	152
retenir	*see* tenir	167	tressaillir	*see* cueillir	141
revenir	*see* venir	171	vaincre		169
revoir	*see* voir	174	valoir		170
rire		163	venir		171
satisfaire	*see* faire	147	vêtir		172
savoir		164	vivre		173
secourir	*see* courir	137	voir		174
séduire	*see* conduire	134	vouloir		175
sentir	*see* dormir	144			

128. acquérir, *to acquire*.

FUTURE
 j'acquerrai, etc.; COND. j'acquerrais, etc.

PRESENT INDICATIVE
 j'acquiers, tu acquiers, il acquiert,
 nous acquérons, vous acquérez, ils acquièrent.

IMPERATIVE
 acquiers, acquérons, acquérez.

PRES. PART.
 acquérant; IMPERFECT j'acquérais, etc.

PRES. SUBJ.
 j'acquière, tu acquières, il acquière,
 nous acquérions, vous acquériez, ils acquièrent.

PAST PARTICIPLE
 acquis; PASSÉ COMPOSÉ j'ai acquis, etc.

PASSÉ SIMPLE
 j'acquis, etc.; IMPER. SUBJ. j'acquisse, etc.

129. aller, *to go*.

FUTURE
 j'irai, etc.; COND. j'irais, etc.

PRESENT INDICATIVE
 je vais, tu vas, il va,
 nous allons, vous allez, ils vont.

IMPERATIVE
 va(s), allons, allez.

PRES. PART.
 allant; IMPERFECT j'allais, etc.

PRES. SUBJ.
 j'aille, tu ailles, il aille,
 nous allions, vous alliez, ils aillent.

PAST PARTICIPLE
 allé; PASSÉ COMPOSÉ je suis allé, etc.

PASSÉ SIMPLE
 j'allai, etc.; IMPERF. SUBJ. j'allasse, etc.

130. s'asseoir, *to sit down*.

FUTURE

je m'assiérai, etc.; COND. je m'assiérais, etc.

PRESENT INDICATIVE

je m'assieds, tu t'assieds, il s'assied,
nous nous asseyons, vous vous asseyez, ils s'asseyent.

IMPERATIVE

assieds-toi, asseyons-nous, asseyez-vous.

PRES. PART.

s'asseyant; IMPERFECT je m'asseyais, etc.

PRES. SUBJ.

je m'asseye, tu t'asseyes, il s'asseye,
nous nous asseyions, vous vous asseyiez, ils s'asseyent.

PAST PARTICIPLE

assis; PASSÉ COMPOSÉ je me suis assis, etc.

PASSÉ SIMPLE

je m'assis, etc.; IMPERF. SUBJ. je m'assisse, etc.

Alternate form of s'asseoir.

FUTURE

je m'assoirai, etc. *or* je m'asseyerai, etc.

CONDITIONAL

je m'assoirais, etc. *or* je m'asseyerais, etc.

PRESENT INDICATIVE

je m'assois, tu t'assois, il s'assoit,
nous nous assoyons, vous vous assoyez, ils s'assoient.

PRES. PART.

s'assoyant; IMPERFECT je m'assoyais, etc.

PRES. SUBJ.

je m'assoie, tu t'assoies, il s'assoie,
nous nous assoyions, vous vous assoyiez, ils s'assoient.

asseoir, *to seat* is conjugated like s'asseoir except that it takes the auxiliary verb avoir.

131. battre, *to beat.*

All forms are regular except:

PRESENT INDICATIVE
 je bats, tu bats, il bat,
 nous battons, vous battez, ils battent.

Like **battre:** **abattre,** *to fell, to beat down;* **combattre,** *to fight,* and
se débattre, *to struggle.*

132. boire, *to drink.*

FUTURE and COND. regular.

PRESENT INDICATIVE
 je bois, tu bois, il boit,
 nous buvons, vous buvez, ils boivent.

IMPERATIVE
 bois, buvons, buvez.

PRES. PART.
 buvant; IMPERFECT je buvais, etc.

PRES. SUBJ.
 je boive, tu boives, il boive,
 nous buvions, vous buviez, ils boivent.

PAST PARTICIPLE
 bu; PASSÉ COMPOSÉ j'ai bu, etc.

PASSÉ SIMPLE
 je bus, etc.; IMPERF. SUBJ. je busse, etc.

133. conclure, *to conclude.*

FUTURE and COND. regular.

PRESENT INDICATIVE
 je conclus, tu conclus, il conclut,
 nous concluons, vous concluez, ils concluent.

IMPERATIVE
 conclus, concluons, concluez.

PRES. PART.
    concluant; IMPERFECT je concluais, etc.
PRES. SUBJ.
    je conclue, etc.
PAST PARTICIPLE
    conclu; PASSÉ COMPOSÉ j'ai conclu, etc.
PASSÉ SIMPLE
    je conclus, etc.; IMPERF. SUBJ. je conclusse, etc.
Like **conclure:** exclure, *to exclude,* and **inclure,** *to include,* except that
the past participle of the latter is **inclus.**

134. conduire, *to conduct, to drive.*

FUTURE and COND. regular.
PRESENT INDICATIVE
    je conduis, tu conduis, il conduit,
    nous conduisons, vous conduisez, ils conduisent.
IMPERATIVE
    conduis, conduisons, conduisez.
PRES. PART.
    conduisant; IMPERFECT je conduisais, etc.
PRES. SUBJ.
    je conduise, etc.
PAST PARTICIPLE
    conduit; PASSÉ COMPOSÉ j'ai conduit, etc.
PASSÉ SIMPLE
    je conduisis, etc.; IMPERF. SUBJ. je conduisisse, etc.
Like **conduire: construire,** *to construct;* **déduire,** *to deduce;* **détruire,**
to destroy; **introduire,** *to introduce;* **produire,** *to produce;* **recon-
duire,** *to lead back;* **réduire,** *to reduce;* **séduire,** *to seduce, to
please;* **traduire,** *to translate;* etc.

135. connaître, *to know, to be acquainted with.*

FUTURE and COND. regular.
PRESENT INDICATIVE
    je connais, tu connais, il connaît,
    nous connaissons, vous connaissez, ils connaissent.

IMPERATIVE
connais, connaissons, connaissez.
PRES. PART.
connaissant; IMPERFECT je connaissais, etc.
PRES. SUBJ.
je connaisse, etc.
PAST PARTICIPLE
connu; PASSÉ COMPOSÉ j'ai connu, etc.
PASSÉ SIMPLE
je connus, etc.; IMPERF. SUBJ. je connusse, etc.
Like **connaître**: **apparaître**, *to appear;* **disparaître**, *to disappear;*
paraître, *to appear;* **reconnaître**, *to recognize;* etc.

136. coudre, *to sew.*

FUTURE and COND. regular.
PRESENT INDICATIVE
je couds, tu couds, il coud,
nous cousons, vous cousez, ils cousent.
IMPERATIVE
couds, cousons, cousez.
PRES. PART.
cousant; IMPERFECT je cousais, etc.
PRES. SUBJ.
je couse, etc.
PAST PARTICIPLE
cousu; PASSÉ COMPOSÉ j'ai cousu, etc.
PASSÉ SIMPLE
je cousis, etc.; IMPERF. SUBJ. je cousisse, etc.

137. courir, *to run.*

FUTURE
je courrai, etc.; COND. je courrais, etc.
PRESENT INDICATIVE
je cours, tu cours, il court,
nous courons, vous courez, ils courent.

Imperative
cours, courons, courez.

Pres. Part.
courant; Imperfect je courais, etc.

Pres. Subj.
je coure, etc.

Past Participle
couru; Passé Composé j'ai couru, etc.

Passé Simple
je courus, etc.; Imperf. Subj. je courusse, etc.

Like **courir: accourir,** *to hasten;* **discourir,** *to discourse;* **parcourir,** *to go over;* **secourir,** *to help;* etc.

138. craindre, *to fear.*

Future and Cond. regular.

Present Indicative
je crains, tu crains, il craint,
nous craignons, vous craignez, ils craignent.

Imperative
crains, craignons, craignez.

Pres. Part.
craignant; Imperfect je craignais, etc.

Pres. Subj.
je craigne, etc.

Past Participle
craint; Passé Composé j'ai craint, etc.

Passé Simple
je craignis, etc.; Imperf. Subj. je craignisse, etc.

Like **craindre: astreindre,** *to compel;* **atteindre,** *to attain;* **contraindre,** *to compel;* **dépeindre,** *to depict;* **déteindre,** *to fade;* **enfreindre,** *to infringe;* **éteindre,** *to extinguish;* **feindre,** *to feign;* **geindre,** *to groan;* **joindre,** *to join;* **peindre,** *to paint;* **plaindre,** *to pity;* **se plaindre,** *to complain;* **rejoindre,** *to rejoin, to meet;* **restreindre,** *to restrain;* **teindre,** *to dye;* etc.

139. croire, *to believe*.

FUTURE and COND. regular.

PRESENT INDICATIVE
    je crois, tu crois, il croit
    nous croyons, vous croyez, ils croient.

IMPERATIVE
    crois, croyons, croyez.

PRES. PART.
    croyant; IMPERFECT je croyais, etc.

PRES. SUBJ.
    je croie, tu croies, il croie,
    nous croyions, vous croyiez, ils croient.

PAST PARTICIPLE
    cru; PASSÉ COMPOSÉ j'ai cru, etc.

PASSÉ SIMPLE
    je crus, etc.; IMPERF. SUBJ. je crusse, etc.

140. croître, *to grow*.

FUTURE and COND. regular.

PRESENT INDICATIVE
    je croîs, tu croîs, il croît,
    nous croissons, vous croissez, ils croissent.

IMPERATIVE
    croîs, croissons, croissez.

PRES. PART.
    croissant; IMPERFECT je croissais, etc.

PRES. SUBJ.
    je croisse, etc.

PAST PARTICIPLE
    crû; PASSÉ COMPOSÉ j'ai crû, etc.

PASSÉ SIMPLE
    je crûs, etc.; IMPERF. SUBJ. je crusse, etc.

141. cueillir, *to pick, to gather.*

FUTURE
je cueillerai, etc.; COND. je cueillerais, etc.

PRESENT INDICATIVE
je cueille, tu cueilles, il cueille,
nous cueillons, vous cueillez, ils cueillent.

IMPERATIVE
cueille(s), cueillons, cueillez.

PRES. PART.
cueillant; IMPERFECT je cueillais, etc.

PRES. SUBJ.
je cueille, etc.

PAST PARTICIPLE
cueilli; PASSÉ COMPOSÉ j'ai cueilli, etc.

PASSÉ SIMPLE
je cueillis, etc.; IMPERF. SUBJ. je cueillisse, etc.

Like **cueillir**: **accueillir**, *to welcome;* and **recueillir**, *to gather, to collect.*
assaillir, *to assail* and **tressaillir**, *to start,* etc. are like **cueillir** except
that the future and conditional are regular.

142. devoir, *must,* etc.

FUTURE
je devrai, etc.; COND. je devrais, etc.

PRESENT INDICATIVE
je dois, tu dois, il doit,
nous devons, vous devez, ils doivent.

IMPERATIVE
———

PRES. PART.
devant; IMPERFECT je devais, etc.

PRES. SUBJ.
je doive, tu doives, il doive,
nous devions, vous deviez, ils doivent.

PAST PARTICIPLE
  dû; PASSÉ COMPOSÉ j'ai dû, etc.
PASSÉ SIMPLE
  je dus, etc.; IMPERF. SUBJ. je dusse, etc.

143. dire, *to say*.

FUTURE and COND. regular.
PRESENT INDICATIVE
  je dis, tu dis, il dit,
  nous disons, vous dites, ils disent.
IMPERATIVE
  dis, disons, dites.
PRES. PART.
  disant; IMPERFECT je disais, etc.
PRES. SUBJ.
  je dise, etc.
PAST PARTICIPLE
  dit; PASSÉ COMPOSÉ j'ai dit, etc.
PASSÉ SIMPLE
  je dis, etc.; IMPERF. SUBJ. je disse, etc.

Like **dire: redire,** *to say again.*

The following verbs are like **dire** except that the 2nd person plural of
  the present indicative ends in **-disez: contredire,** *to contradict;* **se
  dédire,** *to retract;* **interdire,** *to prohibit;* **médire,** *to slander;* **pré-
  dire,** *to predict.*

maudire, *to curse,* is conjugated like **finir** except for the p. part.: **maudit.**

144. dormir, *to sleep*.

FUTURE and COND. regular.
PRESENT INDICATIVE
  je dors, tu dors, il dort,
  nous dormons, vous dormez, ils dorment.
IMPERATIVE
  dors, dormons, dormez.

PRES. PART.
dormant; IMPERFECT je dormais, etc.

PRES. SUBJ.
je dorme, etc.

PAST PARTICIPLE
dormi; PASSÉ COMPOSÉ j'ai dormi, etc.

PASSÉ SIMPLE
je dormis, etc.; IMPERF. SUBJ. je dormisse, etc.

Like **dormir: endormir,** to *put to sleep;* **s'endormir,** to *fall asleep;* etc.

The following verbs are conjugated like **dormir** but the present indica-tive of each is given in full:

bouillir, to *boil:* bous, bous, bout, bouillons, bouillez, bouillent.

mentir, to *lie,* and **démentir,** to *contradict:* mens, mens, ment, mentons, mentez, mentent.

partir, to *leave,* and **repartir,** to *leave again:* pars, pars, part, partons, partez, partent. (Conjugated with auxiliary **être.**)

se repentir, to *repent:* repens, repens, repent, repentons, repentez, repentent.

sentir, to *feel, to smell;* **consentir,** to *consent;* **pressentir,** to *have a presentiment;* **ressentir,** to *feel:* sens, sens, sent, sentons, sentez, sentent.

servir, to *serve;* **se servir de,** to *use:* sers, sers, sert, servons, servez, servent.

sortir, to *go out:* sors, sors, sort, sortons, sortez, sortent. (Conjugated with auxiliary **être.**)

145. écrire, *to write.*

FUTURE and COND. regular.

PRESENT INDICATIVE
j'écris, tu écris, il écrit,
nous écrivons, vous écrivez, ils écrivent.

IMPERATIVE
écris, écrivons, écrivez.

PRES. PART.
>écrivant; IMPERFECT j'écrivais, etc.

PRES. SUBJ.
>j'écrive, etc.

PAST PARTICIPLE
>écrit; PASSÉ COMPOSÉ j'ai écrit, etc.

PASSÉ SIMPLE
>j'écrivis, etc.; IMPERF. SUBJ. j'écrivisse, etc.

Like **écrire: décrire,** *to describe;* **inscrire,** *to inscribe;* **prescrire,** *to pre‹ scribe;* **proscrire,** *to proscribe;* **souscrire,** *to subscribe;* etc.

146. envoyer, *to send.*

FUTURE
>j'enverrai, etc.; COND. j'enverrais, etc.

PRESENT INDICATIVE
>j'envoie, tu envoies, il envoie,
>nous envoyons, vous envoyez, ils envoient.

IMPERATIVE
>envoie(s), envoyons, envoyez.

PRES. PART.
>envoyant; IMPERFECT j'envoyais, etc.

PRES. SUBJ.
>j'envoie, tu envoies, il envoie,
>nous envoyions, vous envoyiez, ils envoient.

PAST PARTICIPLE
>envoyé; PASSÉ COMPOSÉ j'ai envoyé, etc.

PASSÉ SIMPLE
>j'envoyai, etc.; IMPERF. SUBJ. j'envoyasse, etc.

Like **envoyer: renvoyer,** *to send back, to send away.*

147. faire, *to do, to make.*

FUTURE
>je ferai, etc.; COND. je ferais, etc.

PRESENT INDICATIVE
  je fais, tu fais, il fait,
  nous faisons, vous faites, ils font.
IMPERATIVE
  fais, faisons, faites.
PRÉS. PART.
  faisant; IMPERFECT je faisais, etc.
PRES. SUBJ.
  je fasse, etc.
PAST PARTICIPLE
  fait; PASSÉ COMPOSÉ j'ai fait, etc.
PASSÉ SIMPLE
  je fis, etc., IMPERF. SUBJ. je fisse, etc.
Like **faire: contrefaire,** *to imitate;* **défaire,** *to undo;* **satisfaire,** *to satis-*
  fy; etc.

148. falloir, *must,* etc. (impersonal).

FUTURE
  il faudra; COND. il faudrait.
PRESENT INDICATIVE
  il faut.
IMPERATIVE
  ————

PRES. PART.
  ———— IMPERFECT il fallait.
PRES. SUBJ.
  il faille.
PAST PARTICIPLE
  fallu; PASSÉ COMPOSÉ il a fallu.
PASSÉ SIMPLE
  il fallut; IMPERF. SUBJ. il fallût.

149. fuir, *to flee.*

FUTURE and COND. regular.

PRESENT INDICATIVE
 je fuis, tu fuis, il fuit,
 nous fuyons, vous fuyez, ils fuient.

IMPERATIVE
 fuis, fuyons, fuyez.

PRES. PART.
 fuyant; IMPERFECT je fuyais, etc.

PRES. SUBJ.
 je fuie, tu fuies, il fuie,
 nous fuyions, vous fuyiez, ils fuient.

PAST PARTICIPLE
 fui; PASSÉ COMPOSÉ j'ai fui, etc.

PASSÉ SIMPLE
 je fuis, etc.; IMPERF. SUBJ. je fuisse, etc.

Like **fuir:** s'enfuir, *to flee, to escape.*

150. *haïr, *to hate.*

FUTURE and COND. regular.

PRESENT INDICATIVE
 je hais, tu hais, il hait,
 nous haïssons, vous haïssez, ils haïssent.

IMPERATIVE
 hais, haïssons, haïssez.

PRES. PART.
 haïssant; IMPERFECT je haïssais, etc.

PRES. SUBJ.
 je haïsse, etc.

PAST PARTICIPLE
 haï; PASSÉ COMPOSÉ j'ai haï, etc.

PASSÉ SIMPLE
 je haïs, tu haïs, il haït,
 nous haïmes, vous haïtes, ils haïrent.

IMPERF. SUBJ. je haïsse, tu haïsses, il haït, etc.

---

* The **h** is aspirate in all the forms of **haïr.**

151. lire, *to read*.

FUTURE and COND. regular.

PRESENT INDICATIVE
je lis, tu lis, il lit,
nous lisons, vous lisez, ils lisent.

IMPERATIVE
lis, lisons, lisez.

PRES. PART.
lisant; IMPERFECT je lisais, etc.

PRES. SUBJ.
je lise, etc.

PAST PARTICIPLE
lu; PASSÉ COMPOSÉ j'ai lu, etc.

PASSÉ SIMPLE
je lus, etc.; IMPERF. SUBJ. je lusse, etc.

Like **lire**: **élire,** *to elect*.

152. mettre, *to put*.

FUTURE and COND. regular.

PRESENT INDICATIVE
je mets, tu mets, il met,
nous mettons, vous mettez, ils mettent.

IMPERATIVE
mets, mettons, mettez.

PRES. PART.
mettant; IMPERFECT je mettais, etc.

PRES. SUBJ.
je mette, etc.

PAST PARTICIPLE
mis; PASSÉ COMPOSÉ j'ai mis, etc.

PASSÉ SIMPLE
je mis, etc.; IMPERF. SUBJ. je misse, etc.

Like **mettre**: **admettre,** *to admit;* **commettre,** *to commit;* **compromettre,** *to compromise;* **émettre,** *to put out, to emit;* **omettre,** *to omit;* **permettre,** *to permit;* **promettre,** *to promise;* **remettre,** *to put back, to hand to;* **soumettre,** *to submit;* **transmettre,** *to transmit;* etc.

153. mourir, *to die.*

FUTURE
   je mourrai, etc.; COND. je mourrais, etc.

PRESENT INDICATIVE
   je meurs, tu meurs, il meurt,
   nous mourons, vous mourez, ils meurent.

IMPERATIVE
   meurs, mourons, mourez.

PRES. PART.
   mourant; IMPERFECT je mourais, etc.

PRES. SUBJ.
   je meure, tu meures, il meure,
   nous mourions, vous mouriez, ils meurent.

PAST PARTICIPLE
   mort; PASSÉ COMPOSÉ je suis mort(e), etc.

PASSÉ SIMPLE
   je mourus, etc.; IMPERF. SUBJ. je mourusse, etc.

154. mouvoir, *to move.*

FUTURE
   je mouvrai, etc.; COND. je mouvrais, etc.

PRESENT INDICATIVE
   je meus, tu meus, il meut,
   nous mouvons, vous mouvez, ils meuvent.

IMPERATIVE
   meus, mouvons, mouvez.

PRES. PART.
   mouvant; IMPERFECT je mouvais, etc.

PRES. SUBJ.
   je meuve, tu meuves, il meuve,
   nous mouvions, vous mouviez, ils meuvent.

PAST PARTICIPLE
   mû; PASSÉ COMPOSÉ j'ai mû, etc.

PASSÉ SIMPLE
je mus, etc.; IMPERF. SUBJ. je musse, etc.

Like **mouvoir:** **émouvoir,** *to stir;* **s'émouvoir,** *to be stirred;* etc., except that the past participle is **ému** — without the circumflex accent.

155. naître, *to be born.*

FUTURE and COND. regular.

PRESENT INDICATIVE
je nais, tu nais, il naît,
nous naissons, vous naissez, ils naissent.

IMPERATIVE
nais, naissons, naissez.

PRES. PART.
naissant; IMPERFECT je naissais, etc.

PRES. SUBJ.
je naisse, etc.

PAST PARTICIPLE
né; PASSÉ COMPOSÉ je suis né(e), etc.

PASSÉ SIMPLE
je naquis, etc.; IMPERF. SUBJ. je naquisse, etc.

Like **naître:** **renaître,** *to be reborn.*

156. ouvrir, *to open.*

FUTURE and COND. regular.

PRESENT INDICATIVE
j'ouvre, tu ouvres, il ouvre,
nous ouvrons, vous ouvrez, ils ouvrent.

IMPERATIVE
ouvre(s), ouvrons, ouvrez.

PRES. PART.
ouvrant; IMPERFECT j'ouvrais, etc.

PRES. SUBJ.
j'ouvre, etc.

PAST PARTICIPLE
  ouvert; PASSÉ COMPOSÉ j'ai ouvert, etc.

PASSÉ SIMPLE
  j'ouvris, etc.; IMPERF. SUBJ. j'ouvrisse, etc.

Like **ouvrir: couvrir,** *to cover;* **découvrir,** *to discover;* **entr'ouvrir,** *to open slightly;* **offrir,** *to offer, to give;* **souffrir,** *to suffer,* etc.

157. plaire, *to please.*

FUTURE and COND. regular.

PRESENT INDICATIVE
  je plais, tu plais, il plaît,
  nous plaisons, vous plaisez, ils plaisent.

IMPERATIVE
  plais, plaisons, plaisez.

PRES. PART.
  plaisant; IMPERFECT je plaisais, etc.

PRES. SUBJ.
  je plaise, etc.

PAST PARTICIPLE
  plu; PASSÉ COMPOSÉ j'ai plu, etc.

PASSÉ SIMPLE
  je plus, etc.; IMPERF. SUBJ. je plusse, etc.

Like **plaire: déplaire,** *to displease.*

taire, *to say nothing about,* and **se taire,** *to be silent,* are conjugated like **plaire** except that the 3rd person singular of the present indicative is written without the circumflex accent.

158. pleuvoir, *to rain* (impersonal).

FUTURE
  il pleuvra; COND. il pleuvrait.

PRESENT INDICATIVE
  il pleut.

PRES. PART.
  pleuvant; IMPERFECT il pleuvait.

PRES. SUBJ.
 il pleuve.
PAST PARTICIPLE
 plu; PASSÉ COMPOSÉ il a plu.
PASSÉ SIMPLE
 il plut; IMPERF. SUBJ. il plût.

159. pouvoir, *to be able, can,* etc.

FUTURE
 je pourrai, etc.; COND. je pourrais, etc.
PRESENT INDICATIVE
 je peux (je puis), tu peux, il peut,
 nous pouvons, vous pouvez, ils peuvent.
PRES. PART.
 pouvant; IMPERFECT je pouvais, etc.
PRES. SUBJ.
 je puisse, tu puisses, il puisse,
 nous puissions, vous puissiez, ils puissent.
IMPERATIVE
 ——— ——— ———

PAST PARTICIPLE
 pu; PASSÉ COMPOSÉ j'ai pu, etc.
PASSÉ SIMPLE
 je pus, etc.; IMPERF. SUBJ. je pusse, etc.

160. prendre, *to take.*

FUTURE and COND. regular.
PRESENT INDICATIVE
 je prends, tu prends, il prend,
 nous prenons, vous prenez, ils prennent.
IMPERATIVE
 prends, prenons, prenez.
PRES. PART.
 prenant; IMPERFECT je prenais, etc.

PRES. SUBJ.
> je prenne, tu prennes, il prenne,
> nous prenions, vous preniez, ils prennent.

PAST PARTICIPLE
> pris; PASSÉ COMPOSÉ j'ai pris, etc.

PASSÉ SIMPLE
> je pris, etc.; IMPERF. SUBJ. je prisse, etc.

Like **prendre: apprendre,** *to learn;* **comprendre,** *to understand;* **entre-prendre,** *to undertake;* **reprendre,** *to take again,* etc.; **surprendre,** *to surprise;* etc.

161. recevoir, *to receive.*

FUTURE
> je recevrai, etc.; COND. je recevrais, etc.

PRESENT INDICATIVE
> je reçois, tu reçois, il reçoit,
> nous recevons, vous recevez, ils reçoivent.

IMPERATIVE
> reçois, recevons, recevez.

PRES. PART.
> recevant; IMPERFECT je recevais, etc.

PRES. SUBJ.
> je reçoive, tu reçoives, il reçoive,
> nous recevions, vous receviez, ils reçoivent.

PAST PARTICIPLE
> reçu; PASSÉ COMPOSÉ j'ai reçu, etc.

PASSÉ SIMPLE
> je reçus, etc.; IMPERF. SUBJ. je reçusse, etc.

Like **recevoir: apercevoir,** *to catch a glimpse of;* **concevoir,** *to conceive;* **décevoir,** *to deceive;* **percevoir,** *to collect;* etc.

162. résoudre, *to resolve, to solve.*

FUTURE and COND. regular.

PRESENT INDICATIVE
    je résous, tu résous, il résoud,
    nous résolvons, vous résolvez, ils résolvent.
IMPERATIVE
    résous, résolvons, résolvez.
PRES. PART.
    résolvant; IMPERFECT je résolvais, etc.
PRES. SUBJ.
    je résolve, etc.
PAST PARTICIPLE
    résolu; PASSÉ COMPOSÉ j'ai résolu, etc.
PASSÉ SIMPLE
    je résolus, etc.; IMPERF. SUBJ. je résolusse, etc.

163. rire, *to laugh.*

FUTURE and COND. regular.
PRESENT INDICATIVE
    je ris, tu ris, il rit,
    nous rions, vous riez, ils rient.
IMPERATIVE
    ris, rions, riez.
PRES. PART.
    riant; IMPERFECT je riais, etc.
PRES. SUBJ.
    je rie, tu ries, il rie,
    nous riions, vous riiez, ils rient.
PAST PARTICIPLE
    ri; PASSÉ COMPOSÉ j'ai ri, etc.
PASSÉ SIMPLE
    je ris, etc.; IMPERF. SUBJ. je risse, etc.
Like **rire:** sourire, *to smile.*

164. savoir, *to know.*

FUTURE
    je saurai, etc.; COND. je saurais, etc.

PRESENT INDICATIVE
 je sais, tu sais, il sait,
 nous savons, vous savez, ils savent.
IMPERATIVE
 sache, sachons, sachez.
PRES. PART.
 sachant; IMPERFECT je savais, etc.
PRES. SUBJ.
 je sache, etc.
PAST PARTICIPLE
 su; PASSÉ COMPOSÉ j'ai su, etc.
PASSÉ SIMPLE
 je sus, etc.; IMPERF. SUBJ. je susse, etc.

165. suffire, *to suffice, to be enough.*

FUTURE and COND. regular.
PRESENT INDICATIVE
 je suffis, tu suffis, il suffit,
 nous suffisons, vous suffisez, ils suffisent.
IMPERATIVE
 suffis, suffisons, suffisez.
PRES. PART.
 suffisant; IMPERFECT je suffisais, etc.
PRES. SUBJ.
 je suffise, etc.
PAST PARTICIPLE
 suffi; PASSÉ COMPOSÉ j'ai suffi, etc.
PASSÉ SIMPLE
 je suffis, etc.; IMPERF. SUBJ. je suffisse, etc.

166. suivre, *to follow.*

FUTURE and COND. regular.
PRESENT INDICATIVE
 je suis, tu suis, il suit,
 nous suivons, vous suivez, ils suivent.

IMPERATIVE
suis, suivons, suivez.

PRES. PART.
suivant; IMPERFECT je suivais, etc.

PRES. SUBJ.
je suive, etc.

PAST PARTICIPLE
suivi; PASSÉ COMPOSÉ j'ai suivi, etc.

PASSÉ SIMPLE
je suivis, etc.; IMPERF. SUBJ. je suivisse, etc.

Like **suivre: poursuivre,** *to pursue.*

167. tenir, *to hold.*

FUTURE
je tiendrai, etc.; COND. je tiendrais, etc.

PRESENT INDICATIVE
je tiens, tu tiens, il tient,
nous tenons, vous tenez, ils tiennent.

IMPERATIVE
tiens, tenons, tenez.

PRES. PART.
tenant; IMPERFECT je tenais, etc.

PRES. SUBJ.
je tienne, tu tiennes, il tienne,
nous tenions, vous teniez, ils tiennent.

PAST PARTICIPLE
tenu; PASSÉ COMPOSÉ j'ai tenu, etc.

PASSÉ SIMPLE
je tins, tu tins, il tint,
nous tînmes, vous tîntes, ils tinrent. IMPERF. SUBJ. je tinsse, etc.

Like **tenir: s'abstenir,** *to abstain;* **appartenir,** *to belong;* **contenir,** *to contain;* **détenir,** *to detain;* **entretenir,** *to keep in good condition;* **maintenir,** *to maintain;* **obtenir,** *to obtain;* **retenir,** *to retain;* **soutenir,** *to sustain.*

168. traire, *to milk.*

FUTURE and COND. regular.

PRESENT INDICATIVE
> je trais, tu trais, il trait,
> nous trayons, vous trayez, ils traient.

IMPERATIVE
> trais, trayons, trayez.

PRES. PART.
> trayant; IMPERFECT je trayais, etc.

PRES. SUBJ.
> je traie, tu traies, il traie,
> nous trayions, vous trayiez, ils traient.

PAST PARTICIPLE
> trait; PASSÉ COMPOSÉ j'ai trait, etc.

PASSÉ SIMPLE
> ——; IMPERF. SUBJ. ——.

Like **traire: abstraire,** *to abstract;* **distraire,** *to distract;* **extraire,** *to extract;* **soustraire,** *to subtract;* etc.

169. vaincre, *to conquer.*

FUTURE and COND. regular.

PRESENT INDICATIVE
> je vaincs, tu vaincs, il vainc,
> nous vainquons, vous vainquez, ils vainquent.

IMPERATIVE
> vaincs, vainquons, vainquez.

PRES. PART.
> vainquant; IMPERFECT je vanquis, etc.

PRES. SUBJ.
> je vainque, etc.

PAST PARTICIPLE
> vaincu; PASSÉ COMPOSÉ j'ai vaincu, etc.

PASSÉ SIMPLE
> je vainquis, etc.; IMPERF. SUBJ. je vainquisse, etc.

Like **vaincre: convaincre,** *to convince.*

170. valoir, *to be worth*.

FUTURE
> je vaudrai, etc.; COND. je vaudrais, etc.

PRESENT INDICATIVE
> je vaux, tu vaux, il vaut,
> nous valons, vous valez, ils valent.

IMPERATIVE
> vaux, valons, valez.

PRES. PART.
> valant; IMPERFECT je valais, etc.

PRES. SUBJ.
> je vaille, tu vailles, il vaille,
> nous valions, vous valiez, ils vaillent.

PAST PARTICIPLE
> valu; PASSÉ COMPOSÉ j'ai valu, etc.

PASSÉ SIMPLE
> je valus, etc.; IMPERF. SUBJ. je valusse, etc.

171. venir, *to come*.

FUTURE
> je viendrai, etc.; COND. je viendrais, etc.

PRESENT INDICATIVE
> je viens, tu viens, il vient,
> nous venons, vous venez, ils viennent.

IMPERATIVE
> viens, venons, venez.

PRES. PART.
> venant; IMPERFECT je venais, etc.

PRES. SUBJ.
> je vienne, tu viennes, il vienne,
> nous venions, vous veniez, ils viennent.

PAST PARTICIPLE
> venu; PASSÉ COMPOSÉ je suis venu(e), etc.

PASSÉ SIMPLE
> je vins, tu vins, il vint,
> nous vînmes, vous vîntes, ils vinrent. IMPERF. SUBJ. je vinsse, etc.

Like **venir: convenir,** *to agree, to suit;* **devenir,** *to become;* **intervenir,**
to intervene; **parvenir,** *to attain;* **prévenir,** *to warn,* etc.; **provenir,**
to come from; **revenir,** *to come back;* **se souvenir,** *to remember;*
etc.

172. vêtir, *to clothe.*

FUTURE and COND. regular.

PRESENT INDICATIVE
> je vêts, tu vêts, il vêt,
> nous vêtons, vous vêtez, ils vêtent.

IMPERATIVE
> vêts, vêtons, vêtez.

PRES. PART.
> vêtant; IMPERFECT je vêtais, etc.

PRES. SUBJ.
> je vête, etc.

PAST PARTICIPLE
> vêtu; PASSÉ COMPOSÉ j'ai vêtu, etc.

PASSÉ SIMPLE
> je vêtis, etc.; IMPERF. SUBJ. je vêtisse, etc.

173. vivre, *to live.*

FUTURE and COND. regular.

PRESENT INDICATIVE
> je vis, tu vis, il vit,
> nous vivons, vous vivez, ils vivent.

IMPERATIVE
> vis, vivons, vivez.

PRES. PART.
> vivant; IMPERFECT je vivais. etc.

PRES. SUBJ.
    je vive, etc.
PAST PARTICIPLE
    vécu; PASSÉ COMPOSÉ j'ai vécu, etc.
PASSÉ SIMPLE
    je vécus, etc.; IMPERF. SUBJ. je vécusse, etc.

174. voir, *to see.*

FUTURE
    je verrai, etc.; COND. je verrais, etc.
PRESENT INDICATIVE
    je vois, tu vois, il voit,
    nous voyons, vous voyez, ils voient.
IMPERATIVE
    vois, voyons, voyez.
PRES. PART.
    voyant; IMPERFECT je voyais, etc.
PRES. SUBJ.
    je voie, tu voies, il voie,
    nous voyions, vous voyiez, ils voient.
PAST PARTICIPLE
    vu; PASSÉ COMPOSÉ j'ai vu, etc.
PASSÉ SIMPLE
    je vis, etc.; IMPERF. SUBJ. je visse, etc.

Like **voir: entrevoir,** *to catch sight of;* **revoir,** *to see again.*

prévoir is like **voir** except that the future and conditional are regular.

pourvoir is like **voir** except that the future and conditional are regular
    and that the passé simple is **je pourvus,** etc. and the imperfect
    subjunctive **je pourvusse,** etc.

175. vouloir, *to want, to will.*

FUTURE
    je voudrai, etc.; COND. je voudrais, etc.

PRESENT INDICATIVE
  je veux, tu veux, il veut,
  nous voulons, vous voulez, ils veulent.

IMPERATIVE
  veux, voulons, voulez, *or*
  veuille, veuillons, veuillez.

PRES. PART.
  voulant; IMPERFECT je voulais, etc.

PRES. SUBJ.
  je veuille, tu veuilles, il veuille,
  nous voulions, vous vouliez, ils veuillent.

PAST PARTICIPLE
  voulu; PASSÉ COMPOSÉ j'ai voulu, etc.

PASSÉ SIMPLE
  je voulus, etc.; IMPERF. SUBJ. je voulusse, etc.

VOCABULARIES

ABBREVIATIONS

abbr	abbreviation	*interrog*	interrogative
adj	adjective	*intr*	intransitive
adv	adverb	*lang*	language
art	article	*m*	masculine
* (asterisk)	aspirate *h*	*n*	noun
cond	conditional	*obj*	object
conj	conjunction	*p part*	past participle
conjug	conjugated	*p simple*	passé simple
contr	contraction	*par*	paragraph
dem	demonstrative	*pers*	person, personal
dir obj	direct object	*pl*	plural
exclam	exclamatory	*poss*	possessive
f	feminine	*pr*	present
fut	future	*prep*	preposition
imper	imperative	*pron*	pronoun
imperf	imperfect	*rel*	relative
ind	indicative	*sg*	singular
indir obj	indirect object	*subj*	subjunctive
inf	infinitive	*trans*	transitive

FRENCH-ENGLISH

A

à [a] at, in, to, into, for; à moi mine

abandonner [abɑ̃dɔne] to give up

abondant, abondante [abõdɑ̃, abõdɑ̃t] abundant

abord: d'abord [dabɔʀ] at first

absence [apsɑ̃s] f absence

absolument [apsɔlymɑ̃] absolutely

accepter [aksɛpte] accept

accessible [aksɛsibl] accessible

accident [aksidɑ̃] m accident

accompagner [akõpaɲe] to go with

accueillir [akœjiʀ] to welcome

accuser [akyze] to accuse; s'accuser to accuse oneself

achat [aʃa] m purchase

acheter [aʃte] to buy

achever [aʃve] to finish

actuel, actuelle [aktɥɛl] present

actuellement [aktɥɛlmɑ̃] at present

adjectif [adʒɛktif] m adjective; adjectif possessif possessive adjective

administration [administʀasjõ] f administration; une administration financière an office of the Treasury Department

admirer [admiʀe] to admire

adorer [adɔʀe] to love, to adore

adresse [adʀɛs] f address

adresser [adʀɛse] to send

affaire [afɛʀ] f affair; une affaire d'impôt a tax question

affirmativement [afiʀmativmɑ̃] affirmatively

affluent [aflyɑ̃] m tributary

afin de [afɛ̃də] in order to

âge [ɑʒ] m age; Quel âge a-t-il? How old is he?

agent [aʒɑ̃] m: agent de police policeman

agit: s'agir de [saʒiʀ də] to be a question of

agréable [agʀeabl] pleasant

agréer [agʀee] to accept, to approve

agricole [agʀikɔl] agricultural

agriculture [agʀikyltyʀ] f agriculture

aider [ɛde] to help

aile [ɛl] f wing (of bird or of building)

ailleurs [ajœʀ] elsewhere; d'ailleurs besides

aimable [ɛmabl] kind

aimer [ɛme] to love, to like; aimer mieux to prefer

air [ɛʀ] m air

aisé [eze] easy

aisément [ezemɑ̃] easily

ajouter [aʒute] to add

aliment [alimɑ̃] m food

Allemagne [almaɲ] f Germany

aller [ale] to go; **s'en aller** to go away

alors [alɔʀ] then, in that case

Alpes [alp] ƒ Alps

Américain, Américaine [ameʀikɛ̃, ameʀikɛn] an American

ami [ami] *m* friend

amitié [amitje] ƒ friendship; **faire mes amitiés à** to say hello to, give my regards to

amuser [amyze] to amuse; **s'amuser** to be amused, to have a good time

an [ɑ̃] *m* year (*see par 56*)

Angleterre [ɑ̃glətɛʀ] ƒ England

année [ane] ƒ year (*see par 56*)

anniversaire [anivɛʀsɛʀ] *m* birthday

annonce [anõs] ƒ announcement

Antilles [ɑ̃tij] ƒ *pl* West Indies

antiquaire [ɑ̃tikɛʀ] *m* antique dealer

août [u] or [ut] August

apercevoir [apɛʀsəvwaʀ] to see, to perceive

appareil [apaʀɛj] *m* camera

appartenir (à) [apaʀtəniʀ] to belong to

appeler [aple] to call; **s'appeler** to be named

apporter [apɔʀte] to bring

apprécier [apʀesje] to appreciate

apprendre [apʀɑ̃dʀ] to learn

approcher [apʀɔʃe] to approach, to draw near; **s'approcher** to approach

approprié [apʀɔpʀije] appropriate

après [apʀɛ] after; **d'après** according to

après-midi [apʀɛmidi] *m* or ƒ afternoon

Arabie [aʀabi] ƒ Arabia; **Arabie saoudite** Saudi Arabia

arbre [aʀbʀ] *m* tree

arbuste [aʀbүst] *m* shrub

argent [aʀʒɑ̃] *m* money

arme [aʀm] ƒ weapon

armée [aʀme] ƒ army

armoire [aʀmwaʀ] ƒ cupboard

arranger [aʀɑ̃ʒe] to arrange; **s'arranger** to improve, to clear up

arrêt [aʀɛ] *m* stop, stopping

arrêter [aʀɛte] *trans* to stop, to arrest; **s'arrêter** to stop

arrivée [aʀive] ƒ arrival

arriver [aʀive] to arrive, to get to; to happen; to succeed

arroser [aʀoze] to water, to sprinkle

article [aʀtikl] *m* article

artistique [aʀtistik] artistic

Asie [asi] ƒ Asia

asseoir [aswaʀ] to seat; **s'asseoir** to sit down

assidûment [asidymɑ̃] systematically

assiette [asjɛt] ƒ plate

assister à [asistea] to be present at

association [asɔsjasjõ] ƒ association; **association sportive** an athletic organization

assurance [asyʀɑ̃s] ƒ insurance

atteindre [atɛ̃dʀ] to reach

attendre [atɑ̃dʀ] to wait for, to expect; **s'attendre à** to expect

attention [atɑ̃sjõ] ƒ attention

attirer [atiʀe] to attract

aucun, aucune [okɶ̃, okyn] (**with**

ne) not a, no; *pron* none, not a one

au-dessus [odsy] above

augmenter [ɔgmɑ̃te] to increase, raise

aujourd'hui [ɔʒuʀdɥi] today

auparavant [opaʀavɑ̃] before

auprès de [opʀɛdə] near, with

auquel [okɛl] *see* **lequel**

aussi [osi] also, too; **aussi . . . que** as . . . as

aussitôt que [ositokə] as soon as

auto [ɔto] *m* or *f* car

autoroute [ɔtoʀut] *f* freeway, throughway

autre [otʀ] other

autrefois [otʀəfwa] formerly, long ago

avancer [avɑ̃se] to go forward

avant de [avɑ̃də] before; **avant que** before

avec [avɛk] with

aventure [avɑ̃tyʀ] *f* adventure

avenue [avny] *f* avenue

avertir [avɛʀtiʀ] to warn

avion [avjõ] *m* plane; **en avion, par avion** by plane; **avion à réaction** jet plane

avis [avi] *m* advice, opinion

avocat [avɔka] *m* lawyer

avoine [avwan] *f* oats

avoir [avwaʀ] to have; **pour avoir un taxi** to get a taxi; **avoir à** to have to; **avoir beau** to . . . in vain

avril [avʀil] April

B

Balzac [balzak] 19th century French novelist

banque [bɑ̃k] *f* bank

bateau [bato] *m* boat

bavard, bavarde [bavaʀ, bavaʀd] chatty, garrulous

beau, belle, etc. [bo] [bɛl] beautiful; **il faisait beau** the weather was fine

Beauce [bos] *f* rich agricultural region southwest of Paris

beaucoup [boku] much, a great deal

Beaune [bon] city in Burgundy

beauté [bote] *f* beauty

bébé [bebe] *m* baby

Belgique [bɛlʒik] *f* Belgium

besoin [bəzwɛ̃] *m* need

beurre [bœʀ] *m* butter

bien [bjɛ̃] very; well; **bien que** although

bien-être [bjɛ̃nɛtʀ] *m* well-being

bière [bjɛʀ] *f* beer

bijou [biʒu] *m* jewel

billet [bijɛ] *m* ticket

blanc, blanche [blɑ̃, blɑ̃ʃ] white

blesser [blɛse] to wound; **se blesser** to be wounded

bleu, bleue [blø] blue

boire [bwaʀ] to drink

bois [bwa] *m* wood; **en bois sculpté** of carved wood

bois [bwa] *pr ind of* **boire**

bon, bonne [bõ, bɔn] good; l̥ **bon vieux temps** the good old days; **sentir bon** to smell good

bonjour [bõʒuʀ] good morning, good afternoon

bord [bɔʀ] *m* edge

bouledogue [buldɔg] *m* bulldog

bouteille [butɛj] *f* bottle

bouton [butõ] *m* button, knob

bras [bʀɑ] *m* arm; **à bras ouverts** with open arms
brave [bʀav] good, worthy; brave
bref [bʀɛf] in a word
Brésil [bʀezil] *m* Brazil
Bretagne [bʀətaɲ] *f* Brittany
bruit [bʀɥi] *m* noise
brûlant, brûlante [bʀylɑ̃, bʀylɑ̃t] burning, very hot
Bruxelles [bʀy(k)sɛl] Brussels
bureau [byʀo] *m* office; **bureau de tabac** tobacco shop
but [by] *m* goal; **un but commun** a common goal

C

c' *see* **ce**
ça, cela [sa, sla] that, it
cabinet [kabinɛ] *m* private room, study, office (at home)
cacher [kaʃe] to hide, conceal
cadeau [kado] *m* present, gift
Caen [kɑ̃] ancient city in Normandy
café [kafe] *m* coffee; **café noir** black coffee; **café au lait** coffee with hot milk
Le Caire [lə kɛʀ] *m* Cairo
calme [kalm] calm
camp [kɑ̃] *m* camp
campagne [kɑ̃paɲ] *f* country
Canada [kanada] *m* Canada
capitaine [kapitɛn] *m* captain
car [kaʀ] because
carré [kaʀe] square; **un kilomètre carré** one square kilometer
carte [kaʀt] *f* card; menu
carte-postale [kaʀt pɔstal] *f* post card

cas [kɑ] *m* case; **en tout cas** in any case, anyway
cathédrale [katedʀal] *f* cathedral; **cathédrale gothique** Gothic cathedral
cause [koz] *f* cause; **à cause de la pluie** because of the rain
ce, c' [sə] it, that, he, she, they, etc.
ce, cet, cette; ces [sə, sɛt, sɛt; sɛ] this, that; these, those
célèbre [selɛbʀ] famous, celebrated
celui [səlɥi] *m* the one; **ceux** the ones, those; **celui-ci, celui-là** this one, that one, etc.; **celle** *f sing*, **celles** *f pl;* **celle-ci**, etc.
centaine [sɑ̃tɛn] *f* about a hundred
cérémonie [seʀemɔni] *f* ceremony
certain, certaine [sɛʀtɛ̃, sɛʀtɛn] certain; **il est certain** it is certain
certainement [sɛʀtɛnmɑ̃] of course
cesser [sɛse] to stop
ceux [sø] *see* **celui**
Cézanne [sezan] 19th century French painter
chacun, chacune [ʃakœ̃, ʃakyn] each, each one
chambre [ʃɑ̃bʀ] *f* bedroom
champ [ʃɑ̃] *m* field
chandail [ʃɑ̃daj] *m* sweater
changement [ʃɑ̃ʒmɑ̃] *m* change
changer [ʃɑ̃ʒe] to change
chant [ʃɑ̃] *m* song
chanter [ʃɑ̃te] to sing; **chanter faux** to sing off pitch; **chanter juste** to sing on pitch

charge [ʃaʀʒ] *f* charge, load
charger: se charger de [səʃaʀʒe] to take charge of
chat [ʃa] *m* cat
château [ʃɑto] *m* château
chauffeur [ʃofœʀ] *m* driver
Chenonceaux [ʃənõso] famous Renaissance château
cher [ʃɛʀ] dear; **coûter cher** to be expensive
chercher [ʃɛʀʃe] to look for; **aller chercher** to go to get; **chercher à** to try to
cheval [ʃəval] *m* horse
chez [ʃe] at the home, house, apartment, office, store of
chien [ʃjẽ] *m* dog
Chili [ʃili] *m* Chile
Chine [ʃin] *f* China
choisir [ʃwaziʀ] to choose
choix [ʃwa] *m* choice
chose [ʃoz] *f* thing; **quelque chose** something; **autre chose** something else; **pas grand'chose** nothing much; **peu de chose** practically nothing; **dire bien des choses à** to give regards to
chute [ʃyt] *f* fall; **les Chutes du Niagara** Niagara Falls
ci-inclus [siẽkly] herewith
cimetière [simtjɛʀ] *m* cemetery; **Le Cimetière marin** a poem by Paul Valéry
cinéma [sinema] *m* movies; **au cinéma** to, at the movies
clairière [klɛʀjɛʀ] *f* clearing
cœur [kœʀ] *m* heart; **savoir par cœur** to know by heart
coin [kwẽ] *m* corner; **coins perdus** out-of-the-way places

combien [kõbjẽ] how much; **combien de temps** how long
combiner [kõbine] to combine, join
commander [kɔmɑ̃de] to order
comme [kɔm] as; **Comme il vous plaîra** As You Like It; **comme ça** like that; **comme ci comme ça** so-so
commencement [kɔmɑ̃smɑ̃] *m* beginning
commencer [kɔmɑ̃se] to begin
comment [kɔmɑ̃] how; **Comment ça?** How's that; **Et comment!** And how!
commettre [kɔmɛtʀ] to commit
commun, commune [kɔmœ̃, kɔmyn] common
compagnie [kõpaɲi] *f* company
comparé à [kõpaʀea] in comparison with
complet, complète [kõplɛ, kõplɛt] complete; full
compliment [kõplimɑ̃] *m* compliment
comprendre [kõpʀɑ̃dʀ] to understand; **Je n'y comprends rien** I don't understand it at all; **ça se comprend** that is understandable
compte [kõt] *m* account; **se rendre compte** to realize
compter [kõte] to expect, count on
concerner [kõsɛʀne] to concern; **en ce qui concerne l'agriculture** as far as agriculture is concerned
concert [kõsɛʀ] *m* concert
conclure [kõklyʀ] to conclude

condition [kõdisjõ] *f* condition; à quelles conditions in what circumstances; à condition de on condition that

conditionnel [kõdisjɔnɛl] *m* conditional; conditionnel passé conditional perfect

conduire [kõdɥiʀ] to drive, to conduct

configuration [kõfigyʀasjõ] *f* lay (of the land)

confort [kõfɔʀ] *m* comfort

congé [kõʒe] *m* leave of absence, vacation

connaissance [kɔnɛsɑ̃s] *f* acquaintance; faire sa connaissance to meet him, her

connaître [kɔnɛtʀ] to know (*see paragraph 41*)

conseil [kõsɛj] *m* advice

conseiller [kõsɛje] to advise

consentir [kõsɑ̃tiʀ] to consent

conserver [kõsɛʀve] to keep

considération [kõsideʀasjõ] *f* consideration

consoler [kõsɔle] to console, to comfort

construction [kõstʀyksjõ] *f* building

construire [kõstʀɥiʀ] to build

construit [kõstʀɥi] *p part of* construire

content, contente [kõtɑ̃, kõtɑ̃t] happy, glad

continuer [kõtinɥe] to continue, proceed

contraire [kõtʀɛʀ] *m* contrary; au contraire on the contrary

convenable [kõvnabl] proper, correct

convenir [kõvniʀ] to agree, to be suitable

copieusement [kɔpjøsmɑ̃] copiously

corde [kɔʀd] *f* rope

cordialement [kɔʀdjalmɑ̃]; bien cordialement cordially

correspondance [kɔʀɛspõdɑ̃s] *f* correspondence

côté [kote] *m* side; à côté de beside; de l'autre côté on the other side

coucher: se coucher [skuʃe] to go to bed

couleur [kulœʀ] *f* color

coup [ku] *m* blow; tout à coup suddenly

cour [kuʀ] *f* court

courageusement [kuʀaʒøzmɑ̃] courageously

courageux, courageuse [kuʀaʒø, kuʀaʒøz] courageous

couramment [kuʀamɑ̃] fluently

courant [kuʀɑ̃] this month

courir [kuʀiʀ] to run

cours [kuʀ] *m* course; au cours de in the course of

course [kuʀs] *f* errand

court, courte [kuʀ, kuʀt] short

cousin [kuzɛ̃] *m,* cousine [kuzin] *f* cousin

coûter [kute] to cost; coûter cher to be expensive

couvrir [kuvʀiʀ] to cover

craindre [kʀɛ̃dʀ] to fear

crème [kʀɛm] *f* cream

crime [kʀim] *m* crime

criminel [kʀiminɛl] *m* criminal

crise [kʀiz] *f* crisis; crise d'appendicite appendicitis

croire [kʀwaʀ] to believe, to think; **se croire au Pays des Merveilles** to think you are in Wonderland

cru [kʀy] *p part of* croire

cruel, cruelle [kʀyɛl] cruel

cueillir [kœjiʀ] to pick

cuisine [kɥizin] *f* cooking

cuisinier [kɥizinje] *m,* cuisinière [kɥizinjɛʀ] *f* cook

cultivateur [kyltivatœʀ] *m* farmer

culture [kyltyʀ] *f* farming

cygne [siɲ] *m* swan

D

dahlia [dalja] *m* dahlia

Danemark [danmaʀk] *m* Denmark

dans [dɑ̃] in, into; **dans quelques années** within a few years

date [dat] *f* date

davantage [davɑ̃taʒ] more

de [də] of; from; by

décider [deside] to decide

déclarer [deklaʀe] to declare

décoration [dekɔʀasjõ] *f* decoration

découverte [dekuvɛʀt] *f* discovery

décrire [dekʀiʀ] to describe

défaut [defo] *m* fault

défendre [defɑ̃dʀ] to forbid

défini, définie [defini] definite

Degas [dəga] French Impressionist painter

déjà [deʒa] already

déjeuner [deʒœne] to have lunch

délai [delɛ] *m* delay; the time required

délicieux, délicieuse [delisjø, delisjøz] delicious

demander [dəmɑ̃de] to ask; **se demander** to wonder

demeurer [dəmœʀe] to live, to reside

demi-heure [dəmiœʀ] *f* half an hour

demi-tour [dəmituʀ] *m* half turn; **faire demi-tour** to turn around

démonstratif, démonstrative [demõstʀatif, demõstʀativ] demonstrative

départ [depaʀ] *m* departure

dépêche [depɛʃ] *f* telegram

dépêcher [depɛʃe]: **se dépêcher** to hurry

dépendre de [depɑ̃dʀ] to depend upon

dépenser [depɑ̃se] to spend

déplaire à [deplɛʀ a] to displease

déportation [depɔʀtasjõ] *f* deportation

déposer [depoze] to put down, to deposit

dépouiller [depuje] to strip

depuis [dəpɥi] since; for (*when used with pres tense*)

dérangement [deʀɑ̃ʒmɑ̃] *m* bother

déranger [deʀɑ̃ʒe] to bother (someone); **se déranger** to be bothered

dernier, dernière [dɛʀnje, dɛʀnjɛʀ] last

dès que [dɛ kə] as soon as

descendre [desɑ̃dʀ] to go down; **descendre à un hôtel** to stop at a hotel; **descendre de l'autobus** to get off the bus

désert [dezɛʀ] *m* desert

désespérer [dezɛspeʀe] to despair, to give up; **de quoi désespérer** enough to make you give up

désirer [deziʀe] to want

dessin [desɛ̃] *m* drawing, design

destination [dɛstinasjõ] *f* destination

destiné à [dɛstine a] intended for

déterminer [detɛʀmine] to determine

détester [detɛste] to hate, detest

devanture [dəvãtyʀ] *f* shop window

développement [devlɔpmã] *m* development

devenir [dəvnir] to become

devenu [dəvny] *p part of* **devenir**

devoir [dəvwaʀ] must, should, ought, to be supposed to; to owe (*see par 34*)

dévoué [devwe] devoted; **votre bien dévoué** sincerely yours

Diane de Poitiers [djandəpwatje] favorite of Henri II

différence [difeʀãs] *f* difference

dîner [dine] to dine, to have dinner

diplomate [diplɔmat] *m* diplomat

dire [diʀ] to say, to tell; **cela se dit** that is said

direct, directe [diʀɛkt, diʀɛkt] direct; **l'expression directe** direct discourse; quotation

directement [diʀɛktəmã] directly

diriger [diʀiʒe] to direct

discuter [diskyte] to argue, to discuss

disparaître [dispaʀɛtʀ] to disappear

disposition [dispozisjõ] *f* disposal;

à votre disposition at your disposal

distance [distãs] *f* distance; **à quelle distance de** how far, at what distance; **vu à distance** seen from a distance

distinguer [distɛ̃ge] to distinguish

dites [dit] say (*imper of* **dire**)

divers, diverse [divɛʀ, divɛʀs] various

docteur [dɔktœʀ] *m* doctor

donc [dõk] then

dont [dõ] whose, of whom, of which; **l'argent dont j'ai besoin** the money I need

dort [dɔʀ] *pres ind of* **dormir**

douane [dwan] *f* customs

doute [dut] *m* doubt

douter [dute] to doubt; **se douter de** to suspect

doux, douce [du, dus] gentle, soft; **bruit doux** gentle noise

douzaine [duzɛn] *f* dozen

du, de la, des, de, d' some, some of (often not translated in English); from, of, etc.

dû [dy] *p part of* **devoir**

dune [dyn] *f* dune

duquel [dykɛl] *see* **lequel**

durée [dyʀe] *f* duration; **de courte durée** of brief duration, short-lived

dynamite [dinamit] *f* dynamite

E

eau [o] *f* water

échanger [eʃãʒe] to exchange

échantillon [eʃãtijõ] *m* sample

échapper [eʃape] to escape

éclat [ekla] *m* brilliance
école [ekɔl] *f* school
écouter [ekute] to listen
écrier: s'écrier [sekʀie] to cry out
écrire [ekʀiʀ] to write; ça s'écrit that is written, spelled
effet [efɛ] *m* effect; en effet indeed, in truth
efforcer: s'efforcer [sefɔʀse] to try hard
égal, égale [egal] equal; ça m'est égal it's all the same to me
égaler [egale] to equal
Égypte [eʒipt] *f* Egypt
Eiffel: Tour Eiffel [tuʀefɛl] *f* tower 300 meters high (1000 ft. approx.) built in 1889 in Paris
élégant, élégante [elegɑ̃, elegɑ̃t] elegant
élevé [elve] high
elle [ɛl] she; her; herself
éloigné [elwaɲe] distant
emballage [ɑ̃balaʒ] *m* packing
embarquer [ɑ̃baʀke] to embark; to take on
emblème [ɑ̃blɛm] *m* emblem
emparer: s'emparer [sɑ̃paʀe] to seize
empêcher [ɑ̃pɛʃe] to prevent
emplette [ɑ̃plɛt] *f* purchase; faire des emplettes to go shopping
emploi [ɑ̃plwa] *m* use
employer [ɑ̃plwaje] to use, employ
empressé [ɑ̃pʀese]: veuillez agréer mes salutations empressées sincerely yours
en [ɑ̃] *prep* in, to; *adv* from there; *partitive* of them; il en a assez he is fed up with it; il

veut en finir he wants to be done with it; où en est-il? how far along is he?
enchanté [ɑ̃ʃɑ̃te] delighted
encore [ɑ̃kɔʀ] again; pas encore not yet
endormir [ɑ̃dɔʀmiʀ] to put to sleep; s'endormir to fall asleep
endroit [ɑ̃dʀwa] *m* place, locality
enfin [ɑ̃fɛ̃] finally
enfuir: s'enfuir [sɑ̃fɥiʀ] to flee
engrais [ɑ̃gʀɛ] *m* fertilizer
ennuyer [ɑ̃nɥije] to bore; s'ennuyer to be very sad
énorme [enɔʀm] huge
enseigner [ɑ̃sɛɲe] to teach
ensemble [ɑ̃sɑ̃bl] together
ensuite [ɑ̃sɥit] afterwards, then
entendre [ɑ̃tɑ̃dʀ] to hear; entendre parler de to hear of
entendu [ɑ̃tɑ̃dy] agreed, all right; bien entendu of course
enthousiaste [ɑ̃tuzjast] enthusiastic
entier, entière [ɑ̃tje, ɑ̃tjɛʀ] entire, whole
entourer [ɑ̃tuʀe] to surround
entre [ɑ̃tʀ] between; entre eux among them; combien d'entre eux? how many of them?
entrée [ɑ̃tʀe] *f* entrance
entrer [ɑ̃tʀe] to go in
envie [ɑ̃vi] *f* desire
environ [ɑ̃viʀɔ̃] about, approximately
envoyer [ɑ̃vwaje] to send
époque [epɔk] *f* period
équipe [ekip] *f* team, crew
escalier [ɛskalje] *m* staircase
escorter [ɛskɔʀte] to escort

espèce [ɛspɛs] f kind
espérer [ɛspeʀe] to hope
esprit [ɛspʀi] m mind
essayer [esɛje] to try
estampe [ɛstɑ̃p] f print
estimer [ɛstime] to esteem
établissement [etablismɑ̃] m laying; establishment
étage [etaʒ] m story; à deux étages two stories high
état [eta] m state, condition
États-Unis [etazyni] m pl United States
éteindre [etɛ̃dʀ] to extinguish, put out
étendre [etɑ̃dʀ] to stretch; s'étendre to extend
étonnant, étonnante [etɔnɑ̃, etɔnɑ̃t] astonishing
être [ɛtʀ] to be; être censé to be supposed to
étudiant [etydjɑ̃] m, étudiante [etydjɑ̃t] f student
étudier [etydje] to study
Europe [œʀɔp] f Europe
Européen, Européenne [œʀɔpeɛ̃, œʀɔpeɛn] European
eux [ø] they, them
évidemment [evidamɑ̃] evidently
exact, exacte [ɛgzakt] exactly true, correct
exactement [ɛgzaktəmɑ̃] exactly, precisely
examiner [ɛgzamine] to examine
excursion [ɛkskyʀsjɔ̃] f trip
excuser [ɛkskyze] to excuse; s'excuser to apologize
exemple [ɛgzɑ̃pl] m example; par exemple for example
exercice [ɛgzɛʀsis] m exercise

exister [ɛgziste] to exist
expédier [ɛkspedje] to ship
expédition [ɛkspedisjɔ̃] f shipment
expérience [ɛkspeʀjɑ̃s] f experiment
exploser [ɛksploze] to explode
expression [ɛkspʀɛsjɔ̃] f expression

F

façade [fasad] f front, façade
face [fas] f face; face à face face to face
fâché [fɑʃe] angry, sorry, annoyed
facile [fasil] easy
facilement [fasilmɑ̃] easily
façon [fasɔ̃] f way; une façon de parler a way of speaking; de façon à ce que so that
facture [faktyʀ] f bill
faïence [fajɑ̃s] f earthenware, pottery
faillir [fajiʀ] to fail; faillir and infinitive to almost . . .
faire [fɛʀ] to make, to do; faire signe to signal; il fait beau the weather is fine; si ça ne vous fait rien if it's all right with you; cela se fait that is done; faire voir to show; faire bien de to be right in; faire des vers to write poetry; qu'est-ce que ça fait? what difference does that make?
falloir [falwaʀ] to be necessary; must; to require, to take (see par 36)

famille [famij] *f* family

faudra [fodʀa] *future of* falloir

favorable [favɔʀabl] favorable

femme [fam] *f* woman, wife

fermer [fɛʀme] to close

fête [fɛt] *f* festivity, party

février [fevʀie] February

fier, fière [fjɛʀ] proud

fièrement [fjɛʀmã] proudly

fille [fij] *f* girl (as opposed to boy); **jeune fille** girl (especially teen-agers)

film [film] *m* film

fils [fis] *m* son

fin [fɛ̃] *f* end

finance [finãs] *f* finance

financier [finãsje] *m* financier; *adj f* **financière** [finãsjɛʀ] of or pertaining to finance

finir [finiʀ] to finish, to end; **il a fini par** he finally . . . ; **le temps finira par s'arranger** the weather will eventually clear up

fixer [fikse] to fix, to stabilize; **fixer les prix** to fix prices

fleur [flœʀ] *f* flower

fleuve [flœv] *m* river

fois [fwa] *f* time; **une seule fois** a single time

fonctionnaire [fõksjɔnɛʀ] *m* government employe

forage [fɔʀaʒ] *m* drilling

forcer [fɔʀse] to force

formalité [fɔʀmalite] *f* formality

forme [fɔʀm] *f* form

fort, forte [fɔʀ, fɔʀt] *adj* strong; **fort** *adv* very

frais, fraîche [fʀɛ, fʀɛʃ] cool

frais [fʀɛ] *m* cost, expense; **frais d'envoi** cost of shipping

franc [fʀã] *m* franc

français [fʀãsɛ] *m* French (*lang*); **français, française,** *adj* French; **Français,** etc. a French person

franchement [fʀãʃmã] frankly

frère [fʀɛʀ] *m* brother

froid [fʀwa] cold

fruits [fʀɥi] *m pl* fruit

fumer [fyme] to smoke

G

galerie [galʀi] *f* gallery; **Grande Galerie** one of the principal galleries of the Louvre

gant [gã] *m* glove

garantir [gaʀãtiʀ] to guarantee

garder [gaʀde] to keep; **se garder de** to avoid

geler [ʒəle] to freeze

gendarme [ʒãdaʀm] *m* national police

gêner [ʒɛne] to bother

Genève [ʒənɛv] Geneva

genre [ʒãʀ] *m* kind, sort

gens [ʒã] *f pl* people; **des gens riches** rich people

gentil, gentille [ʒãti, ʒãtij] nice

gentiment [ʒãtimã] politely, kindly

Gien [ʒjɛ̃] small town in the Loire valley

gisement [ʒizmã] *m* deposit

glissant [glisã] slippery

gouvernement [guvɛʀnmã] *m* government

gramme [gʀam] *m* gram

grand, grande [gʀã, gʀãd] tall, large

grand'chose [gʀɑ̃ʃoz]: pas grand'chose nothing much

gros, grosse [gʀo, gʀos] large, big

guère [gɛʀ] scarcely (used with ne)

guide [gid] m guide

H

habiller [abije] trans to dress (someone); s'habiller to dress (oneself)

habitable [abitabl] livable, inhabitable

habitant [abitɑ̃] m inhabitant

habiter [abite] to live, reside

habitude [abityd] f habit; d'habitude usually

habituer: s'habituer [sabitɥe] to get used to

*hardi, hardie [aʀdi] bold

*hardiment [aʀdimɑ̃] boldly

*hasard [azaʀ] m chance

Hassi-Messaoud [asimɛsaud] rich oil region in the Sahara

*haut [o] high; en haut de to the top of; parler haut to talk loud; parler bas to talk low

Le *Havre [lə avʀ] m Havre

*hélas [elɑs] alas

hélicoptère [elikɔptɛʀ] m helicopter

hésiter [ezite] to hesitate

hétéroclite [eteʀɔklit] strange

heure [œʀ] f hour; à l'heure on time; de bonne heure early

heureux, heureuse [øʀø, øʀøz] happy

hier [jɛʀ] yesterday

histoire [istwaʀ] f story, history

hiver [ivɛʀ] m winter

*Hollande [ɔlɑ̃d] f Holland

Homère [ɔmɛʀ] Homer

hommage [ɔmaʒ] m homage; agréez mes hommages respectueux sincerely yours

homme [ɔm] m man

honnête [ɔnɛt] honest, respectable

honorer [ɔnɔʀe] to honor

hôpital [ɔpital] m hospital

humeur [ymœʀ] f humor; de bonne humeur in a good mood

I

ici [isi] here; now

idée [ide] f idea

ignorer [iɲɔʀe] to be unaware, not to know

il [il] he, it

île [il] f island; l'Ile d'Orléans island in the St. Lawrence river

Iliade [iljad] f Iliad, Greek epic poem

imaginer: s'imaginer [simaʒine] to imagine

imparfait [ɛ̃paʀfɛ] m imperfect tense

impatience [ɛ̃pasjɑ̃s] f impatience

impératif [ɛ̃peʀatif] m imperative

imperméable [ɛ̃pɛʀmeabl] m raincoat

importer [ɛ̃pɔʀte] to be important; tout ce qui importe all that's important

imposé [ɛ̃poze] imposed, necessitated by

impossible [ɛ̃pɔsibl] impossible

impôt [ɛ̃po] m tax

impression [ɛ̃pʀɛsjõ] f impression

inattendu, inattendue [inatɑ̃dy] unexpected

incliner: s'incliner [sɛ̃kline] to list, to lean

inclus [ɛ̃kly] included; **ci-inclus** herewith

indésirable [ɛ̃deziʀabl] undesirable

indicatif [ɛ̃dikatif] *m* indicative

Indien [ɛ̃djɛ̃] *m* Indian

indiquer [ɛ̃dike] to indicate

indirect, indirecte [ɛ̃diʀɛkt] indirect; **expression indirecte** indirect discourse

industriel, industrielle [ɛ̃dystʀiɛl] industrial

inexploré [inɛksplɔʀe] unexplored

infinitif [ɛ̃finitif] *m* infinitive

ingénieur [ɛ̃ʒenjœʀ] *m* engineer; **ingénieur-chimiste** chemical engineer

inhospitalier, inhospitalière [inɔspitalje, inɔspitaljɛʀ] inhospitable

inoubliable [inubliabl] unforgettable

inscription [ɛ̃skʀipsjɔ̃] *f* inscription, what is written

instant [ɛ̃stɑ̃] *m* moment

intelligent, intelligente [ɛ̃tɛliʒɑ̃, ɛ̃tɛliʒɑ̃t] intelligent

intention [ɛ̃tɑ̃sjɔ̃] *f* intention, meaning

intéressant, intéressante [ɛ̃teʀɛsɑ̃, ɛ̃teʀɛsɑ̃t] interesting, worthwhile

intéresser [ɛ̃teʀɛse] to interest; **s'intéresser** to be interested

intérêt [ɛ̃teʀɛ] *m* interest

intérieur [ɛ̃teʀjœʀ] *m* interior

interrogatif, interrogative [ɛ̃teʀɔgatif, ɛ̃teʀɔgativ] interrogative

intriguer [ɛ̃tʀige] to intrigue

intrus [ɛ̃tʀy] *m* intruder

inverse [ɛ̃vɛʀs] **en sens inverse** in the opposite direction

inversion [ɛ̃vɛʀsjɔ̃] *f* inversion, inverted order

invitation [ɛ̃vitasjɔ̃] *f* invitation

invité [ɛ̃vite] *m* guest

J

jamais [ʒamɛ] ever, never; **ne ...
jamais** never

janvier [ʒɑ̃vje] January

Japon [ʒapɔ̃] *m* Japan

jardin [ʒaʀdɛ̃] *m* garden

jardinier [ʒaʀdinje] *m* gardener

jeu [ʒø] *m* game; **jeu de mots** play on words

jeune [ʒœn] young; **jeune fille** girl

La Joconde [ʒɔkɔ̃d] *f* Mona Lisa

joindre [ʒwɛ̃dʀ] to join; **joindre les deux bouts** to make both ends meet

joli, jolie [ʒɔli] pretty

joliment [ʒɔlimɑ̃] very, quite

jouer [ʒwe] to play; **jouer au tennis** to play tennis

joueur [ʒwœʀ] *m* player

jour [ʒuʀ] *m* day; **de nos jours** these days, in our time

journal [ʒuʀnal] *m* paper

journée [ʒuʀne] day (duration)

juger [ʒyʒe] judge; **juger bon (de)** to see fit (to)

juillet [ʒɥijɛ] July

juin [ʒɥɛ̃] June

jungle [ʒõgl] *f* jungle
jus [ʒy] *m* juice
jusqu'à [ʒyska] until; as far as,
to; **jusqu'à ce que** until
juste [ʒyst] just; **au juste** precisely

K

kilo [kilo] *m* kilogram, 1000
grams (2.2 pounds, approx.)
kiosque [kjɔsk] *m* newspaper
stand

L

là [la] there
la *see* **le**
laboratoire [labɔratwar] *m* laboratory
laisser [lɛse] to leave; to let
lait [lɛ] *m* milk
lancer [lɑ̃se] to throw
Laon [lɑ̃] city northeast of Paris
laquelle [lakɛl] *see* **lequel**
large [larʒ] wide; **la rue a 20
mètres de large** the street is 20
meters wide
largeur [larʒœr] *f* width
le, la, les *art* the; *pron* him, her,
it; them
lendemain (de) [lɑ̃dmɛ̃] *m* the
next day, the day after
lequel, laquelle, lesquels, lesquelles [ləkɛl, lakɛl, lekɛl, le-
kɛl] *rel pron* which; *interrog
pron* which?
leur, leurs [lœr, lœr] their
lever [ləve] to raise; **se lever** to
get up; **le rideau se lève** the
curtain goes up

liberté [libɛrte] *f* liberty
libre [libr] free
lieu [ljø] *m* place; **avoir lieu** to
take place; **au lieu de** instead of
lire [lir] to read
lit [li] *m* bed
litre [litr] *m* liter (9/10 of a
quart, approx.)
livre [livr] *f* pound
livre [livr] *m* book
loin (de) [lwɛ̃ də] far from
Loire [lwar] *f* Loire river
Londres [lõdr] London
long, longue [lõ, lõg] long; **La
Seine a 800 km de long** the
Seine is 800 kilometers long; **le
long des quais** along the quais
longtemps [lõtɑ̃] a long time,
long
longueur [lõgœr] *f* length
lorsque [lɔrskə] when
Louise de Savoie [lwizdəsavwa]
mother of François Ier
Louvre [luvr] *m* former royal
palace that now houses mu-
seums and government offices
lui [lɥi] he, himself; to him, to
her; him
luxe [lyks] *m* luxury
Lyon [ljõ] Lyons

M

machine [maʃin] *f* machine
magasin [magazɛ̃] *m* store
magnifique [maɲifik] wonderful,
magnificent
main [mɛ̃] *f* hand
maintenant [mɛ̃tnɑ̃] now
mais [mɛ] but; **mais oui** of course;

mais si yes I do (*after negative*)

maison [mɛzõ] *f* house; **à la maison** at home

maître [mɛtʀ] *m* master, teacher

mal [mal] *m* evil, pain; **mal au cœur** heartburn; *adv* badly; **pas mal** not bad, quite a bit

malade [malad] sick

malgré [malgʀe] in spite of

malheur [malœʀ] *m* misfortune, unhappiness; **par malheur** unfortunately

malheureusement [malørøzmã] unfortunately

malheureux, malheureuse [malørø, malørøz] unhappy

maman [mamã] *f* mother

mandat-poste [mãdapɔst] *m* money order

manger [mãʒe] to eat

manière [manjɛʀ] *f* manner; **de manière à** so as to

manquer (de) [mãke] to fail; **j'ai manqué de tomber** I almost fell; to be missing; **une assiette manque** one plate is missing

marcher [maʀʃe] to walk

mardi [maʀdi] Tuesday; **le mardi** on Tuesdays

mariage [maʀjaʒ] *m* marriage

marier [maʀje]: **se marier** to get married

mars [maʀs] March

Marseille [maʀsɛj] Marseilles

match [matʃ] *m* game

matin [matɛ̃] *m* morning

mauvais, mauvaise [mɔvɛ, mɔvɛz] bad, wrong; **sentir mauvais** to smell bad

me [mə] me, to or for me, myself

mécontentement [mekõtãtmã] *m* annoyance

meilleur, meilleure [mɛjœʀ] better; **le meilleur** the best

même [mɛm] *adj* same; *adv* even

menacer [mənase] to threaten

mener [məne] to lead

merveille [mɛʀvɛj] *f* a marvel; **à merveille** marvelously; **Pays des Merveilles** Wonderland

mètre [mɛtʀ] *m* metre (39.36 inches, approx.)

mettre [mɛtʀ] to put; **se mettre à** to begin; **se mettre en route** to start

meuble [mœbl] *m* a piece of furniture; **meubles** furniture

meubler [mœble] to furnish

Mexique [mɛksik] *m* Mexico

mien, mienne [mjɛ̃, mjɛn] mine

mieux [mjø] *adv* better; **on ne peut mieux** extremely well

milieu [miljø] *m* middle

minéral [mineʀal] mineral; **l'eau minérale** mineral water

minuit [minɥi] *m* midnight

minute [minyt] *f* minute

mis [mi] *p part of* **mettre**

mobile [mɔbil] movable

mobilier [mɔbilje] *m* furnishings

mode [mɔd] *f* style; **à la mode de** in the style of

moi [mwa] I, me

moindre [mwɛ̃dʀ] *adv* less; **le moindre** the least

moins [mwɛ̃] *adj* less; **le moins** the least; **à moins que** unless; **de moins en moins** less and less; **au moins** at least

mois [mwa] *m* month

moissonneuse - batteuse [mwasɔ-nøz-batøz] *f* combine (harvester-thresher)

moment [mɔmɑ̃] *m* moment; au moment de at the time of; au moment où when

mon, ma, mes [mõ, ma, mɛ] my

monde [mõd] *m* world; du monde in the world, of the world

monsieur [məsjø] *m* gentleman; sir, Mr.; messieurs dames ladies and gentlemen (informal)

montagne [mõtaɲ] *f* mountain

monter [mõte] to go up; to get in (train, car, bus); to go aboard (ship, plane)

montre [mõtʀ] *f* watch

Montréal [mõʀeal] Montreal

monument [mɔnymɑ̃] *m* monument

moquer: se moquer de [sə mɔke də] to kid, make fun of

mort, morte [mɔʀ, mɔʀt] *p part of* mourir

mot [mo] *m* word; un mot short letter

mourir [muʀiʀ] to die

mouvant, mouvante [muvɑ̃, muvɑ̃t] moving

musée [myze] *m* museum

N

nager [naʒe] to swim

naître [nɛtʀ] to be born

national, nationale [nasjɔnal] national

naturellement [natyʀɛlmɑ̃] of course, obviously

ne: ne...pas not; ne...plus no longer; ne...guère scarcely; ne...jamais never; ne...que only; ne...rien nothing; ne...personne nobody; ne...ni...ni neither...nor

né [ne] *p part of* naître

négatif, négative [negatif, negativ] negative

négativement [negativmɑ̃] in the negative

neige [nɛʒ] *f* snow

neiger [nɛʒe] to snow

netteté [nɛtte] *f* clarity

neuf [nœf] nine

nom [nõ] *m* name; noun

nombre [nõbʀ] *m* number

nombreux, nombreuse [nõbʀø, nõbʀøz] numerous

non [nõ] no

notre, nos [nɔtʀ, no] *adj* our; le nôtre [notʀ] our (*poss pron*)

Notre-Dame de Paris [nɔtʀədam də paʀi] cathedral built in 12th and 13th centuries on the Île de la Cité

nourrir [nuʀiʀ] to feed; se nourrir to eat

nous [nu] we; us, ourselves; to or for us, etc.

nouveau, nouvel, nouvelle [nuvo, nuvɛl, nuvɛl] new; de nouveau again

nouvelle [nuvɛl] *f* news

La Nouvelle-Orléans [lanuvɛlɔʀleɑ̃] *f* New Orleans

noyer: se noyer [sə nwaje] to be drowned

nuit [nɥi] *f* night

numéro [nymeʀo] *m* number

O

obéir à [ɔbeiʀ a] to obey
objet [ɔbʒɛ] *m* object; purpose
obliger [ɔbliʒe] oblige
occasion [ɔkɑzjõ] *f* occasion; bargain
occuper [ɔkype] to occupy; **s'occuper de** to take care of
octobre [ɔktɔbʀ] October
œil [œj] *m* eye
œuvre [œvʀ] *f* work
offrir [ɔfʀiʀ] to offer
ombrelle [õbʀɛl] *f* parasol
on, l'on [õ, lõ] one, you, we, they, someone, people
opérer [ɔpeʀe] to operate (on)
opinion [ɔpinjõ] *f* opinion
ordinaire [ɔʀdinɛʀ] ordinary; **d'ordinaire** ordinarily
ordre [ɔʀdʀ] *m* order; **donner l'ordre** to give orders
Orléans [ɔʀleã] city on the Loire river
orner [ɔʀne] to adorn, decorate
oser [oze] to dare
où [u] where, when, in which
oublier (de) [ublie də] to forget
ouest [wɛst] *m* West
outil [uti] *m* tool
ouvert, ouverte [uvɛʀ, uvɛʀt] open; **à bras ouverts** with open arms
ouvrir [uvʀiʀ] to open

P

paiement [pɛmã] *m* payment
paire [pɛʀ] *f* pair
palais [palɛ] *m* palace

panneau [pano] *m* panel
papiers [papje] *m* papers
par [paʀ] by; **par une phrase complète** with a complete sentence
paraître [paʀɛtʀ] to appear
parc [paʀk] *m* park
parce que [paʀskə] because
parcourir [paʀkuʀiʀ] to go through
pardon [paʀdõ] *m* pardon
pare-brise [paʀbʀiz] *m* windshield
parent [paʀã] *m* parent
parfois [paʀfwa] sometimes
parisien, parisienne [paʀizjẽ, paʀizjɛn] Parisian
parler [paʀle] to speak, talk; **parler bas** to talk low; **parler haut** to talk loud
parmi [paʀmi] among
parole [paʀɔl] *f* word
part [paʀ] *f* part; **de ma part** for me
part: à part le pétrole aside from the oil
participe [paʀtisip] *m* participle; **participe passé** past participle; **participe présent** present participle
particulier [paʀtikylje] *m* a (private) person, an individual
particulièrement [paʀtikyljɛʀmã] in particular; specially
partie [paʀti] *f* part; **faire partie de** to be a part of, belong to
partir [paʀtiʀ] to leave, set out
partitif [paʀtitif] *m* partitive
partout [paʀtu] everywhere
parvenir à [paʀvniʀ a] to succeed in

pas: ne. . .pas not
passage [pasaʒ] *m* passage; **de passage à** passing through, temporarily in
passager [pasaʒe] *m* passenger
passé [pɑse] *m* past; **passé composé** compound past tense
passeport [paspɔr] *m* passport
passer [pɑse] to pass, to hand; to spend (time) ; **se passer** to happen
patiemment [pasjamɑ̃] patiently
patience [pasjɑ̃s] *f* patience
patient, patiente [pasjɑ̃, pasjɑ̃t] patient
pauvre [povr] poor; unfortunate
pavillon [pavijɔ̃] *m* lodge; **pavillon de chasse** hunting lodge
payer [pɛje] to pay
pays [pɛi] *m* country; **Pays des Merveilles** Wonderland
paysage [pɛizaʒ] *m* landscape
peindre [pɛ̃dr] to paint
pcine [pɛn] *f* trouble; **à peine** scarcely; **j'ai peine à** I find it hard to; **ce n'est pas la peine** it isn't worth the trouble
peinture [pɛ̃tyr] *f* painting
pèlerine [pɛlrin] *f* cape
pendant [pɑ̃dɑ̃] during; **pendant . . .que** while
penser [pɑ̃se] to think; **je pense à Marie** I am thinking of Marie; **penser de** to hold an opinion about; **que pensez-vous d'elle?** what do you think of her?; **penser** *with infinitive* to expect to
pension [pɑ̃sjɔ̃] *f* room and board; boardinghouse

perdre [pɛrdr] to lose, to waste
permettre [pɛrmɛtr] to permit, make possible; **se permettre de** to take the liberty of
permis [pɛrmi] *m* permit; **permis de conduire** driver's license
Pérou [peru] *m* Peru
personnage [pɛrsɔnaʒ] *m* personage
personne [pɛrsɔn] *f* person
personnellement [pɛrsɔnɛlmɑ̃] personally
perte [pɛrt] *f* loss; **à perte de vue** as far as you can see
peser [pəze] to weigh
petit, petite [pəti, pətit] little, small
pétrole [petrɔl] *m* oil
peu [pø] *m* little; **Dites-nous un peu** Just tell us; **peu à peu** little by little; **c'est peu de chose** it is practically nothing; **à peu près** about; **sous peu** soon
peur [pœr] *f* fear; **avoir peur** to be afraid; **de peur de** for fear that
peut-être [pøtɛtr] perhaps, maybe
pharmacie [farmasi] *f* drugstore
photo [fɔto] *f* photograph
pièce [pjɛs] *f* piece; play
pied [pje] *m* foot; **aller à pied** to walk
pilote [pilɔt] *m* pilot
pipe-line [piplin] *m* pipeline
piqué [pike] annoyed
pire [pir] worse (*adj*); **le pire** the worst
pis [pi] worse (*adv*); **de mal en pis** worse and worse, from bad to worse

placard [plakaʀ] *m* cupboard

place [plas] *f* place; **à votre place** if I were in your place; **de la place** room; **à la place des chevaux** instead of horses; **Place de l'Opéra** large square in front of the Paris Opera

plaindre [plɛ̃dʀ] to pity; **se plaindre** to complain

plaire (à) [plɛʀ a] to please; **s'il vous plaît** if you please (if it is pleasing to you)

plaisir [plɛziʀ] *m* pleasure

plan [plɑ̃] *m* plan; map

planter [plɑ̃te] to plant

pleurer [plœʀe] to cry, to weep

pleuvoir [plœvwaʀ] to rain

plu [ply] *p part of* **pleuvoir**

plu [ply] *p part of* **plaire**

pluie [plɥi] *f* rain

plupart (la) [plypaʀ] *f* most of; **la plupart des gens** most people

plus [ply] more; **plus...que** more than; **plus...plus** the more . . . the more; **plus . . . moins** the more . . . the less; **tout au plus** at most

plusieurs [plyzjœʀ] several

plût [ply] *imperf subj of* **plaire**; **plût au ciel** would to heaven

plutôt [plyto] rather

poésie [pɔezi] *f* poetry

poète [pɔɛt] *m* poet

point [pwɛ̃] *m* point; **au point de vue** from the point of view

poison [pwazõ] *m* poison

police [pɔlis] *f* police; **agent de police** policeman; **police d'assurance** insurance policy

pomme [pɔm] *f* apple

pont [põ] *m* bridge

population [pɔpylasjõ] *f* population

porc-épic [pɔʀkepik] *m* porcupine

porte [pɔʀt] *f* door

portefeuille [pɔʀtəfœj] *m* wallet

porter [pɔʀte] to wear; to carry

portière [pɔʀtjɛʀ] *f* door (of car or train)

portrait [pɔʀtʀɛ] *m* portrait

poser [poze] to put; to ask (a question)

posséder [pɔsede] to possess

possessif, possessive [pɔsɛsif, pɔsɛsiv] possessive

poste [pɔst] *f* post office

poteau-indicateur [pɔto ɛ̃dikatœʀ] *m* signpost

pour [puʀ] to, in order to; for; **pour que** so that

pourquoi [puʀkwa] why

poursuivre [puʀsɥivʀ] to pursue, to trail; **se poursuivre** to be carried on

pourtant [puʀtɑ̃] however

pousser [puse] to grow

pouvoir [puvwaʀ] to be able, can, etc. (*see par 37*); **cela se peut** that is possible

précéder [pʀesede] precede

précis [pʀesi] precise; **à 8 heures précises** at exactly eight o'clock

préférer [pʀefeʀe] to prefer, like better

premier, première [pʀəmje, pʀəmjɛʀ] first

prendre [pʀɑ̃dʀ] to take

préposition [pʀepozisjõ] *f* preposition

près (de) [pʀɛ də] near; **de très près** very closely; **à peu près** about

présence [pʀezɑ̃s] f presence

présent [pʀezɑ̃] m present; present tense

présenter [pʀezɑ̃te] to introduce; **se présenter** to introduce oneself

presque [pʀɛsk] almost

presser [pʀɛse] to press

prêt, prête [pʀɛ, pʀɛt] ready

prêter [pʀɛte] to lend; to attribute

prévenir [pʀevniʀ] to warn

prier (de) [pʀie də] to beg, request

prière [pʀijɛʀ] f prayer, request

pris [pʀi] p part of **prendre**

prise [pʀiz] f the capture, fall; **la prise de Troie** the fall of Troy

prix [pʀi] m price; prize

problème [pʀɔblɛm] m problem

prochain, prochaine [pʀɔʃɛ̃, pʀɔʃɛn] next

proche [pʀɔʃ] adj near

Proche-Orient [pʀɔʃɔʀjɑ̃] m Near East

procurer: se procurer [səpʀɔkyʀe] to get, procure

production [pʀɔdyksjɔ̃] f production

produire [pʀɔdɥiʀ] to produce

produit [pʀɔdɥi] m product

professeur [pʀɔfɛsœʀ] m teacher, professor

profiter (de) [pʀɔfite də] to take advantage of

progrès [pʀɔgʀɛ] m progress

projet [pʀɔʒɛ] m project, plan

promenade [pʀɔmnad] f walk; **faire une promenade** to take a walk

promettre (de) [pʀɔmɛtʀ də] to promise

pronom [pʀɔnɔ̃] m pronoun

pronominal: verbes pronominaux [vɛʀb pʀɔnɔmino] reflexive verbs

prononcer [pʀɔnɔ̃se] to pronounce

prononciation [pʀɔnɔ̃sjasjɔ̃] f pronunciation

proposer [pʀɔpoze] to propose, to suggest

propre [pʀɔpʀ] proper; **les noms propres** proper names

propriétaire [pʀɔpʀietɛʀ] m owner

prospecteur [pʀɔspɛktœʀ] m prospector

prospection [pʀɔspɛksjɔ̃] f prospecting

prospérité [pʀɔspeʀite] f prosperity

provenir (de) [pʀɔvniʀ də] to come from

prudemment [pʀydamɑ̃] prudently, carefully

prudent, prudente [pʀydɑ̃, pʀydɑ̃t] prudent, careful

pu [py] p part of **pouvoir**

puis [pɥi] then, afterwards

puits [pɥi] m well

Q

qualité [kalite] f quality

quantité [kɑ̃tite] f quantity

quart [kaʀ] m quarter

que [kə] rel pron whom, which;

interrog pron what?; *conjunction* that

Québec [kebɛk] city in Canada

quel, quelle, quels, quelles [kɛl] what?

quelque(s) [kɛlk] some; **quelque temps** a little time

quelquefois [kɛlkəfwa] sometimes

quelqu'un, quelques-uns [kɛlkœ̃, kɛlkəzœ̃] someone, some

question [kɛstjõ] *f* question

queue [kø] *f* tail; **faire la queue** to stand in line

qui [ki] *rel pron* who, which; *interrog pron* who? whom?

Quimper [kɛ̃pɛR] city in Brittany; well-known make of pottery

quinzaine [kɛ̃zɛn] *f* about fifteen; **une quinzaine** two weeks

quitter [kite] to leave

quoi [kwa] what; **de quoi** the means, the wherewithal; **il n'y a pas de quoi** don't mention it, you are welcome

quoique [kwakə] although

quoi que [kwakə] whatever

R

raconter [Rakõte] to tell, relate

raison [Rɛzõ] *f* reason

raisonnable [Rɛzɔnabl] reasonable

ralentir [Ralɑ̃tiR] to slow down

rappeler [Raple] to call back; **se rappeler** to recall, remember; **rappelez-moi au bon souvenir de** remember me to

rapporter [RapɔRte] to bring in

rare [RaR] rare

récent [Resɑ̃] recent

recevoir [RəsəvwaR] to receive; to have guests

recherches [RəʃɛRʃ] *f pl* research

réciter [Resite] to recite

récolte [Rekɔlt] *f* crop, harvest

reconduire [RəkõdɥiR] to take (a person) back (home)

reconnaître [RəkɔnɛtR] to recognize

reculer [Rəkyle] to back off, to go backwards, to withdraw

redescendre [RədesɑdR] to go back down

réfrigérateur [RefRiʒeRatœR] *m* refrigerator

refuser (de) [Rəfyzedə] to refuse to

regarder [RəgaRde] to look at

région [Reʒjõ] *f* region

règle [Rɛgl] *f* rule; **en règle** in order

regretter (de) [RəgRɛte] to be sorry, to regret

Reims [Rɛ̃s] Rheims, city northeast of Paris

reine [Rɛn] *f* queen

rejoindre [RəʒwɛdR] to meet, join, catch up with

relation [Rəlɑsjõ] *f* relation

reliquat [Rəlika] *m* balance, remainder

remarquer [RəmaRke] to notice

remercier (de) [RəmɛRsje də] to thank (for)

remettre [RəmɛtR] to deliver; to put back; **remettre en liberté** to set free; **se remettre** to recover

remonter [Rəmõte] to go back up

remplacer [Rɑ̃plase] to replace; **en remplaçant** replacing

remuer [Rəmɥe] to stir

Renaissance [Rənɛsɑ̃s] *f* Renaissance (French Renaissance was 15th and 16th centuries)

rencontre [Rɑ̃kõtR] *f* chance meeting

rencontrer [Rɑ̃kõtre] to meet

rendez-vous [Rɑ̃devu] *m* engagement

rendre [Rɑ̃dR] to give back; **se rendre compte** to realize; **se rendre à** to go to

Renoir [RənwaR] French Impressionist painter

renoncer (à) [Rənõse a] to give up

renseignement(s) [Rɑ̃sɛɲmɑ̃] *m* information

renvoyer [Rɑ̃vwaje] to send back

reparler [RəpaRle] to talk over

repartir [RəpaRtiR] to set out again

répéter [Repete] to repeat

répondre (à) [RepõdRa] to answer

réponse [Repõs] *f* answer; **en réponse** in answer

repos [Rəpo] *m* rest

reposer: se reposer [səRpoze] to rest

représentation [RəpRezɑ̃tasjõ] *f* show, performance

réputation [Repytasjõ] *f* reputation

résidence [Rezidɑ̃s] *f* residence; **résidence habituelle** usual dwelling

résolu [Rezɔly] *p part of* **résoudre**

résoudre [RezudR] to solve

respecter [Rɛspɛkte] to respect

respectueux, respectueuse [Rɛspɛktɥø, Rɛspɛktɥøz] respectful

responsabilité [Rɛspõsabilite] *f* responsibility

ressembler (à) [Rəsɑ̃ble] to resemble, to look like

ressortir [RəsɔRtiR] to go out again

reste [Rɛst] *m* remainder, rest

rester [Rɛste] to stay; to remain; to be left

résultat [Rezylta] *m* result

retard [RətaR] *m* lateness; **en retard** late

retenir [RətniR] to engage, reserve

retomber [Rətõbe] to fall again

retour [RətuR] *m* return; **de retour** back

retourner [RətuRne] to go back

retrouver [RətRuve] to meet, meet again; **se retrouver** to meet

réussir à [ReysiRa] to succeed

réveillé [Revɛje] awake

réveiller [Revɛje] to waken (someone); **se réveiller** to wake up, waken

revenir [RəvniR] to come back

revoir [RəvwaR] to see again; **au revoir** goodbye, I'll be seeing you

Révolution [Revɔlysjõ] *f* the French Revolution began in 1789

riche [Riʃ] rich

rideau [Rido] *m* curtain

rien [Rjɛ̃] nothing; **ne . . . rien** nothing

rigoureux, rigoureuse [RiguRø, RiguRøz] severe

rimer [Rime] to rhyme
rire [RiR] to laugh
risquer (de) [Riske də] to risk
rive [Riv] *f* bank (of river)
rivière [RivjɛR] *f* river
Romorantin [RɔmɔRɑ̃tɛ̃] town southeast of Blois
rosbif [Rɔsbif] *m* roast beef
route [Rut] *f* road; **route du pétrole** oil road
rue [Ry] *f* street
ruiner [Rɥine] to ruin (financially), to bankrupt
Russie [Rysi] *f* Russia

S

sable [sɑbl] *m* sand
sage [saʒ] well-behaved, orderly, wise
sagement [saʒmɑ̃] sensibly, quietly
saharien, saharienne [saaRjɛ̃, saaRjɛn] of the Sahara
Saint-Cloud [sɛ̃klu] suburb on west side of Paris
Saint-Germain-des-Prés [sɛ̃ʒɛRmɛ̃ dɛpRe] popular part of the Left Bank in Paris
saison [sɛzõ] *f* season
salamandre [salamɑ̃dR] *f* salamander
salle [sal] *f* lecture room, exhibition room
salon [salõ] *m* living room
salutation [salytɑsjõ] *f* greeting; **veuillez agréer mes salutations empressées** sincerely yours
samedi [samdi] Saturday; **le samedi** on Saturdays
santé [sɑ̃te] *f* health
la Saône [lason] river flowing into the Rhone at Lyons
sauf [sɔf] except, excepting
savamment [savamɑ̃] learnedly
savant, savante [savɑ̃, savɑ̃t] learned
savoir [savwaR] to know, know how (*see par 40*); **faire savoir** to inform; **je n'en sais rien** I have no idea
sculpture [skyltyR] *f* sculpture
se [sə] himself, herself, oneself, itself, themselves; to or for himself, etc.
sécheresse [sɛʃRɛs] *f* drought
second, seconde [səgõ, səgõd] second
secret, secrète [səkRɛ, səkRɛt] secret
Seine [sɛn] *f* Seine river
séjour [seʒuR] *m* stay, sojourn
semaine [səmɛn] *f* week
sembler [sɑ̃ble] to seem
semence [səmɑ̃s] *f* seed
sens [sɑ̃s] *m* direction; sense
sentiment [sɑ̃timɑ̃] *m* feeling
sentir [sɑ̃tiR] to smell; **sentir bon** to smell good; **se sentir** to feel
sérieusement [seRjøzmɑ̃] seriously
sérieux, sérieuse [sɛRjø, sɛRjøz] serious; **soyez sérieux** don't be silly
service [sɛRvis] *m* service; **service de table** a set of dishes
servir [sɛRviR] to serve; **servir de** to be used as; **servir à** to serve as; **ça ne sert à rien** that's useless; **se servir de** to use; **en vous servant de** using
serviteur [sɛRvitœR] *m* servant

ses [sɛ] *see* **son**

seul, seule [sœl] alone; **une seule fois** a single time

seulement [sœlmɑ̃] only; just

si [si] if; *with imperf* what if; **si grand** so tall; **mais si** oh yes *(denying a negative)*

siècle [sjɛkl] *m* century; **au vingtième siècle** in the 20th century

sien, sienne [sjɛ̃, sjɛn] *poss pron* his, her, its

sieste [sjɛst] *f* siesta, afternoon nap

simple [sɛ̃pl] simple

situation [sitɥasjõ] *f* situation

société [sɔsjete] *f* corporation; society

sœur [sœR] *f* sister

soi [swa] oneself

soif [swaf] *f* thirst; **avoir soif** to be thirsty

soir [swaR] *m* evening

soirée [swaRe] *f* evening (duration)

soixantaine [swasɑ̃tɛn] about 60

soixante-dix [swasɑ̃tdis] seventy

soleil [sɔlej] *m* sun

son, sa, ses [sõ, sa, sɛ] his, her, its, one's

sort [sɔR] *m* fate

sorte [sɔRt] *f* kind; **toute sorte de** all sorts of

sortir [sɔRtiR] to go out; *trans* to take out

Soudan [sudɑ̃] *m* country in North Africa

souffrir [sufRiR] to suffer

souhait [swɛ] *m* wish

souhaiter [swɛte] to wish

souligné [suliɲe] underlined

sourire [suRiR] *m* smile

sourire [suRiR] to smile

sous [su] under; **sous peu** soon

souvenir [suvniR] *m* memory; **rappelez-moi au souvenir de** remember me to

souvenir: se souvenir de [sə suvniR də] to remember

souvent [suvɑ̃] often

soyez [swaje] *imperative of* **être**

sport [spɔR] *m* sport

sportif, sportive [spɔRtif, spɔRtiv] pertaining to sports, athletic

stade [stad] *m* stadium

Stendhal [stɛ̃dal] 19th century French novelist

sucre [sykR] *m* sugar

Suède [sɥɛd] *f* Sweden

suffire [syfiR] to suffice, to be sufficient; **il suffit de** it is enough to

Suisse [sɥis] *f* Switzerland

suite: tout de suite [tudsɥit] immediately

suivant, suivante [sɥivɑ̃, sɥivɑ̃t] following

suivre [sɥivR] to follow

sujet [syʒɛ] *m* subject; **au sujet de** about

superlatif, superlative [sypɛRlatif] superlative

sur [syR] on, over

sûrement [syRmɑ̃] surely

surprendre [syRpRɑ̃dR] to surprise

surpris [syRpRi] *p part of* **surprendre**

surprise [syRpRiz] *f* surprise

surtout [syRtu] especially

survoler [syRvɔle] to fly over

T

table [tabl] *f* table; **à table** at the table

tâcher (de) [taʃe] to try to

taille [taj] *f* size

tant [tã] so much; **tant que** as long as

tapisserie [tapisʀi] *f* tapestry

tard [taʀ] late; **un peu plus tard** a little later

tas [tɑ] *m* pile; **un tas de choses** lots of things

taxi [taksi] *m* taxi

te [tə] you, yourself, to you, for you

tel, telle [tɛl] such

télégramme [telegʀam] *m* telegram

téléphoner [telefɔne] to telephone

télévision [televizjõ] *f* TV

tellement [tɛlmã] so much

température [tãpeʀatyʀ] *f* temperature

temps [tã] *m* time; weather

tenir [təniʀ] to hold; **en tenant compte** bearing in mind, taking into account; **tenir à** to insist upon

terre [tɛʀ] *f* earth; **par terre** on the ground

théâtre [teɑtʀ] *m* theatre

tiens! [tjɛ̃] well!; *imperative of* tenir

tiers [tjɛʀ] *m* third

timbale [tɛ̃bal] *f* cup (of metal)

timbre [tɛ̃bʀ] *m* stamp

tirer [tiʀe] to pull

toi [twa] you, yourself

toit [twa] *m* roof

tomber [tõbe] to fall, to fall down

ton, ta, tes [tõ, ta, tɛ] your

tort [tɔʀ] *m* wrong; **il a tort** he is wrong

tôt [to] soon

toujours [tuʒuʀ] always, still

Touraine [tuʀɛn] *f* region around Tours

tout, toute, tous, toutes [tu, tut, tu, tut] *adj and pron* all; **tout le temps** all the time; **toute l'année** all year; **tous les jours** every day; **tous** [tus] *pron* all; **tout** *adv;* **tout au plus** at most; **tout en faisant des compliments** while making compliments; **tout à l'heure** a while ago, in a little while (depending on the tense of the verb)

toutefois [tutfwa] however

tracteur [tʀaktœʀ] *m* tractor

train [tʀɛ̃] *m* train; **en train de** in the act of; **en train de germer** already sprouting

tranquille [tʀãkil] calm

transport [tʀãspɔʀ] *m* transportation

transporter [tʀãspɔʀte] to transport, carry

travail [tʀavaj] *m* work

travailler [tʀavaje] to work

travers: **à travers** [atʀavɛʀ] through

traverser [tʀavɛʀse] to cross

très [tʀɛ] very

triste [tʀist] sad

tromper [tʀõpe] to deceive; **se tromper** to be mistaken; **se tromper de route** to miss the road

trop [tʀɔ] too; **trop de mal** too much evil, too many bad things

trouver [tʀuve] to find; **comment trouve-t-il le dîner?** how does he like the dinner?; **il le trouve excellent** he thinks it is excellent; **se trouver** to be

T.S.F. [te ɛs ɛf] (**télégraphie sans fil**) *f* radio

tuer [tɥe] to kill; **se tuer** to kill oneself

U

un, une [œ̃, yn] a; one; **l'un, l'une, les uns, les unes** the one, etc.; **l'un et l'autre** both; **ni l'un ni l'autre** neither

usine [yzin] *f* factory, manufacturing company

V

vacances [vakɑ̃s] *f pl* vacation

vais [vɛ] *pr tense of* **aller**

valoir [valwaʀ] to be worth; **il vaut mieux** it is better; **il vaut autant** it is just as well; **il vaudrait mieux** it would be better

vaste [vast] large

vaut [vo] *pres ind of* **valoir**

végétation [veʒetasjɔ̃] *f* vegetation

veille [vɛj] *f* the day before

venant [vənɑ̃] *pr part of* **venir**

vendre [vɑ̃dʀ] to sell; **se vendre bien** to sell well; **on a vendu après décès** they sold after the death of the owner

Vénézuéla [venezɥela] *m* Venezuela

vénézuélien, vénézuélienne [venezɥeljɛ̃, venezɥeljɛn] of Venezuela

venir [vəniʀ] to come; **venir de** (*with inf*) to have just . . .

vente [vɑ̃t] *f* sale; **vente aux enchères** auction sale

verbe [vɛrb] *m* verb

vérité [veʀite] *f* truth; **en vérité** in truth, truly

vers [vɛʀ] *m* verse; **faire des vers** to write poetry

vers [vɛʀ] *prep* towards, about

Versailles [vɛʀsɑj] city west of Paris

vêtement [vɛtmɑ̃] *m* clothing

veuillez [vœje] please (*imperative of* **vouloir**)

viande [vjɑ̃d] *f* meat

victorieux, victorieuse [viktɔʀjø, viktɔʀjøz] victorious

vide [vid] empty

vie [vi] *f* life

vieux, vieille [vjø, vjɛj] old

vif, vive [vif, viv] alive, lively

vilain, vilaine [vilɛ̃, vilɛn] ugly, bad, nasty, disagreeable

village [vilaʒ] *m* village

ville [vil] *f* city

vin [vɛ̃] *m* wine

vingtaine [vɛ̃tɛn] *f* about 20

violemment [vjɔlamɑ̃] violently

violent, violente [vjɔlɑ̃, vjɔlɑ̃t] violent

visiter [vizite] to visit, go through

visiteur [vizitœʀ] *m* tourist

vite [vit] fast, quickly

vitre [vitʀ] *f* window

vitrine [vitʀin] *f* shopwindow; showcase

vivement [vivmɑ̃] keenly, deeply

vivre [vivʀ] to live

voilà [vwala] there is, there are; voilà...que (*with pres tense*) for

voir [vwaʀ] to see; voir p. 437; *see page 437*

voisin, voisine [vwazɛ̃, vwazin] (*noun*) neighbor; (*adj*) near, neighboring

voisinage [vwazinaʒ] *m* neighborhood

voiture [vwatyʀ] *f* car

voler [vɔle] to steal; que je n'ai pas volé that I have earned

volontiers [vɔlõtje] willingly, gladly

vont [võ] *present tense of* aller

votre, vos [vɔtʀ, vo] your

vôtre: le vôtre [ləvotʀ] *poss pron* yours

vouloir [vulwaʀ] to want, desire; je veux bien I am willing;

voulez-vous? do you want to?; je veux dire I mean (*see par 38*)

vous [vu] you, yourself, to or for you

voyage [vwajaʒ] *m* trip; en voyage on a trip; voyage d'agrément pleasure trip

voyager [vwajaʒe] to travel

voyons! [vwajõ] come now! let's see! (*imperative of* voir)

vrai, vraie [vʀɛ] true; à vrai dire to tell the truth

vraiment [vʀɛmɑ̃] really, truly

vu [vy] *p part of* voir

vue [vy] *f* view

W, Y, Z

week-end [wikɛnd] *m* week end

y [i] there; to it, to them; il y a there is, there are; il y a...que *with present tense* for

yeux [jø] *pl of* œil *m* eyes

zéro [zeʀo] *m* zero; zéro heure 12 midnight

zone [zon] *f* zone, fields

ENGLISH-FRENCH

A

a un *m,* une *f*

able: to be able to pouvoir

about *prep* vers; *adv* à peu près, environ; sur, au sujet de; **how about going . . . ?** si nous allions . . .

above sur, au-dessus de; **above all** surtout

absence absence *f*

absolutely absolument

abundant abondant *m,* abondante *f*

accept: to accept accepter

accessible accessible

accident accident *m*

according to d'après, selon

account: on my account pour moi, à cause de moi

accuse: to accuse accuser; **to accuse oneself** s'accuser

acquaintance connaissance *f;* **to make the acquaintance of** faire la connaissance de

acquainted: to be acquainted with connaître

across en face de, de l'autre côté de; **to walk across** traverser

address adresse *f*

administration administration *f*

admire: to admire admirer

advantage: to take advantage of profiter de

adventure aventure *f*

advice conseil *m;* **to give advice to** donner des conseils à

advise: to advise to conseiller de

affirm: to affirm affirmer

affirmative affirmatif *m,* affirmative *f*

affirmatively affirmativement

afraid: to be afraid of avoir peur de

Africa Afrique *f*

African Africain *m,* Africaine *f*

after après; **after spending two weeks . . .** après avoir passé quinze jours

afternoon après-midi *m;* **in the afternoon** l'après midi

afterwards après, ensuite

again de nouveau, encore; **to do again** refaire; **to see again** revoir

against contre

age âge *m*

ago il y a; **a long time ago** il y a longtemps

agree: to agree to consentir à; **to agree with** être de l'avis de

agricultural agricole

ahead devant, là-bas; **up ahead** là-bas; **to go ahead** continuer

air air *m*

alas hélas

Algeria Algérie *f*

alive vivant

all tout, toute, tous, toutes; **all of**

them tous, toutes; **not at all** pas du tout; **in all** en tout

allow: to allow to laisser, permettre de

all right bon, bien, pas mal; **if it is all right with you** si ça ne vous fait rien

almost presque; **I almost ran off the road** j'ai failli quitter la route

alone seul *m*, seule *f*; **to leave alone** laisser tranquille

along le long de; **to take along** emporter; **to come along** accompagner

Alps les Alpes

already déjà

also aussi

although bien que, quoique

always toujours

A.M. du matin

America Amérique *f*

American américain *m*, américaine *f*; **Americans** les Américains

among parmi; **to be among your guests** être des vôtres

amuse: to amuse oneself s'amuser

amusing amusant *m*, amusante *f*

and et

angry: to be angry être fâché

animal animal *m*

announce: to announce annoncer

announcement annonce *f*

annoy: to annoy ennuyer

annoyance mécontentement *m*, ennui *m*

another un autre, une autre; **another time** une autre fois

answer réponse *f*

answer: to answer répondre à

antique dealer antiquaire *m*

anxious: to be anxious to tenir à

any du, de la, de l', des, de, en; **not any** ne . . . pas de; **not any more, not any longer** ne . . . plus

anyone quelqu'un; **not anyone** ne . . . personne

anything tout; **not anything** rien

anyway d'ailleurs

apart: to tell apart distinguer

apartment appartement *m*

apologize: to apologize s'excuser (de)

appendicitis appendicite *f*, crise d'appendicite *f*

apple pomme *f*

appointment rendez-vous *m*

appreciate: to appreciate apprécier

approach: to approach approcher, s'approcher de

appropriate *adj* qui convient

April avril *m*

Arabia Arabie *f*

architect architecte *m*

are: there are il y a; **aren't they?** n'est-ce pas?

arm bras *m*; **with open arms** à bras ouverts

around (*place*) autour de; (*time*) vers

arrive: to arrive arriver

art art *m*

artist artiste *m*

artistic artistique

as comme, pendant que; **as . . . as** aussi . . . que; **so as to** pour que, de façon à

aside à part

ask: to ask demander; to ask someone for information demander des renseignements à quelqu'un

asleep endormi *m*, endormie *f*; to be asleep dormir; to fall asleep s'endormir

assiduously assidûment

astonish: to astonish étonner

astonishing étonnant *m*, étonnante *f*

at à, chez; at the au, à la, à l'; at the Duplessis' chez les Duplessis; at about six o'clock vers six heures

attain: to attain atteindre

attend: to attend: assister à, aller à

attention attention *f;* to pay attention to faire attention à, tenir compte de

attract: to attract attirer

attribute: to attribute attribuer

auction sale vente aux enchères *f*; at auction aux enchères

August août *m*

author auteur *m*

automobile voiture *f*, auto *m*

avenue avenue *f*

avoid: to avoid éviter, se garder de

await: to await attendre

awake réveillé

away: to go away s'en aller, partir; to send away renvoyer

awful: it's too awful for words il vaut mieux ne pas en parler

B

baby bébé *m*

bachelor vieux garçon *m*

back: to be back être de retour; to go back retourner, rentrer; to step back reculer

bad mauvais *m*, mauvaise *f*; vilain *m*, vilaine *f*

badly mal

baggage bagages *m pl*

balance reliquat *m*

banana banane *f*

bank banque *f;* (*river*) rive *f*

bankrupt: to bankrupt ruiner

bargain occasion *f*

be: to be être; (*place*) se trouver; there is, there are il y a; to be out être sorti; to be cold avoir froid; to be right avoir raison; the office is in Paris le bureau se trouve à Paris; I am to je dois; I was to je devais; it is better il vaut mieux; it is just as well il vaut autant

bear: to bear in mind tenir compte de

beautiful beau, bel *m*; belle *f*; beaux *m pl*; belles *f pl*

beauty beauté *f*

because parce que; because of à cause de

become: to become devenir; what became of him? qu'est-ce qu'il est devenu?

bed lit *m*; to go to bed se coucher, se mettre au lit

been été *p part of* être

before (*time*) avant, avant de, avant que, auparavant; (*place*) devant; the year before l'année précédente; before finishing avant de finir

beg: beg to prier de, permettre de

begin: to begin to commencer à, se mettre à; **it began to rain** il s'est mis à pleuvoir

beginning commencement *m*, début *m*

behind derrière

Belgium Belgique *f*

believe: to believe croire, penser

belong: to belong to appartenir à, être à

besides d'ailleurs, en outre, et puis

best *adj* le meilleur, la meilleure, les meilleurs, les meilleures; *adv* le mieux

better *adj* meilleur, meilleure, meilleurs, meilleures; *adv* mieux; **it's better** il vaut mieux; **nothing better** rien de mieux; **to do better** faire mieux (de)

between entre

big grand, grande; gros, grosse

bill facture *f*

billfold portefeuille *m*

bit: a bit un peu

board: on board à bord; **to go on board** monter à bord, s'embarquer; **board and room** pension *f*

boat bateau *m*

bold hardi *m*, hardie *f*

boldly hardiment

book livre *m*

bore: to bore ennuyer; **to be bored** s'ennuyer

born né; **to be born** naître; **he was born in Paris** il est né à Paris

both les deux, l'un et l'autre

bother dérangement *m*

bother: to bother gêner, ennuyer, déranger

bottle bouteille *f*

boy garçon, jeune homme; *pl* jeunes gens

bread pain *m;* **a loaf of bread** un pain

break: to break casser, briser

brick brique *f*

bridge pont *m*

brilliance éclat *m*

bring: to bring apporter; **to bring in (income)** rapporter; **to bring back** rapporter

Brittany Bretagne *f*

broad vaste, large

brother frère *m*

Brussels Bruxelles

build: to build construire; **to have ... built** faire construire

building construction *f*

bulldog bouledogue *m*

burn: to burn brûler

burning *adj* brûlant *m*, brûlante *f*

bus autobus *m*

bush arbuste *m*

business affaire *f*

busy: to be busy être en train de, s'occuper de, être occupé à

but mais, cependant; **nothing but** rien que

butcher boucher *m*

butter beurre *m*

button bouton *m*

buy: to buy acheter

by par, de, en; **by leaving early** en partant de bonne heure

C

cab taxi *m*

Cabinet member ministre *m*

Cairo Le Caire

California Californie *f*

call: to call appeler; **to call back** rappeler; **to be called** s'appeler

calm tranquille

camera appareil (photographique) *m*

camp camp *m*

can (pouvoir) **I can** je peux; **you can** vous pouvez, on peut

Canada Canada *m*

cane canne *f*

cape pèlerine *f*

capital capitale *f*

captain capitaine *m*

car voiture *f*, auto *m;* **by car** en auto

card carte *f;* **to play cards** jouer aux cartes

care soin *m*, souci *m;* **to take care of** s'occuper de

career carrière *f*

careful: to be careful not to se garder de

carriage voiture *f*, carrosse *m*

carry: to carry porter, transporter; **to carry away** emporter

carved sculpté

case cas *m;* **in any case** en tout cas

cashier's window caisse *f*

castle château *m*

cat chat *m*

catch: to catch attraper; **to catch up with** rejoindre

cathedral cathédrale *f*

cease: to cease to cesser de

cemetery cimetière *m*

century siècle *m;* **in the XVIth century** au XVIe siècle

ceremony cérémonie *f*

certain certain *m*, certaine *f*

certainly certainement

chair chaise *f*

chance hasard *m;* **by a lucky chance** par un hasard heureux; **chance meeting** rencontre *f*

change: to change changer de

charge: to take charge of s'occuper de, se charger de; **to be in charge of** s'occuper de

charming charmant *m*, charmante *f*

château château *m*

chatty bavard *m*, bavarde *f*

cheap bon marché, à bon marché

child enfant *m* or *f*

China Chine *f*

china vaisselle *f*, faïence *f;* **a set of china** un service de table

choice choix *m*

choose: to choose choisir

church église *f*

cigarette cigarette *f*

circular circulaire

city ville *f*

clarity netteté *f*

class classe *f*

classicism classicisme *m*

classics classiques *m pl*

clear: to clear up (*weather*) **s'arranger**

clearing clairière *f*

close: to close fermer

closely de près

clothes vêtements *m*

Coca-Cola Coca-Cola *m*

coffee café *m;* **to have coffee** prendre le café

cold froid *m*, froide *f*, frais *m*, fraîche *f;* **it is cold** il fait froid; **I am cold** j'ai froid

college collège *m*

color couleur *f;* what color? de quelle couleur?

combine moissonneuse-batteuse *f*

come: to come venir; to come to (*be present at*) assister à; (*to get near*) s'approcher de; to come out sortir, paraître; to come back revenir; to come in entrer; to come with accompagner; to come from provenir de; to come for venir chercher; to come along accompagner; to have (someone) come faire venir (quelqu'un)

comedy comédie *f*

comfort confort *m*

commit: to commit commettre

common commun *m,* commune *f*

company compagnie *f,* usine *f*

comparison: in comparison with comparé à

complain: to complain se plaindre

complete complet *m,* complète *f*

completely complètement

compliment compliment *m;* to pay a compliment faire un compliment

compose: to compose composer

comprehensible facile à comprendre; that is comprehensible cela se comprend

conceal: to conceal cacher

concert concert *m*

conclude: to conclude conclure

condition condition *f,* état *m;* in good condition en bon état; on condition that à condition que

conduct: to conduct conduire

configuration configuration *f*

conquer: to conquer vaincre

consent: to consent to consentir à

console: to console consoler

construction construction *f*

continue: to continue continuer à, se poursuivre

contrary contraire; on the contrary au contraire

control: to be under (someone's) control dépendre de (quelqu'un)

conversation conversation *f*

convincing convaincant *m,* convaincante *f*

cook cuisinier *m,* cuisinière *f*

cook: to cook faire la cuisine

cool frais *m,* fraîche *f*

copiously copieusement

correspondence correspondance *f*

cost coût *m,* frais *m pl*

cost: to cost coûter

could (pouvoir) I could je pouvais, j'ai pu, je pourrais; I could have j'aurais pu

council conseil *m;* executive council conseil d'administration *m*

count: to count on compter sur; not counting sans compter

country pays *m,* campagne *f;* out in the country à la campagne; a part of the country une région

courageous courageux *m,* courageuse *f*

courageously courageusement, avec courage

course cours *m,* a French course un cours de français; of course bien entendu, naturellement; in the course of au cours de

court cour *f*

cousin cousin *m*, cousine *f*
cover: to cover with couvrir de
cow vache *f*
crazy: to be crazy about adorer
cream crème *f*; **coffee with cream** café-crème *m*
crew équipe *f*
crime crime *m*
criminal criminel *m*, criminelle *f*
crisis crise *f*
criticize: to criticize critiquer, dire du mal de
crop récolte *f*
cross: to cross traverser
cruel cruel *m*, cruelle *f*
cry: to cry pleurer, crier; **to cry out** s'écrier
culture culture *f*
cup tasse *f*; **a silver cup (for a child)** une timbale d'argent
cupboard armoire *f*, placard *m*
curtain rideau *m*
customs douane *f*; **to get through customs** (accomplir) les formalités de douane
cute joli *m*, jolie *f*; gentil *m*, gentille *f*

D

dahlia dahlia *m*
danger danger *m*
dangerous dangereux *m*, dangereuse *f*
dare: to dare oser
date date *f*; **on this date** à cette date
date: to date dater
daughter fille *f*
day jour *m*, journée *f*; **per day, a**

day par jour; **all day** toute la journée; **every day** tous les jours; **that day** ce jour-là; **the day before** la veille; **the next day, the day after** le lendemain; **day after tomorrow** après-demain; **today** aujourd'hui; **some day** un jour; **to our day** jusqu'à nos jours; **these days** de nos jours; **the good old days** le bon vieux temps
dead mort *m*, morte *f*
deal: a good deal of beaucoup de
deal: to deal in faire le commerce de, vendre
dealer marchand *m*, marchande *f*; **dealer in antiques** antiquaire *m*
dear cher *m*, chère *f*
death mort *f*, décès *m*
deceive: to deceive tromper
December décembre *m*
decide: to decide to décider de, vouloir
decline: to decline décliner, refuser de
decoration décoration *f*
delay délai *m*, retard *m*
delicious délicieux *m*, délicieuse *f*
delighted enchanté
deliver: to deliver remettre
Denmark Danemark *m*
departure départ *m*
depend: to depend on dépendre de
deportation déportation *f*
deposit gisement *m*
describe: to describe décrire
desert désert *m*
design dessin *m*

design: to design dessiner; to have designed faire dessiner

desk bureau *m*

despair: to despair désespérer

dessert dessert *m*

destined destiné

determine: to determine déterminer

detest: to detest détester

development développement *m*

devour: to devour dévorer

die: to die mourir

difference différence *f;* it makes no difference ça ne fait rien

different différent *m,* différente *f*

difficult difficile

dine: to dine dîner

dinner dîner *m;* to have dinner dîner

diplomat diplomate *m*

direction sens *m,* direction *f*

disappear: to disappear disparaître

discover: to discover découvrir

discovery découverte *f*

discuss: to discuss discuter

display étalage *m;* on display à l'étalage

displease: to displease déplaire à

disposal disposition *f;* at your disposal à votre disposition

distance distance *f;* from a distance à distance

distant éloigné

distinguish distinguer

do: to do faire; to do again refaire; all you have to do vous n'avez qu'à, il suffit de; to do well to faire bien de; my camera will do mon appareil fera l'affaire

doctor médecin *m,* docteur *m*

dog chien *m*

door porte *f,* portière *f*

dot: at eight o'clock on the dot à huit heures précises

double double; double gallery galerie à deux étages *f*

doubt doute *m;* no doubt sans doute

doubt: to doubt douter de

down: to go down descendre; to put down déposer; downtown en ville

dramatic dramatique

dress robe *f*

dress: to dress s'habiller; to be dressed être habillé; to get dressed s'habiller

drill: to drill (*for oil*) faire des forages

drilling forage *m*

drink: to drink boire; to drink coffee prendre le café

drive: to drive conduire

driver chauffeur *m;* driver's license permis de conduire *m*

drought sécheresse *f*

drown: to drown se noyer

drugstore pharmacie *f*

duke duc *m*

dune dune *f*

duration durée *f*

during pendant, au cours de

duty devoir *m,* fonction *f*

dynamite dynamite *f*

E

each *adj* chaque; *pron* chacun, chacune; each one chacun

eager: to be eager to tenir à
early de bonne heure, tôt
earn: to earn gagner
earth terre *f*, sol *m*
earthenware faïence *f;* **Quimper earthenware** faïence de Quimper
easily facilement
easy facile, simple; **nothing easier** rien de plus facile
eat: to eat manger
economic économique
edge bord *m*
education éducation *f*
effect effet *m*
egg oeuf *m*
Egypt Égypte *f*
Egyptian égyptien *m*, égyptienne *f*
eight huit
eighteen dix-huit
eighth huitième
eighty quatre-vingts
either: either . . . or soit . . . soit; not . . . either ne . . . non plus; nor I either ni moi non plus
elegant élégant *m*, élégante *f*
eleven onze
eleventh onzième
else: something else quelque chose d'autre, autre chose; **nothing else** rien d'autre
elsewhere ailleurs
emblem emblème *m*
employee employé *m;* **Government employee** fonctionnaire *m*
empty vide, inhabité
end fin *f*, bout *m;* **to make both ends meet** joindre les deux bouts
end: to end finir, achever

engineer ingénieur *m;* **chemical engineer** ingénieur-chimiste *m*
England Angleterre *f*
English anglais *m*, anglaise *f*
enjoy: to enjoy aimer, apprécier
enough assez; **it is enough that** il suffit que; **it is enough to** il y a de quoi
enter: to enter entrer; **to enter a room** entrer dans une chambre; **to enter school** entrer à l'école
enthusiastic enthousiaste
entire entier *m*, entière *f*
entirely tout à fait, entièrement
entrance entrée *f*
errand course *f*, emplette *f;* **to do errands** faire des courses
escape: to escape échapper à
escort: to escort escorter
especially surtout
esteem: to esteem estimer
Europe Europe *f*
European européen *m*, europénne *f*
even même
evening soir *m*, soirée *f;* **in the evening** le soir; **every evening** tous les soirs
event événement *m*
eventually dans la suite
ever jamais
every chaque; **every morning** chaque matin, tous les matins
everybody tout le monde, chacun
everyone chacun, tout le monde, on
everything tout
everywhere partout
evident évident *m*, évidente *f*
exact exact *m*, exacte *f*

exactly exactement, justement; **exactly true** exact

examine: to examine examiner

example exemple *m;* **for example** par exemple

excellent excellent *m,* excellente *f*

except, excepting sauf, excepté

exchange: to exchange échanger

exist: to exist exister

expect: to expect compter sur, s'attendre à, attendre, penser; **I am expecting a letter** j'attends une lettre

expensive cher *m,* chère *f;* **to be expensive** coûter cher

explode: to explode exploser, faire exploser

exploration exploration *f*

explosion explosion *f*

extend: to extend s'étendre

extinguish: to extinguish éteindre

extraordinary extraordinaire

eye oeil *m,* yeux *pl*

F

façade façade *f*

face face *f;* **face to face** face à face

factory usine *f,* compagnie *f*

fail: to fail to manquer de

fall chute *f,* prise *f;* **Niagara Falls** les Chutes du Niagara

fall: to fall tomber; **to fall down** tomber; **to fall asleep** s'endormir

familiar familier *m,* familière *f*

family famille *f;* **family life** vie de famille *f*

famous célèbre; **fameux** *m* fameuse *f*

far loin; **far from** loin de; **as far as** jusqu'à; **as far as you can see** à perte de vue; **how far?** à quelle distance?; **how far along is your work?** où en sont vos travaux?

farm ferme *f; adj* agricole; **farm products** produits agricoles

farmer cultivateur *m*

farming culture *f,* agriculture *f*

fashionable à la mode

fast vite; **how fast?** à quelle vitesse?

fate sort *m*

father père *m*

fault faute *f*

favorable favorable

fear crainte *f,* peur *f;* **for fear that** de crainte que, de peur que

fear: to fear craindre, avoir peur de

February février *m*

feed: to feed nourrir; **to be fed** se nourrir; **he is fed up with it** il en a assez

feel: to feel sentir, se sentir, croire; **to feel urged to** tenir à; **to feel sick** se sentir mal, avoir mal au coeur

feeling sentiment *m*

fertilizer engrais *m*

festivity fête *f*

few *adj* quelques; **a few yards away** à quelques mètres; *adv* peu, peu de; *pron* quelques-uns, quelques-unes; **a few of them** quelques-uns d'entre eux, quelques-unes d'entre elles

field champ *m*

fierce féroce

fifteen quinze; **about fifteen** une quinzaine

fifteenth quinzième

fifth cinquième

fifty cinquante; **about fifty** une cinquantaine

fill: to fill remplir de, être plein de; **filled with** plein de, pleine de

film film *m*

finally enfin, finalement, finir par + *inf;* **it finally turned over** il a fini par chavirer

finance finance *f*

financier financier *m*

find: to find trouver

fine beau, belle, beaux, belles; joli, jolie; **the weather is fine** il fait beau; **fine!** entendu!

finish: to finish finir de, achever de

first premier *m*, première *f;* **Francis the First** François premier; **May 1st** le premier mai; *adv* d'abord; **first of all** tout d'abord

fish poisson *m*

fishing pêche *f;* **to go fishing** aller à la pêche, aller pêcher

fit: to see fit juger bon de

five cinq

fix: to fix fixer

flaw défaut *m*

flee: to flee s'enfuir

flower fleur *f*

fluently couramment

fly: to fly voler, aller par avion; **to fly over** survoler

follow: to follow suivre, prendre (une route)

following suivant *m,* suivante *f;*

the following day le lendemain

fond: to be fond of aimer

food aliment *m*

foot pied *m*

for pour, depuis, pendant; **I have been waiting for ten minutes** il y a dix minutes que j'attends; **it has been raining for two hours** voilà deux heures qu'il pleut, il pleut depuis deux heures

forbid: to forbid to défendre de

force: to force to obliger à, forcer à

forget: to forget to oublier de

former: the former celui-là, celle-là, ceux-là, celles-là

formerly autrefois

forty quarante; **about forty** une quarantaine

forward: to go forward avancer

four quatre

fourteen quatorze

fourth quatrième

franc franc *m*

France France *f*

Francis François

frankly franchement

free libre; **to set free** mettre en liberté

freeway autoroute *f*

freeze: to freeze geler

French français *m,* française *f;* **the French people** les Français

Friday vendredi *m*

friend ami *m,* amie *f;* **a friend of mine** un de mes amis, une de mes amies

from de, depuis, d'après; **from the** du, de la, de l', des

front: in front of devant

fruit fruit *m;* **I like fruit** j'aime les fruits

full plein *m*, pleine *f*

fun: **to make fun of** se moquer de

furnished meublé *m*, meublée *f*

furnishings mobilier *m sg*

furniture meubles *m pl*

future futur *m*, avenir *m*

G

gallery galerie *f*

game jeu *m*, match *m;* **a rugby game** un match de rugby

garden jardin *m*

gardener jardinier *m*

gas essence *f*

gay gai *m*, gaie *f*

generally d'ordinaire, d'habitude, généralement

Geneva Genève

gentle doux *m*, doucc *f*

gentleman monsieur *m;* **gentlemen** messieurs

German allemand, allemande

Germany Allemagne *f*

get: **to get** prendre, obtenir, recevoir, se procurer; **to get in, to get into** entrer, monter dans; **to get out** sortir, descendre; **to get off** descendre; **to get there** arriver; **to get up** se lever; **to go to get** aller chercher; **to come to get** venir chercher; **to get used to** s'habituer à; **I don't get it at all** je n'y comprends rien

girl jeune fille *f*

give: **to give** donner; **to give up** abandonner, renoncer à; **to give up hope** désespérer

glad content *m*, contente *f;* heureux *m*, heureuse *f;* **glad to** volontiers

gladly volontiers

glass verre *m*

glove gant *m*

go: **to go** aller, marcher, se rendre; **to go back** retourner; **to go in** entrer; **to go out** sortir; **to go away** partir, s'en aller; **to go up** monter; **to go down** descendre; **to go with** accompagner; **to go and see** aller voir; **to go and get** aller chercher; **to go through** traverser, visiter; **to go ahead** continuer; **what's going on?** qu'est-ce qui se passe?; **don't go out of your way** ne vous dérangez pas; **it couldn't be going better** ça marche on ne peut pas mieux

goal but *m*

good *adj* bon, bonne, bons, bonnes

good-bye au revoir

gothic gothique

govern: **to govern** gouverner

government gouvernement *m*

gradually graduellement

granddaughter petite-fille *f*

grandmother grand-mère *f*

greatly beaucoup, grandement

Greek grec *m*, grecque *f*

green vert *m*, verte *f*

ground terre *f*, sol *m;* **on the ground** par terre

grow: **to grow** *intr* pousser; *trans* faire pousser, récolter

grownup grande personne *f*

guarantee: **to guarantee** garantir

guest invité *m;* **to be among your guests** être des vôtres

guide guide *m*

H

habit habitude *f*

habitual habituel *m*, habituelle *f*

half demi *m*, demie *f;* moitié *f;* **half an hour** une demi-heure; **an hour and a half** une heure et demie

hand main *f*

hand: to hand over passer, donner

happen: to happen arriver, se passer; **to happen to** arriver à, devenir; **what happened to him?** qu'est-ce qui lui est arrivé?

happy heureux *m*, heureuse *f;* content, contente

hard fort; **it was raining so hard** il pleuvait tant, il pleuvait si fort

hardly à peine, ne . . . guère

hat chapeau *m;* **high hat** chapeau haut de forme

have: to have avoir; **to have to** falloir, avoir à, devoir; **to have something done** faire faire quelque chose; **to have coffee** prendre le café

he il, lui, c'

head tête *f*

health santé *f*

hear: to hear entendre; **to hear of** entendre parler de; **to hear that** entendre dire que; **to hear from someone** recevoir des nouvelles de quelqu'un

heart coeur *m;* **to know by heart** savoir par coeur

heaven ciel *m*

helicopter hélicoptère *m*

hello bonjour; **say hello to** dites bien des choses de ma part à, dites bien le bonjour à

help: to help aider à, servir à; **to help oneself** se servir

her *poss adj* son, sa, ses; *pers pron* la, l', lui, elle

here ici; **here is, here are** voici; **here and there** ça et là

herewith ci-inclus

hers le sien, la sienne, les siens, les siennes

herself elle-même

hesitate: to hesitate to hésiter à

high haut *m*, haute *f*, de haut; élevé, élevée; **300 meters high** 300 mètres de haut; **a high price** un prix élevé

him le, lui; **to him** lui, à lui

himself lui-même

his *poss adj* son, sa, ses; *poss pron* le sien, la sienne, les siens, les siennes

hold: to hold tenir

Holland Hollande *f*

home: at home à la maison, chez (moi); **to go back home** rentrer (à la maison)

Homer Homère

honest honnête

honor honneur *m*

honor: to honor honorer

hope: to hope espérer

horse cheval *m*, chevaux *pl*

hospital hôpital *m*, hôpitaux *pl*

hot chaud *m*, chaude *f*

hotel hôtel *m*

hour heure *f;* **half an hour** une demi-heure

house maison *f;* **at your house** chez vous

how comment; **and how!** et comment!; **how much, how many** combien; **how long?** combien de temps?; **to know how** savoir + *inf*

however pourtant, cependant

huge énorme, vaste

humor humeur *f;* **in a good humor** de bonne humeur

hundred cent; **about a hundred** une centaine

hungry: **to be hungry** avoir faim

hunting *f;* **to go hunting** aller à la chasse; **hunting lodge** pavillon de chasse *m*

hurry: **to hurry** se dépêcher; **to be in a hurry** être pressé

I

I je, moi

idea idée *f*

if si, s'; **if only** si au moins

Iliad (the) l'Iliade

imagine: **to imagine** imaginer, s'imaginer

immediately immédiatement, tout de suite

impatience impatience *f*

imply: **to imply** impliquer

important important *m*, importante *f*

impossible impossible

impression impression *f*

in dans, en, à, de; **in Paris** à Paris;
in France en France; **in Canada** au Canada; **in the U.S.** aux États-Unis; **in the XVIth century** au XVIe siècle; **in November** en novembre, au mois de novembre; **in the spring** au printemps; **in summer** en été; **in the fall** en automne; **in winter** en hiver; **in an hour** dans une heure, en une heure; **in the morning** le matin; **at seven in the morning** à sept heures du matin

inconvenience: **to inconvenience** déranger

indeed en effet, vraiment

Indian Indien *m*, Indienne *f*

indicate: **to indicate** indiquer

indirect indirect *m*, indirecte *f*

industrial industriel *m*, industrielle *f*

influence influence *f*

information renseignements *m pl*

inhabitant habitant *m*

inhospitable inhospitalier *m*, inhospitalière *f*

insist: **to insist upon** tenir à

installation installation *f*

instance: **for instance** par exemple

instead: **instead of** au lieu de

insurance assurance *f*

intelligent intelligent *m*, intelligente *f*

interest intérêt *m*

interest: **to interest** intéresser; **to be interested in** s'intéresser à

interesting intéressant *m*, intéressante *f*

interior intérieur *m*

intrigue: **to intrigue** intriguer

introduce: to introduce introduire
intruder intrus *m*
invitation invitation *f*
invite: to invite to inviter à
is est; **it is** c'est; **it is cold** il fait
　froid; **it is better** il vaut mieux;
　it is just as well il vaut autant
island île *f*
it il, elle, ce, cela; **it is** c'est, il est,
　elle est; *dir obj* le, l', la; *ind*
　obj y; **of it** en; **it makes no dif-**
　ference cela ne fait rien
its son, sa, ses

J

January janvier *m*
Japan Japon *m*
jewel bijou *m*
juice jus *m*
July juillet *m*
June juin *m*
jungle jungle *f*
just exactement, tout simplement,
　seulement, ne . . . que; **to have**
　just venir de + *inf;* **it is just as**
　well il vaut autant

K

keenly vivement
keep: to keep garder, conserver,
　tenir
kid: to kid se moquer de; **to kid**
　oneself se faire des illusions
kill: to kill tuer; **to kill oneself** se
　tuer
kilogram kilogramme *m,* kilo *m;*
　five francs a kilogram cinq
　francs le kilo

kilometer kilomètre *m*
kind genre *m,* espèce *f*
kind *adj* aimable
kindness amabilité *f*
king roi *m*
know: to know savoir, connaître;
　to know how savoir + *inf;* **not**
　to know ignorer; **to let someone**
　know faire savoir à quelqu'un
knowingly savamment
known connu *m,* connue *f;* **well-**
　known bien connu, bien connue

L

laboratory laboratoire *m*
lack: to lack manquer de
lady dame *f,* femme *f*
land terre *f*
landscape paysage *m*
large grand *m,* grande *f;* gros *m,*
　grosse *f;* vaste
last *adj* dernier *m,* dernière *f;* **at**
　last enfin; **last night** hier soir;
　last Sunday dimanche dernier;
　last year l'année dernière
last: to last durer
late tard, en retard; **it is late** il est
　tard; **I am late** je suis en retard;
　not later than dès
Latin latin *m; adj* latin *m,* latine *f*
latter: the latter celui-ci, celle-ci,
　ceux-ci, celles-ci
law loi *f*
lawyer avocat *m*
laying établissement *m,* construc-
　tion *f*
lead: to lead mener, conduire; **to**
　lead a life mener une vie
leaf feuille *f*

learn: **to learn** apprendre à, savoir, entendre dire

least *adj* moindre; **at least** au moins

leave congé *m*

leave: **to leave** quitter, s'en aller, partir, laisser; **I left** je suis parti; **I left Paris** j'ai quitté Paris; **I left my watch at home** j'ai laissé ma montre à la maison; **all I have left is** il ne me reste plus que; **to leave alone** laisser tranquille

lecture conférence *f*

left: **to be left** rester; **I have one left** il m'en reste un

lend: **to lend** prêter

less moins de, moins que; **less and less** de moins en moins

let: **to let** laisser, permettre de

letter lettre *f*

liberty liberté *f;* **to take the liberty of** se permettre de

license permis *m;* **driver's license** permis de conduire *m*

lie: **to lie down** se coucher

life vie *f*

like comme; **Isn't that just like John** Voilà bien notre John

like: **to like** aimer, plaire, trouver, vouloir; **did you like it?** est-ce que cela vous a plu?; **would you like to?** voudriez-vous?

list: **to list** (*boat*) pencher, s'incliner

listen: **to listen to** écouter

litre litre *m;* **half a litre** un demi-litre; **five francs a litre** cinq francs le litre

little *adj* petit, petite; *adv* peu; **a**

little un peu; **little by little** peu à peu

livable habitable

live: **to live** vivre; **to live in** demeurer, habiter; **lived in** habité

load charge *f*

loaf: **a loaf of bread** un pain

local local, du lieu, du pays

London Londres

long *adj* long *m*, longue *f;* de long; *adv* longtemps; (*time*) **how long?** combien de temps? depuis combien de temps? (*distance*) **how long is the road?** quelle est la longueur de la route?; **the road is 700 kms long** la route a 700 kms de long; **will it take you long?** vous faudra-t-il longtemps?; **no longer, any longer** ne . . . plus; **as long as** (*time*) tant que, (*since*) puisque

look: **to look** regarder, sembler, avoir l'air; **to look at** regarder; **to look for** chercher; **to look like** ressembler à; **to look over (a place)** visiter

lose: **to lose** perdre

lost perdu *m*, perdue *f*

lot: **a lot of, lots of** beaucoup de, quantité de; **lots of money** une grosse fortune

loud fort *m*, forte *f*, haut *m*, haute *f;* **to speak in a loud voice** parler haut

love: **to love** aimer, adorer; **his loved ones** les personnes qui lui sont chères

lovely joli *m*, jolie *f;* charmant *m*, charmante *f*

low bas *m*, basse *f*; **to speak in a low voice** parler bas

lucky heureux *m*, heureuse *f*; **to be lucky** avoir de la chance

lunch déjeuner *m*

lunch: **to lunch** déjeuner

luxury luxe *m*

M

machine machine *f*

machinery machines *pl*

madam madame *f*

magnificent magnifique

mail: **to mail** mettre (une lettre) à la poste

main principal *m*, principale *f*, principaux *m pl*, principales *f pl*

make: **to make** faire, (*followed by adj*) rendre; **it makes no difference** ça ne fait rien

man homme *m*; **old man** mon vieux

many beaucoup de; **so many** tant de; **too many** trop de; **how many?** combien?

March mars *m*

marriage mariage *m*

married marié; **to get married** se marier

marry: **to marry** se marier

master maître *m*

matter: **to matter** importer; **what's the matter?** qu'est-ce qu'il y a?; **what's the matter with him?** qu'est-ce qu'il a?

May mai *m*

may (pouvoir) **may I?** est-ce que je peux? pourrais-je?

maybe peut-être

me, me, moi

mean: **to mean** vouloir dire

meaning intention *f*, sens *m*, signification *f*

meantime: **in the meantime** en attendant, d'ici là

meanwhile en attendant

meat viande *f*

Mediterranean Méditerranée *f*

meet: **to meet** rencontrer, retrouver, rejoindre, faire la connaissance de; **to meet again** se retrouver

meeting rencontre *f*, réunion *f*

member membre *m*

memory mémoire *f*; **if I remember correctly** si j'ai bonne mémoire

merchant marchand *m*, marchande *f*

meter mètre *m*

Mexico Mexique *m*

middle milieu *m*; **in the middle of** au milieu de

midnight minuit

midst: **in the midst of** au milieu de

might (pouvoir): **I might** je pourrais; **whatever you might think** quoi que vous puissiez croire

milk lait *m*

million million *m*

mind esprit *m*

mine le mien, la mienne, les miens, les miennes; **it is mine** c'est à moi; **a friend of mine** un de mes amis

mineral minéral *m*, minérale *f*

minister ministre *m*

ministry ministère *m*

minute minute *f*

miss: to miss manquer, se tromper de; **one plate was missing** une assiette manquait; **I am missing one plate** il me manque une assiette; **I missed the road** je me suis trompé de route

Mississippi Mississippi *m*

mistaken: to be mistaken se tromper

modern moderne

moment moment *m;* **a moment, for a moment** un moment; **in a moment** tout à l'heure; **at that moment** à ce moment-là

Mona Lisa la Joconde

Monday lundi *m*

money argent *m;* **money order** mandat-poste *m,* mandat *m*

monkey singe *m*

month mois *m;* **in the month of** au mois de; **the 19th of this month** le 19 courant

monument monument *m*

more plus, de plus, davantage; **not . . . any more** ne . . . plus; **more than** (*quantity*) plus de, (*comparison*) plus que; **the more . . . the more** plus . . . plus; **once more** une fois de plus

morning matin *m;* **in the morning** le matin; **every morning** tous les matins; **seven o'clock in the morning** sept heures du matin

mosquito moustique *m*

most la plupart; **most of them** la plupart d'entre eux; **at the most** tout au plus

mother mère *f*

mountain montagne *f*

movable mobile

movie film *m,* cinéma *m*

moving *adj* mouvant *m,* mouvante *f*

Mr. Monsieur

Mrs. Madame

much beaucoup; **very much** beaucoup; **too much** trop; **so much** tant; **not much** (*indef*) pas grand'chose

murder: to murder assassiner

murder assassinat *m*

museum musée *m*

music musique *f*

must (devoir, falloir) : **he must be** il doit être

mutual commun *m,* commune *f*

my mon, ma, mes

myself moi-même

N

name nom *m;* **to be named** s'appeler; **proper name** nom propre

narrow étroit *m,* étroite *f*

national national *m,* nationale *f*

nationality nationalité *f*

naturally naturellement, bien entendu

near *prep* près de, à côté de; *adj* proche; **the day is drawing near** le jour approche

Near East Proche-Orient *m*

necessary nécessaire; **it is necessary** il faut

need besoin *m*

need: to need avoir besoin de

negative négatif *m,* négative *f*

negatively négativement

neighbor voisin *m,* voisine *f*

neighborhood voisinage *m*

neither ni l'un ni l'autre; **neither
. . . nor** ne . . . ni . . . ni

never jamais, ne . . . jamais

new nouveau, nouvel *m;* nouvelle
f; nouveaux *m pl;* nouvelles *f
pl;* neuf *m,* neuve *f;* **New
Year's** le Nouvel An

New Orleans La Nouvelle-Orléans

news nouvelles *f pl;* **a piece of
news** une nouvelle

newspaper journal *m,* journaux *pl*

next prochain *m,* prochaine *f;* **the
next day** le lendemain; **next
time** la prochaine fois; *adv* ensuite, alors; **next to you** près de
vous

nice gentil *m,* gentille *f;* aimable;
it's nice of him c'est gentil de
sa part

nicely gentiment

night nuit *f;* **at night** le soir, la
nuit; **tonight** ce soir; **last night**
hier soir; **that night** ce soir-là

Nile Nil *m*

nine neuf

nineteen dix-neuf

nineteenth dix-neuvième

ninety quatre-vingt-dix

ninth neuvième

no non, ne . . . pas de; aucun,
aucune; **I have no idea** je n'en
sais rien

nobility noblesse *f*

nobody personne, ne . . . personne

noise bruit *m*

none aucun, aucune; ne . . . aucun

noon midi *m*

no one personne, ne . . . personne

nor ni; **neither . . . nor** ne . . .
ni . . . ni

North Nord *m;* **North Africa**
l'Afrique du Nord

not ne . . . pas; **not at all** pas du
tout; **not much** pas du tout, pas
grand'chose

nothing rien; **nothing at all** rien
du tout; **nothing much** pas
grand'chose; **nothing but** rien
que; **practically nothing** peu de
chose; **nothing easier** rien de
plus simple

notice: to notice remarquer

noun nom *m*

novel roman *m*

November novembre *m*

now maintenant

nowhere nulle part

number nombre *m,* numéro *m;*
numbers of servants de nombreux domestiques

O

oats avoine *f*

obey: to obey obéir à

object objet *m*

obviously naturellement

occupation occupation *f*

o'clock heure *f;* **at four o'clock** à
quatre heures

October octobre *m*

of de; **of the** du, de la, de l', des;
of it, of them en

offer: to offer offrir

office bureau *m,* cabinet *m*

official fonctionnaire *m*

often souvent

oil pétrole *m;* **oil company** compagnie de pétrole *f*

OK entendu; **everything is OK**
tout est en règle

old vieux, vieil *m;* vieille *f;* vieux *m pl;* vieilles *f pl;* ancien *m,* ancienne *f;* âgé *m,* âgée *f;* **how old is he?** quel âge a-t-il?

on sur, en, dans; **on time** à l'heure; **on Saturday** samedi; **on arriving** en arrivant

once une fois, une seule fois, autrefois; **once more** une fois de plus; **once a year** une fois par an

one un, une; l'un, l'une; on; **this one** celui-ci; **that one** celui-là; **the one** celui; **the one . . . the other** l'un . . . l'autre

only *adj* seul; *adv* seulement, ne . . . que; **if only** si au moins

open ouvert *m* ouverte *f*

open: to open ouvrir

operate: to operate opérer

operation opération *f;* **in operation** en opération

opinion avis *m*

opposite opposé; **opposite direction** l'autre sens *m*

orange orange *f*

order ordre *m;* **in order to** afin de; **by order of** sur l'ordre de; **everything is in order** tout est en règle

order: to order commander

ornamented with orné de

orphan orphelin *m,* orpheline *f*

other autre; **some . . . others** les uns . . . d'autres; **the other one** l'autre

ought (devoir) : **you ought to go** vous devriez y aller; **you ought to have gone** vous auriez dû y aller

our notre, nos

ours le nôtre *m,* la nôtre *f,* les nôtres *pl*

ourselves nous-mêmes

out: to go out sortir; **to be out** être sorti

outside dehors; **at the outside** tout au plus

over sur, au-dessus de; **over 1000 square kilometers** plus de 1.000 kilomètres carrés; **over there** là-bas

owe: to owe devoir

own: to own posséder, être propriétaire de

owner propriétaire *m or f*

P

pack: to pack emballer, faire ses bagages

packing emballage *m*

page page *f;* **on page 89** à la page 89

paint: to paint peindre

painting peinture *f,* tableau *m*

pair paire *f*

palace palais *m,* château *m*

panel panneau *m*

paper papier *m,* journal *m*

parasol ombrelle *f*

pardon pardon *m*

parent parent *m,* parente *f*

Paris Paris *m*

Parisian Parisien *m,* Parisienne *f*

park parc *m*

parrot perroquet *m*

part partie *f;* **to be a part of** faire partie de

pass: to pass passer; **to pass**

through être de passage, traverser; **passing cars** les autos qui passent

passage passage *m*, (*on a plane*) place *f*

passenger passager *m*, passagère *f*

passport passeport *m*

past passé *m*; **in the past** autrefois

patience patience *f*

patiently patiemment, avec patience

pay: to pay payer; rapporter; **to pay for** payer; **to pay more** payer plus cher; **to pay a compliment** faire un compliment

payment paiement *m*

pea pois *m*; **green peas** petits pois

pear poire *f*

people gens *pl*; monde *m*; on; **the French people** les Français

per: per month par mois

perform: to perform jouer

performance représentation *f*

perfume parfum *m*

perhaps peut-être

permit: to permit to permettre de

person personne *f*

personage personnage *m*

personal personnel *m*, personnelle *f*

personally personnellement

petroleum pétrole *m*

Philadelphia Philadelphie

piano piano *m*; **to play the piano** jouer du piano

pick: to pick cueillir, ramasser; **to pick up (someone)** venir chercher (quelqu'un)

picture photographie *f*, photo *f*, tableau *m*

piece pièce *f*, morceau *m*

pilot pilote *m*

pink rose

pipeline pipe-line *m*

piranha piranha (*kind of fish*)

pity: to pity plaindre

place endroit *m*, lieu *m*; **to take place** avoir lieu; **in your place** à votre place; **out-of-the-way places** des coins perdus

plan plan *m*, projet *m*

plan: to plan avoir l'intention de

plane avion *m*

plate assiette *f*

play: to play jouer; **to play the violin** jouer du violon; **to play tennis** jouer au tennis

player joueur *m*, joueuse *f*; **a card player** un joueur de cartes

pleasant agréable

please: to please plaire à; **please** s'il vous plaît, je vous en prie

pleasure plaisir *m*; **a pleasure trip** un voyage d'agrément

plenty beaucoup de

P.M. de l'après-midi, du soir

poet poète *m*

poetry poésie *f*; **to write poetry** faire des vers

point: on the point of faillir + *inf*

poison poison *m*

police police *f*; **State Police** gendarmes *m pl*

policy police *f*; **insurance policy** police d'assurance

poor pauvre

population population *f*

porcupine porc-épic *m*

possible possible; **that is possible** cela se peut; **it's possible that** il se peut que; **to make possible** permettre de

post card carte-postale *f*

post office bureau de poste *m,* poste *f*

pound livre *f;* **three francs a pound** trois francs la livre

practically presque, à peu près; **practically all you have to do is** il suffit presque de

praise: to praise célébrer, louer; **so lavishly praised** si célébré

precede: to precede précéder

precisely exactement, au juste

prefer: to prefer préférer

present cadeau *m,* cadeaux *pl*

present: at present à l'heure actuelle, à présent

press: to press presser

prettily joliment

pretty *adj* joli *m,* jolie *f; adv* assez

prevent: to prevent empêcher de

price prix *m*

print estampe *f*

prison prison *f*

private *adj* particulier *m,* particulière *f* **private families** des particuliers

probable probable

probably sans doute

problem problème *m,* affaire *f*

produce: to produce produire

product produit *m*

profession profession *f*

professor professeur *m*

profit: to profit profiter de

progress progrès *m*

progress: to progress progresser, avancer, faire des progrès

promise: to promise to promettre de

pronoun pronom *m*

pronounce: to pronounce prononcer

pronunciation prononciation *f*

proper propre; **the proper time to** le moment de; **it is proper** il convient de

propose: to propose to proposer de

prospecting prospection *f*

prospector prospecteur *m*

prosperity prospérité *f*

proud fier *m,* fière *f*

proudly fièrement

prudent prudent *m,* prudente *f*

prudently prudemment

pull: to pull tirer

purchase achat *m,* emplette *f*

purchase: to purchase acheter, se procurer

put: to put mettre; **to put on** mettre; **to put back** remettre; **to put down** déposer

Q

quadruped quadrupède *m*

quality qualité *f*

quantity quantité *f*

quarter quart *m; a quarter of an hour** un quart d'heure; **a quarter past** et quart; **a quarter to** moins le quart

queen reine *f*

question question *f; it is a question of** il s'agit de

quickly vite

quiet tranquille

quietly tranquillement, sagement

quite tout à fait, assez
quote: to quote citer

R

radio T.S.F. *f*
rain pluie *f*
rain: to rain pleuvoir; **it is raining** il pleut; **it was raining** il pleuvait
raincoat imperméable *m*
raise: to raise élever
rare rare
rate: at any rate en tout cas
rather plutôt, assez, un peu
reach: to reach atteindre: **to reach its destination** arriver à destination
read: to read lire
ready prêt *m*, prête *f*
realize: to realize se rendre compte de
really vraiment
rear: to rear élever (un enfant)
reason raison *f;* **there is good reason to** il y a de quoi
reasonable raisonnable
receive: to receive recevoir
recently récemment; **until recently** jusqu'à une date récente
recite: to recite réciter
recognize: to recognize reconnaître
recover: to recover se remettre
red rouge
refrigerator réfrigérateur *m*
refuse: to refuse to refuser de
regards: give my regards to dites bien des choses de ma part à
region région *f*
regret: to regret to regretter de

reign règne *m*
relation relation *f*
relative parent *m*, parente *f*
religious religieux *m*, religieuse *f*
remain: to remain rester
remarkable remarquable
remember: to remember se rappeler, se souvenir de; **if I remember correctly** si j'ai bonne mémoire
Renaissance Renaissance *f*
repeat: to repeat répéter
replace: to replace remplacer
reply: to reply répondre
represent: to represent représenter
reputation réputation *f*
request demande *f,* prière *f*
request: to request prier de
require: to require exiger, imposer
research recherche *f*
resemble: to resemble ressembler à
reserve: to reserve retenir; **to reserve passage** retenir une place
residence résidence *f*
respect: to respect respecter
responsibility responsabilité *f*
rest reste *m*
rest repos *m*
rest: to rest se reposer
retain: to retain retenir
return retour *m*
return: to return retourner; **to return home** rentrer
revolution révolution *f*
rhyme: to rhyme rimer
rich riche; **to be rich** avoir une grosse fortune
richly richement
ride: to ride aller en auto, à bicyclette

right *adj* bon, bonne; **the right road** la bonne route; **at the right time** au bon moment; *adv* **right now** en ce moment; **right away** tout de suite

right: **to be right to** avoir raison de, faire bien de

ring: **to ring** sonner

risk: **to risk** risquer de

rival rival *m*, rivale *f*

river fleuve *m*, rivière *f*

road route *f*

roast beef rosbif *m*

roll petit pain *m*

roof toit *m*

room chambre *f*, salle *f*, place *f*; **living room** salon *m;* **there is room** il y a de la place

rope corde *f*

rose rose *f, adj* rose

royal royal *m*, royale *f*

royally royalement

rugby rugby *m*

run: **to run** courir; marcher; **my car was not running well** mon auto ne marchait pas bien; **to run off the road** quitter la route

Russia Russie *f*

Russian russe

S

sad triste; **to be sad** s'ennuyer

Sahara le Sahara

salad salade *f*

salamander salamandre *f*

same même; **the same** le même, la même, les mêmes; **the same one,** le même, la même; **it's all the same to me** ça m'est égal

sample échantillon *m*

sand sable *m*

satisfied satisfait *m*, satisfaite *f*

Saturday samedi *m*

Saudi Arabia l'Arabie saoudite

say: **to say** dire; **they say** on dit, dit-on; **that is to say** c'est-à-dire

scarcely à peine, ne . . . guère

scholar savant *m*

school école *f*

sculpture sculpture *f*

sea mer *f*

season saison *f*

seat place *f*

second second *m*, seconde *f;* deuxième

secret secret *m*, secrète *f*

see: **to see** voir, apercevoir; **to see again** revoir; **to go and see** aller voir; **to see fit to** juger bon de

seed semence *f*

seem: **to seem** sembler, paraître, avoir l'air de

Seine Seine *f*

seize: **to seize** s'emparer de

seldom rarement

sell: **to sell** vendre, se vendre: **if only our products sold well** si au moins nos produits se vendaient bien

send: **to send** envoyer, expédier; **to send back, to send away** renvoyer; **to send off** expédier

sentence phrase *f*

September septembre *m;* **last September** en septembre dernier

serious sérieux *m*, sérieuse *f*

serve: **to serve** servir; **to serve the purpose** faire l'affaire

set: **set of dishes** service de table *m*

set: to set mettre, poser, fixer, établir; **to set out** partir

seven sept

seventeen dix-sept

seventh septième

seventy soixante-dix

several plusieurs

severe rigoureux *m*, rigoureuse *f*

she elle, c'

shelter: to shelter oneself from s'abriter de

ship: to ship expédier, envoyer

shipment envoi *m*

shipping envoi *m*, expédition *f*

shop magasin *m;* tobacco shop bureau de tabac *m;* shop window devanture *f*

shop: to shop, to go shopping faire des courses, faire des emplettes

shore rive *f*, bord *m*

short court *m*, courte *f*

shortly sous peu; **shortly after** peu après

should (devoir) : you should vous devriez; you should have vous auriez dû

show: to show montrer, faire voir

shrub arbuste *m*

sick malade

side côté *m*

siesta sieste *f*

signal: to signal faire signe à

signpost poteau-indicateur *m*

silly: don't be silly soyez sérieux

silver argent *m*

simple simple

since (*time*) depuis, (*result*) puisque

sing: to sing chanter; to sing in tune chanter juste; to sing out of tune chanter faux

single seul, seule

Sir Monsieur

sister soeur *f*

sit: to sit s'asseoir, être assis; to sit down at the table se mettre à table

site emplacement *m*, lieu *m*

situation situation *f*

six six

sixteen seize

sixteenth seizième

sixth sixième

sixty soixante

skillful habile

skyscraper gratte-ciel *m*

sleep: to sleep dormir

slightest le moindre, la moindre, les moindres

slippery glissant *m*, glissante *f*

slow: to slow down ralentir

small petit *m*, petite *f*

smell: to smell sentir; to smell good sentir bon; to smell bad sentir mauvais

smile sourire *m*

smile: to smile sourire

smoke: to smoke fumer

snow neige *f*

snow: to snow neiger

so aussi, si, ainsi, donc; **so that** pour que; **so as to** pour, de façon à; **so-so** comme ci comme ça; **and so on** et cætera

solve: to solve résoudre

some du, le la, de l', des; *adj* quelque *sg*, quelques *pl; pron* en; quelques-uns, quelques-unes; les uns, les unes; **some of them**

quelques-uns (d'entre eux); some . . . others les uns . . . d'autres

someone quelqu'un

something quelque chose; something else autre chose; something interesting quelque chose d'intéressant

sometimes quelquefois, parfois

somewhat un peu

son fils *m*

song chanson *f*, chant *m*

soon tôt, bientôt, sous peu; as soon as dès que, aussitôt que

sorry: to be sorry to regretter de, être fâché de

sort sorte *f*, espèce *f*

South sud *m; adv* south au sud; southwest au sud-ouest

space place *f*

speak: to speak parler; to speak in a loud voice parler haut; to speak in a low voice parler bas

spend: to spend (*time*) passer, (*money*) dépenser

spite: in spite of malgré

splendid splendide

sport sport *m*

spot endroit *m*

spring printemps *m;* in the spring au printemps

sprinkle: to sprinkle arroser

sprout: to sprout (*seed*) germer

square place *f*

square *adj* carré *m*, carrée *f;* a square kilometer un kilomètre carré

stadium stade *m*

staircase escalier *m*

stamp timbre *m*

stand kiosque *m;* a newspaper stand un kiosque à journaux

standing debout

start: to start commencer; (*on one's way*) partir, se mettre en route

State État *m*

stay séjour *m*

stay: to stay rester, s'arrêter; to stay for dinner rester dîner; he is staying at the Hotel Meurice il est descendu à l'hôtel Meurice

steadily sans arrêt

steal: to steal voler

still toujours, encore

stir: to stir remuer

stone pierre *f*

stop: to stop arrêter, s'arrêter

story histoire *f*

story étage *m*

straight droit *m*, droite *f;* straight ahead tout droit

straw: this is the last straw c'est la fin de tout

street rue *f*

strike (*oil*) découverte *f*

strip: to strip dépouiller de

strong fort *m*, forte *f*

student étudiant *m*, étudiante *f*

study: to study étudier

suburb faubourg *m*

succeed: to succeed in réussir à, arriver à

such un tel, une telle, de tels, de telles; such a mother une telle mère; such pleasant company une si agréable compagnie

Sudan Soudan *m*

sudden soudain *m*, soudaine *f*

suddenly tout à coup

suffer: to suffer souffrir
suffice: to suffice for suffire à
sufficient: it is sufficient to il suffit de
sugar sucre *m*
suggest: to suggest proposer de
suit: to suit convenir à
suitable convenable, qui convient; the most suitable date la date qui convient le mieux
summer été *m;* in summer en été
sun soleil *m*
Sunday dimanche *m*
suppose: to suppose supposer; to be supposed to devoir, être censé
sure sûr *m,* sûre *f;* to make sure s'assurer
surprise surprise *f*
surprise: to surprise surprendre
surprised surpris *m,* surprise *f,* étonné
surround: to surround entourer; surrounded by water entouré d'eau
suspect: to suspect se douter de
swan cygne *m*
sweater chandail *m*
Sweden Suède *f*
swim: to swim nager
Switzerland Suisse *f*
systematically assidûment

T

table table *f;* to sit down at the table se mettre à table
take: to take prendre, emporter, mener, conduire; falloir; how long does it take? combien de

temps faut-il?; it would take two hours il faudrait deux heures; to take up monter; to take out sortir; to take place avoir lieu; to take on (*passengers*) embarquer; to take advantage of profiter de; to take care of s'occuper de
taking prise *f*
talk conversation *f*
talk: to talk parler; to talk about parler de
tall grand *m,* grande *f;* de haute taille
tapestry tapisserie *f*
tax impôt *m*
taxi taxi *m*
teach: to teach enseigner à
teacher maître *m*
team équipe *f*
telegram dépêche *f*
telephone téléphone *m*
telephone: to telephone téléphoner
tell: to tell dire, parler de, raconter; to tell about parler de; to tell oneself se dire; to tell apart distinguer
temperature température *f*
ten dix
tennis tennis *m;* to play tennis jouer au tennis
tenth dixième
terrible terrible
than que, (*with numbers*) de
thank: to thank remercier; to thank for remercier de; thank you merci
that (those) *dem adj* ce, cet *m,* cette *f,* ces *pl;* ce . . . -là, cette . . . -là, ces . . . -là; that *dem*

pron celui *m*, celle *f*, ceux *m pl*, celles *f pl;* cela; **that** *rel pron* qui, que; lequel, laquelle, lesquels, lesquelles; **all that** tout ce qui, tout ce que; **that** *conj* que; **that's a sad story** c'est une triste histoire; **that depends** cela dépend; **that which** ce qui, ce que, ce dont

the le, la, l', les

theatre théâtre *m*

their *poss* leur *sg*, leurs *pl*

theirs *poss pron* le leur, la leur, les leurs

them les, leur; eux, elles; **of them** en, d'entre eux

themselves eux-mêmes, elles-mêmes

then *(time)* alors, puis, ensuite; *(result)* alors, ainsi, donc

theology théologie *f*

there là, y; **there is, there are** il y a; **here and there** çà et là

these *dem adj* ces, ces . . . -ci; *dem pron* ceux-ci *m*, celles-ci *f*

they ils, elles, on, ce

thing chose *f*

think: to think penser, croire, trouver; **to think about** penser à; **what do you think of it?** qu'en pensez-vous?; **I thought it was excellent** je l'ai trouvé excellent

third troisième; **one third** un tiers

thirsty: to be thirsty avoir soif

thirteen treize

thirteenth treizième

thirty trente; **seven thirty** sept heures et demie

this *dem adj* ce, cet *m*, cette *f;* ce . . . -ci, cet . . . -ci, cette . . . -ci; **this** *dem pron* celui *m*, celle *f;* celui-ci, celle-ci; **this one** celui-ci, celle-ci

those *dem adj* ces, ces . . . -là; *dem pron* ceux, ceux-là *m*, celles, celles-là *f*

thousand *adj* mille, *noun* millier *m*

threaten: to threaten menacer

through à travers; **to go through** traverser, visiter, parcourir

throw: to throw lancer, jeter

Thursday jeudi *m*

ticket billet *m*

tie cravate *f*

till jusqu'à

time temps *m*, heure *f*, moment *m*, fois *f*, délai *m;* **a long time** longtemps; **at the time of** au moment de; **at the time when** au moment où; **at this time** en ce moment; **in time** éventuellement; **of the time,** du temps, de l'époque; **to have time to** avoir le temps de; **this is not the time to** ce n'est pas le moment de; **to have a good time** s'amuser bien; **to ask for the time** *(of day)* demander l'heure

tired fatigué *m*

to à, en, pour, chez, vers; **to Arabia** en Arabie; **to Venezuela** au Vénézuéla; **to Paris** à Paris; **it's ten to four** il est quatre heures moins dix

tobacco tabac *m*

today aujourd'hui

together ensemble

tomorrow demain

tonight ce soir

too trop, aussi; **too much, too many** trop de

tool outil *m*

top haut *m;* **to the top of** en haut de

towards vers

tower tour *f;* **the Eiffel tower** la tour Eiffel

town ville *f;* **downtown** en ville

tractor tracteur *m*

tragedy tragédie *f*

trail: to trail poursuivre

train train *m*

transport: to transport transporter

transportation transport *m*

travel: to travel voyager; **to travel through** parcourir

Treasury department administration financière *f*

tree arbre *m*

tributary affluent *m*

trip voyage *m;* **on a trip** en voyage; **to take a trip** voyager; **to have a good trip** faire bon voyage

trooper gendarme *m*

trouble peine *f;* **to have trouble in** avoir de la peine à; **it is not worth the trouble** ce n'est pas la peine

Troy Troie

true vrai *m,* vraie *f;* **exactly true** exact

truth vérité *f;* **to tell the truth** à vrai dire

try: to try to essayer de, tâcher de, chercher à; **to try hard** s'efforcer de; **to try in vain** avoir beau + *inf*

Tuesday mardi

turn: to turn tourner; **to turn over** se retourner, (*boat*) chavirer; **to turn around** faire demi-tour, se retourner

twelfth douzième

twelve douze, une douzaine; **twelve o'clock** (*noon*) midi, (*midnight*) minuit

twentieth vingtième

twenty vingt

twice deux fois

two deux

U

under sous, dessous

understand: to understand comprendre

undesirable indésirable *m*

unexpected inattendu *m,* inattendue *f*

unexpectedly d'une façon inattendue

unexplored inexploré

unforgettable inoubliable

unfortunately malheureusement, par malheur

unhappy malheureux *m,* malheureuse *f*

United States États-Unis *m pl;* **in the U.S.** aux États-Unis

university université *f*

unless à moins que

unlikely peu probable

unpleasant désagréable

until jusqu'à, jusqu'à ce que; **until when?** jusqu'à quel moment?

unusual rare

up: to go up monter; **up the Eiffel tower** en haut de la tour Eiffel upon sur, à

use: to use employer, se servir de; to be used (everywhere) être employé (partout); to be used as servir de; to be used to avoir l'habitude de; to get used to s'habituer à; I used to go j'allais

usual ordinaire; habituel; as usual comme d'habitude

usually d'ordinaire, d'habitude

V

vacation vacances *f pl;* on vacation en vacances

vain: in vain avoir beau + *inf*

various divers *m,* diverse *f*

vegetation végétation *f*

Venezuela Vénézuéla *m*

verse vers *m,* poésie *f*

very très, fort, bien

victorious victorieux *m,* victorieuse *f*

view vue *f;* from the point of view of au point de vue de

village village *m*

violent violent *m,* violente *f*

violently violemment

visit: to visit visiter

visitor visiteur *m*

W

wait: to wait for attendre; to wait in line faire la queue

waiter garçon *m*

wake up: to wake up se réveiller

waken s'éveiller, se réveiller

walk promenade *f;* to take a walk faire une promenade

walk: to walk marcher, aller à pied; to walk into entrer dans; to walk across traverser

wall mur *m*

want: to want vouloir, désirer

warm chaud *m,* chaude *f;* it is warm il fait chaud

warn: to warn avertir, prévenir

was: I was j'étais; I was to je devais

wash: to wash laver; to wash one's hands se laver les mains

waste: to waste perdre

watch montre *f*

water eau *f*

way chemin *m,* route *f;* moyen *m,* façon *f;* on the way to en route pour; all the way to jusqu'à; by the way d'ailleurs; don't go out of your way ne vous dérangez pas; out-of-the-way places des coins perdus; a way of talking une façon de parler; the best way to get there la meilleure façon d'y aller

wealth fortune *f,* richesse *f*

weapon arme *f*

wear: to wear porter

weather temps *m;* how is the weather? quel temps fait-il?; the weather is fine (beautiful) il fait beau

wedding mariage *m*

Wednesday mercredi *m*

week semaine *f;* a week from today d'aujourd'hui en huit; two weeks from today d'aujourd'hui en quinze; all week long toute la semaine; week end week-end *m*

weigh: to weigh peser

welcome: to welcome accueillir, recevoir

well puits *m*

well *adv* bien; **it's just as well** il vaut autant; **to do well to** faire bien de

well-being bien-être *m*

West ouest *m; adv* à l'ouest

what? *interrog adj* quel? quelle? quels? quelles?; **what** *interrog pron* que? qu'est-ce que? qu'est-ce qui? quoi?; **what is?** qu'est-ce que c'est que? **what** *rel pron* ce qui, ce que, quoi; **what is . . .** ce que c'est que; **what!** *exclam* quoi!; **let's see what's up** voyons de quoi il s'agit

whatever quoi que; **whatever he does** quoi qu'il fasse

wheat blé *m*

when quand, lorsque, où, au moment où, au moment de

whenever quand, chaque fois que

where où

whereas tandis que

which? *interrog adj* quel? quelle? quels? quelles?; *interrog pron* lequel? laquelle? lesquels? lesquelles?; **which one?** lequel? laquelle?; **which ones?** lesquels? lesquelles?; **which** *rel pron* qui, que; lequel, laquelle, lesquels, lesquelles; **of which** dont; **in which** où, dans lequel, etc.; **that which** ce qui, ce que, ce dont

while tandis que, pendant que, en, tout en; **a while ago, in a while** tout à l'heure; **while waiting for her** en attendant son retour

white blanc *m*, blanche *f*

who? *interrog pron* qui? qui est-ce qui?; **who** *rel pron* qui; lequel, laquelle, lesquels, lesquelles

whole entier *m*, entière *f*; **a whole cow** une vache tout entière; **whole days** des journées entières

whom? *interrog pron* qui?; **whom** *rel pron* que, qui; **of whom, about whom** dont

whose? *interrog pron* à qui?; **at whose house?** chez qui?; **whose** *rel pron* dont, de qui

why pourquoi

wide large, de large; **how wide is . . . ?;** quelle est la largeur de . . . ?; **ten yards wide** dix mètres de large

widow veuve *f*

wife femme *f*

willing: to be willing vouloir bien

window fenêtre *f;* **shopwindow** devanture *f*

windshield pare-brise *m*

wine vin *m*

wing aile *f;* **a two-story wing** une galerie à deux étages

winter hiver *m*

wise sage

wish souhait *m*

wish: to wish désirer, souhaiter; **I wish to heaven that** plût au ciel que; **to wish good luck to** souhaiter bonne chance à

with avec, auprès de

within dans; **within a few years** dans quelques années

without sans; **without leaving the house** sans sortir de chez elle

woman femme *f*

wonder: to wonder se demander
Wonderland le Pays des Merveilles
wood bois *m;* **carved wood** bois sculpté
word mot *m;* (*spoken*) parole *f;* **in a word** en un mot
work travail *m,* travaux *pl*
work: to work travailler
world monde *m*
worry souci *m*
worry: to worry s'inquiéter; **don't worry** soyez tranquille
worse *adj* pire; *adv* pis; **from bad to worse** de mal en pis
worst *adj* le pire, la pire, les pires
worth: to be worth valoir
worthy brave; bon, bonne; **those worthy policemen** ces braves gendarmes
write: to write écrire
wrong *adj* mauvais *m,* mauvaise *f*
wrong: to be wrong to avoir tort de

Y - Z

yard mètre *m* (*approx*)
year an *m,* année *f;* **every year** tous les ans, chaque année; **every three years** tous les trois ans
yellow jaune
yes oui, si; **yes I do** mais si
yesterday hier
yet encore, déjà, cependant; **not yet** pas encore; **and yet . . .** et cependant . . .
yield production *f,* récolte *f*
you vous, on; tu, te, toi; **if I were you** si j'étais à votre place
young jeune
your votre, ton
yours le vôtre, la vôtre, les vôtres; le tien, la tienne, les tiens, les tiennes; **is it yours?** est-ce à vous?
yourself vous-même, vous-mêmes
zero zéro *m*

INDEX